The Nelson Touch

BY THE SAME AUTHOR

NON FICTION

The Railway Navvies: a history of the men who made the railways
Providence & Mr Hardy (with Lois Deacon)
Passage to America: a history of emigration from Great Britain and Ireland
The Liners: a history of the North Atlantic crossing
Thatcher's Britain: a journey through the promised lands

NOVELS

A Girl for the Afternoons
Southern Cross: a novel of early Australia
Thanksgiving: a novel in praise of America
Empire: a novel of the Texas Republic

COLLECTED JOURNALISM

The Only True History
The Scented Brawl
Movers and Shakers: collected interviews

AS EDITOR

An Indiscretion in the Life of an Heiress: Hardy's unpublished first novel

The Nelson Touch

The Life and Legend of Horatio Nelson

Terry Coleman

OXFORD
UNIVERSITY PRESS
2002

OXFORD

UNIVERSITY PRESS

Oxford   New York
Auckland   Bangkok   Buenos Aires
Cape Town   Chennai   Dar es Salaam   Delhi   Hong Kong   Istanbul
Karachi   Kolkata   Kuala Lumpur   Madrid   Melbourne   Mexico City   Mumbai
Nairobi   São Paulo   Shanghai   Singapore   Taipei   Tokyo   Toronto

and an associated company in Berlin

Copyright © 2002 by Terry Coleman

First published by Bloomsbury, London, 2002

Published by Oxford University Press, Inc.
198 Madison Avenue, New York, New York 10016

Oxford is a registered trademark of Oxford University Press

Library of Congress Cataloging-in-Publication Data
is available at the Library of Congress
ISBN 0-19-514741-3

1 3 5 7 9 10 8 6 4 2
Printed in the United States of America
on acid-free paper

For Lesley and for Vivien; both

CONTENTS

Author's Note and Acknowledgments

This book has been a long time in the gestation. My maternal grandfather served more than forty years in the Royal Navy. On the editorial staff of the *Guardian* I was a very junior colleague of the splendid and modest Mark Arnold-Forster, who was I believe the youngest commander RNVR of the 1939–45 war and who was reputed to have gone into action, with his squadron of MTBs, waving a sabre. We often talked ships. I once went as a reporter to meet Arthur Bugler, who had risen from apprentice shipwright to be dockyard constructor at Portsmouth, and he showed me over *Victory*, calling parts of her by their beautiful and lost names – topgallants and futtocks, seizings and mizens, thimbles and after-ends of horses, helves and hitches and hoggings, vang pendants and falls. After that, wherever I went – English Harbour on Antigua, the tiny island of Nevis, the bay of Cap Haitien, the mouth of the Nile, Naples, Copenhagen – I looked to see where Nelson had been. Then I began to read his manuscript letters, and it became gradually but irresistibly clear that there was more to Nelson than the legend. I did not set out to write a revisionist biography. I should suspect the good faith of anyone who did set out to do that. I started off knowing nothing, but then a pattern emerged. The Nelson of Hotham's action seemed to explain the Nelson of the battle of St Vincent, the hasty Nelson of the Caribbean in 1785–87 ('hasty' is his own description of himself) shed light on the hasty Nelson of Naples, and the Nelson of Naples was very much the man who seized the day at Copenhagen with a *ruse de guerre*. That is how this book came about.

I should like to thank all those who have let me explore the vast archive of Nelson and other papers, or have helped in other ways: the National Maritime Museum, Greenwich, and particularly Mr Alan Giddings of the manuscripts department; the British Library manuscripts room; the Public Record Office, Kew; the Nelson Museum at Monmouth and its curator, Mr Andrew Helme; Mr Anthony Cross of the Warwick Leadlay Gallery, Greenwich, for generous help with illustrations; the London Library; the BL newspaper library at Colindale; the College of Heralds; Bristol University Library; the county record office, Trowbridge; Mr and Mrs Harry Spiro, New York; the New York Public Library; the Houghton Library of Harvard University; the Huntington Library, San Marino, California; and the Pierpont Morgan Library, New York.

And since the way in which a book is produced is of great importance, I should like to thank Rosemary Davidson and Edward Faulkner, of Bloomsbury Publishing, for sympathy in the matter of illustrations, for indicating and demanding proper emendations, and for the most scrupulous copy-editing of an intricate book.

List of Illustrations

IN THE CASE OF portraits, the number in square brackets at the end of the description – e.g. [Walker 67] – is the number of the picture in *The Nelson Portraits*, by Richard Walker, 1998, the standard book of reference, which gives details of the date, medium, provenance, dimensions, copies and other versions made, of each of 238 paintings, prints, medals, and sculptures.

Illustrations in the colour section

NELSON THE YOUNG SEA OFFICER: oil portrait by Francis Rigaud, 1777–81. [Walker 1]. Courtesy National Maritime Museum, Greenwich. The uniform is that of a post captain, but the features are those of the seventeen-year-old lieutenant Rigaud first began to paint. HMS *Boreas*: the sentencing of the seaman William Clark, 16 April 1787. This coloured print, by Louis Ryngal, also shows *Solebay, Maidstone, Rattler,* and *Pegasus* (Prince William's frigate), all at English Harbour, Antigua in 1787. Courtesy Royal Naval Museum, Portsmouth.

THE WEST INDIES AND AFTER: Nelson, watercolour by Cuthbert Collingwood, c1784, done for Mary Moutray, wife of the commissioner at English Harbour, Antigua. [Walker 2]. National Maritime Museum, Greenwich. *Frances Nelson*, pencil sketch by Daniel Orme, c1798. National Maritime Museum, Greenwich. *Chatham royal dockyard*, detail of coloured print, n.d. The print evidently shows a royal visit (see the royal ensign flying by the dockyard steps). In the right foreground a first rate is fitting out. Courtesy Anthony Cross, Warwick Leadlay Gallery, Greenwich.

EARLY YEARS IN THE MEDITERRANEAN: The capture of the *Ça Ira* by the *Agamemnon* in Hotham's action, March 1795, by Nicholas Pocock. National Maritime Museum, Greenwich. *Nelson*, miniature in oils by unknown Leghorn artist, 1794. [Walker 3]. National Maritime Museum, Greenwich.

THE ROMANTIC HERO: Nelson after he lost his right arm at Santa Cruz. Mezzotint by W. S. Barnard, May 1798, after the oil by Lemuel Abbott. [Walker 14, 1]. Anthony Cross, Warwick Leadlay Gallery, Greenwich.

THE CARICATURE: The Hero of the Nile, by James Gillray, December 1798. Nelson is shown in full dress uniform, and weighed down by an exaggerated chelengk and by the scarlet pelisse also given to him by the Sultan of Turkey. [Walker 68]. Anthony Cross, Warwick Leadlay Gallery, Greenwich.

THE BATTLE OF THE NILE: Coloured engraving published by Edward Thompson, October 1798. Anthony Cross, Warwick Leadlay Gallery, Greenwich.

NAPLES, AND THE TWO WOMEN WHO CHANGED NELSON'S LIFE: Nelson by Leonardo Guzzardi, 1799. This is one of four copies made by the artist himself, probably for Nelson. [Walker 79]. The original was sent to the Sultan of Turkey, another is in the old admiralty boardroom, and this version is in the collection of the National Maritime Museum, Greenwich. *Maria Carolina*, Queen of Naples, unknown artist. National Maritime Museum, Greenwich. *Attitudes* by Emma Hamilton, engraved in 1794 by Tommaso Piroli after Friedrich Rehberg. The sitting attitude shows Emma in a pose entitled Penseroso. From *Nelson and his Companions in Arms*, by John Knox Laughton, 1896.

Illustrations in the first black-and-white section

THE FAMILY: Silhouette of the Revd Edmund Nelson, from *The Nelsons of Burnham Thorpe* [a family memoir] by M. Eyre Matcham, London, 1911. Portraits of the Revd William Nelson (later first Earl Nelson), Maurice Nelson, and Catherine Matcham (Nelson's younger sister), from *Nelson's Friendships*, by Hilda Gamlin, 1899.

NELSON'S EARLY PATRONS: Captain Maurice Suckling, stipple after Thomas Bardwell, from *The Life of Nelson*, by A. T. Mahan, 1897. Captain William Locker, engraving by H. T. Ryall after Gilbert Stuart, Clarke and M'Arthur, 1840 edition. Admiral Sir Peter Parker, from an engraving by Ridley, from *Nelson and his Times*, by Lord Charles Beresford, 1897.

TWO GREAT COMMANDERS: Viscount Hood, mezzotint by J. Jones after Reynolds; and Earl St Vincent, mezzotint by C. Turner after William Beechey. Both from *The Royal Navy*, by William Laird Clowse, vol IV, 1897.

THE PRESS GANG: engraving by Barlow after Collings; courtesy Anthony Cross, Warwick Leadlay Gallery, Greenwich.

PRINCE WILLIAM: engraving after a portrait by Richard Cosway; from *Nelson's Friendships*, by Hilda Gamlin, 1899.

THE BATTLE OF ST VINCENT: engraving by Edward Orme after Daniel Orme, 1800; courtesy Royal Naval Museum, Portsmouth.

ANNIHILATION AT ABOUKIR: engraving made for Clarke and M'Arthur's biography, 1840 edition, after the oil by George Arnald. This is one of those engravings whch are somehow more vivid than the original work.

CAPTAIN FOLEY: engraving after William Grimaldi; courtesy Anthony Cross, Warwick Leadlay Gallery, Greenwich.

NELSON IN NAPLES, 1799: Sir William Hamilton, engraving by G. Morghen after Hugh Douglas Hamilton; Ferdinand IV, Francis Caracciolo, and Cardinal Ruffo, all by unknown artists. Queen Maria Carolina, detail of portrait by Elisabeth Vigée-Lebrun.

LATER PATRON: Sir Gilbert Elliot, later first Earl Minto, by unknown artist. FIRST LORD: Lord Spencer, engraving by B. Holl after John Copley, from Clarke and M'Arthur's biography of Nelson, 1840 edition. FAVOURITE, THEN RIVAL: Thomas Troubridge, engraving by M-A. Bourlier after Beechey, courtesy Anthony Cross, Warwick Leadlay Gallery, Greenwich. MISTRUSTED COMMANDER: Lord Keith, mezzotint by Hoppner, from *The Keith Papers*, NRS, 1950.

Illustrations in the second black-and-white section

CONSTANT WIFE: Lady Nelson, from a miniature c1793, which in the 1890s was in the possession of Mrs F. H. B. Eccles, her granddaughter, at Plymouth. From Mahan, 1898.

LADY OF THE ADMIRALTY: Lavinia, Countess Spencer, mezzotint by Charles Howard Hodges after Reynolds, from *British Portrait Engravers* . . . ed. Edmund Gosse, 1906.

THREE ENGLISH PORTRAITS: Top right: mezzotint by Edward Bell, after full length portrait by Beechey, 1800 [Walker 137]. Left: detail of stipple by G. Keating after an oil by Henry Singleton, 1797 [Walker 10]. Bottom left: stipple by William Evans, after the drawing by Henry Edridge, 1797, showing Nelson with the stump of his right arm still unhealed after Tenerife; the ribbon-ties just visible on the right sleeve, which was slit, enabled the wound to be dressed without removing the coat every time. [Walker 5]; from *Nelson in England*, by E. Hallam Moorhouse, 1913.

ENGLISH CARICATURE of October 1798, by James Gillray, shows Nelson extirpating revolutionary crocodiles at the mouth of the Nile. This was done as soon as news of the victory reached England, and

Nelson is shown with a hook to his right arm, which he never had. Courtesy Anthony Cross, Warwick Leadlay Gallery, Greenwich.

TWO ITALIAN PORTRAITS: Left: a fine engraving made by J. Skelton for Pettigrew's life of Nelson, 1849, after the full length portrait of 1799 by the Palermo artist Leonardo Guzzardi, which was in 1849 and is now in the admiralty boardroom. Guzzardi made at least three versions in oil, the first of which was sent to the Turkish sultan in thanks for the chelengk. This is still at Istanbul. Compare the portrait by Guzzardi in the colour section, which is the version Guzzardi made for Nelson himself and is now in the National Maritime Museum. [Walker 77, 79, 82]. Right: Drawing by an unknown Palermo artist, 1799, from *The Nelsons of Burnham Thorpe*, by M. Eyre Matcham, 1911. [Compare Walker 96–101, which are however slightly different].

BATTLE OF COPENHAGEN: A detail from a pen and ink drawing by the Danish artist J. Bang, 1803. An emblematic and composite picture of the engagement. Courtesy National Maritime Museum, Greenwich.

NELSON'S FAVOURITE PORTRAIT: Stipple vignette by James Stow after a pencil drawing by Simon de Koster, 1800. Courtesy Anthony Cross, Warwick Leadlay Gallery, Greenwich. Nelson wrote [see Walker 164] that this 'little outline of the head' was of all prints the most like him. Many versions exist. On the left is the version now used by the Nelson Society; courtesy Derek Hayes.

PARADISE MERTON: The house Nelson bought in 1801, where he lived with Emma Hamilton. Engraving c1804, from *Nelson and His Companions in Arms*, by J. K. Laughton, 1896.

LAST PORTRAIT, by William Arthur Devis, of which this engraving, by Edward Scriven, was made for the frontispiece of William Beatty's *Authentic Narrative of the Death of Lord Nelson*, 1807. Pettigrew does say that Devis saw Nelson just before he left for Trafalgar, but this is a portrait done for the most part not from the life but from the death. Devis went on board *Victory* when she returned to Spithead after the battle, was present at the post mortem, and was commissioned by the surgeon, Beatty, to paint this portrait. It is the only known portrait of Nelson to show him wearing the shade attached to the front of his hat-brim, which protected his good eye from the glare of the sun. Many versions exist. [Walker 197–210]. Courtesy Anthony Cross, Warwick Leadlay Gallery, Greenwich.

STATE FUNERAL: This fabric shows scenes from the death and the funeral – Nelson falling on his quarterdeck, the shallop bringing his body from Greenwich, and the funeral car in front of St Paul's – which appeared in a series of aquatints published by Ackermann in January 1806. The fabric is 26½″ wide and has a vertical repeat of 21″. Courtesy Royal Naval Museum, Portsmouth.

INSIDE ST PAUL'S: This engraving by W. H. Worthington, after a pen and ink sketch by W. Bromley, is one of the illustrations of T. O. Churchill's biography of 1808. It shows the Bishop of Lincoln, who was also Dean of St Paul's, saying the last prayers over Nelson's coffin. In the centre foreground is the Prince of Wales, whom Nelson detested, suspecting him of wishing to seduce Emma, and to his left is the Duke of Clarence. Courtesy Anthony Cross, Warwick Leadlay Gallery, Greenwich. On the coffin were laid a laurel wreath and the cocked hat worn by Nelson. It is obviously a foul-weather hat, and is waterproofed. From *Nelson and His Times*, by Lord Charles Beresford, 1897.

THE ASCENSION OF NELSON: The Christ-like Nelson, wrapped in a white shroud, is raised up by Neptune and offered to Britannia. The artist was Benjamin West, president of the Royal Academy and historical painter to the king. His romantic work was engraved for the first edition of Clarke and M'Arthur's biography of 1809. Compare Gillray's satirical version in the colour section. Courtesy Anthony Cross, Warwick Leadlay Gallery, Greenwich.

Figures in the text

A: Map of the West Indies and central America, 1780, showing Jamaica, where Nelson served and from where he sailed to take part in the disastrous Nicaraguan adventure, and the islands of Nevis, Antigua, and Barbados which he later knew well. Map adapted from *Nelson and His Times*, by Rear-Admiral Lord Charles Beresford, 1897.

B: 'Never a finer night was seen than last night and I am not the least tired.' Facsimile of Nelson's note to his wife as he left her to join the *Agamemnon* in 1793. Courtesy Nelson Museum, Monmouth.

C: Facsimile of part of Nelson's first letter with his left hand, 27 July 1797, after he lost his right arm at Tenerife. In it he asks Sir John Jervis, soon to become Lord St Vincent, for a frigate to convey the remains of his carcass home. From *Nelson and His Companions in Arms*, by J. K. Laughton, 1896.

D: Map of the Mediterranean in 1798, from Gibraltar to Naples and Aboukir, showing the routes taken by Nelson in his pursuit of Napoleon's French fleet. Adapted from *Nelson and His Times*, by Rear-Admiral Lord Charles Beresford, 1897.

E: Map of the battle of the Nile, 1 August 1798, From Clowes's *Royal Navy: a History*, vol IV, 1899.

F: Eighteenth-century Naples, showing the position in 1799 of the rebel castles, the French garrison, the royal palace, and the polaccas in the harbour. Engraving by Guiseppe Pietrasante, from *Nelson and the Neapolitan Jacobins*, by H.C. Gutteridge, Navy Records Society, 1903.

G: Facsimile of part of a letter from Nelson to Emma Hamilton, January 1800, in which he recounts to her his erotic dream of her and two princesses. By kind permission of Mr and Mrs Harry Spiro, New York.

Endpapers

The battle of the Nile, an engraving, made for the 1840 edition of Clarke and M'Arthur's biography of Nelson, after the oil by George Arnald. It shows the moment the French flagship *L'Orient* blew up, which so stunned both fleets that there followed several minutes of silence before the battle was resumed.

. . . and when I came to explain to them The Nelson
Touch *it was like an Electric Shock, some shed tears
all approved, it was new it was simple and from admirals
downwards it was repeated it must succeed if they will
allow us to get at them, You are My Lord surrounded by
friends who you inspire with confidence, some may be
Judas's but the majority are certainly much pleased
with my commanding them.*

Thus Nelson, in one of his last letters to Emma Hamilton,
told her how he explained the plan of attack at Trafalgar to
his captains. And thus was born another part of the Nelson
legend. Like so much of that legend, its origin lies with Nelson
himself. "The Nelson touch" is his own phrase, as is the picture
of the captains moved to tears. We do not have a word that any
one of the thirty-one captains of his fleet wrote on the
occassion.

CHAPTER ONE

Natural Born Predator

NELSON WAS A PARAMOUNT naval genius and a natural born predator, and those who look to find a saint besides will miss the man. The strength of mind is everywhere obvious. He knew he was right, and in action was daring and direct. His originality asserts itself again and again, and so does his quixotic generosity. But in private life, as in war, he was ruthless whenever he had to be, and he could be pitiless. He was a fanatic for duty, at times beyond all sense, and a royalist so infatuated with the divine right of kings that he began to see himself, in revolutionary times, as the instrument of God. This made him a good hater. He hated the American rebels of the thirteen colonies, and the harmless liberal rebels against the Bourbon king of Naples, as unforgivingly as he hated the revolutionary French and then Napoleon.[1]

He often spoke of his soul, as often as he spoke of himself, in the third person. 'Nelson comes, the invincible Nelson' – this to his wife after the Nile. 'Nelson, all that is left of him' – this to a fellow admiral, in a letter listing his wounds. 'Nelson is as far above doing a scandalous or mean action as the heavens are above the earth' – this to the commissioners of the navy victualling board, who suggested he had bought beef too dear. Write to Nelson about beef, and he invokes the heavens.[2]

No one expects so great a marshal as Napoleon, or so implacable a general as Sherman, razing Georgia from Atlanta to the sea, to be a saint as well, but Nelson has been encumbered with his own romantic legend. The real Nelson was a man whose mind was, in his own words, fixed as fate, whose instinct was not just to defeat the enemy but to annihilate him – and he uses the word again and again – as he did at the Nile. That was a new kind of victory. Annihilation was not in the naval tradition of the late eighteenth century, but Nelson was never 'one of us'. Do not look for a rounded man. As a young captain in the Leeward Islands he despised his commander-in-chief for playing the fiddle. But an instinct to annihilate, though not quite the done thing, was a capital quality in a war against Napoleon.[3]

Nelson the living man cannot be held to account for the Nelsonian legend which was so sedulously cultivated after his death, but he did set out to be a hero, and did all he could to advance his own fame. He was an instinctive self-publicist. He first made his name in 1797 at the battle of St Vincent, two accounts of which became classic. Both were his. One he wrote himself and sent to a friend with the suggestion that it should be sent to the newspapers, which it was; and the other, published as a pamphlet by a colonel in the army, relied on what Nelson told him the day after the battle. Thus was established the story of Nelson's patent bridge for taking Spanish ships of the line, by boarding one over the other. The story was challenged, but Nelson's two versions were in print by then, and his fame never looked back.[4]

After Nelson's death his legend grew and thrived. Trafalgar, in 1805, was a great victory, though it was by no means the end of the Napoleonic wars, which lasted another ten years. But it was a victory which was badly needed and it came at the right time, when Napoleon was sweeping everything before him on the continent and had just won the battles of Ulm and Austerlitz. The dead Nelson was seen almost as a redeemer, and was portrayed by Benjamin West in his vast oil painting as a Christ-like figure draped in a shroud and supported in the arms of Neptune while Britannia hovered above. This became the frontispiece to the official biography by Clarke and M'Arthur, which was in part controlled by Nelson's older brother William. It came out in two vast volumes weighing twenty-three pounds, and was a hagiography.[5] It reflected the spirit of the times, and served as an admirable piece of propaganda. Then in 1813 the single most influential biography of Nelson ever to appear was written by Robert Southey, who became poet laureate that same year. The publisher John Murray believed that a short life by Southey would sell well as a midshipman's manual, and it has sold ever since. Few biographers can ever have known less about their subject. Southey probably saw no single paper of Nelson's, his principal informant was his brother Tom who had been a midshipman at Copenhagen, and he wrote what was for the most part an elegant epitome of the unreadable Clarke and M'Arthur. 'I walk,' said Southey, 'as a cat does in a china pantry, in bodily fear of doing mischief, and betraying myself, and yet there will come a good book of it . . .'[6] It was still wartime, and his book, as he said, was a eulogy of a great national hero. It portrayed an almost infallible yet humane Nelson, helped form the legend, and set the tone for many later biographers. It is at times the portrait of an impossible ideal, as when Southey asserts that Nelson never placed musketry in his tops, to pick off enemies at close range, because this was a 'murderous sort of warfare'. This quite misunderstands Nelson the fighting officer. At close range, in action, Nelson's business was killing, and he excelled at his business. At Trafalgar he raked the *Bucentaure* through her stern windows with a carronade loaded with five hundred grapeshot. It must have killed fifty. Warfare is meant to be murderous.

It is now all but two hundred years since Nelson's death. The only comparable British military hero of modern times is Wellington.[7] He was as great a fighter as Nelson, and had, by the age of forty-seven, at which Nelson died, been created a duke and a knight of the garter. He too won a great, remembered battle – his Waterloo to Nelson's Trafalgar. He was in his day as celebrated as Nelson, his funeral was as splendid, and there are in greater London ninety-seven streets or other thoroughfares named after Wellington or Waterloo as against sixty-nine named after Nelson or Trafalgar. But he is now generally known for the wellington boot and for having replied, when threatened with the publication of an ex-mistress's memoirs, 'Publish and be damned' (which he probably did not say or write). Nelson, with his eye patch (which he never wore), and with Emma Hamilton on his one arm, is a more vivid figure.[8] He did of course have the great advantage that he died in battle at the height of his fame, and did not have the misfortune to survive and become prime minister, as Wellington did.

It is an irony that the immortal memory is in part kept fresh by two circumstances which are commonly counted stains upon it. One is Nelson's liaison with Lady Hamilton, and the other his conduct at Naples in 1799 where he acted more like a Neapolitan viceroy than a British admiral, broke a treaty, and imprisoned the rebel leaders in

British ships of war before handing them over to the Bourbon king's executioners. This is something Southey deplored, as a stain on the memory of the Nelson he was helping to create. Early in 1999, three London newspapers gave half a page each to a conference in Naples where Italian academics called Nelson a butcher and a war criminal.[9] A chapter in this book is devoted to the Naples affair. But quite apart from the truth or falsity of the accusations, the remarkable fact is that after two hundred years Nelson is still news.

From all the evidence, these qualities of the man emerge. Always strength of mind amounting to genius, often generosity, always a fascination with women, often uneasiness with his family and with his superior officers, often ruthlessness, always fearlessness.

Often he was generous, giving a boatswain on hard times £100, going out of his way to support the common law wife his brother Maurice left behind, and twice writing privately to the first lord of the admiralty on behalf of a young commander who had been court-martialled and ruined for running his sloop ashore, saying that if he himself had been censured every time he ran his ship into danger he would long ago have been out of the service.[10]

He delighted in women and always noticed them. The commissioner's wife in Antigua who made him feel like an April day; the most beautiful girl of seventeen killed during a bombardment on Corsica; the ladies walking the walls of Cadiz, seen by telescope from his quarterdeck; and the bride, not quite thirteen, of Sir John Acton, prime minister of Naples. This was a marriage which caused Nelson to write to a friend, 'So you see it is never too late to do well. He is only sixty-seven.' And women liked Nelson – his admirals' wives, Lavinia Spencer, wife of the first lord, and girls in England who became *brisk* at the thought of him. Nelson was accused of venery, but if that is a fault in a vigorous man then it is one that Wellington shared in abundance.

Nelson's family have been too little taken into account. At times they tormented him. His father, a clergyman, loved his son but Nelson, in his last years, could not bear the old man's troubled doubts. Nelson was affectionate towards his sisters Catherine and Susannah, but was wary of their husbands. His brother Maurice, at the navy office, was disappointed and not so amiable as he is generally painted. And Nelson's brother William, also a clergyman, was a boorish, grasping scoundrel. In his twenties he went as chaplain with Nelson to the

Caribbean but came home early and then procured a pay certificate from Nelson stating that he had served fifteen months longer than he had.[11] Later he constantly scrounged for deaneries and bishoprics and was a perpetual irritant. Nelson's gentle and constant wife could not stand William, whom even his father thought ambitious, proud, and selfish. This was the brother who after Trafalgar, to honour the victory and the family name, was given the earldom that Nelson in his lifetime was denied.[12]

That Nelson was often ruthless there is no doubt. It is all very well for one Victorian writer to say, in accordance with the legend, that Nelson's nerves were convulsed by seeing seamen punished, and for another to state emphatically that among the many jewels which composed the hero's character, that of humanity was among the most conspicuous, but the log of the *Boreas*, the frigate Nelson commanded at the time of his marriage, shows that in eighteen months he flogged fifty-four of his 122 seamen and twelve of his twenty marines, almost half his people, and that eight of the punishments were for mutinous language.[13] This does not make him a great flogger, but his nerves were plainly not convulsed. And when a fellow admiral objected to the execution of mutineers on a Sunday, Nelson said he would have hanged them though it had been Christmas day. This is not the sensitive Nelson of the legend. It was ruthless, and so was his threat to set fire to the floating batteries he had taken at Copenhagen, 'without having the power of saving the brave Danes who have defended them', burning the men with the batteries. He thereby procured a truce, and stated that his motive in asking for it was humanity, but he needed the truce to save his squadron.[14]

Nelson's fearlessness was perfect. His wife, his father, and the London newspapers urged him in 1797 to leave boarding enemy ships to others, telling him he had glory enough. He took no notice. He lost both his right eye and his right arm not in fleet actions, not even at sea, but on land, the arm quite gratuitously while he was leading what would now be called a commando raid, in which no admiral should have taken part. He had a reckless courage which was best described by Vice-Admiral Philip Colomb, in a sketch of Nelson which appeared in 1899. 'It is impossible to doubt, on the one hand, that these tremendous acts arose out of a sense of duty which in religion would be called fanatical; and on the other, out of some sense of delight of the fox hunting kind, which

I can only explain by supposing bodily fear and the mental power to banish it, the delight being in the moral victory.'[15] His own fearlessness did of course expose others to danger. In the attack which cost him his arm, an attack which he knew to be hopeless and which he later said he made out of pride, he lost twice as many men as died in the whole battle of St Vincent.[16]

At sea, most of all in action at sea, he was all bold originality. On land he was less sure, and in the last five years of his life he was unhinged. He was a generous man who wished his wife dead, half out of his mind with Emma Hamilton but jealously unsure of her, at odds with his father whom he neglected and whose funeral he did not attend, at law with his old mentor Earl St Vincent over prize money, forever complaining that prime ministers never did anything for him, and damning the lords of the admiralty as a set of beasts. At the same time as he was doing the damning, he was writing to Emma: 'I am all soul and sensibility; a fine thread will lead me, but with my life I would resist a cable dragging me.'[17] He would not, he was saying, be dragged even by the admiralty. Yet the man of soul and sensibility who wrote this was still the fearless predator who a few weeks later won the battle of Copenhagen. That too was in his soul.

The immortal memory survives everything, and will survive everything. In 1999 the Royal Naval Museum, in Portsmouth dockyard and in sight of the *Victory*, commissioned a life-size wax figure of Nelson to stand in its new Nelson gallery. It depicts Nelson as he was when he went aboard the *Victory* for the last time, at Portsmouth in 1805, to search out the French and Spanish fleets. Nelson's health and appearance is well documented in contemporary descriptions and paintings. When he set out on his last voyage he had spent only a month at home after two solid years at sea. He was thin, his hair had been white for five years, and he had lost his top teeth. He had lately described himself again and again as worn out, shaken, and old. Yet the Portsmouth museum, after taking careful measurements from the uniform Nelson wore at Trafalgar, and examining hair cut off after his death, produced the effigy of a man whose hair is reddish, who fills out his uniform, and is the image of robustness. No matter that a showcase just behind him shows seven miniatures of a white-haired Nelson. The effigy is of Nelson the legend, and that in its way is perfectly authentic, for the legend has long outlasted the man.[18]

This book is an attempt to tease out the man from the legend, which is not easy, because the two have become so intertwined. The poet Coleridge discovered from one of Nelson's captains that *L'Orient*, the French flagship at the Nile, which famously blew up, may have been fired by some phosphorus-like substance thrown aboard her. But in considering this, as with so much else, it is as well to bear Coleridge's own maxim in mind: 'Facts! Never be weary of discussing and exposing the hollowness of these – every man an accomplice on one side or the other ...'[19] One of the most potent and most universally accepted facts – that of Nelson putting a telescope to his blind eye at the battle of Copenhagen – does not stand examination. In spite of all the evidence, or what appeared to be evidence, it didn't happen. It is a myth. But in general, to distinguish the man from his legend is the less easy with Nelson because the man was himself full of such contradictions and paradoxes. One of them is his relationship with his mentor St Vincent. Nelson and John Jervis, later Earl St Vincent, were the two greatest sea officers of their age. St Vincent, who was born in 1735, was the older of the two by a generation. Nelson as captain and commodore served under him in the Mediterranean. The two men got on marvellously, and few senior officers did get on well with the irascible St Vincent. It was he who in 1801 recommended Nelson to go as second in command to the Baltic and then, in 1803, as first lord, appointed him commander-in-chief in the Mediterranean. It was he who called Nelson a predator, and prized him for it. He believed that Nelson possessed the magic art of infusing his own spirit into others, and told him so.[20] But his belief in Nelson changed. In retirement, St Vincent corresponded frequently with his old friend Dr Andrew Baird, who had known Nelson well and had served with him as fleet physician. In 1814, when St Vincent was in his eightieth year, he wrote a discursive letter to Baird to which he scribbled a postscript: 'Animal courage was the sole merit of Lord Nelson, his private character most disgraceful in every sense of the word.'[21]

How St Vincent came to write that is one of the questions this book will try to answer.

CHAPTER TWO

Well Then, I Will Be a Hero

HORATIO NELSON WAS BORN on 29 September 1758 – two years after Mozart's birth and the year before Wolfe stormed the Heights of Abraham – in the parsonage house at Burnham Thorpe, a village three miles from the northern coast of Norfolk. A man standing on that bleak coast and looking north has nothing but sea and ice between him and the North Pole. Horatio's father, the Revd Edmund Nelson, had been rector of the parish since he came down from Cambridge. His father before him had been a country clergyman, and his mother was the daughter of a baker. There was nothing distinguished, then, about the male line of the Nelsons, except for its tradition of longevity. Horatio's paternal grandmother lived to be 91, and two aunts to 89 and 93. But the female line had some claim to distinction. Edmund Nelson's wife Catherine was a Suckling, and her great great grandmother had been sister to Sir Robert Walpole, prime minister to both George I and George II, who had been created an earl. This connection to nobility was tenuous enough, but it did subsist. Horatio itself was a traditional Walpole family name, and Horatio, second baron Walpole, stood as Nelson's godfather. In the 1760s another branch of the Walpoles, who were distant cousins and lived at Houghton Hall, ten miles or so from Burnham, sometimes remembered to send a brace of pheasants to the Nelsons, and sometimes forgot.

But Edmund Nelson was in no sense a poor parson. He had inherited his two livings from his father, and one was in the gift of Eton College. He kept four servants, and had the means to spend most winters in the milder climate of Bath. Catherine Nelson bore eleven children, of whom eight survived at the time of her death in the winter of 1767. She was forty-two. Horatio was then nine years old. Three of his brothers had died in infancy. Two older brothers, Maurice and William, were fourteen and ten. An older sister, Susannah, was twelve. That left two more brothers and a sister who all later died young, and the youngest of all, Catherine, who was only ten months old at the time of her mother's death. She grew up to be Horatio's favourite. The widowed rector did not remarry. Susannah was apprenticed to a milliner in Bath. Maurice left for London at the age of fifteen to become a clerk in the excise. William and Horatio were educated at the Royal Grammar School in Norwich and at two other schools in Norfolk. William went on to Cambridge and became a parson like his father. Horatio picked up enough Latin to be able to quote the odd tag in his letters, read enough Shakespeare to enable him to misquote from *Henry V*, and was vilely taught French, in which language he could never speak or write a dozen words together. But he always had a natural gift for the written word. His letters can be as vivid, and as self-revealing, as Pepys's.

It is important to recognise that no more is known for sure about the young Nelson than about any other country clergyman's son. His father kept a 'family historical register' which says nothing at all about him until he went to sea at the age of thirteen.[1] All that Nelson ever said he remembered about his mother was that she hated the French. Of course many traditional anecdotes of the young Nelson have been handed down from biographer to biographer. They should be given as much credence as any anecdotes of a man's youth, recalled by others many years later when their subject has achieved greatness. It has also to be taken into account that almost all these stories come from Clarke and M'Arthur's approved biography published soon after Nelson's death. John M'Arthur was a naval journalist, who had been secretary to Admiral Lord Hood and had known Nelson. The Revd James Clarke, who was added for respectability, had been a naval chaplain and journalist, but was by then chaplain to the Prince of Wales. Their work, when it can be checked against the letters and documents it cites, is in a hundred instances inaccurate.[2] Furthermore, in selecting early anecdotes, the joint authors naturally chose tales which revealed in the young Nelson the heroic qualities he displayed as a man. This does not matter with such a story as that of the boy Nelson, lost in a wood on the way to visit his grandmother and believed to have been carried off by gypsies, who when found and asked whether he had not been afraid, replied, 'Fear never came near me, grandmama!'[3] It hardly rings true, but it is of little consequence. The accuracy of some other anecdotes does matter.

The source of such tales had to be the family, but by the time Clarke and M'Arthur were compiling their biography Nelson's father and his brother Maurice were dead, and of his surviving sisters Catherine would have been too young to remember her brother's youth. That left Susannah and William, and it was William, the sanctimonious and grasping elder brother, who insisted on controlling the biography and made himself most objectionable in the process.[4] He was concerned that the work should reflect glory not only on Nelson's memory, which would have been natural, but also on 'the line of Nelsons', by which he meant himself. The bloodline was an obsession with him. William, having been created an earl solely to celebrate the merits of his dead brother, considered himself the proper and principal surviving representative of that bloodline; and he was also a self-seeker in whom no confidence whatever should be reposed. So where a story is at all unlikely, and where its probable source is William, it has to be taken with a large pinch of salt.[5]

Two important anecdotes fit this description. One concerns Nelson taking his lieutenant's examination. We shall come to that. The other is the classic story of how the boy Nelson came to enter the navy.

Nelson's mother had two brothers who had done well for themselves. One was William Suckling, deputy collector in the custom office, who had got Maurice Nelson his post with the excise. The other was Captain Maurice Suckling, a sea officer who had distinguished himself in a Caribbean action in the Seven Years' War. He had then been on half pay for seven years, but in December 1770, when war looked likely with Spain over an obscure dispute in the Falkland Islands, he was given the *Raisonnable*, 64 guns, which was fitting out at Chatham. The story goes that the twelve-year-old Nelson, reading of his uncle's appointment in a county newspaper, exclaimed: 'Do, brother William, write to my father at Bath and tell him I should like to go with uncle Maurice to sea.' At which William did write to Bath, where their father was spending the winter for his health, and he in turn wrote to Captain Suckling, who exclaimed: 'What has the poor Horace done, who is so weak, that he above the rest should be sent to rough it out at sea? Do let him come; and the first time we go into action, a cannon ball may knock off his head and provide for him at once.'[6]

The tale has been told ever since, and doubtless it was agreeable to William that he should be seen to have played an indispensable part in sending his famous brother to sea. But is it likely that Horatio Nelson, who throughout his life was the first to hurl himself into any enterprise, and was always the dominant brother, would have asked William, who was after all only eighteen months his senior, to make the application for him?

At any rate Nelson had taken the first, indispensable step of any would-be sea officer. He had found a captain to take him to sea. Suckling took his nephew on board and rated him midshipman. But the greatest of naval careers nearly came to a rapid end. Spain climbed down and withdrew from the Falklands, the newly commissioned ships were taken out of service, and Nelson would have been on his way home again if Suckling had not asked for the command of a guardship in the Medway, and got one. She was the *Triumph*, 74 guns, and he rated his nephew as captain's servant. Whether a young gentleman was written down as midshipman or captain's servant did not matter. There was no one rank equivalent to officer-cadet in the modern sense. A midshipman was an aspiring officer, but not yet an officer. He was a rating and he could be rated or disrated as his captain pleased, turned ashore or turned before the mast with the common seamen, though this rarely happened. Nelson in his first years at sea served variously as midshipman, captain's servant, and able seaman. Many distinguished officers had once been nominally rated able seaman, but this did not mean they had risen from the lower deck. The crucial distinction was that, however a young gentleman was written down in the ship's books, he had the privilege of walking the quarterdeck with the captain and his officers. If all went well with him he would in time become one of those officers. But it was a hard life, and though he was in no real sense a common seaman he had to learn to do the duties of one: that was indeed one of the requirements of the lieutenant's examination he could take after six years at sea.

In a third rate ship of the line like the *Triumph*, if she were fully manned, six or seven hundred unwashed seamen lived and messed on the gundeck, sleeping in hammocks slung fore and aft and with only fourteen inches of lateral space to swing in. A midshipman was slightly better off. He messed and slung his hammock either in the gunroom, in the sternmost part of the gundeck, or in the cockpit on the orlop deck, midships and on or below the water line, where there was no natural light and little air. On duty he learned navigation from the master or the lieutenants, hauled cables, and climbed into the rigging with the topmastmen. He thoroughly learned his trade and his profession.

So Nelson walked the *Triumph's* quarterdeck, and learned to pilot the ship's cutter from Chatham to Tower Bridge, or from Chatham to the North Foreland, becoming confident in the rocks and sands of the Thames. But service on a guardship which would never leave the Medway was no way for a young gentleman to learn his profession, so Suckling sent his nephew on a voyage with a merchantman, whose master had once served with him. We do not even know the name of this ship or where she went, but her owners traded out of Florida, Bermuda, and the Lesser Antilles. When after a year Nelson returned, having become as he said a 'practical seaman', he was taken back into the *Triumph*, on whose books his name had remained, so that he should lose none of the six years' service required before he could hope to gain a commission. This was a harmless fiction regularly practised.[7]

Then came his first adventure. In 1773 an expedition towards the North Pole was planned. The navy strengthened the two bomb-ketches which were to sail on it. The principal purpose was to make astronomical observations for the Royal Society, though there was speculation that the larger object might be to find a northwest passage to India. An act of George II still offered a reward of £20,000 to any British ship that should do so. It was an age of exploration. The Frenchman de Bougainville had circumnavigated the globe and given his name to the bougainvillea. Captain Cook had discovered the extent of the southern continent later to be called Australia. Among those who at one time sailed with him were George Vancouver, who later surveyed much of the western coast of America, and William Bligh of breadfruit and mutiny fame. Cook, on his second voyage, had crossed the Antarctic circle and was northward bound for Tahiti at the time the Arctic expedition was due to sail. It was an expedition in which Nelson had an ardent desire to take part. As he wrote years later in a memoir, nothing could prevent him using 'every interest' to go with

Captain Lutwidge in the *Carcass*. This meant that his uncle knew that captain. The strange thing is that, having got his way and sailed with the expedition, and traditionally attacked a bear on an ice floe with the butt of a musket (an adventure he never mentioned), Nelson wrote no more than that he was given the command of a cutter with twelve men and prided himself in fancying he could navigate her better than any other boat in the ship.[8] It was left to another midshipman to describe, in his journal, the passage to the far north of Spitzbergen, snowflakes sometimes shaped like icicles and sometimes like stars, the vistas of ten miles of unbroken ice, up to twenty-four feet thick, which threatened to engulf and crush the ships, the walrus crashing against the boats with which the men tried to tow the ships to open water, and the eventual escape.

The expedition returned after five months, having found no north-west passage but having been within ten degrees of the Pole. Nelson at fifteen had been as far north as any man in the navy.

He returned to the *Triumph*, put in another one week and five days' service with Captain Suckling, and was then given a letter of introduction to the master of the *Seahorse*, a small frigate in a squadron which was fitting out for a far eastern voyage. The *Seahorse* took the classical route to the East Indies – to Madeira, south to the Cape of Good Hope, eastwards in the roaring forties, and then north to Madras. In the next two years she touched at Calcutta and Bombay, and sailed as far north and west as Basra in the Persian gulf. It was a thorough tour of the East. He thought Trincomalee in Ceylon the finest harbour in the world, but otherwise recorded nothing of his first, and only, experience of the East.[9] A quarter of a century later he did tell the daughter of an admiral that at one port, which he did not name, he won £300 at cards and then, considering what he might have lost, never played again. The pay of a midshipman was £60 a year, which would hardly have paid his mess bills. Then he took fever, probably the malaria which returned intermittently all his life, and was sent home, a mere skeleton, in the *Dolphin* frigate. The passage took six months. He recovered, but during this first severe illness thought that he should never rise in his profession, and almost wished himself overboard. But then his mind exulted in the idea of patriotism, that the king and country should be his patron. 'Well then,' he told himself, 'I will be a hero, and confiding in Providence I will brave every danger.'[10]

Such was the vision, and such his state of mind on that long passage. But this again is what he is reported, perhaps with advantages, to have told a brother officer many years later. We do not have a single line he wrote at the time. He had sailed to the Caribbean and the Arctic. He had sailed the Atlantic as far south as the Cape of Good Hope, traversed the Indian Ocean, the Bay of Bengal, and the Arabian Sea. He had, indeed, seen more of the world than he ever would again, but his family, who afterwards preserved hundreds of his letters, extraordinarily kept not one from his first five years at sea, nor did he preserve one from them. He arrived back in England, a month or so before his eighteenth birthday, in a time of peace when employment would be scarce, and with little but his ideal of patriotism to sustain him. For a midshipman there was not even the half pay on which many a sea officer without a ship scraped by.

CHAPTER THREE

The Whole Glory of the Service

BUT WHEN NELSON RETURNED to England on board the *Dolphin* in the summer of 1776 not only was his health restored but his prospects had changed beyond anything he could have hoped. For a start, there was war. The thirteen American colonies had rebelled the year before, the shots that rang around the world had been fired at Lexington and Concord, George Washington had forced the British to evacuate Boston and move their headquarters to New York, and the first naval action of the war was fought against an American squadron off Rhode Island. In time of war, there would be employment for an aspiring sea officer. Not only that, but Nelson's uncle, Captain Suckling, had been appointed comptroller of the navy. This was the greatest stroke of luck. The eighteenth century was a time when a sea officer, if he were to flourish, needed 'interest', or influence in the right places. Nelson as a young officer liked to say that he stood for himself and had no great connection, the implication being that he had risen unaided and on his own merit. Now his merits were great, but without the chance of his uncle's advancement he could never have risen as he did. Of Nelson in his mid-twenties it can safely be said that few sea officers had ever enjoyed better interest.

The fount of interest in the navy was the first lord of the admiralty. He could make an officer's career, and received constant requests to do so. The man enjoying the best interest with a first lord was likely to be someone close to him, say a nephew, or a person whose services he needed to keep. Family interest was best. A nephew had a stronger claim than a man of high rank who was personally unknown to the first lord. St Vincent, as first lord in 1801, replied to a petitioner that he had lately refused to promote at the request of four princes of the blood. He liked to prefer those he called 'young men of friendless merit', but kept a sense of proportion and readily procured the promotion of an old friend's grandson.[1]

How Captain Suckling, as the captain of a guardship, had caught the eye of the first lord is not known, but in 1775 he was made comptroller, and Nelson's future was assured. The comptroller was traditionally appointed from among the senior captains, and he became head of the navy board. If the admiralty was the right hand of the navy, its left hand was the navy board. Ultimate power lay with the admiralty which disposed of the navy's ships and its commissioned officers, but the navy board, which was an infinitely larger organisation, ran the navy's dockyards, built, repaired, and supplied its ships, and mustered their crews. It was the civil and administrative branch of the navy. Another comptroller of the period described his powers in these words: 'He is the mainspring belonging to anything that is naval; he must be in every part of it and know everything that is going on, in and out of it ... It is the office of next consequence to the first lord of the admiralty.'[2] Just so. All sea officers of whatever rank would wish to cultivate the comptroller, who by virtue of his office, and because he was a creature of the first lord, was a man of great power. Suckling was also a man whose services the first lord needed. What he asked for his nephew, the first lord was likely to grant. Unless Nelson had been the son of the first lord himself, he could not have had a more powerful patron than Suckling.

The first lord of the time was Lord Sandwich, statesman, sponsor of Captain Cook's voyages, rake, and so keen a gambler that rather than leave the table he had meat brought to him between two slices of bread, thus giving his name to the sandwich. His enemies said of him that he liked to thumb through the pages of Lemprière's *Classical Dictionary* picking out attractive names for new frigates while allowing those frigates he had to decay from neglect.[3] He had first become first lord as far back as 1748, had held the post again in the 1760s, and in 1771 was appointed for a third time to that office. He knew the navy.

Sandwich kept patronage books, leather bound and bearing the gold-tooled title 'Appointment of Officers', in which the names of those recommended for or seeking promotion were set down, in columns which recorded by whom and for what they were recommended, and what the case was.[4] Lieutenant William Williams, recommended by Lord North, who happened to be prime minister, was unsurprisingly promoted master and commander. Lieutenant Young, recommended by the admiral his father, was found employment in the Mediterranean. Lieutenant Samuel Thompson, on half pay, recommended himself 'to be put somehow on full pay'; no outcome is recorded. Those putting forward candidates included the Lord Chancellor, Lord Plymouth (recommending his son), the Bishop of Oxford, and the dukes of Leeds and Kingston. The case stated varied from 'driven from his estates by [Irish] rebels', to 'was round the world with Capt. Wallis', to 'very indigent and unfortunate', to 'slow, but a good man.'[5]

In these books the name of Horatio Nelson appears nine times, first when he was a midshipman on board the frigate *Seahorse* in 1775, in the East. In the column which asks by whom the man is recommended this entry candidly appears: 'Capt. Suckling, his uncle.'[6] When Nelson returned in 1776, the lords of the admiralty wrote to the port admiral at Portsmouth directing him to appoint a well-qualified midshipman to act as fourth lieutenant of the *Worcester*, a ship of the line of 64 guns, under Captain Mark Robinson.[7] The admiral, who of course knew Suckling, duly appointed a young man whom Captain Robinson wrote down in his ship's books as Horace Nelson,[8] who presented himself with letters from Captain Suckling. Robinson took good care of his new young gentleman, introducing him to the port admiral and taking him to dinner with the mayor of Portsmouth. And when they reached Cadiz, it was Nelson rather than one of the more senior officers of the *Worcester*, who was sent ashore with mail for the British consul. During a winter of dreadful weather in the Channel and the Atlantic, Robinson was well pleased with Nelson, who later recalled that the captain felt as easy when Nelson was in charge of a watch, as any other officer in the ship.[9]

But the rank of acting lieutenant was purely temporary. Nelson was paid as a lieutenant and did a lieutenant's duties, but as soon as he left the *Worcester* he would revert to his former rating of midshipman. He still, however, figured in Sandwich's patronage book, and on 9 April 1777 he appeared before three captains to take his lieutenant's examination, without which no man could go further.[10]

The commissioning of officers was the admiralty's business, but by an historical anomaly the examination of young gentlemen to determine whether they were fit to hold a lieutenant's commission was conducted by the navy board. The examinations were by tradition conducted by three captains. During his time as comptroller, Suckling had consistently sat as chairman of the examining board, and he did that day. The other two captains were very different men. Captain Abraham North was ordinary. He had been made lieutenant as far back as 1739 and had been a post captain for twenty-two years, but had seen little sea service. His principal business was as regulating captain of the impress service, the press gang, which in seaports rounded up unwilling men to serve in his majesty's ships. The other captain, John Campbell, was a remarkable man. He had himself been impressed into the navy from a Scottish coaster, went round the world with Anson as master's mate and was afterwards made lieutenant, and became a post captain in 1747. He served in the *Victory* when she was a new ship, commanded a first rate and then a royal yacht, was reputed to have declined a knighthood, and was almost unrivalled as an astronomer and navigator.[11] These three captains stated that Nelson appeared to be twenty years of age – he was not quite nineteen – that he produced certificates from five captains under whom he had served, that he had been at sea for more than six years, and that he could splice, knot, reef a sail, and perform his duty as an able seaman and midshipman.[12] There is a tradition that when Nelson was shown into the room Suckling showed no sign of recognition, and that only when it was clear that there could be no doubt the candidate had passed did he rise from his seat and beg to introduce his nephew.[13] At which the captains are reputed to have expressed surprise at not being informed before, and Suckling to have replied that he had not wished the younker to be favoured. This is a good story but wildly improbable. Captains Campbell and North had been examining for eight years, and with Suckling for the two years since his appointment as comptroller. They knew him and they knew how the system worked. Nor was there anything unusual in an uncle's patronage of his nephew. Such nepotism was expected and openly avowed, as it was in Lord Sandwich's books. Nelson was the only candidate examined that day, which was unusual. At its previous sitting, the week before, the same board had examined five. Furthermore, one of the captain's certificates produced by Nelson was from Suckling, with whom he first went to sea, so it would have been obvious he knew Nelson. The tradition makes a good story, but that is all. Clarke and M'Arthur say the source is William. Nelson did not hint that anything of the sort had happened when he wrote five days later to William, telling him he had passed his 'degree as Master of Arts'.[14]

Not that he did quite have his degree. Passing the lieutenant's examination did not give a man a commission. There was no such thing as a commission in the abstract. It had to be a commission to serve as lieutenant in a certain named vessel. Men who had passed their certificate could wait years for a ship. One unfortunate, given acting rank by Howe of all people, had to wait ten years. A few were never called. Of the ten who passed immediately before and after Nelson, only four received a commission that same year, five waited anything from one year to four, and one was never made.[15] Nelson on the other hand received his commission the very next day, as second lieutenant of the frigate *Lowestoffe*, 32 guns.[16] 'So,' as he continued in his letter to William, 'I am now left in [the] world to shift for myself, which I hope I shall do, so as to bring credit to myself and friends.' He would not quite have to fend for himself. His uncle the comptroller even franked the letter, which saved Nelson the postage.

It was a very good time to begin a sea officer's career. Not only was there war against the rebel American colonies, but in February 1778 Britain declared war on France when she signed an alliance with the Americans. So there was a general war and general employment. If we consider again the ten men who were Nelson's immediate contemporaries, of the nine who were commissioned two progressed no further than lieutenant and one no further than commander, but no fewer than six became post captains. Of these six, one (Philip Gidley King) became governor of New South Wales, and four achieved flag rank. Of these last four, two were knighted.[17]

The captain of the *Lowestoffe* was William Locker, a man of some parts. He had served in the West Indies, North America, India, and China, and sailed with Hawke and Jervis. He had been wounded in the boarding and taking of a more powerful French privateer, and Nelson frequently quoted his advice: 'Lay a Frenchman close and you will beat him.' He and Nelson became close friends. Two-thirds of the existing letters written by Nelson in his first four years as a commissioned officer were to Locker.[18] And to Locker is owed the first portrait of Nelson,

who liked to have portraits of his young officers. Before Nelson sailed
he gave sittings to John Francis Rigaud, a French émigré who had also
painted Joshua Reynolds, William Chambers, and the ceiling of Trinity
House. It was unfinished when Nelson sailed with the *Lowestoffe*, and
was put away for three years. It is the only portrait of Nelson made
before he was changed by recurrent illness and wounds.

In the *Lowestoffe* Nelson sailed for Jamaica, which was the principal
British naval base in the Caribbean. He was an outstanding and fearless
lieutenant. He liked to tell the story of his boarding a captured French
merchantman in a gale of wind and a heavy sea, saying it was an
event which presaged his character, and remarking that it was his
disposition that difficulties and dangers only increased his desire of
attempting them.[19] He was not modest. From Jamaica, with his eye
on the American rebellion to the north, he wrote home to Captain
Suckling about the Yankees who had come down the Mississippi,
plundered the plantations, carried off the negroes, and sold them at
New Orleans. Providence (now Annapolis) had also been taken by the
Americans, and here Nelson added an approving note which gives some
idea of his lifelong contempt for rebels. 'It was retaken by a Kingston
privateer who flogg'd the whole council for giving it up without firing
a shot.'[20]

After Britain declared war on the French, Rear-Admiral Sir Peter
Parker came out as commander-in-chief of the Jamaica station. Here
was a character, an admiral in a line of admirals. His father had been
an admiral, and his own son and grandson became admirals too. As
commodore on the New York station he had already taken Long Island
and Rhode Island.[21] He had served his country well, and believed that
a grateful country should reward its sea officers. He was one of those
officers who also became a member of parliament. In one debate on the
promotion of officers, having spoken on the peril and fatigue of a naval
life, he told the Commons that if neither honours nor emoluments were
to be given to officers who had behaved meritoriously, and gallantly
distinguished themselves, he feared that the mere thanks of the House
(which were frequently voted) would be considered only as an empty
compliment.[22] Sir Peter practised what he preached. He had made a
nephew lieutenant at the age of thirteen, and his son Christophe
post captain at seventeen, with the result that this son later became
rear-admiral at the age of thirty-four; no younger man is known to

have attained that rank.[23] When he arrived in Jamaica, Parker knew Nelson was the comptroller's nephew, and was happy to take an active young man into his flagship, the *Bristol*, which was the classic way of bringing a young man on. In July 1778 Nelson joined Parker as third lieutenant. By September he had, by succession, become first lieutenant of the flagship.[24] He was not quite twenty. By then he had just heard that his uncle the comptroller had died. But as Nelson wrote to his father: 'Even in his last illness he did not forget me but recommend'd me in the strongest manner to Sir Peter Parker who has promised he will make me the first captain.'[25]

So Suckling was succeeded as patron by Parker, and again Nelson could not have had a better sponsor. At home an officer had to rely on the admiralty for employment and promotion. But an admiral who was commander-in-chief of a foreign station had almost equal powers. He could promote whom he wished, and though his promotions would be subject to confirmation by the admiralty, by long tradition such an admiral's appointments to fill death vacancies were always confirmed. And there were deaths enough on the busy Jamaica station, deaths and prizes.

Prizes were a great consolation. In one year Parker's own flagship took three ships, two schooners, and a sloop, carrying cargoes of lumber, staves, rum, sugar, pimento, negroes, and dry goods. The other ships under his command took forty-six more. Typical among them were the *Pirha*, ship, of Rochelle, bound from West Africa to Cap François with 570 slaves; the *Fredericksburg*, an American sloop, with rum, sugar, and salt; and the *Comte de Vergennes*, ship, of Havre, bound from Port au Prince to Bordeaux with sugar, coffee, indigo, and cotton.[26] Most were out of or bound for the ports of St Domingue, now Haiti, then the richest of all French colonies. Prizes formally belonged to the Crown, but by an act of parliament of 1708, to encourage seamen and sea officers, the whole net value of a prize went to those who took her. Parker, as commander-in-chief, took one-eighth of the entire value of any prize taken by a vessel of his squadron, whether he was there or not. The captain of that vessel took a quarter. The lieutenants, of whom in a frigate there might be four, divided another eighth between them. The warrant officers and petty officers – the master, boatswain, chaplain, surgeon, clerks, sailmakers, and incidentally midshipmen – shared another quarter. Then the last quarter was split between all the rest, captain's servants, seamen, and boys. A modest prize of £10,000 taken by a small frigate would yield the captain £2,500, each lieutenant £312, and each seaman £25. This was ten years' pay for the captain and a full year's for each seaman. It was a lottery and an inducement.

Deaths from disease and war continued. The French frigates were typically larger and faster than the British. In late August the *Concorde* took the *Minerva*. Captain John Stott was wounded in the head. A piece of his ear was shot off, his eyesight and hearing taken away by a great swelling, and a ball remained in his face. A few days later the *Active* (Captain William Williams) was taken and towed into Cap François, where she was moored alongside the *Minerva*. Nelson knew both these captains. He wrote to his friend Locker that three hundred British seamen lay in the jails of St Domingue, and that poor Captain Williams had died of a broken heart.[27] By 8 December 1778, losses had been so great that Parker had to make fourteen new appointments in one day. One of them was Nelson, who was made master and commander of the *Badger* brig.[28]

This was a between rank given to officers who commanded vessels smaller than frigates, in effect sloops or brigs. A frigate was a three masted square rigged ship, carrying anything from twenty to forty-four guns, mostly used for commerce raiding or reconnaissance. A sloop carried twenty guns or fewer, and could be either a three masted ship or a two masted brig. Officers in command of sloops were called master and commander because such vessels did not also carry a master – that is to say an uncommissioned navigating officer – as all larger ships did. A commander was called Captain This or That, but that was out of courtesy. He was not a post captain. Commander was the first step in a sea officer's promotion.

Nelson spent only six months in the *Badger*, in a filthy climate and constant rains protecting the settlers in the bay of Honduras from American privateers. But he did everything well and gained the affection of the settlers who, as he did not hesitate to say, voted him their unanimous thanks.[29] On her return to Jamaica, the *Badger* was lying in Montego Bay when the *Glasgow* sloop came in, anchored, and was soon in flames. A steward with a candle had tried to steal rum and a cask caught fire. Nelson was affected by this as he was not afterwards affected in battle, and told Locker he thought the burning

ship a most shocking sight. He saved all her crew.[30] Then in June 1779
he was given the most essential promotion in the career of a sea officer.
A commander could remain a commander for the rest of his days,
without promotion or even employment. Many did. As St Vincent put
it with typical blunt emphasis: 'Seniority upon *that vile list* is no boast,
or ever can be of service to any man.'[31] Many a commander, after his
sloop was paid off, found himself less able to find employment than if
he had remained a lieutenant, and had to live on half pay for years.
In 1790 about 300 lieutenants were employed, as against sixty-eight
commanders. But once an officer was given command of a post ship,
a frigate or larger, he became a post captain. The list of post captains
was inviolable and unalterable, and the order of seniority on it was
determined by the date of a captain's commission. An officer on *this* list
had only to survive, and not be disgraced and dismissed the service, in
order to rise. Employed or unemployed, on full pay or half pay, he rose
as those above him were killed, or died off, or in the fullness of time
became admirals. And when an officer rose to the top of the list of post
captains, he himself was raised, in one of the periodic promotions, to
rear-admiral. Once a man was a post captain, and lived, he would die
an admiral.

In the autumn of 1778 Admiral Parker had bought a captured
French ship into the service, armed her with 28 guns, rated her a
frigate, and renamed her the *Hinchinbrook*.[32] She was a post ship, and
her commander would be a post captain. In June of 1779, when her
first British captain was killed by a random shot from a French ship,
Parker gave Nelson command of her. Since it was a death vacancy it
would be confirmed. As Nelson wrote to his brother William, 'We all
rise by *deaths*. I got my rank by a shot killing a post captain and I
most sincerely hope I shall, when I go, go out of the world the same
way ...'[33] He was made.

The rise in Nelson's fortune in the previous six months is best put
in his own words, written many years later and speaking of another
young lieutenant, but the essence was the same for any sea officer: 'Get
him the next two steps, commander and post, for until that is done,
nothing substantial is effected; then the whole glory of our service is
opened to him.'[34]

Nelson was post, and in command of a frigate bearing the name
Hinchinbrook, which was the name of the estate of Lord Sandwich, who

had preferred him in the first place. He was still not twenty-one. To be post captain so young was extraordinary. Of other admirals, Jervis (later Lord St Vincent) gained that rank at 24, Collingwood at 29, the great Hood at 31. And this rapid early promotion was crucial to his later career, because a captain's promotion to admiral depended not at all on brilliance but entirely on length of service on the captains' list. Unless Nelson had been post captain at twenty he could never have won his first great victory at the Nile. Only an admiral could have commanded the British squadron in that battle. If he had achieved post rank only a year later than he did, he would not have been an admiral in time.

CHAPTER FOUR

The Reduction of the New World

BY AUGUST 1779 THE widespread war was going badly for Britain. What the British saw as a civil war between British subject and British subject was being fought in the thirteen colonies of the American eastern seaboard. The French, having leapt at the chance of helping the American rebels and thereby embarrassing their ancient enemy, had sent a great fleet into the Caribbean. Spain, embracing a French promise to help her recover Gibraltar and Florida, had also entered the war against Britain. The Dutch had signed a treaty of amity with the American rebels. It was a world war. Scattered British armies and fleets were fighting the French from America to India. A French fleet menaced the English channel. Britain was alone, and as beleaguered as she ever was later in the French revolutionary wars. In the American theatre, where Nelson was serving, the thirteen colonies of the eastern seaboard were not the only territories of the New World at risk. Both Florida and Canada were vulnerable. The West Indian colonies were in a larger and strategic sense part of Britain's American possessions, and they were very rich and tempting to an enemy. The French had already taken St Vincent and Grenada. Barbados was disaffected. And Jamaica, the largest and most important of all the British islands, was menaced by Vice-Admiral Comte d'Estaing at St Domingue, only 300 miles to the east. He was at the northern port of Cap François with twenty ships of the line and 25,000 men. At Jamaica, ready to resist this force when it came, were only 6,800 men, five ships of the line, five frigates, and four fire ships. Nelson himself had been given command of Fort Charles, a battery which covered the entrance to the anchorage at Kingston. He wrote home: 'I leave you in England to judge what stand we shall make. I think you must not be surprised to hear of my learning to speak French.'[1] He seems to have meant, as a prisoner of war of the French. This is an unusually realistic letter for Nelson. Later on he never counted odds, or, if he did, never admitted it.

Invasion was expected. The governor himself, Major General John Dalling, published in the Kingston newspaper the cheerful message that he had no reasonable hope of preserving the colony without speedy reinforcement. This, when it reached London, brought a stinging rebuke from Lord George Germain, secretary of state for the colonies: 'Be more cautious of submitting such matters to the public eye, and forego the little temporary popularity which can be obtained by such exposures, when they have a tendency . . . to bring calamity upon the country you are appointed to watch over.'[2]

By December the danger of invasion had passed. D'Estaing did not invade Jamaica but sailed his fleet north to help the Americans at Savannah, and then returned to France. By then Dalling had revived a bold, mad plan that had been in his mind for months, would cost any number of lives, and nearly kill Nelson. France was the principal enemy, but from Jamaica Dalling saw that Britain's Caribbean possessions were dominated, on the map at least, by a great western arc of Spanish provinces and viceroyalties – Mexico to the north, and Guatemala, Nicaragua, New Granada, and even Peru further south. He conceived a plan to cut the Spanish Americas in two, to open a door from the Caribbean to the Pacific, destroy the Spanish dominion of Central and South America, seize the treasures of these provinces, and with such gains redress the losses in North America. It has to be said that the folly was not all Dalling's, and that Germain encouraged the scheme until he saw it had collapsed. Dalling had a copy of Thomas Jefferys's *West India Atlas*, whose commentary listed the glories of the Spanish province of Nicaragua – its plentiful timber, sugar cane, cotton, cattle pastures, and the salubrity of the Lake of Nicaragua itself, which was the largest sheet of fresh water in Central America. The atlas showed that from the port of San Juan del Norte, on the Caribbean coast four hundred miles southwest of Jamaica, the river San Juan ran one hundred and ten miles inland to the lake, which extended westward for another sixty miles. And the lake at one point was only eleven miles from the South Sea, the Pacific. Dalling formed his plan. He would send a force inland from San Juan del Norte. It would ascend the river San Juan, which is now the border between Costa Rica and Nicaragua, as far as the lake of Nicaragua. The only obstacle on the river was the castle of the Immaculate Conception, some miles before the river met the lake. The expedition would cross this lake and then take and ransom the cities of Granada and Leon, which were on or near the lake.[3] Then the land crossing from the lake to the Pacific, as the atlas showed, would be only a few miles. This plan was approved. The troops from Jamaica had to get to San Juan del Norte. Admiral Parker was sceptical of the whole idea but appointed Nelson, who had the most recent experience of the Mosquito coast, to escort the troop transports.

At about this time Nelson wrote to Locker, who had returned home for his health. It was a letter full of news. Kitty Crawford was sending two jars of tamarinds. Of the Jamaica squadron, two men they both knew had been killed, and a third had died of fever. Admiral Parker had promised him the first bigger frigate that became vacant. The *Hinchinbrook* in company with two other frigates had taken four vessels as prizes, and Nelson's share would be about £800. (This was about seven times his annual pay as captain of a small frigate.) And he mentioned that he had been appointed to go with an expedition now on foot upon the Lake of Nicaragua. 'How it will turn out,' he wrote, 'God knows.'[4]

Dalling assembled his force. There were only 200 regulars, assisted by a ragtag of 'volunteers' – freed slaves, seamen without ships, and prisoners from the jails. In command was Captain John Polson, of the 60th Regiment of Foot. The medical officer of the expedition was Benjamin Moseley, MD, who was learned both in *obeah*, negro witchcraft, and in the course of the plague in ancient Athens, but knew little of tropical diseases. 'Enthusiasm was never carried to a greater height,' he said, 'than by those who had promised to themselves the glory of shaking Spain to her foundation. The colours of England were, in their imagination, already even on the walls of Lima.' Moseley did not give way to his patriotic fervour so far as to accompany the expedition, sending instead the younger Thomas Dancer, physician to the Jamaica baths.[5]

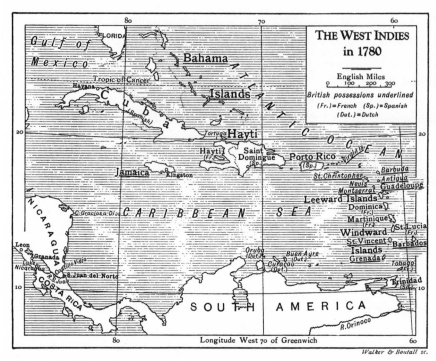

Map of the West Indies and central America, 1780, showing Jamaica, where Nelson served and from where he sailed to take part in the disastrous Nicaraguan adventure (bottom left), and the islands of Nevis, Antigua, and Barbados which he later knew well. Adapted from Nelson and His Times *by Rear-Admiral Lord Charles Beresford, 1897.*

The expeditionary force paraded in Kingston on 3 February, the hundred volunteers among them half-clothed and half-drunk, and then boarded seven transports. Dalling wrote to Germain promising him 'the dominion of Spain in this part of the world'.[6] Germain, writing from London, hoped that a colony with so fine a climate as Nicaragua's could not fail to draw settlers from North America, where many who had been ruined by the rebellion might hope to restore their fortunes by moving to a happier country.[7] The expedition was delayed. Not until seven weeks out of Jamaica did Polson arrive at the mouth of the San Juan, and when he tried to launch his men upriver in their forty-foot canoes, the overloaded boats overturned in the swirling current, and the men were rescued with difficulty. It was here that Nelson stepped in. He offered to accompany the expedition up the San Juan, and take fifty of the *Hinchinbrook*'s people and two of the ship's boats with him.[8] Now this was not his duty. His orders were to escort the transports to the mouth of the San Juan. Parker had been reluctant to approve even this, thinking no good could come of it. But Nelson did go upriver. It was his first, and quite flagrant, disobedience of orders. And then, as Captain Polson put it: 'In two or three days he displayed himself, and afterwards he directed all the operations.'⁹ Polson caught Nelson's spirit. He was saying in those words what St Vincent expressed twenty years later, when he said that Nelson 'possessed the magic art of infusing the same spirit into others'.¹⁰

The expedition, having left its medical supplies behind to save weight, started towards the interior where, as Nelson put it, none but Spaniards since the time of the buccaneers had ever ascended. After a few days of savannah they were in a rainforest, with trees a hundred feet high either side of the river. Then they travelled through jungle. They had arrived two months too late, so near the end of the dry season that the river was low and men became exhausted dragging boats over mud. Alligators were in the river, monkeys and snakes in the trees. One man was bitten near the eye by a snake hanging from a branch. Four hours later, said Dr Dancer, he was dead, 'with all the symptoms of putrefaction and the eye all dissolved'. A Spanish prisoner told them the castle was only five miles further on. Nelson and Lieutenant Despard, an engineer officer, took a canoe, paddled upriver, and in the early morning of 11 April gained their first view of the castle they had to take. It stood on a hill beside the river, and its walls were fifty feet high.¹¹ Nelson was all for bringing up their men and artillery and attacking straightaway. Polson wished to lay siege in a proper military fashion, and wait for reinforcements from the coast. They laid siege for eleven days. A man was struck in the back by the paws of a 'tiger', more likely a jaguar. They did try to undermine the castle walls, but struck solid rock. Nelson came down with what appeared to be dysentery. It was not. He and others had drunk from a clear pool, but, as the Indians discovered, a branch of the poisonous machineel tree was floating in it. Then the rainy season came. Dr Moseley, who was not there, later gave quite the most vivid descriptions of the terrain and climate. Here he is on the rain: 'The torrents of water that fall for weeks together are prodigious ... This bursting of the waters above and the raging of the river below, with the blackness of the nights, accompanied by horrible tempests of lightning and thunder, constitute a magnificent scene of terror unknown but in the tropical world.' Exhausted men were permanently soaked. By now many were suffering not only from dysentery but from yellow fever they had contracted at the coast, which had taken its usual month to incubate. Nelson was prostrate.

Polson was about to invite the castle to surrender when orders came up the river. Among them was one from Admiral Parker, appointing Nelson to the *Janus*, 44 guns. Parker's final act of patronage, keeping his promise of a bigger frigate, saved Nelson's life. He was lifted into a canoe which in three days descended the same river the expedition had taken three weeks to ascend, and taken in a sloop to Kingston where he was carried ashore in his cot. He was cared for by Cuba Cornwallis, a freed Jamaican slave, whose cheerful care and cooling herbs saved more feverish men than ever the hospital did. Dr Moseley described the state of those who returned from Nicaragua, saying it was long doubtful whether those who were thrown in the river, or lay unburied on its banks, a prey to wild beasts, were not in a more enviable state than the survivors. These were harassed by intermittent fever, diarrhoea, dysentery, and painful enlargements of the spleen and liver. Their complexions were very yellow, their bodies emaciated, and their senses at times disordered.

The news Nelson brought back was disastrous. Then, about three weeks after his return, dispatches came from Polson. The castle of the Immaculate Conception, having no well and being out of water, had surrendered the day after Nelson left. Polson was generous to Nelson: 'I want words to express the obligations I owe to that gentleman. He was the first on every service whether day or night, there was scarcely a gun fired but was pointed by him or Lieut. Despard.'[12] Dalling became sanguine again, writing to Germain that the door to the South Sea, the Pacific, was open, and proposing attacks on Chile and Mexico. In his opinion 5,000 regulars marching from Vera Cruz could shake to the very centre the enormous and ill-constructed fabric of Spanish dominion in America. Even Peru might become an easy prey.[13] While his men rotted, he was foreseeing thousands of miles of new empire, and went on to confide the very heart and source of his grand confidence. 'In military matters,' he wrote, 'it often happens that those things that seem of the greatest magnitude in point of difficulty are eventually attended with scarce any seeming hardship & fall with a facility that astonishes.

The reduction of the new world will, I hope, effectively prove the truth of my observation . . .'[14]

When Nelson heard the castle had fallen he wrote congratulating Dalling, and Dalling congratulated him, saying: 'To you, without compliment, do I attribute, in a great measure, the cause.'[15] The two men got on well. In the middle of June, Nelson was at the admiral's house in the mountains, where the climate was kinder than on the coast. But Lady Parker, who liked him and came to think of him as a son, was away, and he wrote this note to his friend Hercules Ross: 'What would I give to be at Port Royal. Lady P not here, and the servants letting me lay as if a dog, and take no notice.'[16] But Nelson appeared to be recovering and warmed to Dalling, admiring the 'loyal spirit' of a man who had served with the Duke of Cumberland in putting down the Stuart rebellion of 1745.[17] Dalling in turn wrote Nelson a glowing testimonial, in the form of a letter to Germain.

> Private.
>
> I have hitherto neglected a piece of justice due to the service of Captain Nelson ... He left his ship in the harbour [of San Juan del Norte], and attended the first division up the river to the fort with some of his seamen, he then dedicated himself to the erecting of the batteries, and afterwards to the fighting them ... I must humbly intreat that His Majesty will be gratiously pleased thro' your lordship to manifest a satisfaction of his conduct, and in case a co-operating squadron should have been determined on for the southern ocean [the Pacific], that he may be employed in that service; as for the service under my direction on this northern one [the Caribbean] Captain Nelson's constitution is rather too delicate, but such minds, my lord, are most devoutly to be wished for governments sake . . .[18]

Dalling gave Nelson a copy of this letter, signed with his own hand, and Nelson did, five years later, make use of it to recommend himself to another secretary of state. But it was no use to Nelson that summer, even if there had been a Pacific squadron. Parker doubted if Nelson would live to get home. Three doctors did a survey on him, and this is their report: 'We have strictly and carefully examined into the nature of the complaints of Captain Horatio Nelson ... and find that from repeated attacks of tertian and quartian agues, and those now degenerated into quotidian, attended with bilious vomitings, nervous headaches, visceral obstructions and many other bodily infirmities, and being reduced to a skeleton, we are of opinion that his remaining here will be attended with fatal consequences, wou'd therefore recommend an immediate change of climate as the only chance he has for recovery.'[19]

Parker sent him home in a ship of the line, attended by John Tyson, who had been his purser in the *Badger*. He was only twenty-one. It was his second passage home in a dying condition. His illness had cost him the *Janus*, and it was a great loss. She was a new 44-gun frigate, a finer ship than he would command for another thirteen years. At the height of Nelson's fame, his father still remembered how reluctant he had been to give up his command.[20] But hope remained. 'I shall recover and my dream of glory be fulfilled,' he told Ross. 'Nelson will yet be an admiral. It is the climate that has destroyed my health and crushed my spirit.'[21]

Dalling's Nicaraguan expedition collapsed and retreated. Germain was savage, calling the adventure ill-conceived and worse executed, and lamenting exceedingly the dreadful havoc death had made among the troops.[22] Dalling still believed he could open a door to the Pacific, but what use would it have been? It would not even have cut off communication between the northern and southern provinces of the Spanish empire, because communication was not by land but by sea. As Fortescue, the historian of the British army, later asked of the whole expedition – if the door had been opened, to what advantage? Seventy years later the forty-niners, crossing from the east to the San Francisco gold rush, followed Dalling's route – up the San Juan, across the Lake of Nicaragua, and then overland to the Pacific. Later still, the route was surveyed as an alternative to the Panama Canal, but nothing came of it.

Dalling was disgraced, recalled, made a baronet, and promoted lieutenant-general. Nelson, when he left Jamaica, did not know the expedition had failed so completely. He did not know that the *Hinchinbrook*, which he had sailed to San Juan del Norte, had lost from disease all but ten of its crew of two hundred.[23] He may have been sceptical at the start of the expedition, when he said God knew how it would turn out, but he did come to believe it would have succeeded if it had started when it should have done, two months earlier and before the rainy season. He got on with Dalling when Parker, his commander-in-chief, did not. Years later, after the Nile, when Lady Dalling wrote to congratulate him, she called him an old friend for whom her husband had a true regard, 'and whose attachment to him I believe to have been equally strong'.[24]

The young Nelson, already a very able captain, admired in Dalling, bad general though he was, the boldness that could envisage cutting the Americas in two, destroying the Spanish empire in America, and then proceeding to the conquest of Mexico, Chile, and Peru. Nelson, as a very junior rear-admiral, later assumed the direction of a large part of Britain's Mediterranean strategy and saw himself as the saviour of Italy. It may have sounded absurd for Dalling to write to the secretary of state that it often happened in military affairs that feats which seemed of the greatest difficulty were achieved in the event without hardship, and with astonishing ease. It sounded absurd because Dalling was incompetent. But from Nelson, later on, those words would have been no more than a simple statement of his own habitual bold instinct.

CHAPTER FIVE

Fair Canada, and the Merest Boy

THE ENGLAND TO WHICH Nelson returned by the late fall of 1780 was far from happy. In the American colonies the land war appeared to be going the way of the British, who had captured Charleston, Carolina, but French troops had arrived as reinforcements at Rhode Island, and at sea only an indecisive action had been fought against the French at Martinique. And London had been under mob rule for several days during anti-Catholic riots led by a retired navy lieutenant, Lord George Gordon. Nelson went to Bath to recover. He stayed there for the winter because it was, as he told his old friend Captain Locker, like Jamaica to any other part of England. He was physicked four times a day, drank the waters three times a day, and was so ill that by the following January he still had to be carried to and from bed. As he put it, he had not yet recovered the use of his limbs, but his inside was a new man. His spirit was reviving. He asked for a copy of the new Navy List.[1]

Something of Nelson's reputation had preceded him to Bath. *The London Gazette* had carried Captain Polson's report that Nelson had volunteered to accompany the troops up the San Juan river, and that scarcely any gun had been fired that was not pointed by him.[2] He was impatient. At the end of January he wanted a ship, but two weeks later he still did not have use of his left arm.[3] William Suckling of the custom office, brother of the late Maurice Suckling, was already lobbying on behalf of his nephew. He wrote to Charles Jenkinson, secretary at war, who was notorious for having the ear of both the king and the prime minister.[4] Jenkinson in turn wrote to Lord Sandwich, still first lord of the admiralty, with whom he had served in government on and off for eighteen years, saying he would be much obliged if Nelson, who was the nephew of the late comptroller of the navy and bore a very good character, could be employed.[5] This is a classical example of the way interest worked. Jenkinson's letter books show that in the previous year he had recommended thirty-four men for various preferments, including a captaincy in the Coldstream Guards, an ensigncy in the 55th of Foot, and a living in Yorkshire. Through Jenkinson, Maurice Suckling, two years dead, could still be called to the aid of his protégé.

By March 1781 Nelson still had a slight fever, but came up to London to view Mr Rigaud's portrait of him, which had been started more than three years before. He was certain it would no longer be the least like him. Rigaud was asked to 'add beauty'. He added a post captain's uniform, and in the background a representation of the Castle of the Immaculate Conception, which had been so uselessly taken at such cost, but the features remained those of the young lieutenant he had started to paint.[6] In London, Nelson visited his brother Maurice, who was now at the navy office. He also saw Lord Sandwich, who, having been reminded by Jenkinson, promised a ship at the first opportunity. He did not go home to Burnham Thorpe to see his father until the summer, seven months after he arrived in England.[7] His older sister Susannah, who was twenty-five, had been rescued from her apprenticeship to a milliner by a legacy of £2,000 from Maurice Suckling and a moderate marriage to Thomas Bolton, a merchant in corn, malt, and coals. Ann, who was nineteen, had been indentured to a lace warehouse in London but had bought herself out with her share of the legacy. Nelson's favourite sister, Catherine, was only fifteen. William had taken orders, and was a curate.[8]

It was wartime, when a captain of any ability or interest would certainly get a ship, and in August Sandwich gave Nelson another frigate, though not much of one. She was the *Albemarle*, 28 guns, a French merchantman taken as a prize. He went down to see her in dock at Woolwich with Maurice and Locker. She was not beautiful, but Nelson was happy with her, saying her hull had a bold entrance and a clean run. He offered a bounty of two pounds to any seaman who signed on, and twenty did, which meant he would not have to press so many.[9]

It was while the *Albemarle* was coppering and fitting out that the dull William began the cadging and lobbying that he continued for the rest of his illustrious brother's life. Could he profitably go to sea as a chaplain? He asked this four times. It was five to one, Nelson replied, that William would not like it. 'If you get with a good man and a gentleman [as captain] it will be tolerable, if not you will soon detest it. It's a chance ...' And at last, for the moment and for that voyage, William desisted.

When *Albemarle* moved down to Sheerness, Nelson was convinced that he would not wish to change a man or an officer in her. In Yarmouth Roads he was convinced his ship could outrun a new 44-gun frigate – that is to say one of the *Janus* kind, which he had been obliged to give up in Jamaica. He was always cheerful about his ship of the moment.

At the Nore in the Thames estuary, late in October, he read bad news of the American war, feared for General Cornwallis, and thought that if something was not done immediately, America was quite lost.[10] It was worse than he knew. Cornwallis had already surrendered at Yorktown, and the land campaign was almost over. And Nelson was ill again, hardly able to get out of bed. For a man still so shaky, his orders for the winter were not ideal. He was to spend it escorting convoys in the Baltic and the North Sea, hanging round for a month waiting for two hundred merchant ships to assemble, and then trying to keep them together. On Tuesday 5 November, *Albemarle*'s log reads: 'Elsinore Road. Fresh gales and rainy. Fired 19 guns it being Gun Powder Plot.'[11] By January 1782, back in the Channel, he was ill again. The weather of the previous month had been the worst he had ever seen, 'with nothing but wrecks all over the coast'. Then he was ordered to Portsmouth to take on eight months' supplies, which meant a long voyage. He had no doubt it was to the East Indies, which he would have liked exceedingly. Chance disappointed him. On 29 January, in a gale, an East Indiaman broke from her anchors and rammed *Albemarle*. She lost her foremast and bowsprit and was stove in on the port side. Nelson was thankful she did not founder, but feared she was so badly damaged she would be paid off, which would leave him unemployed.[12] He made his last appearance in Sandwich's patronage books. '*Person recommended*: Horatio Nelson. *By whom*: himself. *For what*: larger frigate.' This time he got nothing.[13] Lord North's government, having all but lost America, was on its last legs, and collapsed on 19 March, taking Sandwich with it. His long career at the admiralty was over.

So 'the old *Albemarle*', as Nelson was now calling her, was patched up and due to be sent on more convoy work, this time to Quebec, where she was to winter. 'I want much to [get] off from this d – d voyage,' wrote Nelson, 'and believe me if I had time to look a little about me I could get another ship.' He expected Canada to be cold and damp and feared it might make him worse than ever, and sailed unwillingly, still hoping for a better ship and a better station than Quebec.[14] He arrived there in July, having lived on salt beef for eight weeks, with no vegetables, and knocked up with the scurvy. Having delivered his convoy, Nelson cruised off Boston where he escaped in what he called a wonderful manner from four French ships of the line and a frigate, who led him a 'pretty dance' for nine or ten hours before he evaded them first in fog and then in the shoals of St George's Bank, where the larger French ships could not follow. The pilot among those shoals was an American, whose schooner the *Albemarle* had taken as a prize the month before. After the action Nelson told this man that he had rendered them a very essential service, and that it was not the custom of English seamen to be ungrateful. So, with the approbation of his officers, who would be losing prize money, he gave him his vessel and a certificate, which read: 'These are to certify, that I took the schooner *Harmony*, Nathaniel Carver, master, belonging to Plymouth [Mass.]; but, on account of his good services, have given him up his vessel again ... Horatio Nelson, Boston Bay.'[15] It was a typically quixotic act of generosity.

The late fall at Quebec, far from being damp as Nelson had feared, is dry and tonic. As he wrote to his father, he never knew health until he saw fair Canada. He had also seen a girl. She was Mary Simpson, who was the daughter of the provost marshal of Quebec garrison and a belle of that city's balls. *The Quebec Gazette* called her, in verse, a Diana, and 'noble and majestic in her air'. She was sixteen. Then in mid-October Nelson was ordered to New York, which he thought a very pretty job for that late season, with his ship's sails frozen to their yards. There followed, according to Clarke and M'Arthur, a strange incident. Alexander Davison, a merchant and navy agent, found Nelson striding back from his ship into the city, and asked why.

Nelson: 'I find it utterly impossible to leave this place without waiting on her whose society has so much added to its charms and laying myself and my fortunes at her feet.'

Davison: 'Your utter ruin, situated as you are at present, must inevitably follow.'

Nelson: 'Then let it follow, for I am resolved to do it.'

Davison: 'And I also positively declare that you shall not.'[16]

At which Nelson desisted. The source has to be Davison. If it is not, it all becomes even more distant hearsay. If it is Davison, what we have is his recollection nearly thirty years later, and presented with Clarke and M'Arthur's gloss of sentiment. Is it possible that a man who had determined, after San Juan, that his dream of glory would be fulfilled and that he would be an admiral, would have intended to desert ship for a girl? He went to New York. Davison became his lifelong friend, and in later years his prize agent.

The *Albemarle*'s log for 21 November 1782 reads: 'At anchor at Sandy Hook [New York harbour]. Found riding here Rear Admiral Lord Hood with 12 sail of the line & 2 frigates.'[17] Hood had been a friend of Maurice Suckling, having commanded a guardship in Portsmouth harbour and later been commissioner of Portsmouth dockyard while Suckling was one of the town's members of parliament. Hood took to Suckling's nephew at first meeting. Nelson thought that the captains at New York considered prize money the great object and attended to nothing else. For himself, he knew the West Indies to be the 'grand theatre of actions',[18] and asked Hood to take him there. He had found a new patron, and even considered himself a candidate with Hood for a ship of the line, a strange optimism for a man who a month before was supposed to be on the verge of sacrificing his sea career to Miss Simpson.[19] It was a strange optimism in any event. Nelson was twenty-four and the captain of an indifferent frigate. He must have known that the command of a ship of the line, a ship of at least 64 guns, was a remote prospect. But his mind was flying high again, perhaps helped by his introduction to a prince of the blood. This was Prince William Henry, third son of George III, who had sent him to sea. He was serving with Hood on his flagship, and described the first time he saw Nelson. It is a picture of a very young post captain who, from his dress, evidently had only his pay to live on. And since Prince William became, almost fifty years later, William IV, it has the piquancy of being a picture of a genius, at a time when nothing extraordinary was expected from him, drawn by a man of very ordinary abilities who by chance was to become king. It has to be said that the prince did not give this description until many years later, after Nelson's death, when he knew what the young captain had become. Still, this is what he said he remembered:

'I was then a midshipman on board the *Barfleur*, lying in the narrows off Staten Island, and had a watch on deck, when Captain Nelson, of the *Albemarle*, came in his barge alongside, who appeared to be the merest boy of a captain I ever beheld; and his dress was worthy of attention. He had on a full-laced uniform: his lank unpowdered hair was tied in a stiff Hessian tail, of an extraordinary length; the old-fashioned flaps of his waistcoat added to the general quaintness of his figure, and produced an appearance which particularly attracted my notice; for I had never seen anything like it before ... My doubts were, however, removed when Lord Hood introduced me to him. There was something irresistibly pleasing in his address and conversation; and an enthusiasm, when speaking on professional subjects, that showed he was no common being ... I found him warmly attached to my father ...'[20]

Nelson was always warmly attached to kings, and no doubt told the prince so. And his situation in Hood's fleet was flattering to any young man. 'He treats me as if I was his son, and will, I am convinced, give me anything I can ask of him: nor is my situation with Prince William less flattering.' But in the West Indies they were all still in the dark whether it was peace or war.[21] In March, off Cuba, Nelson captured a Spanish launch with several French officers on board, who were making a scientific tour. One of the officers was Maximilian Joseph, comte de Deux Ponts, of whom more will be heard. Nelson, considering them savants rather than combatants, released them.[22]

That same month he mounted a brief attack on Turks Island, north of Le Cap. It was a small action, but had in it characteristics which later became familiar. He fell in with the *Resistance*, Captain James King, who told him the French had lately taken Turks Island. The *Resistance* was a larger frigate, of 44 guns, but her captain, though he had been round the world with Captain Cook, was junior to Nelson on the post captains' list. Nelson determined to retake the island. He took King under his command, as he did the *Tartar*, another frigate, and two brigs. Having collected a small squadron, he summoned the French commander of the island to surrender. When he declined, Nelson sent one hundred and sixty-seven seamen and marines ashore, and ordered the two brigs into the bay to 'batter' the town. This they did for more than an hour, until the evidently superior force of the French induced Nelson to retire. Eight of his men were injured.[23] This was no great action, but here is the young Nelson not hesitating to take four other ships under his command, and not hesitating to batter the capital, Grand Turk, just as he later threatened to batter down Bastia in Corsica and Santa Cruz, Tenerife, and just as he wished in 1799 to batter down the city of Naples.[24] The phrase came easily to him.

It was as well he called off the action. Peace had already come, in February. Hood's squadron was ordered home. Nelson wrote to Locker that, after all his tossing about in various climates, he hoped to be rid of the *Albemarle*. That is how he then spoke of her. He was bringing back twelve dozen bottles of rum for his friend, which he hoped to smuggle through the Custom House.[25]

CHAPTER SIX

Subjects of the Grand Monarque

WHEN JANET SCHAW, A Scottish lady of quality, visited the British Caribbean islands of St Kitts and Nevis in 1774 and 1775, just before the American war, she found thirty-two kinds of fruit – pineapples, oranges, citrus shaddocks, alligator pears – plentiful fish, and meat and poultry of all kinds. Pure, lucid water flowed from marble cisterns, so cold it made the teeth chatter. There was Madeira, port, claret, and champagne, though the ladies did not drink champagne 'as the heat made it fly too much'. Everywhere she found luxury. At dinner the napkins were washed and changed between courses. The men were amorous. The women were modest, dressed lightly in muslins, soft silk tiffities, or glossy lustrings, seldom walked out without a mask or veil, and danced every night.[1] St Kitts was small and Nevis even smaller, a circular island only seven miles across, but Nevis also had its hot springs, and in 1778 a three-storey stone-built hotel was erected here – an astonishing building for the Caribbean – where fifty guests could bathe in five thermal baths. There were 2,000 whites and 9,000 slaves. The principal crop was sugar cane, from which were made sugar, molasses, and rum. It was a land of plenty, where cotton and coffee grew as shrubs.

The great families of Nevis were the Herberts, the Nisbets, the Pinneys, and the Tobins. They were plantation owners and merchants, and tended also to be members of the island council. John Richardson Herbert was president of the council. Of the Pinneys and the Tobins it was said that the former made money and the latter had careers. In

Tobin family history there is a playwright, a general, and an admiral. The Tobins also had opinions. James Tobin, who kept a thousand slaves on his estate, published two pamphlets in which he defended the name of *creole*, and expressed decided views on the upbringing of creole young ladies.[2] He said, first, that he had never thought the name of creole disgraceful. And it was not. Creole was used with no suggestion of inferiority. Nor did it mean half-caste. A creole was a white man or woman who had been born in the West Indies. As to the young women, West Indian planters used, he said, to bring up their daughters themselves, to be excellent housewives and careful nurses. Lately, however, elegant and agreeable young creole women had been sent to boarding school in London, and acquired in these hotbeds of vanity the most romantic and expensive notions, which proved too often the foundation of a life of gaiety, pleasure, and dissipation.

One of the young women Mr Tobin was so concerned about was very likely Frances Woolward, daughter of the island's chief justice, who later married Nelson as her second husband. Whether she was sent to London to complete her education we do not know. She never said so, but then she was a discreet woman. She did have good French, and in her youth spoke it regularly, a facility she probably did not acquire on Nevis.[3] We do however know that the elegant and leisured Nevis described by Miss Schaw was the island on which Frances Woolward grew up.

Then came the war in America. This destroyed the island's trade Traditionally Nevis shipped rum, sugar, molasses, and indigo to the thirteen colonies which were its principal market, and received in return candles, bricks, timber, tar, corn, salt, and horses. The goods Nevis exported were luxuries to the Americans. The goods Nevis imported were essentials. The war was a disaster for the islands. By 1779–80 the price of the sugar they sold had fallen by 25–40%, and that of rum by 37%. The cost of salt they bought had risen by 50–100%, and that of corn 400%.[4] The British forbade trade with the rebellious colonies and the French fleet threatened the islands themselves.

Britain was also at war with the Dutch, and in February 1781 a British fleet under Admiral Sir George Rodney, carrying an army under General Vaughan, took the nearby Dutch island of St Eustatius generally called Statia, and 'everything in and belonging thereto'.[5] Miss Schaw had known Statia, which was only a few miles north of Nevis

It was not a great colony like St Domingue or Jamaica. Nor had it grown rich on its produce, like Nevis. It was a freeport which lived by commerce, and was so rich that it was known as the Golden Rock. There Miss Schaw found a place of vast traffic from every quarter of the globe. The town consisted of one street a mile long, but never had she seen such variety. Here was a merchant selling his goods in Dutch, another in French, a third in Spanish. It was one continued mart of embroideries, silks, flowered muslins, French and English millinery, and silver plate. She bought excellent English gloves for fourteen pence a pair, and English stockings cheaper than she could buy them at home.

Statia in wartime was fair game, since it had been trading with and helping to sustain the thirteen rebel American colonies. Statia had also been tactless enough, back in 1776, to be the first territory to salute the rebel American flag, flown by the brig-of-war *Andrea Doria* of the Continental Navy.[6] But when Rodney and Vaughan took the island they looted it, seizing one hundred and fifty merchant ships in the harbour, and between two and three million pounds' worth of goods and treasure. This greatly alarmed the inhabitants of Nevis, who asked themselves why a French fleet should not follow the example and treat them likewise. From Nevis, John Pinney wrote to his agent in Bristol: 'As the French now ride triumphant in these seas, it is probable my next letter will give you an account of our being subjects of the Grand Monarque [the King of France], if he will permit us so to be – Should this happen, which, I assure you, we have reason to expect daily, we may feel the ill effects of the impolitick and inhuman behaviour of R—y & V—n at St Eustatius.'[7]

A few months later, after Yorktown, when Cornwallis and his army surrendered to the combined forces of France and America, Pinney was lamenting the impending ruin of the few remaining British islands in America,[8] and on 9 January 1782 the inhabitants of Nevis, watching from the semi-tropical slopes of their volcano, saw on the horizon the enemy sails they had feared. They counted twenty-six ships of the line and twenty frigates or smaller craft, which passed the island in line ahead. President Herbert reasoned that any opposition would be little better than madness.[9] Nevis and St Kitts were within two miles of each other, but while the French fleet anchored in St Kitts roads and assaulted the fort of Brimstone Hill on that island, James Tobin and

John Pinney of the Nevis council went on board the French flagship and talked terms. It was all very civilised. The French took formal possession of Nevis. All arms were surrendered. Then the planters took the oath of allegiance to Louis XVI, at which their weapons were handed back. In case of a British counter-attack they would not be obliged to bear arms against King George, but would on the other hand undertake to remain neutral and not assist the British. There was nothing very discreditable about what took place, but nothing gallant either. As the *Annual Register* for 1782 put it: 'It cannot be supposed that such a discontented people should ever make a hearty and vigorous defence . . .' So when the French arrived, Herbert wrote to Admiral de Grasse saying his excellency could depend on every assistance, and sent ten fat sheep for his excellency's table. De Grasse accepted these as testimony of the inhabitants' gratitude, and Nevis was left more or less to govern itself.

The ins and outs of the St Kitts campaign do not concern us. The French fleet moved out to engage a British fleet, which promptly outwitted it by moving into the anchorage the French had vacated. It was a bold and brilliant piece of seamanship. The French fleet then attacked the British at anchor, but was repulsed, thus leaving the French troops on St Kitts without close naval support. But neither could the British fleet land troops to help the besieged garrison, and Brimstone Hill fell to the French. This left the anchorage untenable, and the superior French fleet cruising only five miles out to sea, waiting. The British fleet cut its anchors at night, slipped away in the darkness unnoticed and intact, and sailed to Antigua, leaving de Grasse to discover in the morning that the sea was empty and his adversary gone. The French continued to occupy St Kitts and Nevis until the peace of 1783.

Later on, Nelson came to know all the principal personages in this passage of Nevis's history. He met the Tobins and the Pinneys, in the West Indies and at Bath and Bristol, and did his best to make a young Tobin post captain. He came to know John Richardson Herbert well, and the woman he later married was Herbert's niece. She, as it happened, was away from the island at the time of its conquest by the French, having gone to England with her first husband.

And Nelson certainly knew Hood, who played a great part in the events of 1781 and 1782 in the Caribbean. Hood had been Rodney's second in command at the taking of St Eustatia. This was the action which so alarmed John Pinney of Nevis and many other planters throughout the West Indies. Hood did not get on with Rodney at all, and after St Eustatius he despised him for his rapacity.[10] When the British fleet came to St Kitts, Hood was in command, in the absence of Rodney who had gone home for a few months for his health. It was Hood who first stole the French anchorage, and then slipped away from it at night. But de Grasse's fleet still dominated the Caribbean. Britain might very well have lost Jamaica as well as the thirteen colonies, and the West Indian planters feared the imminent dissolution of the British empire. In April, de Grasse was at Martinique with thirty-five sail of the line and five thousand troops, and intent on Jamaica. It is well to remember that although in the French revolutionary wars there was an assumption, for the most part well merited, of an English superiority at sea, this was not at all so in the American war. It was only at the end of that war that England won her first convincing naval victory. Rodney had returned, and on 12 April he, and Hood, and thirty-six ships of the line defeated the French in the Saintes passage south of Guadeloupe.

It was, said Hood, such a beating as no great fleet had ever received before. Five French ships were taken, among them de Grasse's flagship the *Ville de Paris*, which struck to Hood at sunset. He was astonished that Rodney then gave the order to lie to for the night, seeming more interested in preserving this great prize than in pursuing the flying French. He lamented that the British fleet did not give chase, to which Rodney replied, 'Come, we have done very handsomely as it is.' Hood was bitter, and asserted to a friend that had he been in command the flag of England would have graced the stern of twenty French ships, not five. He characterised Rodney as no more fit to command than he (Hood) was to be an archbishop.[11]

The French fleet was not destroyed. But it was a victory, and Rodney had done enough to save Jamaica and to ensure that a peace on reasonable and not too humiliating terms could be made the following year. The planters of Nevis and St Kitts were gratified to become British subjects once again. Both Rodney and Hood were ennobled, but there was a pecking order in such things. Rodney was created a baron of Great Britain, which gave him a seat in the House of Lords, and Hood a baron of Ireland, which did not. As to the prizes, the fleet taking the entire vast treasure of Statia to England was intercepted by the French and sold at Brest. And even the *Ville de Paris*, the prize so carefully guarded, foundered in a storm on the way home.

After the battle of the Saintes, as the action of 12 April came to be known, Hood took his squadron off St Domingue, then to Jamaica, and then in the fall went north to New York to refit. There, as we have seen, he met the young Nelson. They were like spirits. Nelson in his glory would prove as demanding, as intolerant, and as intolerable a second in command as ever Hood was.

CHAPTER SEVEN

Running at the Ring of Pleasure

IT WAS JUNE 1783 when Nelson, just ahead of Hood's squadron, returned to England after the peace. From then until the following April he was unemployed, but it was an eventful time for him.

At last he got rid of *Albemarle*, having been ordered to pay her off at Portsmouth. From there, late in June, with the main part of Hood's fleet just having come in sight round the point of St Helen's, on the Isle of Wight, he was writing to Locker, with whom he was always frank, that he fancied his people, his ship's company, would be pretty quiet as long as they were not set on by some of the ships lying in port. He had got on well with his 'good fellows', but these were turbulent times. The crews of some ships at Portsmouth were almost mutinous, demanding to be paid off there and then, but *Albemarle*'s whole company offered to sail with him again if he got another ship, which he thought must flatter any officer.[1] But he had no idea of going to sea – indeed his chances of doing so were small, since so many ships were being laid up. He was put on half pay which, for the captain of a sixth rate like *Albemarle*, was about £60 a year, paid half yearly in arrears.[2] But this poor sea officer had great connections. Lord Hood took his protégé to a levee at St James's Palace, where he met the king, who was 'exceedingly attentive'. Then he went to Windsor to take his leave of Prince William, who was about to leave on a grand tour of Europe.[3] It was a time, with the peace recently concluded, when many Englishmen flocked to the continent.

London in summer was hot, and Nelson wanted to get away to

Norfolk. But he was ill again, and was cooped up for fourteen days in his lodgings in Salisbury Street, south of the Strand. The houses were new, but the road was narrow and close to the Thames, which stank at low tide. He went to his uncle Suckling's for a day or two, at Camden Town, which was almost rural, and breathed a little fresh air. Not until late August, with his brother Maurice, did he take the King's Lynn diligence and travel to his family at Burnham Thorpe.[4]

By October, Nelson too had the urge to travel on the continent, to learn French. It is one of the curiosities of his life that he never did learn any. He considered a knowledge of the language of the principal enemy essential to a sea officer,[5] and did well in everything else he ever put his mind to, but there he failed. Before he left England he paid a visit of gratitude to his old mentor Admiral Sir Peter Parker in Essex. Parker and his wife, back from the West Indies, had bought an estate and were pulling down the old house and building a new one. 'Thanks to Jamaica for the money,' Nelson remarked.[6] Parker had been lucky in his stations and had made one of the greatest fortunes in prize money ever amassed by any admiral. For himself, Nelson told his brother William, he wished to be rich only to serve his family.[7]

Then in late October Nelson and a friend, Captain James Macnamara, crossed the channel from Dover to Calais and began an expedition into northern France. Nelson's accounts of this escapade read racily, as he and his companion were two young men on the loose. Macnamara was a bold spirit.[8] Nelson called him Mac, he was a frigate captain met in Jamaica days, and later on he killed a man in a duel. As to their tour, Nelson said Sterne's *Sentimental Journey* was the best description he could give of it. Straight off the Dover packet, the two of them breakfasted at Monsieur Grandsire's house, whose mother had kept it when Hogarth painted his 'Gate of Calais'. Then they travelled the fifteen miles to Marquise in a chaise pulled by what Nelson called rats of horses where they found an inn he called a pigsty. There they were shown into a room with two straw beds, and for supper were served two pigeons on a dirty cloth, with wooden-handled knives, and next morning went on to Boulogne. The town was full of English visitors, which Nelson supposed was because the wine was so cheap. From there to Montreuil they passed through the finest corn country they had ever seen, and then through fine woods and noble forests. At Montreuil they put up at the same house and with the same jolly landlord, Nelson said, who had recommended La Fleur as servant to Sterne. Sixty noblemen's families lived in the town and owned the vast plain round it, but the rest were very poor. The game was the finest they ever saw – pheasants, woodcock, snipe – and cheap: partridges twopence a brace, fifteen pence for a noble turkey.

They left with regret and went on by way of Abbeville to St Omer, which, as Nelson said, was what they should have done in the first place. It was a large city, well paved and well lighted, not the dirty, nasty town they had expected. There they settled. They had gone round in a circle, travelling a hundred and fifty miles to end up at a town only thirty miles from Calais, but there they found consolation. They lodged with a pleasant French family. One agreeable young daughter of the house made their breakfast, another their tea, and both came to play cards in the evening. 'Therefore,' said Nelson, 'I must learn French if 'tis only for the pleasure of talking to them, for they do not speak a word of English.' Nelson had read Sterne, and in such passages sounds as if he were attempting a sentimental journey of his own.

There were many English at St Omer, and for the sake of his French, which was coming on very slowly, Nelson tried to avoid them. He particularly avoided two navy captains, Alexander Ball and James Shepard, whom he thought great coxcombs, because they wore not only their uniforms, which in France was strange, but also epaulettes in the French style. He held them a *little cheap* for wearing any part of a Frenchman's uniform. It is true that epaulettes became no part of British naval uniform until 1795, but Ball was no coxcomb and later, in the Mediterranean, became one of Nelson's 'band of brothers'. At St Omer, Nelson found the Andrews family. Mr Andrews was a clergyman, and he had two beautiful young daughters. Nelson wrote to William, saying in the arch tone he often took with his brother, 'I must take care of my heart, I assure you.'

Then there was bad news from home. Nelson's sister Ann died at Bath in November, having caught a chill coming out of a ballroom after dancing. She was twenty-four, and in the Nelson family was the nearest in age to Horatio. William Suckling wrote to tell Nelson of the death, and that the Revd Edmund Nelson's grief was intolerable.[9] Ann was the fourth of his eleven children to die. Nelson's actions here are hard to follow. He said he was made melancholy; Macnamara had been to a ball but his own mind was too much taken up with his sister's death for him to take part in any amusement. He feared for his father's health, and said he very nearly went home to him. He could easily have done this since he was only in the Pas de Calais, but he did not. Three weeks after Ann's death he wrote to William asking him for god's sake to send news of their father, but in the same letter he wrote ecstatically about going to dine with one of the Andrews girls, and also reported that he had received an invitation from a man who would one day be a sovereign prince of Europe and an absolute monarch.

The monarch-to-be was the comte de Deux Ponts, one of the savants Nelson had arrested off Havana in the last days of the war, and then released. He was much grander than Nelson had known, turning out to be a general in the French army, the holder of the French order equivalent to the Garter in England, and heir of the Elector of Bavaria. He had invited Nelson to Paris. Nelson was pleased.[10] Of the girl, Elizabeth Andrews, he spoke as he almost always did of a woman or a ship at first sight. She had such accomplishments, he said, that if he had a million pounds he was sure he would have made her an offer of them.[11] He then asked William whether their lottery tickets had yet been drawn. All this in the letter which he began with his grief at the 'shocking event' of his sister's death, and with his concern for his father.

Nelson did not in the end go home until January 1784, two months later, and then it was to settle a few accounts and for his own health, since the winter was cold in northern France, and cold, as he said, was death to him. When he wrote to tell William he would probably be back, he said he would buy six or seven halves of tickets for the Irish lottery, for by having that number of chances something might turn up, and that he would probably stretch as far as Bath, where his father was, for a few days. He then said he must conclude, as he was engaged to the most accomplished woman his eyes ever beheld – 'And when a lady's in the case, all other things they must give place.' He is quoting a couplet from John Gay, writer of *The Beggar's Opera*.[12]

At about this time he wrote a celebrated letter to his uncle William Suckling.[13] 'There arrives in general a time in a man's life (who has friends), that either they place him in life in a situation that makes his application for anything farther totally unnecessary, or give him help in a pecuniary way, if they can afford, and if he deserves it. The critical moment of my life is now arrived, that either I am to be happy or miserable: – it depends solely on you. You may possibly think I am going to ask too much. I have led myself up with hopes you will not – till this trying moment. There is a lady I have seen, of a good family and connexions, but with a small fortune, – 1,000*l* I understand. The whole of my income does not exceed 130*l* per annum. Now I must come to the point: – will you, if I should marry, allow me yearly 100*l* until my income is increased to that sum, either by employment, or any other way? A very few years will turn something up, if my friends will but exert themselves.'

He then asked his uncle, if he would not give him the money, whether he would get him either a guardship or some employment in a public office where his attendance would not be necessary. Or he understood the Indian marine service was to be under the command of a navy captain, and that was a situation he would like. He was asking, then, for the Indian service, or a sinecure, or for a guardship which would normally go to a very much more senior and less active captain. Nelson then ended in this manner: 'You must excuse the freedom with which this letter is dictated; not to have been plain and explicit in my distress had been cruel to myself. If nothing can be done for me, I know what I have to trust to. Life is not worth preserving without happiness; and I care not where I may linger out my miserable existence.'

The tradition is that Suckling gave him the money he asked for. Nelson plainly had marriage in mind, and it must have been then that he wrote and made his father a promise which the old man recalled to him many years later. 'I well remember,' he told Nelson in early 1800, when his son had returned to England to be fêted as a hero, 'that upon my receiving a wound, you promised to heal it, by giving me another daughter.'[14] But Nelson did not marry Miss Andrews, and we do not know whether she refused him or whether he never asked. Within a week after his return to England in January his mind was on other things. He was back in Salisbury Street, and telling William that London had so many charms that his time had been taken up running at the ring of pleasure.[15] He had received sixteen guineas for their winning lottery tickets, and used this whole sum to buy more tickets – a considerable gamble for a man to whom sixteen guineas represented three months' half pay, and strange for a man who said he had never gambled since he was a midshipman.[16] And he said he would visit their father in Bath before he left England again in two or three weeks.[17]

He then began his excursion into politics and into the general election of 1784. The political situation was complex. After Lord North's downfall a coalition ministry had failed, and when in December 1783 the younger Pitt was called upon to form a government he was greeted with derision. He was only twenty-four, a year younger than Nelson. He had great difficulty even assembling a cabinet. An election became inevitable, and Nelson threw himself into it. To him, politics was a simple matter of Pittites and Foxites. He loved the Pittite tories and loathed the Foxite whigs. He had no doubt Pitt's ministry would stay in, in spite of Charles James Fox 'and all that party'. He had become a political animal. When a dissolution was first threatened, he rather hoped there would be one, so that people would have an opportunity of sending to Parliament men who would support their interests, and 'get rid of a turbulent faction who are striving to ruin their country'.[18] Pitt was member for Cambridge University, and William Nelson, as a master of arts of that university, had a vote there. Lord Hood, a recent hero of the Saintes, would be a tory candidate for Westminster, where Fox held one of the two seats. Hood was only an Irish peer and could therefore stand for a seat in the House of Commons. Nelson, back in London, had dined with Hood, who said his house was always open, and the oftener Nelson came the happier it would make him. Captain Robert Kingsmill had a seat to fight, and he was a friend both of Locker and of Nelson, who had stayed with him two years before on his return from Jamaica. It was common for sea officers to hold parliamentary seats. Admiral Parker did, and so had Maurice Suckling. In January 1784, with a dissolution imminent, Nelson was going the rounds of London as one of the Hood party, and was himself as likely a candidate as any. Then he visited Lord Howe, first lord of the admiralty, who asked him if he would like a ship – a question to which there could be only one answer.[19] So by the end of January, he was writing that he was done with politics; let who would get in, he would be left out. But he plainly was not done: in the same letter he declared that Mr Pitt would stand against all opposition, and that an honest man would in time get the better of a villain.[20]

By this time, three months after his sister's death, Nelson had at last been to see his father in Bath and reported him to be as well as he could ever remember him. 'Keep his mind at rest,' he told William, 'and I do not fear but he will live these many years.' For himself, he was thinking of returning to France. 'I return to many charming women, but *no charming woman* will return with me.'[21] Miss Andrews was no longer the lady in the case. His only reason for returning to France, or so he said, was to learn French, though he professed to hate the country and its manners. His invitation from the comte de Deux Ponts had been renewed. The count had sent a second letter inviting Nelson to France in the spring, offering him any service he might wish for. He then became more explicit. 'You will see hier, very pretty midshipmans, which I dare say will teach you French with a new method, which will pleas you & improve you very fast.'[22]

The count had mistaken his man. Nelson never did return to France. In March he was given the *Boreas* frigate, and hoped she would be ordered to the East Indies. William asked by what interest he got a ship, and for once he asked an apt question. If Hood had put in a good word for Nelson it was not only because he knew him to be a good sea officer, but also because Nelson had worked in Hood's interest. Nelson, answering his brother's question, replied that having served with credit was his recommendation to Lord Howe.[23] This was naïve. Howe hardly knew Nelson. And Nelson had no sure political sense either. He wrote to his brother that he hoped he would vote for Pitt. William, at Cambridge, was going to vote in the whig interest, because the grand whigs had more church preferments in their gift, and because he hoped that his distant Walpole kinsmen, whigs and the descendants of whigs, would put something his way. Nelson also assured William that Fox would be unkennelled at Westminster. He was not. In the general election of April 1784, Hood topped the poll there, but Fox took the city's second seat. Across the country the Foxites lost 160 seats and Pitt was returned with the largest parliamentary majority ever attained.

By then Nelson was preparing to take the *Boreas* to sea, and knew his destination was not the East Indies but the Caribbean again, this time the Leeward Islands. And William was renewing his importunities. Although he was no longer a penniless curate, having just been made rector of Little Brandon in Norfolk, he wanted to go to sea as his brother's chaplain. Nelson saw no objection to William's taking a trip for a few months and returning by the winter, and told him to come, bringing his canonicals and sermons, but no servants.[24]

Nelson would have other passengers. He was taking out Lady Hughes, wife of Rear-Admiral Sir Richard Hughes, and their daughter

Rosy, who hoped to marry in the West Indies. He could not refuse since Hughes would be his commander-in-chief in the Leewards.[25] He had to put up with the discomfort, because the Hughes women would take up much of his own cabin, and the expense, because they would eat at his table. The Hughes's son, Richard, would also be on board as a midshipman. Nelson complained that everyone was asking him to take someone or other, and the ship was full of young midshipmen. One of them was George Andrews, brother of Elizabeth, so she and Nelson seem to have parted with no hard feelings.

Boreas lay at Woolwich. Nelson did not easily get her down the Thames and round to Portsmouth. First the damned Thames pilot – it made Nelson swear to think of it – ran her aground where she lay in so little water that people could walk round her till the next high tide. Then it blew a gale, and then it snowed in April. Then in the Channel he got into a quarrel with a Dutch Indiaman on which sixteen British seamen claimed to have been detained by force. The Dutchman had chosen the wrong captain to argue with. He handed over the men but kept their chests and clothes on pretence that they were in his debt, whereupon Nelson seized his ship. The chests were given up. Nelson assured the admiralty he had shown the Dutch master every politeness and attention.[26] Then, to complete everything, he got into a scrape at Portsmouth. In a last run at the ring of pleasure he took a girl riding on the common when their horses ran away, carrying them into the town through the London gate, across town, and then making for another of the city gates where there was a wagon in the road so that a horse could hardly pass. 'To save my legs, and perhaps my life, I was obliged to throw myself from the horse, which I did with great agility, but unluckily upon hard stones, which has hurt my back and my leg, but done no other mischief. It was a thousand to one that I had not been killed.'[27]

At Portsmouth, Lady Hughes, 'a fine talkative lady', came on board with her daughter. And there Nelson met Captain Kingsmill again. He had been elected to Parliament for a Cornish seat, and had come to Portsmouth to take possession of his guardship and of what Nelson called his 'land-frigate' – his wench in that port.[28] It was Kingsmill, exercising his new privilege as a member of parliament, who franked Nelson's letter, saving him the postage, and added a few words on the cover: 'Nelson's last, I imagine: he sailed today. He is a very good young man; and I wish him every enjoyment of life.'[29]

CHAPTER EIGHT

Let My Heart Speak for Me

BOREAS WAS A SMALL frigate, and Nelson was irritated that she was so crowded. The day before he reached Madeira he made a list of the thirty-three people on his quarterdeck. There were the Hugheses, his three lieutenants, his brother, the lieutenant of marines, the purser and his wife, the surgeon, and twenty-two young gentlemen, most of whom he was taking out to oblige other captains. Of these, only eight were later commissioned. Of the rest, two were dismissed for duelling, one went to America, and the rest probably found it impossible in peacetime to get the first step to lieutenant.[1]

At Madeira the frigate's distinguished passengers were received with three cheers and brought ashore in the Spanish governor's state barge. George III's birthday, 4 June, happening to fall while they were there, his and his queen's health and that of his thirteen royal children was drunk in as many bumper toasts. William Nelson preached a sermon. A calm cruise of sixteen days brought them to Barbados.[2] Nelson's abiding concern was at the 'incredible expense' of the admiral's wife and daughter. By the time he reunited them with Sir Richard Hughes they had cost him £200 to entertain, and Lady Hughes showed her gratitude by presenting Nelson with a silver tea-caddy ladle worth five shillings.[3] There was some consolation. At Bridgetown, James Wallis, the *Boreas*'s first lieutenant, noticed that 'it was no small satisfaction to Captain Nelson to find himself senior captain, and second in command to the station'.[4]

But he took against Hughes straightaway, thinking that he and all

about him were ninnies, and most of the captains geese. He derided
Hughes for living in a boarding house at Barbados, not at all in the
style of a British admiral, and for playing the fiddle.[5] 'Therefore,' he
wrote to Locker, 'as his time is taken up tuning that instrument, you
will consequently expect the squadron is cursedly out of tune.'[6] He
disliked Lady Hughes's 'eternal clack', thought the islanders a sad set,
and detested the country. Most of all he thought his admiral allowed
himself to be duped by the islanders into admitting the Yankees to
a trade with the islands which the navigation laws had forbidden
since the American colonies had become independent and therefore
foreign. 'They will first become the carriers,' he said, 'and next have
possession of our islands, are we ever again embroiled in a French war.
The residents of these islands are Americans by connection and by
interest, and are inimical to Great Britain. They are as great rebels as
ever were in America . . .'[7]

There was much truth in this, but the way in which Nelson went
about convincing his admiral was tactless. He demanded to know
whether it was not his duty to ensure that the islands' trade was
with the British and not with Americans. Hughes said he had no
orders. Nelson said this was odd since every captain was furnished
with the navigation act, which he then produced and read aloud. At
which the admiral, who could hardly do otherwise, told him to carry
out the act, and Nelson went away and turned away rebels, as he called
them. A month later, to his astonishment, another order came from the
admiral, saying he had taken good advice and requiring captains not
to hinder Americans from coming in if the islands' governors chose to
allow them.[8]

One governor who did admit Americans was General Shirley of the
Leeward Islands. As Nelson put it, 'Mr Shirley I soon trimmed and
silenced.' Shirley was insulted, and retorted that old generals were not
in the habit of taking advice from young gentlemen, to which Nelson
replied: 'I have the honour, sir, of being as old as the prime minister
of England, and think myself as capable of commanding one of his
majesty's ships as that minister is of governing the state.'[9] That at any
rate was the recollection of Nelson's first lieutenant. It rings true.

Nelson then set about trimming and silencing the admiral too. This
time he did not just go and read him the law. He wrote him a letter of
defiance.[10] 'I beg leave to hope that I may be properly understood . . .

Whilst I have the honour to command an English man of war, I shall never allow myself to be subservient to the will of any governor, nor to co-operate with him in doing *illegal acts.* They shall make proper application to me, for whatever they want to come by water.' As if this were not enough, Nelson then said he understood Hughes's order to admit foreigners into the ports had been founded on an opinion of the attorney-general (probably of Barbados), and finished with this astounding sentence: 'How the king's attorney-general conceives he has a right to give an illegal opinion, which I assert the above is, he must answer for. I know the navigation laws.'

An admiral of any temper would have sent Nelson home. An admiral of any subtlety would have sent him to survey every beach, inlet, and freshwater spring on the furthest and most obscure islands of the station, and kept him on that essential service. Only three captains on the station, Nelson, Collingwood, and Collingwood's younger brother Wilfred, tried to hinder the American trade, and Nelson alone seized any vessels, the others being 'fearful of being brought into scrapes'.[11] Nelson was not fearful. He seized six American vessels and was indeed in a scrape.

It was not the first. He had also picked a quarrel over a commodore's broad pendant flown by Commissioner Moutray of the Antigua dockyard. This was a trivial matter, important only because it shows Nelson standing on his dignity and on the letter of the law. Commodore was not a substantive rank in the Royal Navy. It was a temporary appointment held by a senior captain given the command of a squadron or holding the acting command of a port; and a commodore, becoming for the moment a flag officer, flew his own pendant. John Moutray was a post captain twenty-one years Nelson's senior on the list.[12] Because he had accepted the civil post of commissioner at Antigua, he would have been considered as retired from active service, and he irritated Nelson by still wearing his post captain's uniform. Then, in December 1784, Hughes ordered that in his absence Moutray should fly a commodore's broad pendant.[13] In February 1785, entering English Harbour, Antigua, Nelson took issue with this pendant. Now Moutray was past sixty, and unwell. His much younger wife, Mary, had been one of the few people Nelson had taken to on his first arrival in Antigua the previous fall. She was about thirty, an amused, polished woman, more than pretty. She had entertained both Nelson and the older Collingwood, and in her house they drew each other's likenesses, both of which she kept. She had, Nelson wrote, been *very very* good to him, and without her he would almost have hanged himself. She was his dear, sweet friend, who made him feel 'really an April day, happy on her account'. He called her a treasure. When she and her husband went home to England he walked up the hill to their house and wrote that even the trees dropped their heads, and the tamarind trees died, all was melancholy, and the road covered with thistles.[14] He was plainly in love with her.

This did not induce him to behave civilly to her husband. It was not as if he acted impulsively. He knew perfectly well what he was about.[15] The admiral had sent him a written order to obey Moutray when he was at English Harbour, saying Moutray had orders to hoist a commodore's pendant on any ship in his port he might think proper.[16] When he received this order, Nelson first replied demanding to see Moutray's commission from the admiralty.[17] Then he marked that rash letter 'Not sent', and composed another. This said that whenever Moutray was in commission as a commodore or captain it would be his duty to obey him, but until then he never would obey any order of his. 'I have ever felt myself since my arrival in this country second officer in command of his majesty's ships upon this station and in English Harbour and elsewhere when you are not present ... I beg leave to assure you sir with all respect, that should anyone so far forget himself as not to pay me that attention my situation as senior captain demands, that I shall take proper notice of it.'[18]

A month later he took the *Boreas* into English Harbour and saw the commodore's pendant flying on the frigate *Latona*, Captain Charles Sandys. Nelson several times referred to Sandys in his letters as 'Little S—', and thought that what with his grog and his women he was, in spite of his good heart, unfit to command a king's ship, his own being 'the merest privateer'.[19] Sandys was junior to him, and Nelson summoned him on board and demanded to know by what right he flew the pendant. Sandys said it was by Moutray's orders. What followed was an examination, part of which went like this:

Question [Nelson] – Sir, you have acted wrong, to obey any man who you do not know is authorised to command you.

Answer [Sandys] – I feel I have acted wrong; but being a young captain, did not think fit to interfere in this matter ...

Nelson then sent a long letter, containing fifteen lines of such verbatim dialogue, with a plentiful commentary, to the secretary of the admiralty in London. He trusted that he knew his duty too well to obey any half-pay captain and begged their lordships' indulgence to hear the reasons for his conduct, that it might never go about in the world that he ever had an idea to dispute the orders of his superior officer.[20]

If Nelson had deliberately set about stroking everyone the wrong way he could hardly have done better. It was true there was a strictly legal point to all this. Could a half-pay commissioner act as commodore? Strictly, no. But it was a trifle. Nelson had made a great fuss, written to the admiralty challenging his admiral's authority, and wasted everyone's time. For this sort of conduct a captain would normally have had his head bitten off. By the 1840s, when Sir Nicholas Harris Nicolas, the compiler of Nelson's complete dispatches and letters, looked for their lordships of the admiralty's reply to Nelson, it was not to be found. He could only say that the admiralty told Nelson he should have submitted his doubts to the admiral.[21] This is too mild a rebuke to be believed. As for the Moutrays, they must have been forgiving people. Two weeks after the premeditated challenge to the commissioner's pendant, Nelson was telling his brother William that Moutray was very ill and would be going home to England, and that Mrs Moutray had promised to make herself known to Catherine Nelson if they should be together at Bath the next winter. 'What an acquisition to any female to be acquainted with,' he said. 'What an example to take a pattern from.'[22] Captain Moutray died in England soon after his return.

To go over the admiral's head in the matter of the pendant was one thing. Nelson soon did better than that. He was up to his ears in the American trade, Hughes was doing nothing, and Nelson was burning with indignation, saying of the Americans, of the customs, and of his admiral, that he hated them all.[23] Then in March 1785 he wrote not just to the secretary of the admiralty – which few captains ever dared to do, but which he had already done in the matter of the pendant. He wrote not just to the first lord, which would in itself have been thought outrageous in a young captain. He wrote directly to one of his majesty's principal secretaries of state; to Lord Sydney, who as home secretary was also in those days responsible also for the West Indian colonies. This was the man after whom Sydney in New South

Wales was named, when he was responsible for that colony too. What Nelson wrote was a grand remonstrance.[24] He wrote that it was not to incriminate any individual, but to vindicate his character as an officer from the aspersions thrown upon it by the inhabitants of St Kitts and Nevis, that he troubled his lordship. The character of an officer was his greatest treasure: to lower that was to wound him irreparably. He had only done his duty in suppressing the American trade, but as a result the people in general, from the highest to the lowest, had not only neglected paying him the attention his rank might have made him expect, but had also called him an injurer of the colony. He gave an example of the way the trade went on. An American vessel appeared. Her master swore his vessel leaked, or had sprung a mast, or made some excuse of that sort. Then the customs granted a permit for him to land the whole or part of the cargo to pay for repairs, under which permits the Americans landed innumerable cargoes.

What had particularly stung Nelson was that, the day before he wrote his letter, an American brig had come into St Kitts. The master said she was in distress. Nelson told him he would inspect the ship. People then came out from the shore in boats, and the master told them his story. 'Now, my lord,' Nelson wrote, 'let my heart speak for me.' It had been dispersed all over the island that in the night he intended to turn the vessel out of port and that she would certainly sink before morning, and people thought him cruel and unjust. This, as the honour of his gracious king and his country were at stake, had made him take the liberty of addressing his lordship, for far from treating the American cruelly he had sent an officer, a carpenter, and some men to take care of the vessel, which they did by pumping her all night, and in the morning she was moved into a safe harbour.

'My name,' he wrote, 'is most probably unknown to your lordship; but my character as a man, I trust, will bear the strictest investigation: therefore I take the liberty of sending inclosed a letter, though written some years ago, which I hope will impress your lordship with a favourable opinion of me. [He enclosed the letter from Governor Dalling after the Nicaraguan adventure, suggesting Nelson should be given command of a South Seas squadron and that such minds as his were devoutly to be wished for government's sake.] I stand for myself; no great connections to support me if inclined to fall: therefore my good name as a man, an officer, and an Englishman, I must be very careful of. My greatest pride is to discharge my duty faithfully, my greatest ambition to receive approbation for my conduct.'

In all Nelson wrote four more letters to Sydney – all in his own hand. Merchants and shipowners had taken out writs for £40,000 sterling against him, and to avoid arrest he had to stay on board for eight weeks without setting foot on land. Nelson then even sent a formal memorial, or petition, to George III, saying in the covering letter that he was persecuted, that his constitution was weak, and that his situation was cruel.[25]

He received no answer to all this for six months, until September 1785. 'I should have answered your first letter by the April packet,' wrote Sydney, 'had it not been reported at that time that you had died in the West Indies soon after the date of it, but as I have the satisfaction of learning that the report was ill founded, I am now to acquaint you that your letters with your memorial have been laid before the king.' The king had directed the law officers of the crown to defend the law suits against Nelson.[26] When he received this, Nelson replied in his most heightened vein. 'Allow me without placing vanity in view to say that ... this mark of attention from great officers of state will bind me if possible faster than ever to the service of my country ... I am now convinced that while I do my duty to my country, I shall always experience the same flattering marks of attention, when I fail in that may I fall unpitied ...'[27]

But the matter was not settled, and neither Nelson nor the merchants desisted. The day before he wrote thanking Sydney for great marks of attention, Nelson wrote to Cuthbert Collingwood, 'I am to get to Nevis with all expedition to catch Yankees. My dear boy, I want some prize-money.'[28] The islanders for their part had found a new legalism to help them, and their lawyers were asserting that the law, strictly interpreted, allowed only customs officers and not sea officers to arrest ships. To counter this, Nelson was writing to his uncle William Suckling, at the custom office in London, asking him to get the official solicitor's opinion on his own contention that 'the 3rd [Act] of George the Third, chapter 22nd, section 4th' did permit him to seize ships. Having committed this view to paper, he then congratulated himself, exclaiming to Suckling: 'Well done, lawyer Nelson!'[29]

Whether in the end the American trade was that much diminished is doubtful. The navigation act was an unworkable piece of law in the

Caribbean. In 1784 the lieutenant governor of Jamaica had allowed free trade with the United States in provisions and lumber.[30] He had no powers to do this, but he did. And Sydney himself, in response to Governor Shirley at St Kitts, had said in April 1785 that while it must be understood that his majesty's servants could not encourage illicit intercourse with the Americans, they were at the same time 'by no means disposed to countenance any measures that [might] be looked upon as oppressive by the island . . .'[31] Confronted with the passionate representations of Nelson, the secretary of state could only come down on the side of the act, but his reply did confine itself to the narrow point of supporting Nelson's defence against his pursuers.

In the end the Treasury thanked Sir Richard Hughes, who had wavered and done nothing, for his activity and zeal in protecting British commerce. At which Nelson complained, in a letter to Locker, 'I feel much hurt that after the loss of health and risk of fortune, another should be thanked for what I did against his orders. I either deserved to be sent out of the service, or at least had some little notice taken of me. They have thought it worthy of notice, and have neglected me . . .'[32]

For not being sent out of the service he could thank Hughes's good nature and indolence. Nelson showed himself then, and remained throughout his career, a fanatic for duty.[33] If he failed in his duty he hoped to fall unpitied. Now his plain ordinary duty, with which most captains contented themselves, was to obey his admiral, but he conceived a higher duty to an act of parliament. In the pursuit of that higher duty he did what no other captain in the squadron did, and seized American ships. Only in a most attenuated sense was it his duty to write to Sydney, but he saw it that way, and did so. It was unwise, and it was not common sense, but those were not considerations to which Nelson ever gave a thought. It could have ruined him, and he knew it, but he was still impelled to do it. And then there is the suddenly heightened tone of the sentence: 'Now, my lord, let my heart speak for me.' Nelson's vigour shows through everything he wrote. Among his contemporaries as sea officers, only St Vincent had such a command of language. But when Nelson wrote he permitted himself more than the occasional dramatic apostrophe. 'My soul soars above such considerations,' he would write many years later to a fellow admiral, about prize money.[34] No doubt his soul often did, but all the same he had told Collingwood, at Nevis, that he was going after prizes.

One other great theme of Nelson's life is illustrated in Sydney's reply, and that is death. Sydney had heard he had died. Frequently in his brilliant career Nelson thought he was dying. Five years earlier, in Jamaica, he had been dying of malaria, dysentery, and perhaps yellow fever. From the Mediterranean in 1799 he wrote that he could quit life with a smile. To St Vincent, after Copenhagen, he wrote of soon going to heaven. To Lord Minto he wrote in 1804, 'What is man? A child of the day.' Nelson was not only frightfully wounded, he suffered at various times from what appeared to be consumption and angina. When his mind was perturbed, his body suffered. In a fight he was always fit, but he survived in an intermittently dying state throughout the years of his glory.[35]

CHAPTER NINE

I Perceive the Contrary Effect

IT WAS ON NEVIS that Nelson met Frances Nisbet and married her. They are first mentioned together in a letter from an unknown woman friend to Mrs Nisbet, probably written early in 1785 at a time when Nelson had made himself notorious by arresting American ships.

'We have,' she says, 'at last seen the little captain of the *Boreas*, of whom so much has been said. He came up just before dinner, much heated and was very silent: yet seemed, according to the old adage, to think the more. He declined drinking any wine: but after dinner, when the president, as usual, gave the three following toasts, the king, the queen and royal family, and Lord Hood, this strange man regularly filled his glass, and observed, that these were always bumper toasts with him: which having drank, he uniformly passed the bottle, and relapsed into his former taciturnity. It was impossible, during this visit, for any of us to make out his real character; there was such a reserve and sternness in his behaviour, with occasional sallies, though very transient, of a superior mind. Being placed by him, I endeavoured to rouse his attention by showing him all the civilities in my power; but I drew out of him little more than yes and no. If you, Fanny, had been there, we think you would have made something of him; for you have been in the habit of attending to these odd sort of people.'[1]

The friend might have thought Fanny was used to odd people because of her first marriage. She was the daughter of William Woolward, senior judge of Nevis, who had died in 1779. In the same year she married Dr Josiah Nisbet, who had attended her father. Nisbet came from a Scottish family who had emigrated to Nevis and bought a plantation there. He went from the West Indies to Edinburgh to take his medical degree, and then returned to practise in Nevis.[2] After their marriage, the Nisbets went to live in Salisbury, England, where his maternal relatives the Webbes had a house. A son, also Josiah, was born in 1780. Dr Nisbet died after a short illness in Salisbury in October 1781. He was said to have died insane.[3] His goods were sold by auction. The catalogues, to be had at all the principal inns, listed 'all the neat mahogany and other furniture, some curious china jars and other china, bedspreads, bed, and bedding, a well-tuned harpsichord in a neat mahogany case, &c &c.'[4]

This was during the American war, which was no time to return to the West Indies, so Mrs Nisbet stayed with the Webbes in Salisbury and then with the Pinneys in London. There is one vignette of her in London in August 1783. John Pinney and his wife had just arrived from Nevis. Their two sons, who had been staying at Salisbury, were unexpectedly brought to the Pinneys' London lodgings late at night, and the Pinneys, not having seen their sons for some time, took them for strangers. At which Mrs Nisbet, who was with them, exclaimed, 'Good God! Don't you know them, they are your children?' Mrs Pinney was so affected that she set her own head dress in a blaze with the candle, at which the boys cried out, and Pinney extinguished the blaze before it could do any injury. 'Such a scene,' he wrote, 'of distress and joy, I never before experienced.'[5]

Late in 1783, her bed, bedding, and well-tuned harpsichord having been sold, Mrs Nisbet returned to Nevis with her three-year-old son. There she settled down to keep house for her maternal uncle, Mr Herbert, president of the island council. He had dealt with the French when they took the island, and dealt just as capably with Nelson.

In the spring and summer of 1785 Nelson was confined to his ship for fear of being arrested if he went ashore. But he could not be arrested on a Sunday,[6] and early one Sunday Herbert hurried out of his room half dressed, and exclaimed, 'Great God, if I did not find that great little man of whom everybody is so afraid, playing in the next room, under the dining table, with Mrs Nisbet's child.' Nelson was known to like children. That summer, Nelson met Fanny as well as her son, and by August he was writing to her from Antigua that did he possess a million his greatest pride and pleasure would be to share it with her. A cottage with her would be better than a place with any other he had yet met. He wrote that common sense told him what a good choice he had made. 'But come,' he continued, 'don't say: "What a vain young man is this, 'tis a modest way of telling me I have given a proof of my sense by accepting him."'[7]

This is the first letter we have of Nelson to Fanny. He was already assuming that she had accepted him. But he was also anxious to hear from Mr Herbert. He did not need his permission to marry Fanny, who was a widow and could dispose of herself. He did need Mr Herbert's good wishes, because he was poor and Herbert was rich, and Fanny might be something of an heiress. Nelson was straightforward about it. In the following eighteen months before their marriage, he made seven applications to Herbert, who was always amiable and always counselled delay. Perhaps he did not wish to lose the accomplished manager of his house.

Nelson's first letter then went on racily. He told Fanny that the admiral was in high spirits at having left his wife in Barbados, was acting like a bachelor, and making 'quite a — of himself'. About Kelly (another captain), Nelson said he could tell quite a long history, but would only say, 'I hope he is constant.' These last five words are written in the cryptic symbols of a simple code, suggesting there was already some degree of complicity between Nelson and Fanny. He went on to write that Little Sandys, the captain he had rebuked for flying Moutray's pendant, had twice proposed marriage and been twice refused. Then he told Fanny the story of Miss Whitehead's elopement from St John's to St Kitts with Captain S, a friend of Fanny's and 'a gentleman well versed in the business of carrying off young ladies'. One evening, Miss W was playing the harpsichord to her mother when after two or three tunes she got up, walked out of the room, downstairs through the yard and into the bathing house, out of the window into Captain S's arms, and was not missed until they were sailing out of the harbour. 'Set them merry. I hope they will never be anxious to run from each other.' Then there was a mention of Mrs Moutray in England, from whom Nelson had had a letter. He wished Fanny knew her because their minds and manners were so congenial.

So apart from its opening, about his good sense and hers, and about Herbert's necessary approval, this was a letter about elopements, proposals, and general gallantry. Nelson spelled her name wrong on the cover, as Mrs Nisbit, just as he spelled it wrong on his second letter, as Mrs Nisbitt.[8] But his first letter suggested a degree of chatty intimacy, and as good as assumed she had accepted him. This fits in with Nelson's letter to his brother William at the end of June when he hinted that he might be married within a month.[9] At some time he made another effort to learn some French, perhaps with her help, since she spoke the language well enough. A vellum-bound copy of the *Boreas*'s log for the time contains, at the back, twenty-three pages of French exercises in his hand. It is mostly formal grammar, nothing that would help him in conversations with the officers of French ships, except for one phrase: 'Que vous craignissiez – that ye might fear.'[10]

It has become traditional to assert that Fanny Nisbet took Mrs Moutray's place in Nelson's affections. Mary Moutray had been unattainable, and seems in any case to have preferred Collingwood's company, but she had left a gap. What man would not have wanted to find another woman who could make him feel like an April day? And there is no reason why Nelson should have been less than ardent, or why he should have been less bold with a woman than he was in every other regard. He liked to run at the ring of pleasure. He did not expect a man to live celibate. When his uncle Suckling unexpectedly remarried in 1786, Nelson wrote to his brother William: 'It will add to his felicity, for had he not done that, he must have kept a woman . . .'[11] And later, someone who knew Nelson very well in this sense later caused the following words to be written: 'It is not to be dissembled [that Nelson], though by no means ever an unprincipled seducer of the wives and daughters of his friends, was always well known to entertain rather more partiality for the fair sex than is quite consistent with the highest degree of Christian purity.' This is from James Harrison's biography of 1806 which was written using materials in Emma Hamilton's possession, with her encouragement, and perhaps at her dictation.[12]

And it is, not so strangely, from this same source that Fanny's reputation for coldness comes. Those who knew her liked her and admired her spirit. But she was reticent, and almost all her correspondence with Nelson remained unknown throughout the nineteenth century. The

letters were found in 1898,[13] but were not widely known until they
were published in 1958. So she was for the most part a shadowy, cool
figure compared with the earthily abundant Emma, and this natural
comparison was much assisted by a savage passage from Harrison. This
undoubtedly came from Emma, who hated Fanny and blackened her at
every opportunity. The passage describes Nelson's return home from
the Mediterranean in late 1800, and says that 'at the obvious coldness
of her ladyship ... the warmth of his affectionate heart felt a petrifying
chill, which froze for ever the genial current of supreme regard that had
hitherto flowed with purity through the inmost recesses of his soul.'[14]
Harrison's book was forgotten, but that depiction of Fanny became part
of the lasting myth. It was not true. They were well matched and got on
well from the first. Nelson was a slight man, no more than five feet six
inches tall, but full of energy. Fanny was also slight, dark haired, and
given to a rapid movement of the hands when she spoke. The pity is
that their early correspondence is one-sided. We have only his letters.
No letter from her exists before 1794. It was Nelson's intermittent
custom to burn the letters he received. We have no early letters from
his father, and none from Locker to Nelson, so that we cannot know
if the friend to whom he confided so much ever advised him to act less
rashly in, say, the matter of the American trade.

By September 1785, Nelson was spelling Mrs Nisbet's name correctly, addressing her as 'my dear Fanny', and saying he had heard
from Herbert, who wanted to defer matters but loved her too well,
Nelson believed, not to let her marry the man of her choice. But there
had also been a cooling off. He had not married within a month. But in
November he had written a long letter to William Suckling asking, as
he had with Miss Andrews two years before, for the money to marry.
He first described Fanny, and did so with remarkable inaccuracy. He
said his attachment was of long standing, when he had at most known
her for eight months and perhaps only for five, and that she was
twenty-two, when she was twenty-seven, his own age. (Clarke and
M'Arthur absurdly say she was not yet eighteen, though she had a
five-year-old son.) And Nelson said she had been brought up by her
mother's brother, Mr Herbert, since infancy, her mother and father
having died when she was two: this was wrong too, for though her
mother had died while she was a child, her father had survived until
just before her marriage, when she was twenty. So he got Fanny wrong,

but he did give a living picture of John Richardson Herbert.

'Herbert is very rich and very proud, – he has an only daughter, and this niece, who he looks upon in the same light, if not higher. I have lived at his house, when at Nevis, since June last, and am a great favourite of his. I have told him I am as poor as Job; but he tells me he likes me, and I am descended from a good family, which his pride likes; but he also says, "Nelson, I am proud, and I must live like myself, therefore I can't do much in my lifetime: when I die she shall have twenty thousand pounds; and if my daughter dies before me, she shall possess the major part of my property. I intend going to England in 1787, and remaining there my life; therefore, if you two can live happily together till that event takes place, you have my consent." This is exactly my situation with him; and I know the way to get him to give me most, is not to appear to want it; thus circumstanced, who can I apply to except you? ... I think Herbert will be brought to give her two or three hundred a year during his life; and if you will either *give me*, I will call it – I think you will do it – either one hundred a year, for a few years, or a thousand pounds, how happy you will make a couple who will pray for you for ever.'[15]

If Nelson and Herbert had talked good families, then Herbert had the advantage. Nelson had the Sucklings and the distant Walpoles. The Herberts, of whom Fanny's mother had been one, came from a long line of the Earls of Pembroke and Montgomery. The third earl had been lord chamberlain, and the eighth had carried the sword at the coronation of George I. George Herbert the poet was one of the same family. A cadet branch of the family settled in Nevis in the early seventeenth century.[16]

One of Nelson's minor distractions at this time was his brother William, who had come out with him as chaplain in June 1784, was known by the seamen as 'the bishop', and remained with the ship only three months before returning in September for his health. He had since, several times, expressed a desire that his pay should continue. In February 1785 Nelson assured William he would keep him on the books as long as he could. In March, when William had written about coming out again, Nelson said he could come whenever he pleased and, as to his previous pay, he would send a certificate but was not certain about paying him, for the muster-master had checked him absent. The idea of coming out was abandoned by August, William having inherited a family living worth £700 a year, fourteen times the pay of a navy chaplain.[17] But that still left the back pay. On board the *Boreas*, in a document dated 31 December 1785, Nelson wrote the following:

> These are to certify the principal officers and commissioners of his majesty's navy that the Revd William Nelson serv'd as chaplain on board his majesty's ship under my command from the 27th day of June 1784 to the date hereof (although there was no room to enter him upon the books 'till Septr 1784) during which time he regularly performed divine service except he was absent upon leave.[18]

This is in Nelson's hand, and signed by him. He was certifying that William had served fifteen months longer than he had, when for almost all that time he had been the other side of the Atlantic. The certificate could only have been valid if William's time at home counted as time 'absent upon leave'. If this certificate had been presented to the navy board it would have been a fraud both by William Nelson and his brother. Sea officers were broken for less. The fact that it still exists among Nelson's papers suggests that it was not presented, but the very writing of it is inexplicable. The following year he did write again to William saying he had his warrant in his bureau, but thought it a chance he would be paid as he had not actually been on board: 'However, that we'll try when *Boreas* gets home.'[19]

As for Fanny, Nelson said that his whole life should be an attempt to make her happy, and assured her that he would always consider her dear son as one of his own. He looked for harpsichord strings for her in Barbados, which he called 'Barbarous island', writing from there to say that if he had taken her advice and not seized any Americans he would now be with her, but duty was the great business of a sea officer.[20] The very next day he was writing to the East India Company in London on something emphatically not his business. A British ship under American colours had been trading in China and Bengal and was selling off her cargo of tea and saltpetre at Saint Eustatius. He could only regret that the *Boreas* was not there, 'or let me assure you that I should have thought it my indispensable duty to have gone to St Eustatia, and demanded the ship and cargo, which I hope to have been able to prevail upon the Dutch to have given up ...'[21] He was lucky not to have been there. Memories of Rodney's looting were fresh enough at Statia, which was after all both a free port and Dutch, to have made such a demand inflammatory and foolish. That summer of 1784 he was very ill. It was probably his recurrent malaria, but the doctors thought it a consumption. There is a sentence in a letter to Locker which shows the state he was in. 'I think I have wrote lately to Kingsmill [his political friend from the 1784 election] but really I have been since June so very ill till lately that I have only a faint recollection of anything which I did.'[22] By August he was recovered, he thought from taking a pint of goat's milk each morning, and he was writing to Fanny most vigorously. 'As you begin to know something about sailors, have you not often heard that salt water and absence always wash away love? Now I am such a heretic as not to believe that faith: for behold every morning since my arrival [at Antigua], I have had six pails of water at day-light poured upon my head, and instead of finding what the seamen say to be true, I perceive the contrary effect . . .'[23] Any man who writes like that to a woman probably knows that what he perceives as he looks down at himself, she has perceived too.

In July 1786 Hughes had gone home, leaving Nelson as senior captain in temporary charge of the station until the admiral's successor came out. As soon as Hughes went, Nelson turned his mind towards zealously righting abuses in the Antigua dockyard.[24] He was on his own, and received no orders from the admiralty for the five months until January 1787. The previous month, Prince William Henry was sent out to his station.[25] This was the young prince whom Nelson had met in New York harbour on board Lord Hood's flagship in 1782, when the prince was a midshipman. After returning home, he had spent nearly two years in the courts of Europe, falling in love at Hanover with the fourteen-year-old Princess Charlotte of Mecklenburg-Strelitz, his mother's niece, having affairs with the daughter of a merchant and the daughter of a general, and with others. 'Oh for England,' he wrote to his brother the Prince of Wales, 'and the pretty girls of Westminster; at least such as would not clap me or pox me every time I fucked.'[26] In April 1785, when Nelson was arresting American ships, Prince William was, as he again told his brother, pursuing his amours 'with a lady of the town against a wall'.[27] In June, back in England, he was passed for lieutenant by a full board of the admiralty and joined the *Hebe* at Portsmouth, where his mentor Hood was now commander-in-chief. In April 1786 the admiralty made him post captain into the frigate

Pegasus. In her he was sent first to Halifax and then to the West Indies to visit such islands as he thought fit, with orders to return to Halifax the following May.[28] In the Leeward Islands he would be under Nelson's command.

Nelson and the prince met at Dominica on 2 December 1786. William asked straightaway how Nelson was officered, at which he replied pretty well. William said he wished he could say so too, but his gave themselves such airs that he could not bear them. Next day, a French frigate having come in from Martinique to pay her respects, William said to his first lieutenant, Isaac Schomberg, in Nelson's presence, that he had ordered his men to have their uniform jackets on. Schomberg replied that he thought the cloth too warm for the country, but that if his royal highness chose he would have them put on directly, and Nelson heard, from the manner in which this was spoken, that all was not right.[29] At Antigua the state of the *Pegasus* was found to be so bad – leaking, seams open, and some of her bolts so loose as to be drawn out by hand – that she had to be careened.[30] While this was done, William occupied the commanding officer's house, and chose to dine there only with Nelson, inviting none of his own officers.

As Nelson saw, there was trouble. He knew Schomberg because he had been first lieutenant of the *Canada*, a ship of the line which had served with Hood at St Kitts and later at the Saintes. He was thirty-four, a most experienced lieutenant, unlucky to have achieved no further promotion, and at the time of their meeting in Dominica more battle-hardened than Nelson. Hood had especially sent him to the *Pegasus* to help the inexperienced William. But William was too stiff to think himself in need of help, and Schomberg was not tactful in offering it.[31] Nelson at the time was beginning to be strict in his own ship, thinking he would be stricter as he grew older, and that in a new ship he would be indifferent whether he ever spoke to an officer in her, except on duty.[32] This was not a recipe for a happy ship. Some of Nelson's increasing strictness probably communicated itself to Prince William, who was already distant enough with his own officers. So the meeting of Nelson and the prince, in such a place and such a time, was in every way unfortunate for them both.

Nelson accompanied William round the islands, and within ten days was writing to Fanny that the prince was a gallant man, volatile but with great good humour. At Antigua there had been three nights' dancing which never broke up till near day, and Nelson had only two or three times been in bed before morning. He said he really loved to honour the prince or he could not have gone through with it. He also sprung on Fanny the news that the prince was insisting on attending their wedding and giving the bride away.[33] To Locker he wrote that the prince had foibles like private men's, but they were far overbalanced by his virtues, and that in the professional line he was superior to two-thirds of the captains' list.[34] He said this of a man who was only just twenty-one, who was in his first command which he had held for less than eight months, and who was in trouble with his officers. The prince's racketing continued. His overbearing animal strength began to weary even so active a man as Nelson. 'How vain are human hopes,' he wrote to Fanny. 'I was in hopes to have been quiet all this week. Today we dine with Sir Thomas [Shirley, recently made a baronet], tomorrow the prince has a party, on Wednesday he gives a dinner in St John's to the regiment, in the evening is a mulatto ball, on Thursday a cock fight, dine at Col Crosbie's brother's and a ball, and on Friday somewhere but I forget, on Saturday at Mr Byam's the president [of Antigua].' By mid-January, still kept from Nevis, he was complaining to her: 'What is to attend on princes, let me attend on you and I am satisfied. Some are born for attendants on great men, I rather think that is not my particular province.'[35]

Worse was to come. On 22 January Schomberg sent a boat ashore without William's express permission. For this trivial act he was reprimanded in writing for neglect of duty. He had already been confined by the prince on some other matter and forced to apologise in front of the other officers.[36] He asked for a court martial to clear his name, at which Nelson, as senior captain, put him under arrest, and the prince said he would try him for mutiny after his court martial and that if he were found guilty he would be 'hung or broke'. The prince was also convinced that William Hope, his third lieutenant, was at the bottom of it all, in which case he would try him too for promoting mutiny and sedition. He recounted all this in a letter to Hood, asking him to keep it from the king.[37] A few days later Nelson issued a general order that any officer who frivolously asked for a court martial would be tried under the 14th and 19th Articles of War. These forbade the delaying or discouraging of service, mutinous assembly, and contemptuous behaviour. He had no doubt Schomberg would be broken.[38]

There was no going back from all this. There were at the time in Antigua two young gentlemen who saw some of what went on. Both were only fourteen at the time, but both later attained high rank. Thomas Byam Martin, then captain's servant on board the *Pegasus*, later admiral of the fleet, noticed a complete change for the worse in the captain when they reached the Leewards, in particular the many petty restrictions placed on the officers.[39] William Hotham, later a full admiral but then a midshipman in the *Solebay*, which joined the squadron soon after the *Pegasus*, thought Nelson was quick and active in everything he did or said, never even in trifles irresolute, but 'had not much the appearance or the manners of a gentleman'.[40]

While Schomberg was under arrest Nelson at last found strings for Fanny's harpsichord. He wrote to her that a man was 'cracking his head' tuning the instrument, and then that he would send it up to her by his servant, safe and well tuned. He was still anxious about Herbert, who had now suggested their marriage could best wait till they got to England. 'I objected to the latter for many reasons for the ill natured part of these islands would say that I had only been playing the fool with you. Nothing else passed but I dare say Mr Herbert will do everything which is handsome on the occasion. I hope he will for your sake for it would make me unhappy to think I had taken you from affluence to a small pittance.'[41]

For three months Nelson had been taking the prince from island to island, firing twenty-one gun salutes as his royal highness was received at each place, and being kept by this duty from Fanny. And it was the prince who in the end determined when the marriage should take place. On 6 March Nelson wrote to Fanny from St Kitts saying he felt most awkward. The prince had told him that if he was not married the next time he went to Nevis it was improbable they would be there together again, that Nelson had promised not to marry without his being present, and that he would be much mortified if impediments were thrown in the way.

'He intends it as mark of honour to me,' wrote Nelson, 'and as such I wish to receive it ... He told me this morning that since he has been under my command he has been happy, and have given me to understand that there is no doubt whenever he may be placed in a high situation that I will find him sincere in his friendship. By keeping in his esteem there is no doubt but that I shall have my right in the service if nothing more. I hope Mr Herbert can have no objection, especially if he considers how much in my interest it is to be well with the prince.'[42]

The prince stayed a week on Nevis. A few days before the wedding, he met Fanny for the first time and found her a pretty and sensible woman.[43] He tried to persuade Herbert to make a settlement on Fanny, but Herbert declined.[44] He may also have considered that he, and not a chance prince, should have given his niece away. At any rate, the president and council of Nevis spent £800 of public money entertaining their royal guest. A hundred gentlemen sat down to dinner with him, seventy ladies danced at a ball, and the prince was entertained with horse races and cock fighting.[45] The wedding took place not in church but at Herbert's plantation house, Montpelier, on 11 March 1787. Nelson received his bride from the hands of the future William IV.[46] Like Napoleon he had married a creole heiress whom, like Napoleon, he would later abandon.

Meanwhile Schomberg remained under arrest for more than a hundred days, because there were not the five captains on the station required to hold a court martial. The prince's orders were to return to Halifax, and when he arrived Nelson had punctiliously told him that nothing could allow him to vary these orders, as they were drawn up with the king's approbation. But by May 1787 the prince, fearing that there would not be enough captains for a court martial at Halifax either, suggested that justice required he should return by way of Jamaica, where there would be enough to form a court. In this way, the prince said, his own 'uneasiness of mind' could be settled, and the affair of the 'unhappy and deluded' lieutenant settled. Nelson had forgotten his scruples, and at the prince's request he not only ordered the *Pegasus* to return by way of Jamaica; he also sent the *Rattler* sloop with her, not only to increase the number of captains at Jamaica but also 'to carry home his royal highness's despatches, which he must be very anxious should reach the king before any reports get to him'.[47]

Nelson was preparing to leave himself. He told his brother William that the officers of his squadron would not be sorry to part with him as they thought he made them do their duty too strictly: as to the islanders, they hated him and would give a *bal champêtre* upon his departure.[48] To Locker he wrote that no man had more illness or trouble on the station, but on the other hand he was married to an amiable woman who he was morally certain would continue to make him a happy man for the rest of his days.[49] Fanny and Mr Herbert sailed for England in the *Roehampton* West Indiaman. Herbert seems to have declined the offer of a passage home in the *Boreas*, which Nelson said was certainly as clean as a loaded sugar ship, though the accommodation might not be so elegantly fitted up.[50] The *Boreas* sailed for England on 4 June 1787. By then Nelson was very ill again, and some did not expect him to reach home alive.[51]

CHAPTER TEN

Nelson Found Wanting

NELSON RECOVERED ON THE passage home and arrived at Portsmouth in the *Boreas* in July 1787 with sixty gallons of rum and a hogshead of madeira for Locker, and was there reunited with Fanny. But he was in trouble with his crew, having punished John Kelley, George Hoskins, and John Chilcott with twenty-four strokes of the cat for using mutinous language.[1] Strictly, only a court martial could order a man more than twelve lashes. It was a rule often broken, but not in a happy ship. He was also, on several heads, in trouble with the admiralty. The first and worst trouble was over Prince William, for having allowed him to sail to Halifax by way of Jamaica, to make the prince easy in his mind. The admiralty did not share Nelson's concern for his royal highness, and was much dissatisfied that he had authorised the prince to decline to furnish a complete muster book to the muster clerk at Antigua dockyard.[2] A muster book showed the number of men on board, and had to be produced when their pay or rations were drawn. Unless the prince was defrauding the admiralty by attempting a false muster, drawing for more men than he had, this was a matter of form, and why the prince should have declined to produce his books, and why Nelson should have permitted him to do so, is a mystery which probably has something to do with Nelson's views on the divine right of princes. As was often the case with the prince, his own accounts of the matter show him in a bad light. He said that soon after he arrived, in December 1786, one of the storekeepers at the Antigua yard asked him for his muster book which he refused. This was in the presence of

Nelson and another captain, and with Nelson's 'entire approbation'. It is easy to see how Nelson, particularly with a third party there, felt unable to tell William to recant.[3] The prince later refused, in spite of a direct admiralty order, to produce muster books at Halifax or Cork, calling the shipyard officers insolent.

Asked why he had let the prince go by way of Jamaica, Nelson said he hoped that the commander-in-chief there might have found some way of preventing a court martial.[4] This was a new tack for him to take, since all along he had done all he could to bring one about. But a court martial had been avoided. Commodore Alan Gardner at Jamaica had finessed his way round what was obviously trouble. He said that, never losing sight of his royal highness's elevated station, he had considered it his duty to heal and conciliate the dispute. 'I gave him my honest and open opinion, that . . . with the want of evidence on the part of his royal highness, it would be highly improper for me to suffer a court martial to be held . . .'[5] So the prince, finding himself in what he called the singular predicament of having no witnesses to support him, allowed Schomberg to withdraw his request for a court martial, while the commodore, in response to the prince's counter-demand that Schomberg should be removed from the *Pegasus*, allowed him to go home.[6]

Nelson did not know that his own lack of finesse had frustrated a scheme hatched between the king and his ministers to keep the dissolute Prince William gainfully employed, out of trouble, out of debt, and out of England for three years, in effect to exile him. The secret out-letters of the admiralty for 1786 are more concerned with William than with any other subject. There are letters to the commanders-in-chief at Halifax, Jamaica, and Barbados and the Leeward Islands.[7] One of these letters, addressed to Sir Richard Hughes, fell into Nelson's hands because Hughes had gone home. The most detailed orders were those sent to Commodore Sawyer at Halifax, which was where the North America station was based since the loss of the thirteen colonies. William was to be under his command. The prince was to acquire a knowledge of his majesty's possessions and islands in North America and the West Indies. In the West Indies he could go where he pleased, but each summer he should return to Halifax. Sawyer's orders ended: 'You are therefore hereby required and directed to take his royal highness under your command and, from time to time, to detach him to the West Indies in the winters, and to employ him as part of your squadron in the summer months, until the end of the year 1789 . . .'

Nelson unknowingly frustrated this plan.

This capital matter aside, there was the matter of the promotions Nelson had made in the Leewards. He had made Wallis, his old first lieutenant in the *Boreas*, commander of the *Rattler* sloop, and another officer third lieutenant of the *Pegasus*. The admiralty declined to confirm either, at which Nelson protested that he would be looked upon as an officer who arrogated to himself powers with which he was not invested. The admiralty was unmoved. Wallis had to wait another seven years for his promotion to commander.[8] In attempting to justify his power to promote, Nelson also pointed out that this was only one of the powers Hughes had given him. Another was the right to hold courts martial, which he had also exercised. If it turned out that he did not have this power either, the results might have embittered his future days, for he had tried William Clarke of the *Rattler* for desertion. Although it was peacetime, and Clarke had made no real attempt to desert, openly hanging around the island of Antigua, he had been convicted, and the only sentence was death. 'Thus,' wrote Nelson, 'was I near, if not cutting the thread of life, at least of shortening a fellow-creature's days. The law might not have supposed me guilty of murder, but my feelings would have been near the same.' As it happened, Prince William had interceded for a pardon for Clarke, who was not hanged. But this explanation served only to get Nelson into deeper trouble. A few days later their lordships acquainted him of their surprise at finding the pardoned man had been discharged from the navy, and wanted to know why. It appeared that Nelson could only have reprieved the man, not pardoned him, and even if the man had been properly pardoned he had no claim to be discharged. Instead of simply acknowledging this technical irregularity, Nelson persisted in defending himself, and with the most specious argument. 'I had always understood,' he replied, 'that when a man was condemned to suffer death he was from that moment dead in law; and if he was pardoned, he became as a new man; and there being no impress, he had the choice of entering or not his majesty's service. There was no want of a good man to supply his place.'[9] Lawyer Nelson again, but it was doing him no good.

Then there was the matter of Nelson's having appointed Joseph

King, the supposedly insane late boatswain of the *Boreas*, as sail maker's assistant at the Antigua yard. He had no authority to do this, he had driven the officers of the yard mad, and they protested. To the admiralty Nelson replied that he had indeed appointed the man; that as to King's being insane he was merely struck with the sun; and that as to the yard officers' objections: 'I know not of remonstrances – I never allow inferiors to dictate.'[10]

Meantime, at Portsmouth, Nelson had flogged three more of his men for leaving the ship's boat and going ashore. His plentiful allegations of habitual fraud in West Indies shipyards were taking up the time of Sir Charles Middleton, who had succeeded Nelson's uncle as comptroller of the navy board. The Duke of Somerset had not yet acknowledged his investigations into the victualling board.[11] And Nelson was writing to George Rose, secretary to the treasury, trusting that his exertions on the Leeward Islands station in stopping the illegal trade with America, were not forgotten.[12] He was also continuing his correspondence with Prince William, the cause of so much trouble to him, in terms which showed that he was not wholly aware that this royal connection was doing him no good.[13] 'I am interested,' he said, 'only that your royal highness should be the greatest and best man this country ever produced . . . When I go to town, I shall take care to be presented to his majesty [the king] and the Prince of Wales, that I may be in the way of answering any question they may think proper to ask me. Nothing is wanting to make you the darling of the English nation, but truth. Sorry I am to say, much of the contrary has been dispersed . . .'[14]

Nelson did not know it, but Lord Howe, the first lord of the admiralty, was much displeased with the prince. He had just received news that Gardner had prudently avoided court-martialling Schomberg, but was irritated that the prince had also, without apparent cause, refused another of his lieutenants, Hope, the certificate of service without which he could not be paid. The prince's version was that Hope deserved a court martial too, but that it was impossible to court martial everyone who deserved it, 'either for want of evidence, or from other motives, such as humanity'. Howe hoped this 'unpleasant business' could be terminated without any further public transaction.[15]

Nelson was stuck at Portsmouth with a slow fever, and uncertain as to when *Boreas* would ever be taken out of commission and her men paid off. He wrote to Locker that he would get his tamarinds smuggled in to him, as the duty on them was so enormous. Fanny was with him. Then there was a bustle about war with the Dutch, and men were needed. Nelson was ordered to the Nore, where *Boreas* was used as a receiving ship for men rounded up by the press gang. Eleven hundred men were pressed one Friday night. In time of war, or threatened war, there were never enough volunteers, for as Dr Johnson had said, no one who could contrive to get himself into jail would go to sea, for being in a ship was being in a jail with a chance of being drowned, and a man in jail had more room and commonly better company.[16] Parties were sent out under a lieutenant to round up more or less able-bodied men between eighteen and fifty-five. A few were exempt – some fishermen, colliers, and whalers, and some could buy themselves out – but the rest were as good as shanghaied. It was a sordid business and Nelson was, besides, parted from his wife, whom he had left in London while he was anchored in the Thames estuary. 'We are here laying seven miles from the land,' he wrote to his brother William, 'and I am as much separated from my wife as if I were in the East Indies . . .'[17]

He had not, as he had confidently promised Prince William, been to see either the king or the Prince of Wales. Captains of press gang ships rarely did. He had however asked Lord Howe not just for a frigate, but for a ship of the line.[18] He returned to *Boreas* at the Nore, where he flogged five more of his seamen for being drunk and leaving their duty on shore. A week later he flogged no fewer than six of his people on one day, five receiving twelve lashes each for disobedience, and William Ingrams twenty-two for mutinous language.[19]

In December he received a letter from Prince William.[20] 'In my opinion Nelson we were both to blame: you in sending the *Pegasus* and *Rattler* down to Jamaica and me in asking and proposing it. I was greatly surprised to see the matter taken up so seriously and severely by the admiralty but we both know who is at the bottom of the whole. Your observation is just, it is sufficient for a man either to be respected in his profession by me or to be my friend to be disliked by Lord Howe.' For a royal prince this was of no great consequence. For Nelson it was dangerous talk. His entire future could depend on the good opinion, or the whim, of the first lord.

But Nelson was hasty. He described himself as such in evidence he gave at the Old Bailey at the time. James Carse, a seaman from the *Boreas*, cut Sarah Hayes's throat in a bawdy house at Shadwell and was tried for murder. There was no doubt he had killed the woman, but there was a question whether he was sane. Two witnesses said he had acted oddly, seemed in sad trouble, and thought a whole gang of people were after him. Nelson, when he was called to give evidence of Carse's state of mind, said he was a quiet, sober, melancholy man. 'When I heard of this affair, I said, if it is true he must be insane, for I should as soon suspect myself, and sooner, because I know I am hasty; he is so quiet a man . . .' When he was questioned further, Nelson volunteered for a second time – and this was on oath – that he was hasty and Carse was not. He said Carse had been struck with the sun, at Antigua he thought, and then he said twice, first to counsel and then to the judge, that he had been affected in the same way. 'I myself have been struck in the brain, so that I was out of my senses.' Carse was found guilty and sentenced to death, but reprieved.[21]

By then, *Boreas* was at last paying off. Her people did not this time volunteer to serve in any other ship Nelson commanded. In the eighteen months since April 1786, he had flogged sixty-six of his one hundred and forty-two seamen and marines – eleven for mutinous language, one for striking a master's mate, and one for trying to desert.[22] That was almost half his people. Far from having a ship of the line, Nelson was on half pay, with no ship at all. There is a report, emanating from Clarke and M'Arthur, that Nelson at this time was so irritated that he told the senior officer in the Medway he rejoiced at being paid off, as it was his firm and unalterable determination never to set foot on a king's ship again. As soon as he went to town he would wait on the first lord and resign his commission. According to the story, this was happily prevented by Nelson's receiving a very civil letter from Howe, who wanted to see him and offered to present him to the king at the next levee, when he was honoured with a gracious reception.[23] There is a little truth here, and a lot of embroidery. It is highly improbable that Howe summoned him to London. Nelson twice tried and failed to see him. There is no evidence that he saw the king. But there is no doubt about his irritation. Twenty years later, Fanny wrote: 'He once talked of the Russian service – in short he was so dissatisfied at the ill usage particularly when at the Nore that I am certain he would never have gone to sea if he had had a fortune.'[24] The Russian service would not then have seemed too outlandish. After the peace of 1783 at least twenty English captains served in the Russian navy, and the grand admiral of the Russian fleet was English.[25] But Fanny perhaps misread her husband's real and evident irritation. No doubt he stormed about from time to time saying he would never again go to sea, but the thing he wanted most in the world was a ship and he never stopped trying.

In the autumn of 1787, while Nelson fumed at the Nore, Fanny was writing to her father-in-law, looking forward to meeting him. She had never seen any country remotely like Norfolk. The rector was more conscious of the shortcomings of his bleak landscape than she was. '[She] seems to think it will not be many weeks before she visits these Arcadian scenes: rivers represented by a puddle, mountains by anthills, woods by bramble bushes; yet all in taste, if not hid by snow.'[26] But Nelson was detained and the visit postponed. The old man was living quietly and alone. His youngest daughter Catherine, Katty, had that January married George Matcham, a man who had made a fortune in India, and they were living in some style at Barton Hall, nearby. At Burnham Thorpe, their father's domestics were in bed by half-past seven, and the rector by nine. Nelson was his favourite son, and when he spoke of him it was always as Horace, never Horatio. But months passed, and Nelson still did not go to see him. At first this was because he could not, but after the *Boreas* paid off he still did not go. Prince William had invited him to Plymouth, where he told Locker he found the prince respected by all: 'Many of the rising people must submit to act subordinate to him, which is not so palatable; and I think a lord of the admiralty [he meant Howe] is hurt to see him so able, after what he has said about him.'[27]

But by then the prince was not respected. No one doubted his seamanship. His ships were spick and span to the point of mania, and the logs he submitted to the admiralty did not record the business of his ship day by day, as every other captain did, but watch by watch and hour by hour.[28] When he was not flogging his men he did look after them. In one letter from the West Indies he recommended that they should be issued with sheets. 'Sheets,' he said, 'are infinitely easier cleaned, and less liable to receive, retain, and communicate infection, than the woolen material furnished to seamen for bedding.'[29] But he was incompetent at managing his officers, and incapable of obeying the orders of his superiors. The admiralty was running out of patience with him, if not quite yet out of deference. Hood, who had been the prince's mentor and was now commander-in-chief at Portsmouth, had taken Schomberg into his own flagship, the *Barfleur*, as first lieutenant. This could not have been done without Howe's approval and was an open rebuke to the prince. When Hood wrote to tell the prince what he had done, William replied that he wanted words to express his feelings, and made what amounted to a threat. 'Much as I love and honour the navy, yet, my lord, I shall beyond doubt resign if I have not a satisfactory explanation from both your noble lordships.'[30]

It is a pity that Hood could not maintain silence and simply await his royal highness's welcome resignation. But it was the king who had sent his son to sea, and Hood replied with a courtly and devastating letter. He had flattered himself that he had so thorough a knowledge of his royal highness's condescending goodness of heart as to think he could not wish the ruin of any man. Schomberg was an excellent officer and a sensible well-behaved man. Though his royal highness had been pleased to withdraw his friendship and good opinion, which, said Hood, was very painful, yet it was some consolation to him that he had forfeited what he so strongly prized only from doing an act of justice to a deserving officer, who had no prospect of being promoted except by him. He would never cease to pray for his royal highness's health, glory, and happiness, etc.[31]

To which the prince replied that he was infinitely uneasy, for it was the general topic of conversation that Lord Hood supported Schomberg in opposition to him. On cool reflection, he thought Schomberg too contemptible an object to be the cause of his breaking his connection with his lordship, but he entreated that the man's name should never be mentioned again. And so on. But there was in that letter one sentence which went too far: '... I felt vastly hurt that you placed him in the *Barfleur* first lieutenant without having previously consulted me whether it would have been acceptable or not.'[32] This, from a very junior captain to a sea officer of great renown, was intolerable, even if the captain was a prince. Hood concluded the unhappy correspondence by replying with a letter full of words like honour, glory, happiness, duty, regard, and esteem, which did however contain the deadly question: 'But how was it possible, sir, as you are pleased to suggest, that I could consult your royal highness in the business?'[33]

The admiralty and the prince were on bad terms and Nelson was taking the prince's part. At Plymouth all was bonfires, routs, ringing of bells, and balls till two in the morning. William's brothers, the Prince of Wales and the Duke of York, were with him, and the three carried on what amounted to a rowdy court, and a court in opposition. All three were more or less estranged from the king, all were seen as his political opponents, and none loved Pitt or his administration. It was bad company for a young sea officer, but Nelson did not see this.

On his way to Plymouth, Nelson had left Fanny at Bath, and after visiting the prince returned to her there. His father would normally have wintered at Bath himself, but had given that up because the expense was too great now that he had to support both Maurice and his youngest son Suckling – Maurice in London and often in debt, and Suckling who was going up to Cambridge to read divinity. The rector's longing to see his favourite son breathes through his letters to Katty, and yet he was becoming apprehensive of meeting Fanny, kindly though she had written. 'I have requested him [Horace] not to think of bringing his lady and suite to Burnham till his other visits are at an end. Indeed I am in no haste to see and receive a stranger . . . I believe she will form a valuable part of our family connections, but every power of mine is in decay. Insipid, whimsical and very unfit for society in truth . . .'

Fanny's seven-year-old son Josiah, Nelson's stepson, had already been sent into Norfolk to go to school. But not until eleven months after his return to England did Nelson go to see his father, and then only for a short visit. He did not take his wife with him. He did at this time ask Prince William if he could get Fanny an appointment in the princess royal's household,[34] and when nothing came of that he at last took her to Norfolk, though not to his father but to stay with the Matchams. She found the climate not so temperate as Nevis. When Nelson eventually took his wife to Burnham Thorpe, she and his father got on well from the start. Captain and Mrs Nelson had not intended to stay, only to pay a visit before they went to France where Fanny was going to help her husband in another attempt to learn French. But, as Fanny put it, Mr Nelson's joy was so great that he told them they had given him a new lease of life, that they had better not have come to him at all than to have cheered him and then left him.[35] So they agreed to live together. The rector found Fanny a great consolation, and was always solicitous for her. He wished she had a little society. He also noticed that she and Horace had never felt so cold a place, and spent much time in bed.

In the end they spent more than three years in Norfolk. Nelson was five years without a ship. It has often been thought extraordinary that the most brilliant admiral of his time should have remained unemployed for so long. But Nelson was not then a brilliant admiral but a young captain who had been lucky in his early promotion, lucky to have had five commands by the time he was twenty-five, and more than lucky to have had any ship at all in peace time. There had been peace since 1783. Nelson had been given the *Boreas* in 1784 because of his political interest. In 1787, when he returned, there was still peace, and any captain would have been fortunate to get a ship. Many of the most able sea officers had spent years unemployed and on half pay. As a captain, Sir Peter Parker, Nelson's patron, had spent eleven years on half pay. John Jervis, later Lord St Vincent, had spent seven. It was usual. There were few ships to have. Late in 1789 only fifty-five post ships were in commission at all, and competing for these were 427 post captains, 172 of them senior to Nelson.[36] So even if Nelson had been in good standing, his chances of a ship would have been small. But he was not in good standing. There were two excellent reasons why he was not.

The first was that in the Leewards he had been a brilliant pest. In the trivial matter of a commodore's pendant flown at Antigua he had written reams to a secretary of the admiralty who had better things to do. In the matter of the American trade he had fallen out with Admiral Hughes, Commissioner Moutray, Governor Shirley, and every merchant in the Leewards. He had questioned his admiral's orders, and then not only gone over his head to the admiralty, but over the admiralty's head to the secretary of state for the colonies. He had inundated the navy board and the board of ordnance with his complaints about dockyards. He had even pestered the prime minister. 'To Mr Pitt I have sent everything, and an opinion, which perhaps I may be wrong in doing, that if he is as thoroughly convinced of the frauds as I am, to pass an act ...'[37] It was not the business of young sea officers to propose acts of parliament to prime ministers. All this had been capped by the Schomberg affair. And when the admiralty rebuked him, he answered back. Nelson had no idea how many people and how many interests he had offended, and he still expected a ship.

The second reason he did not get one was the way he went about it. Thanks to Maurice Suckling's connections he had twice met Sandwich.

Thanks to Hood's connections he had met Howe. He was used to meeting first lords, something most captains rarely did, and getting what he wanted. So he had confidently asked Howe for a ship of the line, and when after some months no ship at all was offered, he wrote him a letter which could hardly have been better designed to annoy. 'I have twice, since my arrival in town [from Bath, in May 1788] done myself the honour of calling on your lordship in order to pay my personal respects and to assure you, that as I have always been, so I continue, ever in readiness to undertake any service to which the admiralty may think it proper to appoint me. My zeal for his majesty's service is as great as I once flattered myself your lordship thought it.'[38] Such a letter would finish any officer with Howe, so Nelson was lucky that a new board of admiralty was appointed two months later, in August 1788. The Earl of Chatham, the prime minister's older brother, became the new first lord, and Lord Hood a member of the board. Nelson straight-away went up to London and presented himself to Hood, who asked after Fanny, was very civil, and assured Nelson that a ship in peace time was not desirable, but that if there was a war, Nelson would have a good ship.[39] This was a tactful way of putting things, from a man not known for his tact.

Two months later, hearing that his old friend Cornwallis was going out to the East Indies as commodore with a squadron, Nelson wrote to him, and again received a reply whose tact should once again have told him where he stood. Cornwallis wrote that it would have given him great pleasure to have him in one of his ships, that he remembered Nelson was partial to the Far East, but that his 'fireside' was so changed since then that he dared not name him to the admiralty: however, if more ships were sent out . . .[40]

So Nelson was disappointed again, but instead of taking the hint and lying low for a bit, he asked the new first lord for a guardship. Chatham sent his regrets in two lines.[41] At this time Nelson read Dampier's *New Voyage Round the World*, of 1697, and thought it the finest thing he had ever read. He cultivated his father's garden, sometimes digging for the purpose of being wearied. He spent days in the woods bird-nesting, giving the eggs to Fanny who always went with him. Mr Nelson, looking at Fanny, saw that she was happy with her son when he was home for the holidays, but wondered whether exclusion from all the world could be comfortable to a young woman. 'Her attention to me,' he said, 'demands my esteem, and to her good husband she is all he can expect.'[42] A letter came from Nevis, worlds away. George Forbes wrote that he had seen a harpsichord belonging to Mrs Nelson, 'without wires or indeed anything, much unglued and upon the whole not worth freight'. He offered £10 for it.[43] It was the second harpsichord Fanny had lost – the first sold up at Salisbury after her first husband's death, and this second one left to come unglued at Nevis. At Burnham Thorpe she had nothing to play.

That July the Paris mob stormed the Bastille. Nelson asked Locker whether there was any idea of Britain being drawn into a quarrel by 'these commotions on the continent', but he had little hope of it, was starting out as a farmer for amusement, and not building his hopes 'on such sandy foundations as the friendships of the great'.[44] But then his bitterness returned, and he wrote an astonishing letter to Hood. We do not have the letter, but we do have Hood's reply.[45] From the first part, it is evident that Nelson in his disappointment was blaming the disfavour in which he found himself on his having supported Hood in the Westminster election of 1784. Hood wrote that he was sorry any officer should have done himself an injury by helping him, but believed Nelson was the *only* one who had suffered. 'And I am really concerned you did that,' he said, 'since you have thereby fallen under the displeasure of your *noble* friends who have in my humble opinion not shown much liberality of mind by such displeasure.' Who these noble friends can have been is not clear. Prince William is the only one who comes to mind.

Nelson in his letter had obviously mentioned his own good services because Hood's reply continued: 'I am ready to own that I have often with much pleasure heard your zeal & exertions spoken of in the handsomest manner, whilst you was in the West Indies, respecting illicit trade; but I am equally sorry to say, that I have as often heard you censured for the advice you gave (which is upon record at the admiralty) for a refusal of the complete muster book to the naval officer [at the Antigua dockyard], and for putting Lieut. Schomberg under an arrest – you well know my sentiments on that subject, as I candidly expressed them to you in the several conversations we had on your return to England. At the same time I made allowances for your situation, and always said I thought it right and just they should be made.'

So there it was. The greater part of Nelson's trouble was the manner in which he had deferred to the prince, whose commanding officer he was, by arresting Schomberg and by allowing the prince, for his greater ease of mind, to come home by way of Jamaica. But the most extraordinary part of Nelson's letter is that which Hood answered in his last paragraph. Hood wrote: 'When I accepted the offer of a seat at the admiralty board I had no selfish view, but did it merely from friendship to Lord Chatham whom I love and to whom it had been my pride & ever will be so, to look to his honour and reputation regardless of myself – & preserving great caution against the imputation of having any degree of power, beyond any other colleague – but should I have the power of assisting any wish of yours I shall embrace it with pleasure, but with respect to your appointment as a commander-in-chief that is totally beyond what I could attempt.'

Was Nelson suggesting that Hood had accepted a lordship of the admiralty from selfish motives? And what can he have meant by an appointment as commander-in-chief? He was a sea officer without a ship of any kind. He had never commanded more than a small frigate. He had recently solicited a guardship, which would have been an honourable but not an active post. For his last year in the Leeward Islands, after Hughes's departure, he had been senior captain, but the admiralty had made it clear on his return that he had not possessed the power of an acting commander-in-chief. The only certain inference is that Nelson, having nothing and the prospect of nothing, was aiming very high. Hood's is a remarkably civil reply. He was a man with a bite, he was very much Nelson's senior, and Nelson's letter was at the very least impertinent. He was presuming a great deal on the goodwill of an admiral he had met in New York six years before, in wartime, who had then put himself out to get Nelson attached to his squadron, and had mentioned, perhaps lightly and in conversation, the possibility of a ship of the line for Nelson, one day. Now the admiral was a lord of the admiralty, and Nelson had overstepped himself.

Nelson did not know that Hood at the time also thought himself hard done by, believing there never was a man who had lent himself to a government with the zeal he had done, and yet was still so neglected. Nelson had touched a raw spot when he mentioned the 1784 election. Hood's conviction was that he had been pressed by Pitt to stand against Fox, 'one of the most disagreeable situations [in which] an officer could be placed'. And when in 1788 he had accepted the post of lord of the admiralty he had done so not only for love of Lord Chatham but also to accommodate the government, and was 'beggar'd and thereby broken hearted'. This was how he put it to his older brother, Rear-Admiral Alexander Hood, and he was putting it a bit strong. It was true that a lord of the admiralty would lose some of the perquisites of a serving admiral, but what Hood really wanted was the ceremonial and lucrative office of vice-admiral of England, which he had asked for but was not given.[46]

Back in Norfolk, Nelson knew nothing of all this. He was still encumbered with the correspondence he had brought on himself about West Indian frauds, still laying papers before the navy office and the attorney-general. In the spring of 1790, while he was away at a fair buying a pony, the first of two writs was served on Fanny. It was from American captains claiming damages of £20,000. Nelson wrote to the Treasury saying he did not deserve this affront and demanding official support or he would be off to France, presumably to get out of the jurisdiction. According to Fanny, all arrangements for the trip were made. Nelson was to go, and she and Maurice would follow ten days afterwards. Treasury support was promised by return of post.[47]

But Nelson did not want another French tour. He wanted a ship. In April 1790 a dispute with Spain blew up over the Nootka Sound, off Vancouver Island. Spain was demanding that her sovereignty over the American Pacific coast should be recognised, the British cabinet in return asserted a right to trade on that coast, and this could have provoked a war since Spain at the time had a treaty of alliance with France. A British squadron of forty-six ships was fitted out, and when he heard of the 'bustle' Nelson immediately set off for London and wrote to the admiralty as soon as he arrived. He was offered nothing, and wrote to Prince William, who had just been created Duke of Clarence, that his not being appointed to a ship was very mortifying. He could not find words to express what he felt, and when he reflected on his royal highness's condescension in mentioning him to Lord Chatham, he was the more hurt and surprised. He still did not realise that his princely friend had no interest at all with the government or with his father the king. When in 1789 he was created Duke of Clarence and voted £14,000 a year, he had straightaway asked for more, and was told by the king that he had entirely estranged himself from his parents and that no more money could be expected 'whilst the dignity of character is forgot, and only dissipation and extravagance is pursued'.[48] Nelson seems to have had no more idea of this than he had suspected, when he proposed Fanny as a lady-in-waiting to the princess royal, that Prince William would have been the last to be consulted in the choosing of his sister Charlotte's household. This was public gossip in the newspapers, but Nelson was blind to it.

In July 1790, in spite of his rebuff of the previous year, he again applied to Hood, and Hood, who was a forgiving man, gave him a plain reply: 'Lord Chatham has so long a list of captains pressing for employment and powerfully recommended that I can be of no use to anyone at present but should hostilities commence you cannot remain unemployed. I can only say you shall not, if I can prevent it . . .'[49] Nelson could not take no for an answer. Two months later he wrote directly to Chatham asking for the *Raisonnable* ship of the line – the first ship in which he had ever served, as a midshipman, with his uncle.[50] There was no reply. At Burnham Thorpe, while Nelson was in London, Fanny showed her father-in-law the letters in which her husband had asked for ships, and the replies refusing them. The Revd Edmund Nelson was an unworldly man, but he still knew something about patronage, because that was how he had attained the little he had. As he admitted, the few advantages he had had were from early connections, 'improved by conduct such as they did not see was amiss'. That puts it neatly. Once, when Maurice had needed help, George Matcham had suggested approaching the Lord Chancellor, whom the old man had known as a boy. To this suggestion, the rector replied: 'You suppose that I was once in a habit of friendly intercourse with Lord Thurlow. No such thing. Near 40 years ago his lordship, then a youth, visited a neighbour and friend of mine. From that house as a saunterer he often called, walked, chatted, or took tea, as it might happen. There it ended. The whole parish of Swaffham separately, much more as a collective body, might with the same propriety ask a favour as a remembrance that he once breathed their salubrious air . . .'[51]

Still, when Fanny showed him Horace's plentiful correspondence, he wrote to his son in London, saying he ought to consider how to act to justify his own character. It ought to be made known why was he so marked as to render any application fruitless – merely for supporting the dignity and character of a person of rank [Clarence], for which he was now, as it were, persecuted. What had passed between Nelson and Hood ought to be known, so long as the confidences of friendship were not broken. He thought his son ought to ask for an audience with the Prince of Wales.[52] Nelson's father did not know that the prince counted for nothing with the admiralty. Neither he nor his son knew how hopeless the case of Captain Nelson was at that moment. Because, though the Nootka Sound squabble had been settled, Lord Chatham had nevertheless just made a great number of new post captains. He had been puzzling how many to make for the previous three weeks and had shown Hood the list and asked him to reduce it, but to Hood's mind it was of no consequence whether he made twenty-five or thirty-five, and he declined to reduce it or add to it.[53] In the end no fewer than forty-four officers were made post in December, among them Isaac Schomberg and William Bligh, who had only that March returned to England after being cast adrift by the crew of the *Bounty*.[54]

In such a way were the entire futures of sea officers decided. And nothing could have made it clearer that at that moment Nelson's prospects were non-existent. Chatham, with this list of young officers three weeks in his pocket, was hardly likely to have given Nelson a thought; nor, evidently, did Hood put in a word for him. But Nelson never gave up. In March 1791 he was in London bowing to royalty. In February and March 1792 he was again there for at least a month, 'bowing to the high and mighty potentates'.[55] And this although he knew from his brother Maurice at the navy office that the navy was being reduced to about 15,000 men. His bows brought him nothing, but he took every opportunity to write to the Duke of Clarence, renewing his expressions of attachment, saying he had again asked Chatham for a ship, but hardly expected an answer.[56] Perhaps this latest request was the celebrated one in which he told their lordships he would be grateful for the command of a cockle boat. This would not have helped him either. He knew, and the admiralty knew, that a post captain, if he were given anything, could be given nothing less than a post ship. The reply, from the admiralty secretary, was brief: 'Sir, I have received your letter of the 5th instant, and I have read the same to my lords commissioners of the admiralty.'[57]

Before he received this reply, Nelson had an unusually long and outspoken letter from Clarence, who went so far as to 'lament that Lord Chatham should so far not attend to the good of the king as to keep out of employment good experienced & zealous officers like you my worthy friend'. He then asked how Nelson stood with Lord Hood.[58] This brought a torrent of a reply: 'We have not for a long time had any communication with each other. Our familiar correspondence ceased on a difference of opinion. In the Spanish armament [of 1790], when almost the whole service were called forth, I asked Lord Hood to interest himself with Lord Chatham, that I might be appointed to a ship. His lordship having declined doing it, *and made a speech never to be effaced from my memory, viz. that the king was impressed with an unfavourable impression of me*, has prevented my troubling him again for his interest or influence. However, in consideration of our former intimacy, whenever I have gone to London, I have hitherto thought it right to leave my name at his lordship's door. I certainly cannot look on Lord Hood as a friend, but I have the satisfaction of knowing, that I never gave his lordship just cause to be my enemy.'[59]

The words in italics are in Nelson's draft of the letter, but not in the copy he sent to Clarence. Clarke and M'Arthur suggest that he might have thought the words improper in a letter to the king's son. The king might indeed not have been delighted that Captain Nelson had let his son make a fool of himself in the Schomberg case. Nelson continued his letter to Clarence with reports of disaffection in Norfolk, where prices had risen but wages had not, and labourers could not afford candles, soap, or shoes. He wrote about agitators going from ale house to ale house inciting poor people to pay no taxes. He said a person of the name of Priestley – this was the celebrated Joseph Priestley, Unitarian minister, one of the discoverers of oxygen, and author of a pamphlet vindicating the early principles of the French Revolution – was one who had 'held this language', and he asked why he was not arrested. (Nelson's father had a different opinion of Priestley, thinking him 'a good man, notwithstanding evill reports'.[60]) Nelson was afraid, though he did not say so in as many words, of a rising on the French model. In his letter to the prince he did say that poor labourers had been seduced by promises and hopes of better times, and that his royal highness would not wonder at this when he was told that they were really in want of everything to make life comfortable. He wrote, and then deleted this too, perhaps also as unsuitable reading for a king's son, that hunger was a sharp thorn and that people were in want of food, clothes, and coal.

In 1799, after the Nile, when he was a hero, Nelson wrote in a sketch of his life that in 1790 he had made use of every interest to get a ship, but in vain, as there was a prejudice at the admiralty against him which he could neither get at nor in the least account for.⁶¹ If he believed this he was deluding himself. He knew perfectly well why he did not get a ship. In the five years from 1787 to 1792 he made no fewer than thirteen direct applications to Howe, Chatham, Hood, and to the secretary to the admiralty, besides several other applications through friends and acquaintances. He maintained his bows to high and mighty potentates. The fact was that he had irritated and alienated all those who could be any use to him, and had kept only the goodwill of the Duke of Clarence, who had been the principal cause of his disfavour and whose interest was worse than useless. It all went back to a reason which was stated in a letter from Howe, as first lord, to Hood, in July 1787, two days before Nelson brought the *Boreas* into Spithead on his return from Nevis. 'I am sorry,' wrote Howe, 'that Capt Nelson, whom we wished well to, has been so much wanting in the endeavours, which I think could not have failed of success if they had been judiciously exerted, to dissuade the prince from the idea of going so prematurely to Jamaica ...'⁶² Nelson, whom they had wished well, had been found wanting. After that he was overlooked time after time. In November 1792 Hood, needing to find a captain for the *Pegasus*, the Duke of Clarence's old ship, gave her to William Domett, three years junior to Nelson on the list but a steady man.⁶³ If the peace had lasted, the great Nelson would have been lucky ever to get another ship again, and no one would know his name.

The peace did not last. By January 1793 war was inevitable, and Nelson was in London, from where he wrote: 'My dear Fanny, – *Post nubila Phoebus* – your son will explain the motto – after clouds come sunshine. The admiralty so smile on me that really I am as much surprised as when they frowned. Lord Chatham yesterday made many apologies for not having given me a ship before this time, but that if I chose to take a 64-gun ship to begin with I should be appointed to one as soon as she was ready, and that I should as soon as in his power be removed into a 74 ... Everything looks like war. One of our ships looking into Brest has been fired on. The shot is now at the admiralty.'⁶⁴

Nelson was all confidence again. Did Chatham, except out of formal politeness, make apologies? Nelson saw it that way. He should have a 74 as soon as it was in Chatham's power? That was a turn of phrase he should have been familiar with. It had earlier not been in Chatham's 'power' to give him a guardship. Nelson was given not a 74 but a 64, the smallest ship of the line he could have been offered, a type almost obsolete. But he had a ship.

By February it was war. The *Agamemnon* was fitting out at Chatham. Captain and Mrs Nelson came to London. On 4 March, having taken his place in the Chatham coach, to go to his ship, Nelson wrote a note to Fanny, who as her father-in-law had noticed was all a man could expect in a wife:

'My dear Fanny, – Never a finer night was seen than last night, and I am not the least tired.'[65]

Facsimile of Nelson's letter to his wife Fanny as he left her to join the Agamemnon *in 1793. Nelson Museum, Monmouth.*

CHAPTER ELEVEN

The Horror, and the Benefit to the Nation

BEFORE NELSON LEFT ENGLAND, Mr Herbert had died. Since he had been reconciled to his daughter, his niece Fanny did not prove the heiress she and Nelson expected. He left £4,000 to Nelson, which at three per cent would bring £120 a year, more than half his pay, but at the same time he lost the £100 a year Herbert had been paying towards Josiah's education. Nelson showed little disappointment. The will did settle the question of Josiah's future. He had not been destined for the navy. Nelson could have borne him, even at seven years old, on the books of the *Boreas*, which would have counted towards the six years at sea before he could take his lieutenant's examination. That was a common enough fiction. But on Mr Herbert's death it became plain that it would take more than Nelson had to bring Josiah up in another profession, so he went as a midshipman in the *Agamemnon*.

Nelson thought her as good a ship as, at first acquaintance, he had thought all his others, but she retained his affections. She had fought at the battle of the Saintes, and had since been laid up at Chatham where Locker, who was now commodore there, could assist in her fitting out. She sailed admirably, Nelson said better than any ship in the fleet. He was with Hood's squadron, but did not know they were bound for the Mediterranean until late June, after they had paid a formal visit to Cadiz. The Spanish at the time were allies. Six captains dined with the Spanish admiral on board the *Concepcion*, 110 guns – larger than any British ship – and saw the arsenal and the dockyards where four first rates were being built, very fine ships but shockingly manned. He was certain that if the English captain had got their barges' crews on board one of their first rates they could have taken her. 'The dons may make fine ships – they cannot however make men.'[1] At Cadiz Nelson was disgusted by a bull fight, and wrote to Fanny that he would not have been displeased to see some of the dons tossed. 'How women can even sit out, much more applaud, such sights, is astonishing. It even turned us sick and we could hardly go through it: the dead, mangled horses with entrails torn out, and the bulls covered with blood, were too much.'[2]

Six weeks later, off Toulon, he was again writing to Fanny, saying he looked back on his being united to such a good woman as the happiest period of his life; and that since he could not show his affection to her, he did so doubly to Josiah, who was a really good boy. Lord Hood had offered him a 74, but he had declined it. 'As the admiralty put me into a sixty-four, there I stay.' There is a touch of pride in this; but he gave Hood as his reason that he did not wish to lose his officers. He ended by saying he did not think the war could last long, for a civil war was inevitable in France. It was reasonable to think so. In Brittany and the Vendée, royalists had risen against the new republic, and many in the southern ports of Marseilles and Toulon would do the same. Nelson said France would be dismembered. The guillotine was at work every day. A ship's master from Marseilles had told him there were now only two kinds of people in France – the one drunk and mad; the other with horror printed in their faces, starving. Peace with England was what they wanted, and Provence would willingly put itself under the protection of England; but what was the use of sending a great fleet to the Mediterranean without troops to act with it?[3]

A list exists in Nelson's hand of twenty-one French ships of the line in Toulon harbour, with notes on the political persuasions of their officers and men. The captains of seven were 'doubtful' – unlikely to support a rising against the revolution – having been promoted from pilots or from the command of fire ships. (Pilot was the French equivalent of master. It was rare in the *ancien régime* for a commoner to reach higher rank.) Other captains, previously the equivalent of British post captains or lieutenants, were marked as of 'sound principles', that is to say royalists. The flagship, the immense *Commerce de Marseille*, was in two minds: the admiral and captain were both sound, but the other officers and the men were Jacobins.[4]

By 23 August the French fleet was in disorder, some officers willing to surrender, others wanting to come out and fight. A deputation of citizens from Toulon went on board Hood's flagship wishing to acknowledge Louis XVII, the son of the executed king, as their sovereign.[5] Hood made a proclamation to the deputies: for four years they had been involved in a revolution which had plunged them into anarchy. After having destroyed their government, factious leaders had assassinated the virtuous, and constantly held forth the idea of liberty while robbing the people of it. 'Everywhere they have preached respect to persons, which everywhere in their name has been violated; they have amused you with the sovereignty of the people, which they have constantly usurped . . . A situation so dreadful sensibly afflicts the coalesced powers [Britain, Austria, Prussia, Spain, Holland, and Piedmont Sardinia]; they see no other remedy but the re-establishment of the French monarchy.' Then Hood made an offer, which gives a pretty fair idea of the power of a British vice-admiral of the time: 'If a candid and explicit declaration in favour of monarchy is made at Toulon and Marseilles, and the standard of royalty hoisted . . . the people of Provence shall have all the alliance and support her Britannic majesty's fleet under my command can give; and not an atom of private property of any individual shall be touched, but protected. And when the peace takes place, which I hope and trust will be soon, the port with all the ships in the harbour, and forts of Toulon, shall be restored to France . . .'[6]

These terms were accepted. But as Nelson had asked, what use was a fleet without an army? On 25 August he was sent with dispatches for Turin asking for 4,000 Sardinian troops, and then to Naples to ask for 6,000 Neapolitans. He would have liked to stay longer, to see the British fleet enter Toulon, but had to sail immediately. On his passage to Naples he wrote to Fanny: 'What an event this has been for Lord Hood. Such a one as history cannot produce its equal. That the strongest place in Europe, and twenty-two sail of the line &c, should be given up without firing a shot, it is not to be credited.' He finished his letter in the Bay of Naples where he was lying-to at night, in sight of an erupting Vesuvius, whose 'throws of fire' were grand.[7] Nothing, he said, could be finer.

Nelson had not been sent as Hood's representative to the court of

Naples. Hood knew from Nelson's conduct with Prince William that he was no diplomat. He was sent because *Agamemnon* was the fastest sailer of all the ships of the line in the fleet, and he should have handed his papers to the British ambassador. But when he anchored at Naples, the king himself came out into the bay to meet him. Nelson went on board the king's barge to report the taking of Toulon and the need for troops, and it was to Nelson that King Ferdinand declared the British were the saviours of Italy and of his kingdom in particular. Then Nelson went ashore to present Hood's papers to the ambassador, Sir William Hamilton, and met his wife.[8]

Naples in 1793 was a mixture of the primitive and the polished. After London and Paris it was the third largest city in Europe. The recent excavations of Herculaneum and Pompeii made it an essential part of an English gentleman's grand tour. The new palace at Caserta was intended to be as grand as Versailles. But Naples was the capital of the kingdom of the Two Sicilies – virtually all Italy south of Rome, and the island of Sicily – most of which remained in feudal poverty. The king, Ferdinand IV, was a Bourbon known as *Il Re Nasone*, King Nosey, on account of the size of his nose, a man happier in the company of fishermen than of his own courtiers. The real government rested with his queen, Maria Carolina, a daughter of Empress Maria Theresa of Austria, and with her favourite and prime minister John Acton, a man of English extraction who had commanded the Neapolitan navy before rising to higher things. Hamilton, who had been British ambassador since 1764, was the grandson of the Duke of Hamilton, and was a dilettante, a connoisseur of paintings and Roman vases, and a vulcanologist who had climbed Vesuvius twenty times. He had married as his second wife Emma Hart, who became celebrated as Emma Hamilton, but in 1793, when Nelson first met her, she was not known as the notorious adventuress who is so familiar to history. In Naples she was the British ambassador's wife, who had been his mistress before he married her. Some English visitors doing the grand tour noticed her Lancashire accent, all noticed her beauty, and some may have known she had often posed for George Romney – at a spinning wheel, or as Circe, or as a devout seamstress, or as Saint Cecilia – but that was all. Few knew that she had started life as a blacksmith's illiterate daughter, had a child out of wedlock at sixteen, was taken up by a rake by the name of Charles Greville, and was then handed on

The Revd William (1757-1835), the grasping older brother, always scrounging for deaneries, who was made an earl after Horatio's death.

Silhouette of Nelson's father, the Revd Edmund Nelson (1722-1802), with whom Nelson fell out over his separation from his wife Fanny.

Maurice (1753-1801), Nelson's oldest brother, a clerk in the navy office, who felt 'degraded' that he never rose to be a commissioner.

Nelson's favourite sister Catherine Matcham.

The rectory at Burnham Thorpe, Nelson's birthplace.

NELSON'S EARLY PATRONS

In the eighteenth-century navy a young
sea officer needed 'interest' above all else.
Nelson was fortunate in this matter.

Suckling *Right: Nelson's maternal uncle
Maurice Suckling, who first took him to
sea as a midshipman and then, becoming
comptroller of the navy in 1775, got his
nephew a lieutenant's commission at the age
of seventeen. Stipple after Thomas Bardwell.*

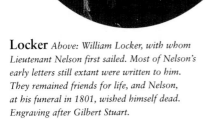

Locker *Above: William Locker, with whom
Lieutenant Nelson first sailed. Most of Nelson's
early letters still extant were written to him.
They remained friends for life, and Nelson,
at his funeral in 1801, wished himself dead.
Engraving after Gilbert Stuart.*

Parker *Right: Sir Peter Parker, who, when he
commanded the Jamaica station, promoted Nelson
post captain at twenty. He became one of the richest
of all admirals, from prize money, and as admiral
of the fleet was chief mourner at Nelson's funeral.*

Two Great Commanders

Hood *Samuel, first viscount Hood, (1724-1816) won his peerage at the battle of the Saintes in the American war. He was a friend of Nelson's uncle, Maurice Suckling, took the young Nelson to the West Indies in 1783, and later presented him to George III. Nelson supported him in the election of 1784, but Hood disapproved of Nelson's conduct with Prince William, and he and Nelson fell out. But Nelson was with Hood in the Mediterranean in 1793, and thought him the greatest sea officer he ever saw. Hood was governor of Greenwich Hospital when Nelson's body lay there in state. Mezzotint by J. Jones after Reynolds.*

St Vincent *John Jervis, first earl St Vincent (1735-1823), won his earldom at the battle of that name, when Nelson famously broke the line. In 1798 he gave Nelson command of the squadron which won the battle of the Nile. He regarded Nelson as a brilliant predator who inspired others, and gave him command of the anti-invasion campaign of 1801, in the Channel. But the two men quarrelled over prize money and Nelson's liaison with Emma Hamilton. In the end, St Vincent wrote that animal courage was Nelson's sole merit, 'his private character most disgraceful in every sense of the word.' Mezzotint by C. Turner after William Beechey.*

The press gang *There were never enough volunteers to man the navy in war time, so ships lacking men sent out parties under a lieutenant to shanghai able-bodied men, as in this lampoon of 1790. In 1787, Nelson's frigate, Boreas, in the Thames estuary, was used as a receiving ship for men rounded up in this way. Eleven hundred men were pressed one night. This engraving, entitled 'Manning the Fleet', is engraved by Barlow after Collings.*

Prince William, *third son of King George III, was created Duke of Clarence in 1790, and succeeded to the throne in 1830 as William IV. His father was determined he should go into the navy, and as a young post captain he served in Nelson's squadron in the Leewards in 1786-7. At Nelson's wedding he insisted on giving away the bride. He also insisted on court-martialling his first lieutenant, which embroiled Nelson in all sorts of trouble. William hoped to become first lord of the admiralty, and Nelson expected much from his royal patronage. But the prince was constantly out of favour with the King and his ministers, and his patronage was more a hindrance than a help. Engraving after a portrait by Richard Cosway.*

Key to the Large Print & Picture of ADM.ˡ NELSON's Boarding the Spanish Ships, in L.ᵈ S.ᵗ VINCENT'S VICTORY.

1. Cap.ᵗ Berry.
2. Adm.ˡ Nelson.
3. Cap.ᵗ Noble.
4. Lieu.ᵗ Pearson 69 Reg.ᵗ
5. Lieu.ᵗ Withers.
6. O Brien, a Spanish Priest.
7. Cap.ᵗ P. Spicer.
8. Lieu.ᵗ Jesú Asbit.
9. Cap.ᵗ Miller.
10. Soldier of the 69ᵗʰ
11. Fearney an English Sailor.
12. Hooper the Sailor who Struck the Spanish Ensign.
13. Ramsay, one of the Admirals Barge men.
14. Spanish Sailor.
15. Ignace Fene the first Lieu.ᵗ Spanish.
16. Don Francisco Xaver Winthuysen the Spanish Adm.ᵗ
17. Don Tomas Dikuena, the Spanish Captain.

The battle of St Vincent This action, on St Valentine's Day, 1797, was fought between fifteen English ships of the line under Sir John Jervis and a Spanish fleet of twenty-seven ships. Jervis triumphed and was made Earl St Vincent. Nelson famously broke away from the line of battle, and boarded the San Nicolas, 112 guns, over the San Josef, 80, calling this action 'Nelson's patent bridge'. This account was challenged by his brother officers, but was the beginning of Nelson's fame. For his part, he was made a knight of the Bath.

At the time of the battle Nelson was a commodore, not an admiral as he is described in the engraving. But this etching, by Daniel Orme, was published three years after the event, in 1800, when Nelson was a rear-admiral, and already celebrated as the victor of the Nile. The dying Spanish admiral (bottom left, No. 16) surrendered his sword to Nelson, who gave it to one of his bargemen, William Fearney, (top right, No. 11) who, as Nelson wrote in a letter to his wife, tucked it under his arm 'with the greatest sang froid.'

Annihilation at Aboukir *The battle of the Nile, on 1 August 1798, was the first example in modern naval history of a fleet not just beaten but annihilated. Of the French fleet of thirteen ships, eleven were taken or destroyed. Here Bruey's flagship, L'Orient, is seen as she blows up. The ship in the centre is Hallowell's Swiftsure, and another English ship, on the left, is seen doubling the French line. The original oil is by George Arnald. This engraving was made for Clarke and M'Arthur's biography of Nelson.*

Captain Thomas Foley, *in the* Goliath, *led the first five ships inside the French fleet, between the enemy and the shore, thus doubling the line and making the victory more devastating. Nelson's flag captain, Berry, wrote in his account that Nelson had foreseen the manoeuvre, but almost all other witnesses agree that the initiative was Foley's, who had the advantage of new and accurate French charts of the bay. Foley was present off Toulon in 1793 and at the battle of St Vincent in 1797, and was captain of the Elephant, Nelson's flagship, at Copenhagen. He lived until 1833 and died a full admiral and a knight of the Bath. Engraving after William Grimaldi.*

NELSON IN NAPLES 1799
Extirpating rebels and jacobins

The other people in the story.

The king *Ferdinand IV, who wanted his kingdom back.*

The ambassador *William Hamilton, the political master, who managed Nelson's 'impetuosity' and strung Cardinal Ruffo along.*

The queen *Maria Carolina:* *'A massacre would not cause me the slightest grief.'*

The man Nelson hanged
Francesco Caracciolo, Neapolitan commodore, who was 'fool enough to quit his master', and fired on the king's ships.

The king's viceroy
Cardinal Ruffo, who took Naples with his holy mob and made a peace treaty that Nelson repudiated.

A later patron *Sir Gilbert Elliot, later Baron and Earl Minto (1751-1814), was viceroy of Corsica in 1793 and thought Nelson an Homeric hero. In 1797 he was a witness of the battle of St Vincent, and later told the first lord Nelson was the fittest man to command the squadron that won at the Nile. But he thought Nelson made a fool of himself with Emma, who 'crammed him with trowelfuls of flattery'.*

The first lord *George, second Earl Spencer (1758-1834), was first lord of the admiralty 1794-1801. In his administration the battles of St.Vincent, Camperdown, and the Nile were won. He did much to advance Nelson's career, but later said neither Nelson's own interests nor those of the country would be served by his staying in the Mediterranean. Mezzotint after John Copley.*

Favourite, then rival *Thomas Troubridge (1758-1807) fought with Nelson at St Vincent and the Nile, and was his favourite captain in the Mediterranean. Nelson got him a baronetcy. But when Troubridge was made a lord of the admiralty in 1801 Nelson was jealously convinced he was 'lording it' over his own chief, and they fell out. Drowned in 1807. Engraving by M-A. Bourlier after Beechey.*

A mistrusted commander *Lord Keith (1745-1823), was at Toulon in 1793, took Cape Town in 1795, and in 1799 was c-in-c in the Mediterranean when Nelson, his junior but a hero after the Nile, twice disobeyed his orders to send ships to Minorca, preferring to protect Naples. Keith became c-in-c Channel, and arranged the exile of Napoleon to St Helena. Mezzotint after Hoppner.*

by him to his uncle William Hamilton with the recommendation that a cleanlier, sweeter bedfellow never existed. Emma protested at this handing on, but by late 1786, in Naples, had settled in well enough to tell Sir William that she was obliged to play whist that evening but would much rather 'play at *all-fours*' with him.[9] She also did her famous Attitudes, with the aid of a few shawls, impersonating classical figures, which in 1787 so captured the visiting Goethe that he said she realised in movements and transformations what thousands of artists would have liked to express.[10] By 1790 Hamilton was writing to his friend Sir Joseph Banks saying he had not neglected the study of 'the animal called woman', that Emma had infinite merit and no princess could do the honours of his house with more ease and dignity than she did, but that he was not thinking of marrying the girl.[11]

But next year he did marry her, in England, privately and by special licence. Romney painted his last portrait of her, entitled 'The Ambassadress', and back in Naples she was accepted by the queen and by the English women there. 'She is really an extraordinary being,' Hamilton wrote to the Earl of Orford, better known as Horace Walpole, '& most grateful to me for saving her from the precipice into which she has good sense enough to know that she must inevitably have fallen . . . It has often been remarked that a reformed rake makes a good husband. Why not vice versa?'[12] She had her generous side, and sent her old grandmother £20 each year for Christmas: 'I have 2 hundred a year for nonsense, and it would be hard not to give her twenty pounds, when she has so often given me her last shilling.'[13] Hamilton had not only married her but educated her so that her French was that spoken in any European court and her Italian, so he said, was better than his. She was not only a famous beauty and the ambassador's lady, but also Maria Carolina's closest female friend. They corresponded almost daily. Maria Carolina was a sister of Marie Antoinette. On the execution of the queen's brother-in-law, Louis XVI, Emma had sent her condolences and received in reply a coloured print of the dauphin of France, under which Maria Carolina had written that this innocent child cried out for vengeance, which she looked to Emma's generous nation to provide.[14]

Nelson stayed six days at Naples, and took Josiah ashore with him. He dined with the king, who placed him on his right. The 4,000 troops were promised. Nelson wrote to Fanny: 'Lady Hamilton has been wonderfully kind and good to Josiah. She is a young woman of amiable manners, who does honour to the station to which she is raised.'[15] He did not see her again for another five years.

He returned by way of Leghorn, the port of Tuscany, 160 miles northwest of Rome, where he found that the crew of a French frigate had just deposed their captain, made the lieutenant of the marines captain of the ship, and their former captain sergeant of marines. 'What a state,' he said, 'they are mad enough for any undertaking.' He returned to Toulon to find Hood quite as he used to be and respected by all. White flags flew from all the ships and forts, and Nelson was confident that by November the allies would have 30,000 troops, when the whole of the country would fall to them, for they hated the Paris convention. He was then given command of a squadron of frigates off Corsica and the coast of Italy, and so he was not at Toulon when the city fell. But he heard Hood never had more than 4,900 reliable troops. By mid-December it was clear that he could not hold a city and harbour surrounded by 40,000 French troops occupying the dominating heights, and against artillery directed by the young Captain Buonaparte.[16] When Nelson touched at Leghorn just before Christmas 1793 the news was bad. A refugee had arrived there and told the sad tale. Nelson wrote to Maurice in London: 'Report has just arrived of Toulon being destroyed by 60,000 Convention troops . . . A man running away makes things worse probably than they are, but something very bad has taken place.'[17] So it had. Hood had abandoned Toulon. He took off 15,000 French royalists, but as many more were left to the mercy of a suddenly republican mob, hundreds were drowned trying to scramble from the quays into boats, and the city burned. What did not burn as it should have done was the French fleet. Only thirteen French ships of the line and some frigates were taken off by the British or destroyed. Eighteen ships of the line survived intact, enough to constitute a formidable French Mediterranean fleet.

About the loss of Toulon, Nelson wrote to the Duke of Clarence and to Fanny on the same day. To the duke, he said: 'The quitting Toulon by us, I am satisfied, is a national benefit; both in money, for our contracts will be found to have been very extravagant, people seemed to act as if fortunes were to have been made instantly; and in saving some of our gallant English blood, which, when the muster comes to be taken, will appear to have flowed plentifully. The destruction of the fleet and arsenal, and indeed of the harbour of Toulon, for a number of years, is a great benefit to England. I have only to regret it could not have been done on the first day of our entrance.'[18]

And to Fanny: 'It is all true. Everything which domestic wars produce are multiplied at Toulon. Fathers are here without families, families without fathers. In short all is horror which we hear. The lord [Hood] put himself at the head of the flying troops and was the admiration of all but the torrent was too strong. Many of our posts were carried without resistance. At others, where the English were, everybody perished. I cannot write all, my mind is truly impressed with grief. Each teller makes the scene more horrible.'[19]

Nelson's information was wrong, and so therefore were his conclusions. The fleet and arsenal had not been destroyed, and neither had the harbour been made useless. Leaving Toulon would save money, but could only be a benefit to the nation if the city had not been worth taking in the first place. Nor had it really been taken at all. Nelson might, with the ruthless directness that came instinctively to him, wish the arsenal and harbour could have been destroyed on the first day, but that was not the bargain. Hood's proclamation had promised alliance and support, that private property should be protected, and that the port and the ships in it should be restored. But against this, Nelson also displayed, in his letter to Fanny, his grief at the horror of it all. He was not there, and he saw nothing, but just as each teller made the scene more horrible, so Nelson made the scene more terrible in his own mind, and long remembered it.

Now that Toulon was gone, Britain needed another base in the Mediterranean. The obvious choice was Corsica, where the patriot leader Paoli had organised an insurrection against the French and favoured a union with Britain. By February 1794 Nelson was already exploring the northern tip of the island, and one morning anchored the *Agamemnon* off the little village of Maginaggio, where the French revolutionary flag was flying. He sent a messenger on shore to say that he had come to deliver the residents from the republicans, but that if a musket was fired he would burn the place down. When the commandant of an old fort defied him, telling him not to address a defenceless place but to go to Bastia or Calvi where he could have his answer, Nelson struck the flag with his own hand, ordered the republican tree of liberty to be cut down, and destroyed five hundred tuns of wine.[20] It was not the most glorious action for a British ship of the line. Nelson did afterwards go to both Bastia and Calvi, the two fortress towns of the island, and believed he deserved much of the credit for taking both.

The taking of these two towns is a history of bickering between the army and navy.[21] The navy wanted to storm the towns, the army to blockade and besiege them. Hood insisted he was supreme commander, which Lieutenant General David Dundas denied. Nelson wanted to act even more precipitately than Hood. Lieutenant Colonel John Moore, who had been sceptical of Hood's conduct at Toulon, became scathing of what he saw in Corsica.[22] Early in March, the army camped at San Fiorenzo on the west coast, now St-Florent, twelve miles west of Bastia. Nelson, who always loved a land campaign, went ashore at Bastia on the northwest coast and wrote to Fanny that he could storm the town with five hundred men, that armies went slow but seamen went forward, and that his seamen were what British seamen ought to be, and really minded shot no more than peas.[23] And he also saw, for he always noticed women, that the French bombardment killed several women in the camp, and a most beautiful girl of seventeen. Such, he wrote, were the horrors of war.[24]

While Nelson, by Hood's authority, was establishing himself as the commander of all naval forces on land,[25] and while the army was declining to take part in an attack, the British admiral and the British general were exchanging courtesies. Hood, replying to General Dundas's opinion that an attempt to reduce Bastia would be most visionary and rash, said it appeared to him very much the reverse, and that he was ready to undertake it at his own risk and with his own force. He also reminded Dundas that his power had ceased with the evacuation of Toulon, and that the troops and ships were now at his (Hood's) disposal. Dundas ironically invited Hood to show his commission from the king for the supreme command, but then walked off and went home.[26] 'Lord Hood,' said Moore, 'enters into the subject little further than to say, "Take Bastia," just as he would say to a captain, "Go to sea." He conceives they are both to be done with equal facility.'[27] Nelson for his part considered that not to attack would be a national disgrace, and that he had rather be beat than not make the attempt. What, he asked Sir William Hamilton in a letter he wrote to Naples, would the immortal Wolfe (the victor of Quebec in

1759) have done? Nelson should have known better than this: he had served in Quebec and must have known that the Heights of Abraham, up which Wolfe had attacked, were nothing to the mountains round Bastia. Nelson commanded the seamen brought ashore from the fleet, but felt he got little credit for it: 'I am everything,' as he told his uncle Suckling, 'yet nothing ostensible.'[28]

Seamen dragged guns down scrubby ravines and up mountain slopes. The news came that Corsica was to become English and be ruled like Ireland, governed by its own laws. Sir Gilbert Elliot, the late brief commissioner of Toulon, was to be viceroy. Moore told Elliot the only chance of taking the town was to blockade the harbour, which might be done equally well whether the heights were attacked or not. Even Hood warned Nelson against firing unless there was an object to fire at, but Nelson was writing to Fanny that a brave man died only once, but a coward all his life long. He called the expedition almost a child of his own, and had no doubt of victory. The army ought to be shot for allowing a handful of brave men to fight unsupported. The seamen had fired 20,000 shot and shell at the town. Not a soldier had fired a musket.[29]

Bastia was starved out on 23 May. After the surrender, Moore walked over the ground, and found the enemy's advance post could only have been taken by a force descending a mountain path in Indian file, which must have suffered great loss. He said Hood's proposals for a land attack were absurd. He had never advanced one inch, and if he had must have been cut up. Nelson put things differently: 'Lord Hood has gained the greatest credit for his perseverance and I dare say he will not forget that it was due to myself in great measure that this glorious expedition was undertaken.'[30]

The British then turned to Calvi on the west coast. A new general had come out from England, and was soon complaining that the army must lose many brave men because of Hood's vanity. The seamen, with a new town to bombard, were dragging cannons up more mountains, and carrying shot and shell.[31] Nelson had already had a narrow escape at Bastia in April. The diary of a fellow captain, Thomas Fremantle, reads: 'Dine with Nelson, take a view of the new battery at Torga. Walking with Nelson from thence a shot knocked him down and covered me all over with dirt. Determine never to go the short way again.'[32] Nelson was hit again at Calvi. At first he called it a smart slap in the face. Two

days after that he wrote to Suckling that he had been wounded in the
head by stones, that his right eye was cut entirely down, and that he
could distinguish light from dark, but no object. 'Such is the chance
of war, it was within a hair's breadth of taking off my head.' But in
the same letter he seemed as much concerned that Hood's letter about
Bastia, as published in *The London Gazette*, gave him no more credit
than it did to another captain who had done nothing.[33] Nelson saw
himself as the prime mover. Hood, though praising Nelson, naturally
saw himself as the first. Nelson never lost an opportunity to remind
Hood that every gun was dragged by his seamen, under a heavy fire
of grapeshot.

Calvi surrendered on 10 August. The garrison numbered 300 French
and 247 Corsican republicans. Nelson said that the British losses
were trifling, but they were not. Lugging artillery up mountains had
exhausted his men. The 'Lion Sun' had claimed upwards of a thousand
sick out of two thousand, and the others were not much better than so
many phantoms. His ship's company and the whole army were worn
out, except himself. All the other officers were scarcely able to crawl.
Elliot, the viceroy to be, wrote to London that Calvi had cost them very
dear.[34] This was true. Nelson might say that generals hated sailors,
because sailors were too active for them, but Moore had been right:
simple blockades would have achieved what Nelson achieved at great
cost by his incessant activity.[35] One of the officers who died at Calvi
was Lieutenant James Moutray, aged twenty-one, a godson of Hood's
and the son of Mrs Moutray whom Nelson had so adored on Antigua,
and of the commissioner to whose broad pendant he had taken such
exception.[36] As to Nelson's own eye, it was only after he left Corsica
that he gave to Fanny any idea of the extent of the injury. Stone
splinters struck him in the face. 'Yet I most fortunately escaped by
only having my right eye nearly deprived of its sight ... However
the blemish is nothing, not to be perceived unless told.'[37] For his
services ashore on Corsica he asked for the pay of a brigadier general,
again writing over the head of the admiralty to the secretary at war
in London. He was refused.[38]

Nelson's first duty after Corsica took him to Genoa. Again it was
not a diplomatic mission. His orders were to deliver papers to the
British minister there, who bore the splendid name of Francis Drake.
This simple duty turned into a state visit. The *Agamemnon* arrived in

the harbour in thick weather, and when she flew the union jack at the fore-topgallant masthead, which was the signal for a pilot, this was taken for the flag of a vice-admiral and Nelson received a salute of fifteen guns. Then Mr Drake was not in the city, so Nelson paid his respects to the government himself. Genoa had been for centuries a prosperous city state, once a rival of Venice, and still had a doge. As Nelson put it, Britain's purpose was to keep peace and harmony with Genoa, a harmony which had been upset the previous year when a British squadron had taken a French frigate in Genoese waters. Nelson thought the city the most magnificent he ever saw, grander than Naples. He was sure Genoa was too rich and magnificent to allow the *sans-culottes* to enter the city, and that when Frenchmen turned their thoughts towards Italy, the Italian states would unite against their common plunderers. When, next day, Mr Drake had still not appeared, Nelson waited on the doge himself and was received in some style, the doge advancing to the middle of the room to meet him. Then, as Nelson told Hood, he felt it absolutely necessary to say something civil, so he said he had come to pay his respects to his serene highness, and that he would preserve the strictest attention to the neutrality of Genoa. The doge in return accorded Nelson the honours of a senator, and ordered the captain of the guard to open the city gates to him at any time he pleased.[39] Eighteen months before, Nelson had been fretting in Norfolk. Since then, first at Naples and then at Genoa, he had been grandly received – at Naples because Ferdinand had come out to meet the *Agamemnon*, and at Genoa because the British minister was away. On neither occasion had he been sent with any powers of negotiation, but he had acquired the taste.

To Fanny, in a letter describing the magnificence of Genoa, Nelson said he hoped to quit such grand scenes, and return to England where all his charms were placed. Throughout the time they had been separated, his letters to Fanny were more than affectionate. Once, in reply to her question whether she should go to Bath, he said: 'I have only to *order* that you do what you like and give you full power to give my assent to your own wishes, that is settled.'[40] He told her not to be afraid of spending money, and that he longed for her letters. He even told her, when she knew he disliked music, that he pleased himself with hopes of hearing her play the pianoforte when they were again snug at Burnham. He told her that Josiah was happy on board, in high spirits, and much grown, and that they were going from Leghorn to spend a day at Pisa together. It was evidently still an affectionate marriage although, by late 1794, he had a mistress at Leghorn. Little is known of her. Fremantle, the frigate captain who had nearly been blown up with Nelson at Bastia and a man who later knew Emma Hamilton well, has four entries in his diary which show he dined with Nelson and 'his dolly'. One entry says that Nelson made himself ridiculous with her.[41] In February 1795 he instructed a merchant at Leghorn, from whom he regularly bought port and champagne, to give his 'female friend' £10, and to pay her house rent. And there is one brief letter of his to Adelaide Correglia, an opera singer at Leghorn, who may have been the friend. It reveals more about his French than about her, and reads: 'Ma chere Adelaide, Je suis partant cette moment pour la mere, une vaisseau Neapolitan partir avec moi pour Livorne, croire moi toujours, votre chere amie, Horatio Nelson.'[42]

After Hood went home to recover his health, the acting commander-in-chief in the Mediterranean was Vice-Admiral William Hotham. He was a safe man who had served with Rodney and Howe, but he was not a dasher. Under his command, Nelson took part in the first fleet action of his life in March 1795, off Genoa, though he impatiently called it a brush not a battle, since the French would not close with Hotham's fleet.[43] Still, it was a bloody brush and it lasted three days. The French had sent fifteen ships of the line from Toulon to retake Corsica. The best-known and traditionally accepted account of the action is Nelson's own.[44] Both fleets manoeuvred all day on 12 March. On the next morning Hotham, with fourteen sail, gave the signal for a general chase. The *Ça Ira*, a large French second rate, the biggest two decker Nelson had ever seen, carried away her fore and main topmasts. The British frigate *Inconstant* fired at the *Ça Ira*, but then had to leave her. The *Agamemnon*, being a fast sailer, was ahead of the rest of the fleet and drew up with the *Ça Ira*. What Nelson was aiming to do was rake her from astern, while keeping out of reach of her broadside. When he was within a hundred yards he ordered his helm a starboard, shivered his sails, and gave the Frenchman his whole broadside, double-shotted, which raked through her from stern to stem. It was the most murderous fire which could be brought to bear on a ship, travelling through the length of her. The *Ça Ira* was so much bigger a ship that she could, said Nelson, have taken the *Agamemnon* in her hold, but in her disabled condition she was helpless against such fire, and after two hours was a wreck with her sails hanging in tatters. Nelson said providence saved his brave fellows, who worked the ship about the Frenchman's stern and quarters with as much exactness as if they had been working into Spithead.[45] In the early afternoon, when Hotham saw other French ships coming up to save the *Ça Ira*, he ordered Nelson away. Next day, after a more general pursuit, the *Ça Ira* lost all her masts and the *Censeur*, a 74 which had been towing her, lost her main mast, and both struck their colours. Nelson ordered his first lieutenant to board them. This was George Andrews, brother of the Miss Andrews he had courted at St Omer. The *Ça Ira* lost in all three hundred and fifty men, the *Agamemnon* only thirteen wounded, though 'her sails were ribbons and all her ropes were ends'.[46] The wind by now was such that the French kept their distance. The battle was indecisive. That is Nelson's account. No ship could have been in a more hopeless position than the disabled *Ça Ira*, which had no chance against a fast, manoeuvrable, and determined enemy. Nelson said that her captain, who paid him the highest compliments, did him more credit than Hotham.[47]

And that is the point. Nelson's account has all the signs of being a riposte to Hotham's dispatch, a setting straight, as Nelson would have seen it, of the record. For Hotham mentioned Nelson only once in his dispatch, and he did not say that Nelson took the *Ça Ira*. What Hotham wrote was this: 'The signal was given for a general chase, in the course of which, the weather being squally, and blowing very fresh, we discovered one of their line of battle ships to be without her topmasts, which afforded to Captain Fremantle of the *Inconstant* frigate (who was then far advanced on the chase) an opportunity of shewing a good proof of British enterprise, by his attacking, raking, and harassing her until the coming up of the *Agamemnon*, when he was most ably seconded by Captain Nelson, who did her so much damage as to disable her from putting herself again to rights ...'[48] A French account tells much the same story, saying the captain of the *Inconstant* attacked the *Ça Ira* with such skill and judgment as did him the highest honour, and that Nelson in the *Agamemnon* then came up, and was soon afterwards joined by the *Captain*, a 74.[49] James's standard naval history of 1822–25 adopts Hotham's version. Nelson has the advantage that he became a hero, but he was ungenerous to say merely, as he did in his account, that 'the *Inconstant* frigate fired at the disabled ship, but receiving many shot, was obliged to leave her'. Fremantle was a friend, the man who was nearly blown up with him one evening at Bastia. But Nelson did not like to be thought of as seconding anyone, even most ably. The difference between Hotham and Nelson is one of emphasis. Hotham probably considered that for Fremantle in a frigate to press an attack on an eighty-gun ship of the line, even if she was disabled, was an act of great courage, and so put him first. And as to the striking of the *Ça Ira*, Nelson does not say in as many words that she struck her flag to him, only that he sent his first lieutenant to board her and hoist English colours.[50] Everyone agreed the *Ça Ira* had fought gallantly. Hotham's dispatch also said, which was manifestly true, that the French intentions, to retake Corsica, had been frustrated. Two French ships of the line had been taken, and one British 74 ran ashore and was lost.[51]

Nelson had no doubt at all of the part he had played, and was critical of his admiral. 'I have only to thank God,' he told Fanny, 'that next to the wind, which carried away the *Ça Ira's* topmast, the success of our action rested chiefly on the conduct of the *Agamemnon* and as all allow it I feel proud on the occasion.'[52] And then there is this celebrated passage, written three days later and also to her: 'In short I wish to be an admiral and in the command of the English fleet. I should very soon either do much or be ruined. My disposition can't bear tame and slow measures. Sure I am, had I commanded our fleet on the 14th, that either the whole French fleet would have graced my triumph, or I should have been in a confounded scrape. I went on board Hotham so soon as our firing grew slack in the van, and the *Ça Ira* and *Censeur* struck, to propose to him leaving our two crippled ships, the two prizes, and four frigates, to themselves, and to pursue the enemy, but he is much cooler than myself and said, "We must be contented. We have done very well," but had we taken 10 sail and allowed the 11th to have escaped if possible to have been got at, I could never call it well done ... We should have had such a day as I believe the annals of England never produced but it can't be helped.'[53]

Nelson's expostulation to Hotham has been compared to Hood's to Rodney after the battle of the Saintes in 1782. Hood said that had he commanded, he would have taken upwards of twenty enemy ships, and Rodney, as commander-in-chief, replied saying come, they had done very handsomely as it was. Hood and Nelson had much in common, not least an intolerant impatience. But the Saintes was a rout, with the

French in full flight, whereas the two fleets off Corsica were never fully engaged, and Hotham's main business was to protect Corsica and the precious base it provided for the English fleet, which he did.

When the prisoners from the *Ça Ira* and the *Censeur* were brought ashore, six of the officers were asked to dinner by the viceroy. 'To describe their appearance,' said Lady Elliot, 'is impossible, but my own idea of them was a gaol-delivery. We had the two captains of the *Ça Ira*; the first was a decent looking man, the second conveyed to me the notion of blue beard; their filth was shocking . . . They were so much surprised at the civility they met with, that they tried to be civil in their turn, saying Monsieur et Madame et Votre Excellence. They seemed very proud of their conduct and really did fight like dragons. They said to the last they looked to assistance from their fleet, and are now so enraged against their admiral that they said they hoped he was by this time guillotined.'[54]

The French admiral did stand in some danger of the guillotine. By the beginning of 1795, hating the revolution or having no taste for the harsh discipline imposed by the committee of public safety, many seamen had simply disappeared. Only three thousand remained at Toulon to man the eighteen seaworthy ships of the line, less than a quarter of their proper crew. When a nominal twelve thousand men were raised, nearly two-thirds of these had never been to sea before. Gun crews, ten men to each cannon, often had only one experienced gunner among them. Nevertheless, Rear-Admiral Martin was ordered to prepare his fleet, transport ten thousand troops to Corsica, and retake the island. The political representative, Letourneur, a sort of commissar, knowing nothing of the sea, went on board many of the ships and harangued the crews – electrified them, he said – so that they swore to conquer or die. He then accompanied Martin on his flagship. After the inconclusive action, which the French saw as a defeat, Martin himself wrote to the committee of public safety that he lacked the capacity to command so large a squadron. In less than a year he had been promoted from lieutenant to captain to rear-admiral.[55]

There is one other sidelight to Hotham's action. One of the fourteen ships of line under his command had been the *Tancredi*, a Neapolitan 74 commanded by Francesco Caracciolo. A few months earlier, Nelson had written to Hamilton at Naples, saying they all loved the captain of the *Tancredi*.[56] After the engagement, Hotham was joined by his nephew, also William Hotham, who was a frigate captain. When he was a midshipman he had seen Nelson in the West Indies. He wrote in his private papers that during the battle off Corsica, Nelson had been jealous of Caracciolo and had asked Admiral Hotham to reprimand the Neapolitan officer who, he said, had repeatedly got in his way during the action. Hotham declined and, when Nelson protested, said: 'If he was in your way during this action his bravery merits praise rather than reproof.'[57]

Long before the action off Genoa, Nelson had been hoping to go home with Hood. In the Mediterranean he had rediscovered his admiration for the man who had bluntly told him why he would not get a ship during the peace. At first they became 'tolerably good friends'. Then Hood was 'very kind'. At Bastia, Nelson was saying that though Hood was upwards of seventy he had the mind of a man of forty, and that he had not a thought separated from honour and glory.[58] By September 1794 he was writing to Fanny that Hood was the greatest sea officer he ever knew, and that only envy could say anything against him.[59] When Hood went home in October, Nelson could not go with him because a ship of the line could not be spared from the Mediterranean. Hood had gone home only to recover his health, he was still a lord of the admiralty, and he was expected to return with reinforcements. At Bath he and Lady Hood took Fanny to a play, and he told her Nelson had never looked better.[60] But many things were held against him. The army had complained bitterly of his high-handedness at Toulon and on Corsica. In March 1795 his name did not appear as one of a new admiralty board under Lord Spencer. He was still due to return to the Mediterranean command, but, having made demands for more ships which the government would not meet, was in May, while he was at Spithead waiting to depart, ordered to strike his flag. He never served at sea again, and the next year was made Governor of Greenwich Hospital.[61] When he heard the news Nelson exclaimed, 'Oh, miserable board of admiralty. They have forced the first officer in our service away from his command.'[62] By October, he was writing to Fanny, with some hyperbole, that if Hood had stayed he was almost certain that the British would at that moment have possessed all Provence.

That June, Nelson did have the consolation of being made a colonel of marines. This was a sinecure given to four of the most senior post captains; it meant Nelson was held in regard again, and gave him a colonel's pay as well as his post captain's. Nelson thanked Spencer, and in the same letter mentioned his damaged eye. He knew Spencer had told Hood that he doubted whether such a pension could be granted as would be for the loss of a limb, and said he would not press the matter. But he did say this: 'I have only to tell your lordship, that a total deprivation of sight for every common occasion in life, is the consequence of the loss of part of the crystal of my right eye.'[63]

In July, Hotham with a fleet of twenty-three ships of the line had another chance of engaging the French fleet south of Hieres, but both fleets were becalmed, and thus, said Nelson, ended the 'second meeting with these gentry'.[64] By August he was writing to Elliot, viceroy of Corsica, that both he and the *Agamemnon* were worn out and must soon be laid up for repairs.[65] In October he told the Duke of Clarence, the former Prince William, that he had been in action 112 times since his arrival in the Mediterranean, and twice wounded, though thank god not dangerously, and that he hoped some day to receive some honour from the king's hand. 'Your royal highness,' he wrote, 'I hope will before a very long time be placed in that situation which both your birth, abilities and rank in our service entitle you to.'[66] The duke had the notion that he might one day soon become first lord, and perhaps Nelson shared that hope.[67] He wrote to Fanny: 'He seems to remember our long acquaintance with much seeming affection. God knows what may ever arise from this acquaintance. However, we are certain no harm can come from it . . . One day or other he may be useful to me.'[68]

Then in November 1795, from Vado bay where he was cooperating with an Austrian general in unsuccessfully trying to drive the French from the Genoese riviera, Nelson wrote one of his most surprising letters. It reads: 'Dear Sir, I have just received your letter of September 29th, and will be open and sincere in my declaration, that I will not attempt to come into parliament but in support of the real whig interest – I mean the Portland interest . . .' He went on to say that if he were thought an eligible person to sit in the House of Commons he would manifest the same zeal there as he had done so repeatedly against the French. If the gentlemen (presumably those wishing him to stand) were satisfied, the Duke of Portland should be applied to through Lord and Lady Walpole: Lord Hood would support him.[69]

This can be seen as a renewal of the political ambitions Nelson had shown in 1784, when he had tried for a seat. But he had changed his ground. Whatever he called himself, he was a tory, and a Pitt-ite. Portland was a grand whig, but he had become wary of the possible effects of the French revolution in England, and taken office under Pitt as home secretary, leaving Fox to lead a whig rump of only forty members. So for Nelson to support Portland was not too great a change. But for him to say that application should be made to the duke through the Walpoles was droll. They were his distant relations, but they remained what they had been in 1784, when he had told his brother William that as to his (William's) having enlisted under the banners of the Walpoles, he might as well have enlisted under the banners of his grandmother, for the Walpoles were 'the merest set of *cyphers* that ever existed . . .'[70]

The gentlemen making the proposal were from Ipswich. It came to nothing, and, as Nelson told Fanny, he could not say he was sorry, though he would like to be in Parliament if he could be 'to a certain degree independent'.[71] Whatever Nelson's views had become, he did not stand for Parliament that year or ever. Nor, worn out as he was, did he come home at the end of 1795.

CHAPTER TWELVE

I Shall Come Laughing Back

HOTHAM HAD GONE HOME, and as soon as Nelson met his new commander-in-chief in the Mediterranean he knew they were congenial. Sir John Jervis was a sea officer of genius. He had fought with Wolfe at Quebec, and was a post captain before Nelson was born. He had just assisted in the capture of Guadeloupe and Martinique. He was a man who loathed slackness, and he was a fighter. He demanded from each captain incessant attention to his duty – 'that, in short, his whole soul and body should be in it'.[1] But 1796 was going to be a bad year. France was about to conquer much of Italy. Both Nelson and Elliot foresaw this. Elliot, as viceroy of Corsica, described his kingdom as like Scotland with a fine climate, and had ironically considered building himself a summer palace in jasper and porphyry, but always had a sense that his viceroyalty was temporary. The liberty of Europe, he thought, had never been in such danger, and he could not help fearing they would soon see a great part of the Roman empire revived, but with Paris as its capital. The submission of Italy would mean the abandonment of Corsica and the withdrawal of the fleet. His wife, observing the danger to Mantua and Milan, put matters more bluntly, asking what could be done against the French and the inclination of the people wherever they went: 'The poor in all states are more numerous than the rich, and are all favourable to the new system of plunder and the chances before them.'[2]

Nelson, cruising off Toulon in late February, saw thirteen French ships of the line ready for sea. He believed they might be joined by a fleet from Cadiz, and then perhaps by another from Brest, and that this great fleet, escorting troop transports, would then take Leghorn; then there would be nothing to prevent a French progress to Rome and Naples. 'What will the French care for the loss of a few men of war? It is nothing if they can get into Italy. This is the gold mine and what, depend upon it, they will push for.'[3] Parma and Modena had paid large sums of money to the French and concluded treaties in which it was stipulated that certain pictures were to be sent to Paris. Revolutionary France wanted the Louvre to be the finest art gallery in the world, and was prepared to loot Italy to achieve this ambition. The Pope had offered ten million crowns to keep the French from Rome, but they had refused unless the Apollo Belvedere, the most famous Roman statue of the son of Zeus, was shipped to Paris.[4] The Directory, which had superseded the Convention in Paris, sent orders to Buonaparte that if Rome wanted to negotiate the first demand should be that the Pope should order public prayers for the success of French arms, and that statues, paintings, libraries, and even clocks should be taken to compensate France for the expenses of his visit.[5] Nelson's view was that Italy was being lost by the imbecility of its states and by the fears of its princes.[6]

He was impatient and summary. When he was blockading Genoese ports, he was shot at from one of them, Finale, twenty miles west of Genoa. At which he sent a message to the governor of the town saying that he would never fire on a Genoese town unless first fired at, but that the inhabitants would then have to take the consequences.[7] He was dissuaded by Elliot, who was twice thanked by Jervis: 'I am very glad that you have a little damped the ardour of Nelson respecting the republic of Genoa. He is an excellent partisan but does not sufficiently weigh consequences.' In another letter, he wrote that Nelson was the best and fittest fellow in the world, yet his zeal did now and then – not often – outrun his discretion.[8] Nelson was worn out and exasperated. It was three years since he sailed from England; he wrote to Fanny that no one could have supposed a ship could have been kept abroad so long or the war lasted so long. If England was determined to go on, she would soon be alone. In June, he moved at last from the 'poor old *Agamemnon*', which was in a miserable state, a tub floating on the water, into the *Captain*, 74. He wrote that he was in the field of glory, and would one day have a *London Gazette* to himself. 'I am known in

Italy, not a kingdom or state where my name will be forgot . . .'[9] Jervis made him a commodore, flying his own broad pendant. His flag money and salary as colonel of marines gave him about £1,600 a year, and in the two years from June 1794 to 1796 he had received £2,227 in prize money. It was not riches, but he was no longer poor.[10]

In July the French did take Leghorn. To protect Corsica against attack, Nelson then took Porto Ferrajo in Elba. But the British position in the Mediterranean was falling apart. When Spain, encouraged by French successes, declared war on Britain in early October, orders had already been received to leave Corsica. At Bastia, all at first was panic and tears. Sixty sail were in the harbour: French sympathisers among the Corsicans were threatening to sequester these vessels and all property, until Nelson told them that if there was the smallest molestation he would 'batter the town down'. The Corsicans ran, £200,000 worth of property was saved, and not sixpence left behind. Nelson took off the viceroy.[11] Then he wrote to Locker: 'I remember when we quitted Toulon we endeavoured to reconcile ourselves to Corsica; now we are content with Elba – such things are . . .'[12] But it was soon worse than that. 'We are,' he told Fanny, 'preparing for an evacuation of the Mediterranean . . . I lament in sackcloth and ashes our present orders, so dishonourable to the dignity of England . . .'[13] When Naples signed a peace treaty with France, there was nothing to stay for, and the British retreat from the Mediterranean was all but complete.

After his brief visit in 1793, Nelson did not see Naples again until 1798. Elliot, however, did go there. After the loss of Corsica he took up a roving mission and visited Rome and Naples. At Naples, the treaty with France notwithstanding, he was given a cordial welcome by the king and queen, and fell for them rather as Nelson later did. Ferdinand took Elliot round a silk manufactory of which he was proud, and where he was greeted as a father. Maria Carolina conducted him arm in arm round the San Carlo opera house which was lit up for the occasion. And he met Emma Hamilton, whom he described as having the easy manners of a barmaid, but then, by candle light, she did her attitudes. 'They,' said Elliot, 'set Lady Hamilton in a very different light from any I had seen her in before; nothing about her, neither her conversation, her manners, nor figure announce the very refined taste which she discovers in this performance . . .' At a state banquet, he could not help recollecting that the last public royal dinner he had attended was at Versailles, where

Marie Antoinette was in all her glory and lustre. Then, he said, there had been much less probability of her dreadful reverse than there was in 1796 of a catastrophe to her sister Maria Carolina. The queen, who had courage, vigour, and firmness, was far from cheerful.[14]

Taking Elliot with him, Nelson joined Jervis with his squadron of fifteen ships of the line near Cape St Vincent, on the southwest coast of Portugal, and brought him the news of a Spanish fleet at sea, out of Cartagena. Jervis prepared for action, Nelson hoisted his broad pendant in the *Captain*, and Elliot and one of his suite, Colonel John Drinkwater, transferred to the frigate *Lively* and became distant witnesses of the imminent battle. Out of the mist after dawn on 14 February 1797, St Valentine's day, appeared first eight, then twenty, then twenty-five Spanish ships of the line. Seven of them were larger than any ship in the English squadron. The Spaniards were in two loose formations. Jervis took his ships in line through the gap, and then signalled them to tack consecutively, to engage the van of the larger Spanish group. The *Captain* was last but two in the English line and would have taken an age to get anywhere near a Spanish ship. It was here that Nelson disobeyed orders. It was not the first time, but it was the first famous disobedience. He did not wait to tack and follow the line. He instantly wore his ship – that is, came around by turning her head not into the wind but away from it – and took a short cut to engage with the three huge ships at the head of the Spanish division – the *San Josef*, 112, the *San Nicolas*, 80, and the *Santissima Trinidad*, 130. Captain Collingwood in the *Culloden* came to Nelson's assistance. Broadsides were exchanged at pistol range for an hour, after which the *Culloden* was crippled and the *Captain* a wreck. She was alongside the *San Nicolas*, which was entangled with the *San Josef*. Nelson boarded first one Spaniard and then, across her, the other. Of the four Spanish ships taken that day, he took the surrender of two. Night came on and the greater part of the Spanish fleet put back to Cadiz.

It was a victory and, given the apparent strength of the Spanish fleet, a surprising one. But as Nelson had said when he first saw the splendid ships of the line at Cadiz in 1793, the Spanish made very fine ships but they were shockingly manned.[15] Some, with a crew of eight hundred men, had only eighty experienced seamen, and the rest were landsmen or soldiers. Their rate of fire was often only a fifth that of the British. And Jervis's opinion of the Spanish was that no English officer with tolerable nerves should be under any apprehension from them, 'ill manned, worse appointed, and beaten in imagination before they leave the port . . .'[16] But what had happened on St Valentine's day? Nelson had disobeyed orders, as none of the thirteen other captains had done. The permanent fighting instructions of 1744 stipulated a line of battle, in which, ideally, British ships should engage enemy ships broadside to broadside. Admiral Byng, in 1756, had been shot for disobeying these instructions – as Voltaire put it, to encourage the others. But Byng had had the misfortune not to win. At St Vincent, Jervis had broken the rules by passing through the gap between the two groups of Spanish ships, and Nelson in his turn disobeyed Jervis's signal to tack in line, but only the better to get at the enemy. What he did was instinct, and it succeeded. And Jervis liked Nelson. But the fact is that in his dispatch to the admiralty the day after the battle he did not mention Nelson's name, let alone his capture of two ships. Jervis, as was often the custom, also wrote a private letter to Lord Spencer, first lord, in which he did name names. First he praised Troubridge for leading the squadron through the enemy in masterly style. Then he said that Nelson 'contributed very much to the fortune of the day, as did Collingwood'. He went on to say that Captain Berry led the boarders on to the two Spanish ships, and was immediately followed by Nelson, who took possession of them both. He then mentioned five other officers.[17]

Nothing there gives Nelson the principal credit for the victory. But apart from Jervis's brief dispatches, almost everything else we know about the action comes from Nelson himself, and he diligently ensured that his version should be known. The account of his boarding the *San Nicolas* by jumping through the quarter gallery windows, the breaking down of cabin doors and the firing of pistols, his ascent to the quarter-deck of the *San Josef* and his acceptance there of the surrender – all that is Nelson's. 'On the quarter deck of a Spanish first rate, extravagant as the story may seem, did I receive the swords of vanquished Spaniards; which, as I received, I gave to William Fearney, one of my bargemen, who put them with the greatest sangfroid under his arm . . . thus fell these ships.' This account, entitled 'A Few Remarks Relative to Myself in the *Captain*, in which my Pendant was Flying on the Most Glorious Valentine's Day, 1797', he sent to the Duke of Clarence, having had it signed by Captains Miller (his flag captain) and Berry.[18]

A second version also exists, substantially the same but in his own handwriting, in which he adds three incidents which have found a place in most biographies. He writes that after the action the *Victory*, Jervis's flagship, saluted the *Captain* with three cheers, as did every other ship in the fleet, and that when at dusk he went on board the flagship, Jervis embraced him on the quarterdeck. Then he finishes with an anecdote and a recipe. The anecdote goes as follows: 'N.B. There is a saying in the fleet, too flattering for me to omit telling – viz., "Nelson's Patent Bridge for boarding first rates," alluding to my passing over an enemy's 80-gun ship . . .' Then follows Nelson's recipe for cooking Spaniards: 'Take a Spanish first rate and an 80 gun ship and after well *battering* and *basting* them for an hour keep throwing in your *force balls*, and be sure to let these be well *seasoned* . . . then skip into her quarter gallery window sword in hand and let the rest of your boarders follow as they can . . . then you will only have to take a hop skip and jump from your stepping stone and you will find yourself in the middle of a first rate quarter deck with all the dons at your feet. Your olla podrida may now be considered as completely *dished* and fit to set before his majesty.'[19] He sent this account to Fanny, and to Locker, saying he was at perfect liberty to insert it in the newspapers. To his uncle William Suckling he wrote that *Nelson's Patent Bridge* would be a saying never forgotten in the fleet.[20]

Nelson's account did appear in *The Times* and *The Sun*.[21] This was not the only printed account to appear. Colonel Drinkwater had been, with Elliot, a distant witness of the battle. His much longer account, with engravings, had much authority, but it was, again, Nelson's version of events. It came about in this way. The morning after the battle Nelson found Drinkwater, who pointed out that he would be taking the news to England, and asked for particulars. Nelson gave them at length. It is in this account that he is described as himself leading the boarding party on the *San Josef*, vehemently exclaiming, 'Westminster Abbey! or, glorious victory!'[22] As for Elliot, he thought Nelson was 'a hero beyond Homer's' and that nothing in the world was more noble than the action of the *Captain* from beginning to end. The day Elliot left for England in the *Lively*, Nelson told him too that he dreaded a baronetcy, which he might have expected, and that rather than take an hereditary honour without a fortune to support it, he would prefer an honour which died with the possessor.[23] This may appear strange, since he was eager for honours. A baronetcy, though it left a man a commoner, conferred a higher rank than that of a knight. Against that, a knighthood of the Bath carried with it a distinguishing red sash, and would give him the letters K.B. after his name. Elliot was a man with great interest with Portland, the home secretary, and with Spencer, the first lord. He was likely to get Nelson what he wanted. Jervis did not understand Nelson's reasons. A month after the battle he wrote to the admiralty secretary, Evan Nepean, whom he knew well, saying: 'Nelson is the modestest of all human beings, yet the title of baronet could not be better applied than to him.'[24] Jervis was an acute man, but of all Nelson's virtues modesty was not one.

Nelson's view of the battle *was* challenged, in the most circumstantial way, by Rear-Admiral William Parker, whose flag was flown in the *Prince George*. He wrote to Nelson readily admitting the credit due to a brave man, but went on to show that the *Prince George* and two other ships had played a greater part than Nelson allowed. Very soon after the *Captain* commenced firing on the two Spanish ships she had, contrary to Nelson's statement, four British ships pressing close behind her to assist. And as to the *San Josef*, the *Prince George* had fired on her from 1.20pm until she struck her colours at 4.05 or 4.10. Admiral Parker was saying in effect that when Nelson boarded the *San Josef* she had already struck. 'Believe me,' he wrote, 'neither they [the officers and company of the *Prince George*] or myself expected to meet an account so different to the real statement of that action.'[25]

The accounts are not incompatible. Nelson assumed the *San Josef* surrendered to him, because he had boarded. She could, however, already have struck to the *Prince George*. Indeed, this is likely. But Nelson could not easily accept Parker's account because it detracted from the notion of his patent bridge for boarding first rates, which he was convinced would never be forgotten. It was a better story anyway. Parker's letter had substance, but Nelson acknowledged it in a brief note, saying he could not enter into the subject.[26] The story of the patent bridge became history. At St Vincent, as well as in Hotham's action, Nelson's account prevailed.

Whatever had happened, a victory was a victory and government was likely to be grateful. It was a dark time. Buonaparte was advancing through the Tyrol to Vienna. Mantua had surrendered to the French. The first mutinous rumblings of discontent among the fleet at Spithead, off Portsmouth, were making themselves heard. The ships' crews were half of them pressed men and unwillingly in the navy at all. Some were Irish and naturally disposed to hate the English. And they had many other grievances besides. Navy pay was the same as it had been in the days of Charles II, more than a hundred years before. Soldiers had lately been given a rise, but not seamen. When a seaman was wounded, his pay stopped. Rations were often shortweight, and no vegetables at all were given out in port. Nor were men often allowed ashore even after a long passage, for fear they would desert. Added to all this, there were a few who were attracted to the idea of a revolution in the French style. This was very much in the public mind. So that when the *Lively* landed Sir Gilbert Elliot and his suite at Plymouth they were met by desponding looks from people whose minds were full of mutinies and rumours that the French and Spanish fleets had united. They feared ruin at home and invasion from abroad, so when they were told of the victory they could hardly believe it. And such was the panic caused by a run on the provincial banks that the Bank of England itself had just suspended payments in cash, and only fifteen guineas in gold could be collected in Plymouth from the port admiral and his friends, to pay the travelling expenses to London of the former viceroy.[27]

The rewards followed. Jervis was made Earl St Vincent, after the place of the battle; two of the junior admirals were made baronets and a third governor of Newfoundland, and Nelson got the Bath. It was a medieval honour which had been restored in 1725, thus creating what Horace Walpole, a most distant kinsman of Nelson's, called 'an artful bank of thirty-six ribbands, to supply a fund of favours in lieu of places'.[28] It pleased Nelson's father who, when he learned of it, wrote to his son: 'My dear K.B. – As much as these two letters are of value, in your estimation so far, they add to my pleasing sensation; firmly believing that no honor or worldly advancement will change your disposition, composed of humility, benevolence, gratitude, and reverence towards the divine author of all good ...'[29] Nelson had a victory, a sash, a fame which his talent for self-publicity greatly assisted if it did not create, and he also had a wound in his belly. 'Not near so much hurt as the doctors fancied,' he said. 'Only a contusion and of no consequence.'[30] He was incapable of playing down his part in a victory, but instinctively made light of a wound. Six days after the action he was made a rear-admiral. This was in no sense a promotion for the battle. The admiralty did not know the battle had taken place, and promotions to admiral were never made for that reason. Nelson was one of nine post captains of 1779 all made rear-admiral of the blue on the same day. All but two of the others outlived him but none achieved distinction.

Fanny, who was at Bath, learned indirectly that her husband was safe. Lady Saumarez, wife of Sir James Saumarez who was captain of the *Orion* at St Vincent, heard from her husband and came running to tell her. At a concert, the audience all made their bow to her. She wrote her husband a letter full of joy and anxiety. 'What can I attempt to say to you about boarding. You have been most wonderfully protected. You have done desperate actions enough. Now may I indeed I do beg, that you never board again. *Leave* it for *captains* . . . Tomorrow is our wedding day, when it gave me a dear husband and my child the best of fathers.'[31]

This letter of Fanny's crossed with two of Nelson's. In the first he said that the more he thought of the late action the more it appeared a dream. He believed there would be enough prize money for a cottage and a piece of ground, which was all he wanted. For years while he was away Nelson wrote about cottages, which he had been barely able to tolerate during his five years on the beach. In his second letter he wrote: 'I shall come one day or other laughing back when we will retire from the busy scenes of life.' And then he went on to write about Josiah, who had not served the six years before he could become a lieutenant. Nelson said he had written to his brother Maurice at the navy office to see if he could not get 'a little cheating done' for the boy, by giving him fictitious time on board men of war. It worked. Jervis made Josiah a lieutenant. The boy was sixteen.[32]

Nelson was back blockading Cadiz when he received a letter from the Duke of Clarence telling him he really did not need to have been wounded at St Vincent to complete his fame, which had been long established. This was one of the few sensible things Clarence ever told Nelson. The duke then went on to deplore the mutinies in England. 'But paint to yourself the fleet at Spithead, during a war, for a whole week, in a state of mutiny . . . Pardon my gloom, but I have a very great stake in the country, and a family of young children to protect.'[33] The young children the duke had to support were two sons and a daughter by the great comic actress Dorothea Jordan, who had been his mistress

since 1791. She had given him the third child just after the battle of St
Vincent, and soon afterwards also gave a benefit performance at Drury
Lane for the widows and orphans of the fleet. She remained his mistress
until 1811 and bore ten of his children.

Nelson, of course, took no notice of the duke's warnings, or of
Fanny's, and was not content with a passive blockade of Cadiz. He
attacked at night with gunboats, launches, barges, and a bomb vessel
which lobbed shells into the city. The Spaniards replied by sending out
their own barges, and Nelson found himself in the thick of hand-to-
hand fighting in open boats, with swords. Twenty-six Spaniards were
killed in one boat. Nelson's cockswain, John Sykes, twice saved his life
by interposing himself between Nelson and a Spanish sabre. Nelson
this time escaped unwounded. Sykes was severely wounded, and never
recovered. It was, Nelson said of himself, at this time that his personal
courage was perhaps more conspicuous than at any other part of his
life.[34] His shells scarred the city. 'News from Cadiz,' he wrote to
St Vincent, '. . . the town was on fire in three places; a shell that
fell in a convent destroyed several priests (that no harm, they will
never be missed); plunder and robbery going on – a glorious scene of
confusion.'[35]

Then came the hangings. In the fleet the mutinies in England were
certainly seen as the beginnings of a revolution. After Spithead came the
Nore, which was much more violent. Nelson denounced the mutineers
as scoundrels and would have been happy to command a ship against
them.[36] As reinforcements came out to Jervis, they brought discontent
with them. On the *St George* two of her men were sentenced to death for
sodomy, and many of the crew came onto the quarterdeck to demand
that their captain, Shuldham Peard, should intercede with St Vincent
to commute the sentence. He assured them the men would hang, and
they did. Then two men slipped into Peard's cabin and warned him of
an impending mutiny. He read the Articles of War, which threatened
death for all manner of offences, and his chaplain preached a sermon.
When this did not quell the people, he seized four men and had
them court-martialled for seditiously, mutinously, and traitorously
conspiring to deprive him of his ship.

The trial, before two admirals and ten post captains, lasted two days,
and the report runs to fifty closely written quarto pages. The charge
was not mutiny itself but conspiracy, and the evidence was mostly of

mutterings and whispers. The men were found guilty and sentenced to death.[37] They asked for five days to prepare in which, said St Vincent, they would have hatched five hundred treasons. He wrote to Lord Spencer, first lord, that the 'most daring and profligate' of the four had confessed to the clergyman who attended him that the plan had been in contemplation for six months, with four other ships; this was not evidence, but it was a breach of the confessional. He ordered the four to be hanged the next day, though it was a Sunday, and insisted also that they should be hauled up by their own shipmates. Next morning St Vincent surrounded the *St George* with twenty barges and pinnaces, and with gunboats ordered to fire on her if necessary, and the men were hanged by their shipmates. Vice-Admiral Charles Thompson, who was second in command of the squadron and had been president of the court martial, protested at this profanation of the sabbath, at which St Vincent promptly sent him home. Nelson felt differently. He wrote to congratulate St Vincent on the speedy finish of the business, even though it *was* a Sunday. And to the admiral's flag captain he wrote: 'Had it been Christmas Day instead of Sunday, I would have executed them. We know not what would have been hatched by a Sunday's grog; *now* your discipline is safe.'[38]

For months the Cadiz squadron had been on the look out for the viceroy of Mexico, who was said to be bringing treasure ships from Vera Cruz and Havana. The hope at first was that the approaching treasure ships would force the Spanish fleet out of Cadiz to protect them, and that another fleet action would be fought.[39] But by March 1797, Nelson was thinking that the viceroy's ships might take refuge in the island of Tenerife, six hundred miles to the southeast, and was planning to seize them there.[40] He had in mind the precedent of Blake, who in 1657 had destroyed six Spanish galleons laden with silver in the harbour of Santa Cruz, Tenerife, and then sailed out again. But Nelson, who always wanted to act the general, favoured a land attack to reduce the city and seize the ships. 'But now comes my plan,' he wrote to St Vincent, 'which could not fail of success, would immortalise the undertakers, ruin Spain, and has every prospect of raising our country to a higher pitch of wealth than she ever yet attained . . .' He proposed that a naval squadron should land troops, cut off the city's water supply, and in three days seize six or seven million sterling. He wanted the troops, and suggested that the army and navy should share the prize money. If such an attack succeeded, and there were that many millions, St Vincent's share would have been £375,000 and Nelson's £45,000. He told his chief that a thousand men would do the business. 'The rest must follow – a fleet of ships, and money to reward the victors. But I know with you, and I can lay my hand on my heart and say the same – It is the honour and prosperity of our country that we wish to extend.'[41] Nelson had also written to John M'Arthur – formerly Hood's secretary, later one of Nelson's biographers, but at that time acting as a prize agent in London – mentioning the mines of Mexico and Peru. And though he did ask what such mines would signify compared to the honour of fighting the dons, it is plain that he was thinking as grandly of Spanish treasure there for the taking as Governor Dalling had, seventeen years before, in his Nicaraguan campaign.[42]

The army did not accept the bargain proposed by Nelson, but when St Vincent learned that the *Principe de Asturias* lay at Tenerife, the plan nevertheless went forward. There would be no soldiers. About nine hundred men would now be enough, seamen and marines. Nelson had twenty scaling ladders made, each of which ten men could mount at the same time. 'Ten hours,' he said, 'shall make me either a conqueror or defeat me.'[43] The expedition set off under Nelson, with three seventy-fours, three frigates, a cutter, and a mortar boat. One of the frigates was the *Seahorse*, commanded by Captain Fremantle, late of the *Inconstant*. He carried on board his new wife Betsy, who was pregnant. She was a witness of some of the action. Troubridge was to lead the land attack, and storm the town. The *Asturias*, her full and entire cargo, and all other cargoes and treasure which might be on the island, together with the town, its forts, and its garrison, were demanded in an ultimatum drawn up in Nelson's hand: if these claims were not met, he wrote, the horrors of war would fall on the inhabitants of Tenerife, for he would destroy Santa Cruz and the other towns in the island.[44]

Santa Cruz was meant to be taken by surprise by troops landing at night. But the first attack, on 21 July, lacked all surprise because a gale and a strong current ensured that Troubridge and his force were still more than a mile offshore when dawn broke. Betsy Fremantle wrote in her diary: 'Friday, July 21st. It was late when the three frigates got in shore and day light by the time the troops were landing, they therefore returned without doing anything . . . Saturday, July 22nd. We anchored in a small bay at a short distance from the town but out of gunshot. The troops landed again this morning and had a most tiring and fatiguing day, for no good what so ever they went at the top of a high hill the enemy on another of them they stayed till the evening, almost dead with fatigue hunger and thirst, they were obliged to return on board.'

By 24 July nothing had been achieved. Nelson decided to lead another attack himself, under the batteries of the town. At eight in the evening he wrote to St Vincent that by the next day his head would probably be crowned with either laurel or cypress, and that should he fall he was confident the Duke of Clarence would take a lively interest in Josiah. Then he had supper with the Fremantles before going off on the expedition. Betsy wrote: 'They are all to land in the town. As the taking of this place seemed an easy and almost sure thing, I went to bed after they were gone, apprehending no danger for Fremantle.'[45] She was wrong. This second attack was a disaster. Between six and seven hundred men embarked at eleven at night. In the dark most of the boats missed the mole – a stone pier eighty yards long, which in any case led straight to the citadel – and were stove in by a raging surf, in which all the scaling ladders were also lost. The defenders opened up with thirty or forty cannon. The *Fox* cutter was hit below the water line and foundered with a shriek and the loss of ninety-eight men. Many of the attackers were killed by grapeshot and musket fire, but more than three hundred seamen and marines did take a convent in the main square, only to learn at daybreak that the Spanish garrison was eight thousand strong. Troubridge's ammunition was wet, and his men had no food. There are then two versions of what happened.

The British version – set forth in Nelson's and Troubridge's accounts – is that Troubridge, with some coolness, sent a captain with a message proposing that the British should be allowed to re-embark their men, that the governor should supply boats to do this, and that in return the British squadron lying offshore would promise not to molest the town. The governor for his part invited the British to surrender, at which the captain replied that Troubridge directed him to say that if the terms offered were not accepted within five minutes the attackers would set the town on fire and attack the Spaniards with bayonets, 'on which the governor instantly closed with the terms'.[46]

This does seem too pat. The Spanish version is that Troubridge made four approaches to the governor. First he sent a sergeant and two Spaniards with a message that unless the main square was surrendered he would burn the town. The governor made no reply. Then Troubridge sent a captain, who was conducted in blindfold and with a roll of drums, and repeated the threat; he was sent back. Then he sent two friars from the convent, with demands to surrender the wealth in the royal treasury: they were too afraid to return. Finally Troubridge sent in Captain Samuel Hood, who did not threaten to burn or demand treasure but made what honourable terms he could.[47] The governor then took the badly wounded into his hospital, provided boats to take the remnants of the attackers off, sent them casks of wine and bread, and offered refreshment to the ships while they lay in the bay. Both sides agree on the generosity of the governor, and Nelson wrote to thank him for his humanity.[48]

However the retreat was negotiated, the action was a disaster. Nelson, doing without the army, and with fewer than a thousand seamen and marines, had directed a land battle in which he, as a rear-admiral, and five post captains, were committed to the thick of the fight. Rank for rank, that is as if a battalion of soldiers were to have been personally led into action by a major general and five full colonels. Two of the five boats that had found the mole the night before were those commanded by Captain Fremantle and by Nelson. Since they were so near the citadel they walked into heavy fire. Fremantle was badly wounded. As Nelson stepped ashore his right arm was shattered by grapeshot above the elbow. Josiah, who was with him, bound the wound with silk handkerchiefs, and Nelson was rowed out to the *Theseus*, where his arm was amputated high up.[49] A great sea officer had suffered his second terrible wound, like his first, not in any fleet action, not even at sea, but on land. He had lost the sight of his right eye arranging the besieging artillery at Calvi, which was hardly his proper business. He had lost his right arm leading what would now be called a commando raid, which was certainly not a flag officer's business. But then it was not a flag officer's business to board a Spanish man of war, as he had at St Vincent, or to scuffle with swords in open boats, as he had off Cadiz. It was not his proper duty. It was not profitable in any way. It did the state no service. It did him no service: as the Duke of Clarence had told him, he really did not need to be wounded to complete his fame. And it was not done. No flag officer had done the like for a century or more.

The attempt on Tenerife could never have been as grand as Nelson had at first hoped. His first plan had been to encounter the viceroy of Mexico and a treasure fleet, to take the island with an army, and ruin Spain. By the time he set out he had no army, he knew there was no viceroy on the island, and he expected to find only one Spanish ship. Nothing he did could have ruined Spain. As to the second attack, which he led himself after the first had failed, he knew it was futile. He said as much. When he reached home he wrote to his friend Sir Andrew Snape Hamond, comptroller of the navy. 'Had I been with the first party, I have reason to believe complete success would have crowned our endeavours.' He knew he did not have any such reason, because he knew by the time he wrote those words that there had been eight thousand soldiers in the Spanish garrison. But it is the next sentence that matters. 'My pride suffered; and although I felt the second attack a forlorn hope, yet the honour of our country called for the attack, and that I should command it. I never expected to return, and am thankful.'[50]

His pride had suffered. He knew it was a forlorn hope. He never expected to return. That night 148 officers and men did not return from Santa Cruz; twice as many were killed in the attack as in the whole battle of St Vincent.[51]

In a letter to his sister Katty, written when the idea of the attack first came to him, Nelson said: 'Perhaps I may *laughing come back* rich in the praises of all mankind friends & enemies, I will not brag of my purse at present I am not sixpence richer for the war but my road has hitherto been the path of honor not of wealth but I hope riches will now flow in a gentle manner to me.' He underlined the words 'laughing come back', the same words he had written to his wife. Katty endorsed the letter: 'The last letter I recvd from the best of brothers written with his right hand.'[52]

CHAPTER THIRTEEN

The Making of the Legend

'ALTHOUGH THE ENTERPRISE HAS not succeeded,' St Vincent wrote to the admiralty, in a dispatch which was published in *The London Gazette*, 'his majesty's arms have acquired a very great degree of lustre.'[1] That is how it was seen. Tenerife was a disaster, but it was the beginning of Nelson as a legend. The battle of St Vincent – and particularly Nelson's patent bridge – had made his name famous, but it would have been a temporary fame which, as he well knew, would have been overtaken by the victor of the next naval action.[2] Tenerife, though a defeat, was full of dash. The leading of an attack he ought never to have led, and the loss of his right arm, gave him the character and the form which were ever after instantly recognisable. His empty right sleeve was pinned across his coat, his figure was frail, his hair was white, and he was Nelson.

Again he made light of his wound. He reported: 'Rear admiral Nelson, his right arm shot off.' In a covering letter, written with his left hand, he said he had become a burden to his friends and useless to his country, and asked St Vincent to promote Josiah. He added as a postscript: 'You will excuse my scrawl, considering it is my first attempt.'[3] When he rejoined the fleet he said a left-handed admiral would never again be considered useful, and that he would make room for a better man to serve the state. To which St Vincent replied, 'Mortals cannot command success; you and your companions have certainly deserved it . . .' And he made Josiah, at the age of seventeen, master and commander.[4]

To his wife, Nelson wrote: 'It was the chance of war, and I have great reason to be thankful; and I know that it will add much to your pleasure in finding that Josiah under God's providence was principally instrumental in saving my life ... I beg neither you or my father will think much of this mishap ...' He was coming home and the first they would hear of him would be at the door. At Portsmouth, when they anchored, he was immediately rowed ashore, though the weather was so bad that no one else thought of leaving the ship that day, and went straight to Bath where he was reunited with Fanny and his father.[5]

Facsimile of part of Nelson's first letter with his left hand, dated 27 July 1797, after he lost his right arm at Tenerife. In it he asks Sir John Jervis (soon to become Earl St Vincent) for a frigate to convey the remains of his carcass home. From J.K. Laughton's Nelson and His Companions in Arms, *1896.*

He had been at sea for four and a half years. He had sent Fanny a lawn gown from the gulf of Genoa, some Naples sashes from off Cadiz, and from Leghorn silk shawls such 'as a most elegant woman' might like. He wrote to her about revolutions in Europe. She wrote to him about revolutions in dress since he left her: waists lengthened, petticoats fashionably shortened above the ankle, little or no heel to the shoes, and long gloves none less than three shillings a pair. When Bath was cold in February she wrote that the sunshine she needed must come from the Mediterranean. When he was made a knight of the Bath, and she became Lady Nelson, she said it sat as easy upon her as if she had been born to it. When he told her he would come laughing back, she replied that those words gave her a pleasure, a something none could feel except those sincerely attached to a husband. 'They are,' she wrote, 'fine feelings but exquisitely painful.'[6] When he did come back he had lost the sight of an eye, and the stump of his arm was not yet healed. She learned to dress it. She acted as his amanuensis. He began a letter to Locker, managed seventeen words, and then she took over and wrote the rest to his dictation. They went to London where he consulted five doctors, among them Dr Moseley of the Nicaraguan campaign. A ligature binding one of the arteries had not come away, the wound was still septic, and there was talk of amputating even higher up until a wise physician suggested they should do nothing and wait.[7] He wrote to St Vincent: 'I found my domestic happiness perfect, and I hope time will bring me about again; but I have suffered great misery. My general reception from John Bull has been just what I wished . . .'[8]

He appeared twice at court, where the king observed that Nelson had lost his right arm, but that his country still had a claim for a bit more of him.[9] That was late in September. He was still in pain in mid-October, when Duncan beat the Dutch at Camperdown, taking nine ships of the line. London was illuminated to celebrate the victory, and a mob pounded on the door of the house in Bond Street where Nelson was staying, demanding to know why the house was dark. He still needed laudanum to sleep. When the mob were told who was there they withdrew, saying, 'You will hear no more from us tonight.'[10] When the wound healed in December, after five painful months, Nelson left a note at the parish church of St George in Hanover Square, to be read out at a service the following Sunday. It read: 'An officer desires to return thanks to almighty god for his perfect recovery from a severe wound, and also for the many mercies bestowed upon him.'[11] He was granted a pension of £712 a year, given the freedom of the City of London, and was present in St Paul's cathedral on 19 December when the king and royal family attended to give thanks for the sea victories of the war – the Glorious First of June over the French, St Vincent over the Spanish, and Camperdown over the Dutch. Ministers, royal dukes, ambassadors, and the queen's maids of honour walked in procession.[12] Nelson was a bit sour about Duncan's victory, 'the last action,' he said, 'being the best', and anyway, since it was off the coast of Holland, much the closest to home. As he wrote to a captain who had been with him at St Vincent: 'Had our battle been in the channel, it would have been so much the better for us.'[13]

But the fame of Nelson's patent bridge survived. Rear-Admiral Parker, who had written to Nelson to vindicate his own ship's part in the action, and received short shrift, was in an impossible position. As he explained to a friend, by the time he saw Nelson's account in the newspapers and wrote his letter, Nelson was away with the Santa Cruz expedition, and when he returned had lost his arm. 'I had no immediate answer; it was left with the commander in chief, by whom he desired it to be delivered to me after he was gone to England, as I was told to prevent a rejoinder; but with assurances that no offence was meant to him by me, and that he never thought it could be understood that both ships had struck to him ... I receive in words, what I suppose was thought he should not commit to paper, for I believe he had advice upon the occasion.'[14]

The story of the night Nelson was wounded grew with the telling. When he fell, he was said to have exclaimed, 'I am a dead man', and was rowed back to the ships under the fire of the batteries. At this moment the *Fox* cutter was hit and many of her people, said one account, 'were rescued from a watery grave by Nelson himself, whose humane exertions on this occasion added considerably to the agony and danger of his wound'. The first ship the boat could reach was the frigate *Seahorse*, on board which Betsy Fremantle was awaiting the return of her husband. Nothing could induce the admiral to board the frigate, though he was told it might be at the risk of his life if they attempted to row to another ship. 'Then I will die,' he said, 'for I would rather suffer death than alarm Mrs Fremantle by her seeing me in this state, and when I can give her no tidings whatever of her husband [who was wounded in the arm].' Betsy makes no mention of this in her diary. Then, when they reached the *Theseus*, Nelson refused a chair, insisted on climbing up the side, and his arm was immediately taken off. To climb the side of a 74 is no small effort for a fit man with all his limbs, but all witnesses say Nelson did it. William Hoste, a midshipman on board, described him, 'his right arm dangling by his side, whilst with the other he helped himself to jump up the ship's side'. Fanny, in an account given after Nelson's death, said he walked up the side of the ship, with Josiah keeping close so that he could have caught him had he slipped. But although she states that the boat saved two or three men from the cutter, she does not say Nelson had a part in this himself, which has to be right. Only in legend could so slight a man, so badly wounded, have hauled drowning men from the sea.[15]

There was a demand for pictures of the hero.[16] Fanny had a miniature which Nelson had had painted for her at Leghorn in 1794. Most people thought it a likeness. Nelson did not, but Fanny cherished it. She lent it to the engraver Robert Laurie, who in November had for sale a mezzotint showing a one-armed rear-admiral with the sash and order of the Bath, with the battle of St Vincent being fought in the background. Daniel Orme produced a 'grand historical' painting showing Nelson receiving the Spanish admiral's sword on the quarterdeck of the *San Josef*, the first of the many patriotic and triumphal tableaux in which he appeared; this too appeared as a print. Orme also made a delicate pencil drawing of Fanny in early 1798. He was better as a miniaturist than as a painter on the grand scale, and this drawing has the virtue of being one of the only three likenesses of Fanny. It shows her as a woman in her late thirties, not vivid but pretty, wearing a light-hearted bonnet and the high waistline she had described to her husband. And Orme's little oval engraving of a sketch of Nelson's head for the historical picture became a bestseller when it was published on 14 February 1798, the anniversary of St Vincent.

The best-known painting done at this time was by Lemuel Abbott, versions of which have been reproduced a thousand times. Two of Nelson's mentors lived at Greenwich Hospital, on the river. Lord Hood was governor and Locker lieutenant governor, and they occupied separate wings of what was then, as now, one of the greatest ranges of buildings in London. In October, before his wound healed, Nelson and Fanny, with Elliot and his wife, dined at Greenwich, and Locker, who more than twenty years before had commissioned the Rigaud, insisted on a new portrait.[17] There is no single great portrait of Nelson. It is a pity Locker did not suggest the young Thomas Lawrence, but he had made his name early with a portrait of the queen, and would have been expensive. The man chosen was Abbott, who had painted Hood and St Vincent. The artist's oil sketch is by some way the best, catching as it does both Nelson's strength of mind and his frailty. Abbott then painted about forty other finished versions variously romanticised and bedizened with orders and medals. None equalled the sketch. By the time Nelson was fit to go to sea again, there were five engravings of him, several portraits, and a marble bust which was shown at the Royal Academy and later went through many editions in plaster, terracotta, and bronze.

And as a knight of the Bath he had a coat of arms, the crest of which showed, on a wreath of colours, 'the stern of a Spanish man of war proper, thereon inscribed *San Josef'*. The colours were those of the Spanish flags Nelson had taken from the *San Nicolas* and *San Josef,* which had also been exhibited at the service of thanksgiving at St Paul's. Nelson's patent bridge was now immortalised by the College of Heralds, and the ship which Parker contended had struck not to Nelson but to him was established on Nelson's coat of arms.

On his return to England, the now famous Nelson had renewed his acquaintance with many men he had known in his earlier life. The port admiral at Portsmouth, who immediately gave him leave to go to Bath without waiting for the admiralty's orders, was Sir Peter Parker, who in Jamaica had made him a post captain at twenty. At Bath and Bristol he was the toast of the Tobins and Pinneys, late of Nevis, with whom Fanny had often stayed during his long absence. Mrs Pinney said that her husband John talked in his sleep about Nelson.[18] The Duke of Clarence wanted to be one of the first to shake him by his left hand.[19] At St James's palace he met old Lord Howe, who in 1784 had given him a ship for politics' sake. At Greenwich of course he met Locker, who had taught him how to lay his ship alongside a Frenchman, and Hood, whom he had alternately adored and execrated. It was Hood who told Fanny after the battle of St Vincent that Nelson had immortalised himself, and who, when she showed him Nelson's account of his share in the action, said he would show it where it would be of service.[20] Hood still had some interest, but Nelson had found a more powerful patron in Gilbert Elliot, who loved the navy and thought Nelson a Homeric hero. Since his return he had been created Baron Minto, and he did not hesitate to use on Nelson's behalf the same interest that would soon make him ambassador to Vienna and then governor-general of India.

Nelson was also finding that he had a little interest himself. He first wrote to Lord Chancellor Loughborough, who had many church benefits in his gift, asking for 'a small provision for the youngest son of my venerable father'. This was for Suckling Nelson, who had just taken holy orders. Nelson asked only that Suckling should be inducted into one of his father's livings, which he was happy to vacate. The chancellor complied with this request and offered to do anything else he could to serve his relatives.[21] William Nelson had been lobbying his brother to help him to a cathedral stall, having heard it was a *fixed* and *certain* thing he was to have the first preferment ministers had to dispose of. He was convinced Nelson could do it. He went on and on, finishing his importuning with these words: 'Pray continue your bows to the great seal [the chancellor]. Who knows what may happen now the iron is hot.'[22] Four days later he was back. Who was to have the canonry at Winchester, and what about the vacancies at Winchester, Bristol, Gloucester, St Paul's, Windsor, Oxford, Westminster, Canterbury, and Worcester?[23] It was all shameless. After Loughborough made his offer, Nelson told William, who replied that a prebend in any cathedral was his wish – 'the larger the income the better'.[24]

Nelson also met the man whose good opinion and interest would, for the next four years, be more important to him than any other's. This was the second Earl Spencer, first lord of the admiralty. The Spencers had risen to prominence and riches under the Tudors and Stuarts, and been given their earldom by George III. The family's country seat was at Althorp in Northamptonshire, which possessed perhaps the finest private library in Europe. Spencer House in London was a gilded palace. Lord Spencer's sister Georgiana was Duchess of Devonshire. His wife Lavinia was a society wit who as a girl had known Samuel Johnson, Edward Gibbon, and Joshua Reynolds. Spencer was a grand whig, one of those who in the war had agreed to serve under Pitt. He had succeeded Lord Chatham at the admiralty in December 1794, when Nelson was in the Mediterranean. Nelson had at first railed against what he called the gross neglect of the new admiralty board, saying Chatham had done better sleeping.[25] Later, of necessity, he became reconciled to the new first lord. They were men of the same age.[26]

It is Lavinia Spencer who gives us one of the classical descriptions of Nelson, and one of the best-known anecdotes. 'The first time I ever saw Nelson,' she said, 'was in the drawing room at the admiralty; and a most uncouth creature I thought him. He was just returned from Tenerife, after having lost his arm. He looked so sickly, it was painful to see him: and his general appearance was that of an idiot; so much so, that when he spoke, and his wonderful mind broke forth, it was a sort of surprise that riveted my whole attention.' This is vivid but must be treated with caution. Lady Spencer as she is there reported was speaking in 1815, seventeen years after the event, and comes to us, apparently verbatim, from the diary of Lady Shelley, a gossip who retailed hearsay news of the courts of Paris, St Petersburg, and other capitals, and gave picturesque descriptions of Pitt, Canova the sculptor, Byron, Wellington, and any other great persons who crossed her path in the drawing rooms of London.[27] One day in 1815 she was at Lady Spencer's when an admiral who had been one of Nelson's captains came in, and the conversation turned to Nelson. In her diary entry for that day she gets things wrong, saying Nelson called on Lady Spencer daily in 1798, which he did not, and that Lord Spencer appointed him to the Mediterranean command, which he did not. So her report of Lady Spencer's conversation must be taken with a pinch of salt, and it must also be taken into consideration that she was writing in knowledge of Nelson's later passion for Emma Hamilton, which she deplored. But here, as it is recorded in the same passage from the diary, is Lady Spencer's famous story of Nelson and Fanny at her dinner table, years before:

> I should explain that, although during Lord Spencer's adminis-
> tration, no sea captain ever returned without being asked to dinner
> by us; I made it a rule not to receive their wives. Nelson said, that
> out of deference to my known determination, he had not begged to
> introduce Lady Nelson to me; yet, if I would take notice of her, it
> would make him the happiest man alive. He said he felt convinced
> that I must like her. That she was beautiful, accomplished; but, above
> all, that her angelic tenderness to him was beyond all imagination.
> He told me that his wife had dressed his wounds, and that her
> care alone had saved his life. In short, he pressed me to see her,
> with an earnestness of which Nelson alone was capable. In these
> circumstances, I begged that he would bring her with him that day

to dinner. He did so, and his attentions to her were those of a lover. He handed her to dinner, and sat by her; apologising to me, by saying that he was so little with her, that he would not, voluntarily, lose an instant of her company.

While Nelson was living in London, attending his various ceremonies, his father felt rather cut off in Bath. He was grateful that his son had 'availed himself of his publick character' to get the living transferred to Suckling, but he knew Nelson was 'panting to be in actuall service'.[28] It was Fanny, and not Nelson, who told him that they had gone to Norfolk to look at a house they might buy. Late in September 1797 Nelson bought Round Wood, a house near Ipswich, for £2,000. The auction catalogue described it as set in fifty acres of rich arable land and as having two genteel parlours, three wine vaults, four bedrooms, two dressing rooms, a well planted garden, a dairy, and a large barn.[29] Nelson did spend most of January at Bath with his wife, father, and brother William. His sisters Susannah and Catherine were visitors. The Marquess of Lansdowne gave him a place in a box at the theatre, and, in thanking him, Nelson said: 'Generally some of the handsomest ladies in Bath are partakers in the box, and was I a bachelor I would not answer for being tempted; but as I am possessed of everything which is valuable in a wife, I have no occasion to think beyond a pretty face.'[30]

As soon as Nelson was fit, he had asked for a ship and was given the *Vanguard*. Edward Berry, who had been with him at St Vincent, was to be his flag captain. He was about to marry Louisa Foster, daughter of a Norwich doctor, and Nelson recommended he should do so speedily, as he might be called upon at any hour. He did, and Mrs Berry became one of Fanny's closest friends.[31] As soon as he had a ship, Nelson was off to London again, to be near Chatham where she was fitting out. He would not have wanted to be at his new house in the country at the time, and in any case there was a sitting tenant who had to be given six months' notice. Fanny was unable to move there until the following May, with Nelson's father.[32] By then Nelson had sailed and was back with St Vincent's fleet. 'My mind feels composed and quiet,' she wrote, 'when I consider how very lately I have seen you. God grant that we may not be very long before we meet and then I shall hope we may live for some years together without being so very often separated.'[33]

Before Nelson joined him, St Vincent received a letter from Lady

Spencer asking for his patronage of a young lieutenant, the Hon. Bladen Capel. She said there was nothing she would not do to have Mr Capel known and patronised by his lordship. Given who she was, it was a request likely to succeed. She then went on to speak of Nelson, so that however dramatised Lady Shelley's diary may be, we do know something of what Lady Spencer felt about him. She wrote: 'I hope you will find Sir Horatio tho' not grown much more substantial yet, better than could have been expected after his various losses . . . He is a very delightful creature & I hope I shall see him once more – tho' when I consider how little there is left of him, I cannot be sanguine in such expectations.'[34]

CHAPTER FOURTEEN

The Nile, and the Happy Instrument of God

IN THE EARLY MONTHS of 1797 northern Italy was falling rapidly to the French. Mantua had surrendered, and the pope had ceded the Romagna, Bologna, and Ferrara. At the same time Napoleon was marching on Vienna through the Tyrol. Then, in April, reports from Leghorn made the British government apprehensive of a great French fleet and army assembling at Toulon. What was the purpose of this armament? To attack Naples and Sicily, to take an army to Spain and from there march to Portugal, or pass through the straits of Gibraltar and invade Ireland? To find out, the admiralty resolved to send a squadron into the Mediterranean, a sea which the British had abandoned at the end of 1796. Getting wind of this, and naturally believing as a former commissioner of Toulon and former viceroy of Corsica that the British ought to check the enemy's dominion in 'the whole of that great world', Lord Minto took it on himself to call at the admiralty. There he told Spencer that Nelson would be the fittest man in the world for such a command, whose name was dreaded by the enemy and inspired confidence in all others, and whose disposition to act in concert and harmony with those on shore had been conspicuous on every occasion. Except that he had always got on well with Minto, Nelson's disposition was not of that nature at all, for he had conspicuously and often quarrelled with the army, but the rest was true. And besides, as Minto pointed out to Spencer, Nelson was as well acquainted with the Mediterranean as the first lord was with the room he was sitting in.

Spencer replied that *if* such a squadron were sent, it would be left to Lord St Vincent to name the officer to command it. However, when he wrote to him, he would suggest his own opinion that Nelson was the proper man. Not, he said, that the measure *was* determined on, and the greatest secrecy was essential. Next day Minto wrote to Nelson and told him all about the conversation.[1] He was by then at Cadiz, where he received letters from Fanny, who was still at Bath, telling him about rumours of invasion. Bath was full of country families supposing it a safe place. She had heard that all the empty houses in Suffolk were to be taken over by the government for barracks, and feared for Round Wood. He replied that if the house were taken it would be instantly given back, because if she was left in the street he would strike his flag and come home to protect her. But the admiral, he said, and this was *secret*, was going to detach him with a small squadron, so she must not be surprised if she did not hear from him for some little time.[2] St Vincent had already written to Spencer that Nelson's arrival had given him new life, and, before he received any orders from England, sent him off with three ships of the line and three frigates to reconnoitre Toulon. Nelson took a French corvette and learned that Buonaparte had been inspecting 12,000 troops which had embarked in transports at Toulon. No one knew where the fleet was going, and Buonaparte himself was not expected to go with it.[3] Two days later, the *Vanguard* almost foundered in a storm. Nelson told Fanny he firmly believed it was the almighty's goodness to check his consummate vanity. 'Figure to yourself a vain man on Sunday evening at sunset walking in his cabin with a squadron about him who looked up to their chief to lead them to glory ... Figure to yourself this proud conceited man, when the sun rose on Monday morning his ship dismasted his fleet dispersed and himself in such distress that the meanest frigate out of France would have been a very unwelcome guest.'[4] He had been towed into St Peter's island, in Sardinia, and was refitting.

By then St Vincent had received four letters. Two were from the admiralty. The first was a 'most secret' order from their lordships, saying they were sending reinforcements, and that when they arrived St Vincent was to detach a squadron of twelve of the line under a discreet flag officer into the Mediterranean. The second was a private letter from Spencer, who wrote that the fate of Europe might depend upon the appearance of a British squadron in the Mediterranean, and that he thought it almost unnecessary to suggest the propriety of putting it under the command of Sir H. Nelson. Lord Minto's advocacy had had its effect. The admiralty's letter mentioned only a discreet flag officer; Spencer's letter, written a few days after Minto's visit, named Nelson.[5]

The third and fourth letters were both from Naples, asking for help. One was from Sir William Hamilton, whom St Vincent assured that he was sending a powerful squadron. The other was from Emma Hamilton, and to it St Vincent, an austere man who could not bear women on board a king's ship, made a flirtatious reply. 'I feel myself highly honoured and flattered by your ladyship's charming letter ... The picture you have drawn of the lovely Queen of Naples and the royal family, would rouse the indignation of the most unfeeling of the creation, at the infernal designs of those devils, who, for the scourge of the human race, are permitted to govern France. I am bound by my oath of chivalry to protect all who are persecuted and distressed, and I would fly to the succour of their Sicilian majesties, were I not positively forbid to quit my post before Cadiz. I an happy, however, to have a knight of superior prowess in my train, who is charged with this enterprize, and will soon make his appearance, at the head of as gallant a band as ever drew sword or trailed pike.' He signed himself her true knight and devoted servant.[6] Now St Vincent had probably never met Emma, but he owed the Hamiltons something, since Sir William's mother, Lady Archibald Hamilton, had persuaded his unwilling parents to let him go to sea.[7] But it is droll that it was the austere St Vincent who, with such a letter, sent Nelson, his knight of superior prowess, off to Naples and to Emma Hamilton.

By then Nelson was already in the Mediterranean, so St Vincent sent Troubridge after him with nine ships of the line, to make his squadron up to twelve. These appointments caused anguish in the fleet. Troubridge was by no means the most senior captain, which irritated those who were passed over. And Nelson was junior to all three of St Vincent's flag officers, and two of those were Sir William Parker and Sir John Orde. Sir William, made a baronet after the battle of St Vincent, was the officer who had civilly challenged the notion of Nelson's patent bridge. Sir John had been governor of Dominica when Nelson was a young captain in the Leeward Islands, and they had met when Nelson was conducting Prince William from ball to ball. Orde had some interest; his brother Thomas had been secretary to the treasury, and had just been made a peer. When they protested, St Vincent told both Parker and Orde that he had been ordered to appoint Nelson. With some murmuring, which St Vincent considered a foul slander, Parker accepted this.[8] Orde did not, considering it a slight to him that Nelson should have been detached 'on a service of the greatest national importance, I might say of the greatest eventual importance to the world'.[9] There was a long history of bad blood between him and his commander-in-chief. St Vincent, on the quarterdeck of his flagship, which is to say more or less in public, had turned on his heel and left Orde; he had berated him for carrying two midshipmen he considered unfit; he had by implication accused two of Orde's lieutenants of 'c—', by which was meant cowardice, that word being by convention never written in full in the navy. If half of Orde's complaints were true, he had been badly used. St Vincent was a stickler for discipline; he ran a tight fleet but not always a happy one. The wife of one captain, after he gave orders that none of his officers should sleep ashore when in port, famously gave a bumper toast: 'May the next glass of wine choke the wretch.'[10] St Vincent peremptorily ordered Orde home. Orde asked for a court martial on St Vincent, which was refused, and then, calling his commander-in-chief's conduct tyrannical and deceitful, challenged him to a duel, which was forbidden by the king.

Among Nelson's squadron were the *Culloden*, the *Theseus*, the *Vanguard*, the *Minotaur*, the *Swiftsure*, the *Zealous*, the *Orion*, the *Goliath*; and among their captains were men who became celebrated as Nelson's band of brothers – Miller, Ball, Berry, Louis, Hallowell, Samuel Hood, Saumarez, Foley.[11] Nelson's orders gave him enormous powers in the whole Mediterranean and beyond. He was to seek and pursue the French fleet and army out of Toulon and then sink, burn, or destroy it. He was to exact whatever provisions he needed from any ports, and any port which refused (excepting only those of Sardinia) was to be considered hostile. He could pursue the French squadron to any part of the Mediterranean, Adriatic, Morea [southern Greece], or even into the Black Sea.[12] He was given full powers extending 2,000 miles from his commander-in-chief at Cadiz, over the Mediterranean and beyond, and over the coasts of Europe, Africa, and Asia. Yet he was still the fourth most junior admiral, out of an active list of ninety-four, in the Royal Navy.[13]

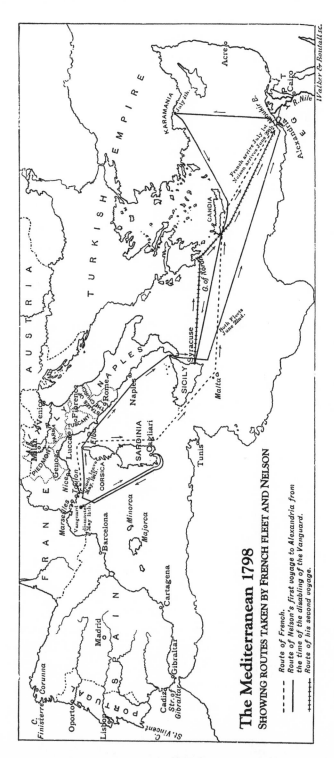

Map of Mediterranean in 1798, from Gibraltar to Naples and Aboukir, showing the routes taken by Nelson in his pursuit of Napoleon's French fleet. Adapted from Nelson and His Times, by Rear-Admiral Lord Charles Beresford, 1897.

For three months after he received these orders, Nelson received no others. What he did was at his own discretion, and would be on his own head.[14] He did not know Buonaparte had sailed from Toulon on 19 May, did not know that he took and looted Malta within a month, and did not know he had been reinforced by fleets from Genoa and Elba so that he commanded a force of 50,000. On 22 June Nelson's squadron and the French probably passed each other in the night south of Sicily, but he could not know because he had no outlying frigates to scout for him. The three frigates of his original reconnaissance flotilla had lost him in the storm which nearly wrecked the *Vanguard*, and never rejoined.[15] Again and again in his letters he lamented the lack of them. 'Was I to die this moment, *want of frigates* would be found stamped on my heart.'[16] He had only the *Mutine* brig. He did not even know that the French had stayed in the Mediterranean until on 14 June he 'spoke a Tunisian cruiser, who reported he had spoke a Greek on the 10th who told him that on the 4th he had passed through the French fleet, of about 200 sail as he thought, off the NW end of Sicily steering to the eastward'.[17] His knowledge was as flimsy as that, hearsay upon hearsay. He knew nothing definite until he sent Troubridge into Naples on 17 June, where he learned that the French fleet had been off Malta on the 8th. By then, he was beginning to suspect, as he wrote to Spencer, that the French had a 'scheme of possessing Alexandria and getting troops to India ... by no means so difficult as might at first view be imagined'.[18] This was a bold leap of reasoning on his part. He went to Alexandria on 29 June, found nothing, and went back to Syracuse in Sicily to water and provision his squadron. He had been off Naples, off Malta, off Egypt, off Syria, a round trip of 1,800 miles, and was as ignorant as he had been four weeks before.[19]

Back in England, Nelson's wife and brother wrote him letters typical of themselves. Fanny, at Round Wood, was anxious. The newspapers had said Nelson was at Naples, but had gone off to Malta. Captain Berry's wife was with her, 'a very pleasant young woman'. John Thompson, a seaman from the *Agamemnon*, had called. He had happened to be at an ale house nearby, was asked if he knew Nelson, and said he did monstrous well, having sailed with him for five years, and then they told him Nelson's house was close. He had been a prisoner in France, was thin, and could hardly eat. Fanny said she was writing opposite her husband's new portrait by Abbott, which she described as her sincere friend and companion in his absence.[20] William Nelson wrote in a different tone. 'I hope you will not forget your promise to me that you would remind the lord chancellor of what passed between you & him about a church dignitary for me; – you know I am always sanguine & looking forward to great things for you, & therefore if you should be able to lay hold of this Hero of Italy, the Terror of Europe, your business will be done indeed, & a peerage I should think will be one sure reward ... But I am running on I know not whither, & am building castles in my imagination which may never be realised.'[21]

The English newspapers became sceptical of Nelson's chances. Even *The Times*, which was in the government's pocket, wrote that it was most unaccountable that a French fleet of near two hundred sail should have eluded Nelson for so long a space of time.[22] Rumours abounded. One day Buonaparte was reported taken prisoner. Another day, Nelson was victorious but dead. Fragments of reports came in from Trieste, Leghorn, and Milan. The *Herald*, losing patience, gave this opinion: 'It may be too much for us to say, that [Nelson] has not the quality, which Buonaparte seems to have, vulgarly called long-headedness. It is clear, however, that he is now unfortunate ... perhaps it may not be amiss to employ the gallantry of Admiral Nelson under the good fortune of others, until his turn comes round ...'[23]

The Morning Chronicle, an opposition paper, was hardest on Nelson, saying all fond hopes of him were disappointed, and that if he had returned to Syracuse without having met the Conqueror of Italy, and if Buonaparte, with all his immense force, had arrived at Alexandria, this was disastrous for England. Nelson was distinguished for enterprise and gallantry, but his warmest friends would admit that a commander of more experience would have been preferable. St Vincent himself ought to have taken on Buonaparte. If Nelson had arrived at Alexandria before the enemy, and left, he could not have been instructed that to prevent Buonaparte's arrival at that port was the great object of his mission, as upon that depended the salvation of India. Any other destination would have been a mere buccaneering scheme of plunder; but India was a plan of national overthrow.[24]

This was very acute. Nelson had not been so instructed, although by then he was convinced that Buonaparte was after India.[25] It was not until 28 July, when he had again taken his squadron eastward from Syracuse, that he learned that the French were in Egypt.[26] They had been there since 29 June, the same day Nelson left. He had just missed them. His famous 'activity' had betrayed him. If he had waited a few hours he would have seen them and been in among the transports and their escorts. In effect, the battle of Trafalgar would have been fought seven years before its time, and Buonaparte might have been taken and never become first consul or emperor. It is one of the great ifs of history. As it was, by the time Nelson heard, Buonaparte had landed at Alexandria, won the battle of the pyramids, and taken Cairo.

Nelson set sail a second time for Alexandria and in the afternoon of 1 August, came upon the French fleet of thirteen ships of the line and four frigates in Aboukir bay, a few miles northeast of Alexandria. Vice-Admiral Brueys's flag flew in a splendid ship of 120 guns, whose successive names were a brief illustration of recent French history. She had been launched at Toulon in 1790, when the king was still on the throne, and named *Le Dauphin Royal*; in 1792, out of revolutionary fervour, she was renamed *Le Sans-Culotte*; in 1798 she was renamed again after the expedition on which Buonaparte was taking her, and became *L'Orient*.[27] The bay is nearly semicircular and stretches between Aboukir point to the west and the Rosetta mouth of the Nile on the east. The French position should have been strong. Thirteen ships of the line were moored in line astern across the bay, north to south, in a compact line of battle, protected by the batteries of Aboukir island to the northwest, and on the land side by shoals of unknown shallowness. Nelson approached. Here report and legend become mixed. He was said hardly to have eaten or slept for the previous few days, but on sighting the enemy to have called for dinner to be served, and on rising from the table to have said: 'Before this time tomorrow, I shall have gained a peerage of Westminster Abbey.' This is unlikely. He always preferred St Paul's, thinking that the abbey, being on low ground by the Thames, would soon sink into the water.[28] What is sure is that he intended from the first to fight that day.

Strong though his position appeared to be, Brueys had been surprised. His ships were undermanned, most of them lacking as many as two hundred of their proper crew. He had parties ashore digging wells, and other seamen ashore to protect the working parties from continual Bedouin attacks. The decks of his ships were cluttered. *L'Orient*'s people were painting ship. Brueys did not expect a fight that day, but the English squadron came on steadily towards him, at some three knots. He had not enough men to get under sail and engage at sea even if he had wished to. By five he saw that Nelson intended to fight that day, and made the signal to engage at anchor.[29]

The wind was from the NNW. Nelson meant to attack the French van and centre, approaching from the head of the enemy line.[30] To do this risked running ashore on the shoals. Troubridge in the *Culloden* did run aground and was stranded throughout the action. None of Nelson's officers knew the bay, and they came in sounding as they went. Foley, who had a recent French chart, led the way. At this point, before a shot was fired, Nelson had done three bold things which few other commanders would have dared, and which went far to determining the course of the battle. He had attacked immediately, he had concentrated his forces on the enemy's van and centre, and in order to do this he had risked the shoals. Had his squadron gone aground – as the *Culloden* did – he would have been helpless. But he had calculated rightly.

There is another factor which determined the outcome. The French ships were at single anchor, and where there was room for them to swing there was also enough water for the British ships to enter. The first five British ships, led by Foley in the *Goliath*, rounded the head of the French line and went inside, between the French and the shore, and anchored there. Nelson's flagship and five others then took the outside, the sea-side, of the French line, which was thus attacked from both sides. There is no agreement whose plan this was. Berry, who wrote the account of the Nile generally credited, implies that the decision was Nelson's. Saumarez says the decision was not preconcerted, but was Nelson's, though made only a minute before its execution: how in that case it would have been communicated is not easy to see. Foley probably led the ships inside without any previous order or arrangement. His friends later claimed with some vigour that the idea was his, and the weight of evidence is on Foley's side.[31] If the manoeuvre had been Nelson's, it would have been in his nature to say so: he had not kept silent in Hotham's action or at St Vincent. Whoever was the author of the tactic, it was that which in the end made the French defeat so overwhelming.

No shots were fired as the fleets converged. The first cannon was fired at half-past six, at sunset, when the leading ships were within pistol range of each other. In half an hour it was dark. The Nile was a battle fought at night and at anchor. The French ships had not even run out their guns on the shore side. Under cross fire, the van ship, *Le Guerrier*, was dismasted in twelve minutes; after another ten minutes the second and third ships, *Le Conquérant* and *Le Spartiate* were dismasted. By half-past eight, *L'Aquilon* and *Le Peuple Souverain* were taken. By then both the French and British admirals were wounded. Brueys's wound was mortal: he was nearly cut in two by a shot in the belly and insisted on being left to die on his quarterdeck. Nelson thought his wound was mortal too. He was struck on the forehead by flying langridge, iron shrapnel. A flap of skin fell over his eye, and this and the copious blood blinded him. Berry caught him as he fell. He said, 'I am killed; remember me to my wife', and was taken below.[32] At five to nine *L'Orient* caught fire, and the blaze illuminated the darkness. One paragraph from an account by Rear-Admiral Blanquet shows the state of the French at that moment. 'The *Tonnant* cut her cable, to avoid catching fire from *L'Orient*. The English ship that was on *L'Orient*'s larboard quarter, so soon as she had done firing at her, brought her broadside upon the *Tonnant*'s bow, and kept up a very heavy raking fire. The *Heureux* and *Mercure* conceived that they ought likewise to cut their cables. This manoeuvre created so much confusion among the rear ships, that they fired into each other, and did considerable damage.'[33] The English ships on either side of the French van had fired into each other, but not so chaotically. Of *L'Orient*'s crew of a thousand men, only seventy saved themselves.[34] At ten she blew up. Masts, yards, cannons, bodies, and blazing wreckage were thrown to a vast height and rained down on the ships of both squadrons. The shock was so great that the battle ceased, and for a space of some say three minutes, others ten, others fifteen, there was only silence. Twenty miles away in Rosetta, Vivant Denon – courtier to both Louis XVI and Buonaparte, diplomat, artist, and a pillager of genius who made the Louvre what it became – saw from a tower a strong burst of light, then heard the dreadful explosion, and then observed the profound silence which followed.[35]

After that all was butchery and wreck. The ships at the rear of the French line were unable, because of the direction of the wind, to come up to the aid of the rest of the squadron, and were themselves successively picked off. Ship fouled ship. Two French ships ran ashore. In the noise, confusion, smoke, darkness, and terror a man knew only what happened near him, and no one report agrees with another. There

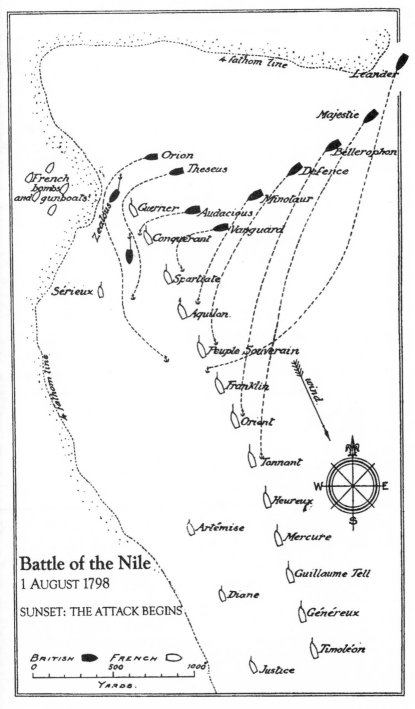

Battle of the Nile

1 AUGUST 1798

SUNSET: THE ATTACK BEGINS

BRITISH ● FRENCH ▯

0   500   1000

YARDS.

From Clowes's Royal Navy: a History, *vol IV, 1899.*

is no coherent report, because nothing coherent happened. There i
one dream-like anecdote of the *Alexander*. After the explosion an(
the silence, she renewed her fight with the French 84 alongside her
the Frenchman's fire slackened and then ceased, and yet she made n(
sign of surrender. The first lieutenant of the *Alexander* approached hi.
captain, Alexander Ball, and told him that though the hearts of hi:
men were as good as ever, they were exhausted and scarcely capabl(
of lifting an arm. He asked whether, since the enemy had stoppe(
firing, the men could lie down by their guns for a short time. Bal
agreed. 'Accordingly,' the story goes, 'with the exception of himself
his officers, and the appointed watch, the ship's crew lay down, each
in the place to which he was stationed, and slept for twenty minutes
They were then roused; and started up [as Ball expressed it] mor(
like men out of an ambush than from sleep, so co-instantaneously did
they all obey the summons. They recommenced their fire, and in a few
minutes the enemy surrendered; and it was soon after discovered, that
during that interval, and almost immediately after the French ship had
first ceased firing, her crew had sunk down by their guns, and there
slept, almost by the side, as it were, of their sleeping enemy.'[36]

The battle rolled on that night, and then intermittently for another
day and night. Nelson recovered, and on the morning of the third day
wrote a dispatch to St Vincent, beginning, 'My lord, almighty God has
blessed his majesty's arms in the late battle, by a great victory . . .'[37]
Of the thirteen French ships of the line, nine had been taken, two had
burned, and only two had escaped. It was an annihilation new to naval
warfare. 'Victory,' said Nelson, 'is not a strong enough name for such
a scene as I have passed.'[38] And when Howe later congratulated him
he replied that if he had not been wounded and stone blind, he would
have taken every ship.[39]

Nelson was later anxious to demonstrate to Spencer, to Minto, and to
the world that *L'Orient* struck before she caught fire.[40] He could not
have known himself because he was below, wounded, when it happened,
and it does not seem to matter one way or the other since the result
was the same. What is clear is that she was not only the flagship but a
treasure ship. Nelson reported that she carried £600,000 in gold coins,
ingots, and diamonds. This was the treasure to finance Buonaparte's
Indian expedition. She also carried a printing press, and the priceless

loot taken two months before from the moribund knights of Malta. The force of the explosion was such that cannon weighing three tons were twisted by the blast and hurled two hundred and fifty yards.[41]

It has never been established how *L'Orient* came to burn. She was newly painted, and had pots of paint on board, which would catch easily. It may also have been that she had on board the Greek fire which some French ships had carried, a sort of phosphorus which would burn under water, and whose flames could not be extinguished by water. Nelson had always said he deplored this, as he did the firing of red hot shot, which he called a diabolical practice.[42] There is another possible explanation, and it comes from Ball, the captain who let his exhausted men sleep by their cannon. Five years later, when he was governor of Malta, he told Samuel Taylor Coleridge – the poet, and friend of Wordsworth – that just such a flammable material had been carried in his own ship. This is Coleridge's account, which he wrote that he received from Ball himself. 'He [Ball] had previously made a combustible preparation, but which, from the nature of the engagement to be expected, he had purposed to reserve for the last emergency. But just at the time when, from several symptoms, he had every reason to believe that the enemy would soon strike to him, one of the lieutenants, without his knowledge, threw in the combustible matter; and this it was that occasioned the tremendous explosion of that vessel, which, with the deep silence and interruption of the engagement which succeeded to it, has been justly deemed the sublimest war incident recorded in history.'[43]

If Ball had made such Greek fire and had it on board, it is difficult to believe that Nelson would not have known. He was intimate with Ball. If the French did have such a weapon, and Nelson was going into battle and hazarding his own ships, it is unlikely that he would have left himself at a disadvantage. It would have been his duty not to. And if such a weapon were used, this might explain Nelson's anxiety to establish that *L'Orient* had struck *before* she caught fire, so that she might therefore be seen to have been defeated by traditional and more gentlemanly methods. But how far is Coleridge's account to be believed? It did not come from an isolated meeting between him and Ball. In 1804, Coleridge went to Malta, where for some fifteen months he met Ball daily, became his secretary, and revered him, calling him 'a man above his age'.[44] The two men worked and dined together. Printed proclamations in Ball's name were put out by Coleridge. Ball talked freely to his secretary, who recorded some of his remarks in a private journal which was not published in his lifetime. Coleridge's journal for 4 July 1804 contains this passage: 'Brave Tars – eager as Tygers for battle. &c &c – Sir A.B. assured me, that the men on board our most glorious Warships *often run from their Quarters* tho' it was made a point to hush it up/ that it was the British *officers* & our Discipline/ yet believed their Men too braver & steadier than any other nation except Danes and Swedes –'[45]

So Ball was prepared to be indiscreet. By that time, whatever his earlier feelings, Coleridge had no sympathy for the French cause: the same entry in his journal contains an anecdote of Napoleon's ruthlessness. Against that, Coleridge in Malta was addicted to opium. The truth about the fire remains a matter of conjecture, but *L'Orient* burned much faster than ships usually burned. Ball's account is said by a biographer of 1849 to have been denied by British officers, whom he does not name, and to be 'contrary to the spirit and character of British warfare'.[46] It does not seem to have been mentioned since then. It is not easy to see why burning a ship by any method should be thought so uncharacteristic. Three years later, in the channel, against a French invasion flotilla, Nelson told St Vincent he proposed to make what he called an 'infernal' of one of the bomb ketches, and run it into Boulogne. And in the plan for his concerted attack on that port he said that each boat should carry 'a carcase, or other combustible, with a match, ready to set the enemy's vessels on fire'. A carcase was an iron incendiary shell 'filled with a very fiercely flaming composition of saltpetre, sulphur, resin, turpentine, antimony, and tallow'.[47] It might not have been quite cricket, but it was done.

After the victory Nelson sent Berry to Cadiz with dispatches for St Vincent. He sent a lieutenant who was a good linguist to take the news to the governor of Bombay, by way of Aleppo and Basra. And then, in case Berry was intercepted on his way down the Mediterranean, he sent duplicate dispatches to London, by way of Naples. By long tradition, the first lieutenants of ships of the line were promoted to commander after a victorious battle.[48] So also, by long tradition, was the bearer of good news. For this duty Nelson chose Thomas Bladen Capel, who happened to be the young officer for whom Lady Spencer had put in a good word with St Vincent earlier that year when Nelson returned to the Mediterranean. He was the most junior of the eight lieutenants of the *Vanguard*, but was the son of the Earl of Essex. He had been entered on the books of a frigate at the age of five, though he did not appear in the flesh for another ten years. Two days after the Nile, Nelson made him master and commander of the *Mutine* brig, with orders to take her to Naples, hand her over to his lieutenant, and then take his dispatches overland to London.[49] Berry was indeed captured, and so it was Capel who brought the dispatches to London. St Vincent was a man who thought there was a great lack of seamanship and that the young people coming forward were for the most part frippery and gimcrack.[50] When he learned of Capel's promotion he said: '[He] will receive all the incense and kisses of Lady Spencer and other heroines.'[51]

When the news came, Lady Spencer also blew some incense to Nelson. She wrote: 'Captain Capel just arrived! Joy, joy, joy to you, brave gallant, immortal Nelson! May that great God, whose cause you so valiantly support, protect and bless you to the end of your brilliant career. Such a race surely never was won. My heart is absolutely bursting with different sensations of joy, of gratitude, of pride, of every emotion that ever warmed the bosom of a British woman – and all produced by you, my dear, my good friend. And what shall I say to you for your attention to me, in your behaviour to Captain Capel? . . . What incalculable service have you been of to my dear Lord Spencer! And as wife of this excellent man, what do *I* not feel for *you all*, as executors of *his* schemes and plans!'[52] Mr Capel, formerly the most junior lieutenant of the *Vanguard*, then rapidly commander of the only precious brig Nelson had, was promoted post captain two months after he brought the good news.

Nelson after the Nile was much taken with God. To Lord Spencer he wrote that in the battle the hand of God was visible from first to last. He told his brother William that the hand of God had been visibly pressed on the French. And to Sir William Hamilton at Naples he wrote: 'Almighty God has made me the happy instrument in destroying the enemy's fleet; which, I hope, will be a blessing to Europe. You will have the goodness to communicate this happy event to all the courts in Italy . . .'[53]

When *L'Orient* blew up, a great chunk of her mainmast landed on the *Swiftsure* whose captain, to remind Nelson that he was mortal, had a coffin made out of it, and sent it to him with a letter: 'Herewith I send you a coffin made of part of *L'Orient*'s main mast, that when you are tired of life you may be buried in one of your own trophies – but may that period be far distant, is the earnest wish of your obedient and much obliged servant, Ben. Hallowell.' Nelson had it placed upright against the bulkhead of his cabin, behind the chair at which he sat at dinner.[54]

CHAPTER FIFTEEN

The Family, and the Great Stage of Life

CAPEL DID NOT ARRIVE in London with his news until 2 October, two months after the victory, but in the weeks before that the newspapers reported rumour after rumour. The first scent of an English victory came, strangely enough, from the Paris papers that came in the Hamburg packet. *L'Echo* said that Buonaparte had himself put to sea and defeated Nelson, who had then shot himself. Then *Le Redacteur*, the official journal of the Directory, reported that a sea battle had been fought, with an obstinacy of which history did not offer an example, on the coast of Bequières (Aboukir), that the French admiral's ship was burned, two or three had foundered, and that others, French and English, had been driven ashore.[1] Next day *Le Clef du Cabinet* carried a self-congratulatory piece which amounted to an admission. The event, said the paper, had doubtless been lamentable, and the picture of men and ships buried in the deep was certainly affecting; but what was this loss compared to the triumph of Buonaparte in Egypt, the descent of the French on Ireland, and the success in St Domingue, not to mention the taking of Malta?[2] On 27 September both *The Times* and *The Morning Chronicle* reported a dispatch from the British minister in Constantinople, who had been told by the Turkish government, who had been told by the governor of Rhodes, that he had been told by the master of a French brig that on 31 July he had seen an English squadron attack the French fleet at Bequières and that *L'Orient* was already on fire when he came away. It was distant hearsay, but close enough. Next day Sir Francis Baring, the banker, received a letter from his nephew, who lived in Albania, saying Nelson had taken seven ships of the line.[3] The day after that came another report, from the British minister in Vienna, that the whole French line of battle was sunk, taken, or destroyed, except for two ships.[4] This was too good to be true, but the day after that Capel arrived with Nelson's own dispatch, and it was true.

The rejoicing was great. Hood said Nelson had preserved the greater part of Europe from anarchy, distress, and misery.[5] At the admiralty, Lady Spencer wrote her joyful letter. Outside, in Whitehall, a joyful mob insisted on every person of genteel appearance pulling off his hat, and when six officers, coming along, were ordered 'to pay the same compliment to the mobility', and refused, the populace tried to knock their hats off and the officers drew their swords.[6] Lady Spencer wrote another letter, to St Vincent, expressing her delight that her husband's naval administration had witnessed three victories which, since naval records had been kept, in England or any other country, were not to be equalled. 'Your magnificent achievement saved this country – Lord Duncan's saved Ireland, & I must hope . . . Nelson's saves India.'[7]

Nelson said in his dispatch that he had been wounded in the head and obliged to be carried off the deck. *The Times* said he was 'severely hurt by a splinter, which struck his head and eyes'.[8] Lord Duncan was in London, and it was he who sent a reassuring messenger to Fanny and the Revd Edmund Nelson at Ipswich, telling them that when Capel last saw him Nelson had been in the greatest spirits, walking the deck and recovered from his wound.[9] This was kind of Duncan; Fanny had been 'tormented and almost killed' by the many rumours.[10] The messenger also brought her the letter Nelson had sent by Capel. It was brief: 'My dearest Fanny, – I am thank God as much better as could be expected, and what I hope will make Europe happy is the certain destruction of the French army. The people of the country [Egypt] are rising against them every hour. Such are the blessed fruits of our conquest. Victory is certainly not a name strong enough for such a scene as I have passed. I shall most probably be in England in November, but more of this hereafter . . .'[11]

From Bath, Catherine Matcham wrote to her brother: 'I am all anxiety to hear, more particularly being apprehensive the wound may be over the *bright eye*, and as a sister, I may be allow'd to think of appearances, as all the ladies will be looking at you, for you see all the young ladies looking very *brisk*, when they hear you are not an *old* man ... I daresay [William] thinks the *mitre* is very near falling upon *his head*. Now he will be *very great* in his own eyes. Poor fellow, he has his good qualities, though he has an odd way of showing them ...' Her husband George, whom Nelson did not like, added a postscript warning him of the dangers of returning, since the young women had the serious intention to eat him up alive, 'and god knows ... your physical corporal substance will not go much further than a sprat, but I suppose they mean to intoxicate themselves with the spirit'.[12]

The *Chronicle* remarked that Nelson was rather unlucky in his own person, as he rarely escaped without a wound, but if the hurt to his head left a scar, it could be hidden with a coronet.[13] For there was no doubt that Nelson would be made a peer. The only question was to what rank in the peerage he would be raised. After St Vincent, Jervis had been made an earl, though that was exceptional, since before the action he had already been promised a barony as soon as he decided by what title he would like to be known.[14] For Camperdown, Duncan was made a viscount, the next rank down. There was no doubt that the annihilation at the Nile was the greatest of the three victories. The decision was not the king's, but the cabinet's. The day after Capel returned, Hood met Pitt, who told him Nelson would certainly be made a viscount.[15] Hood told Fanny, and asked her by what titles Nelson would like to be known. She replied: 'The first title certainly Alexandria.' That was for the viscountcy. Then (since a viscount would also be given a barony) she said that both she and his father thought he would like the second to be Baron Nelson.[16] Meanwhile, probably having been asked for his advice, William Windham, the secretary at war, wrote to Spencer: 'Though Nelson has fulfilled so magnificently all the hopes that could be conceived of him I cannot wish him to be put on a level with Lord St Vincent; at the same time, that I conclude there is not a thought of placing him below Lord Duncan.' He thought Nelson ought to stand somewhere between them, but there was nothing between earl and viscount. He hoped there was no idea of placing him below Duncan because he had not been commander-in-chief.[17] Windham was member for Norwich, and, like Nelson, a Norfolk man. They had both gone on the same arctic expedition in 1773, though Windham did not make a career in the navy. The point he made was a strong one. Nelson had not been commander-in-chief in the Mediterranean, only the rear-admiral commanding a detached squadron, but St Vincent had been two thousand miles away at Cadiz.

The same day as Windham wrote his letter, Spencer sent for Maurice Nelson of the navy office, told him his brother would be made a peer, and asked by what title he would like to be known. Maurice said they had never spoken on the subject, but rather wished the family name might be retained. Spencer agreed, but no rank in the peerage was mentioned. Next day, when the admiralty secretary told Maurice that his brother was to be only a baron, he was so hurt and surprised that he just bowed and took his leave.[18] So it was decided. Spencer wrote to Nelson telling him he was a baron of the United Kingdom by the name, style, and title of Baron Nelson of the Nile, and of Burnham Thorpe in the county of Norfolk, and that this was the highest honour ever conferred on an officer of his standing in the service, who was not a commander-in-chief.[19] Hood said that in his humble opinion a more flimsy reason was never given, and that this was the general opinion of a grateful country.[20] Vice-Admiral Goodall, who had been with Nelson at Hotham's action in 1795, began a letter to Nelson saying he would be showered with deserved honours and that his wound be an additional mark of dignity, but then learned while he was writing that there was to be only a barony. At which he added, '... 'tis not enough ... I shall clamour for more, but shall not rest till I hail you viscount. This is an age wherein titles are not spared in the favourable moment.'[21] Even Nelson's father, who did not care for honours, remarked that the peerage was not what the public was fully satisfied with.[22] The Nelson family was made much of. Fanny was presented to the queen, but remained 'mortified' that her husband was not to be a viscount, as strong a word as she ever used.[23] Maurice was asked by Pitt to a great dinner, but continued dissatisfied with what had been done for his brother, and hoped that the king would confer another peerage on him when he returned home.[24]

Maurice was also dissatisfied with what his brother had not done for him. He was the oldest of the surviving Nelson brothers, five years older than Horatio and four years older than William. He is generally regarded as an amiable man, and compared to William he was. But he was discontented. He had started as a boy in the excise office, in a clerkship procured for him by one Suckling uncle, and then moved o a clerkship in the navy office got for him by another Suckling uncle, Maurice Suckling, when he was comptroller of the navy. About this time he was also, through the interest of the comptroller, appointed purser of a sloop by Lord Sandwich. He too could have gone to sea, but he did not take the post.[25] With one break of three years when he worked as an army commissary, buying supplies in England for Lord Moira's forces in their excursions into Brittany and to Ostend, he spent his life as a clerk in the navy office, though clerk meant more than the word would now suggest.[26] He was considered a gentleman, and had the ability to improve a midshipman's service record in the ledgers, which gave him a little patronage. He lived with a Mrs Sarah Ford, and a series of his letters to her exists, written when he was away in Exeter buying hay in bulk for Lord Moira and she remained at home near London.[27] He writes to her as Dear Sukey, and sends her £10 and a dozen snipe, but when she wants to come to see him he tells her he must have taken leave of her senses. He complains of his lodgings, and says Exeter absolutely stinks, even worse than Edinburgh old town, 'for in every street you see men, girls & boys doing that which delicacy permits my naming'. He does not sound a happy man. After many years at the navy office he earned an annual salary of £300, twice that of a frigate captain but without the chance of prize money, and prize money, in the fall of 1798, was a sore subject with Maurice. He was offended when after the Nile he received only three lines from his brother, telling him Davison would be acting as agent for the Nile prizes. He wrote in reply: 'I am free to confess to you that I feel myself not a little hurt at my not having been named with Mr D. as one of the agents to your squadron it might have put something in my pocket at least it would have stop'd peoples mouths who repeatedly say there must have been some misunderstanding between you and me . . . I have no doubt you have sufficient reason and whatever it may be I submit and content myself in present degrading situation, degrading I call it because I cannot reach the top of my profession . . .'[28] The top of his profession would have been a post as commissioner of the navy, which Nelson often tried to get for him but never did.

William of course was not satisfied, either for Nelson or for himself. He wrote that if any addition were made to the barony, he would remind his brother that the Orford title (an earldom which had distant family connections) was extinct. Not, he said, that he ever wished to see the name Nelson forgotten. He also hoped that Parliament would add a pension to the title. Then he got on to the subject nearest his heart saying he had read in the papers that the king expected some church preferment would be given to Nelson's father and brother. And he busied himself devising a full dress livery for Horatio's servants. His idea was for a coat lined with yellow, the collar and cuffs black velvet the collar embroidered with worsted lace, shag breeches, one or two gold epaulettes, and a gold laced hat, something like Lord Walpole's full dress. The buttons were to have *San Josef* crests on them.[29]

At least eleven prints came out after the Nile, five by Gillray, two by Rowlandson, and one by Cruikshank. Rowlandson showed Nelson drinking with his brave tars and with two turbanned Egyptians smoking hookas. Gillray's 'Extirpation of the Plagues of Egypt' showed Nelson, with a hook for a right hand, vanquishing a swarm of crocodiles Cruikshank showed him leading two weeping crocodiles, with the faces of Fox and Sheridan, who opposed the war, and the Directory of France looking on terror-struck.[30] The previous year's prints, made after St Vincent, were still selling. Nelson was one of the most widely depicted of men, and new songs came out every day on the battle of the Nile.[31]

When Parliament reassembled in November the praises were renewed In the Lords, Minto once again showed himself the most uncritical of all Nelson's friends, adding his voice to what he called 'the full chorus of all Europe, and of the whole world', and saying the action had contributed more to the salvation of the world than perhaps any other single event recorded in history. He said that he had witnessed with his own eyes the battle of St Vincent, in which his illustrious friend performed prodigies of valour never to be surpassed unless by the battle of Aboukir, for it was the peculiar privilege of his friend that there had been few actions of his which could be surpassed, unless by some other of his own. Nelson's was the sort of spirit which without an instant's hesitation could attack on one day the whole Spanish line with his single ship, and, on another, a superior French fleet moored and fortified within the islands and shoals of an unknown bay. What could he add to these two short facts?[32] Next day in the Commons Pitt proposed a motion to give Nelson and the next two male heirs of his body a pension of £2,000 a year, to start from the date of the battle. General George Walpole said he thought Nelson entitled to still higher honours than those bestowed on him. The argument that he had commanded only a detachment was absurd; it was the same as to say that more attention should be paid to rank than to merit. This expressed the popular opinion, but Walpole was the last man Nelson would have wanted to speak on his behalf. He was a younger son of the Walpoles of Wolterton with whom Nelson and Fanny had occasionally stayed, and Nelson's very distant cousin, but he was also a Foxite. Earlier that year he had stood as second for a man who challenged Pitt to a duel. Now, a few months later, it was he who stood up to take Nelson's part.[33] To Walpole's remarks, Pitt made a disingenuous reply. He said first that he would not enter into the question whether the rewards conferred on Nelson were equal to his merit. He would only say that his glory did not depend on the rank to which he might be raised in the peerage. His achievement would be perpetuated in the memory of his countrymen and all Europe. Nor did he think that it was the title of baron, viscount, or earl that could enhance his consideration with Englishmen. His claim to their gratitude and admiration would always rest upon the intrinsic merits of his victory. Having said this, Pitt side-stepped, and did say a few words on Walpole's point about paying attention to rank in the distribution of honours. This, he said, was not an absurd idea, and it was a matter not for the House but for the Crown (by which he meant the government). He would satisfy himself by saying that in no instance within his recollection, where the merits of the achievement were equal, had an inferior officer been distinguished by the same honour as an officer of higher rank.[34] So he was admitting that Nelson's rank had determined the reward. And victory or no victory, Nelson the saviour was still a very junior admiral. General Walpole's was not the only support Nelson would have found distasteful. Fox himself, in an address to the electors of Westminster in October, proposed a toast to Nelson and the gallant tars of Great Britain, but then also gave toasts to The Majesty of the Common People ['great applause'] and to The Cause of Liberty all over the World, toasts to which Nelson, with his unquestioning royalist views, could not have drunk.[35]

When she was in London, Fanny could attend the queen's receptions, called drawing rooms. At Bath she moved in the best society. A favourite quickstep was christened 'Lady Nelson's Fancy'. But she was spending most of her time at Round Wood with Nelson's father, and Round Wood had been a mistake. Even in summer it was exposed, being the highest spot for ten miles. She saw nobody, because there were no families to visit. She wished she had something cheerful to write to Nelson, but evidently did not, and complained it was difficult to get good food – no fish, and the poultry very bad. She was also anxious about Josiah, and, when someone from St Vincent's fleet said everyone spoke well of him, hoped it was true.[36] At this time, through her friends the Pinneys, she had a memorial tablet put up in Nevis to the memory of her father William Woolward, who died in 1779, and to her mother Mary. The inscription read: 'This tablet is erected by their only daughter Frances Herbert: who was first married to Josiah Nisbet M.D.: and since to Rear-Admiral Nelson: who, for his very distinguished services, has been successively created a Knight of the Bath; and a peer of Great Britain by the title of Baron Nelson of the Nile.' It was like Fanny to commemorate her parents, and in the inscription not only to recite with pride the achievements of her second husband, but also to remember her first. On the back of the draft of the inscription some ungenerous hand has written the date, October 1798, and these words: 'As her ladyship approved of this she must have been sensible that the less that was said of her father the better.'[37]

Fanny read the newspapers to Nelson's father, who could not do it for himself. When he wrote it was in the huge, childish letters of a man who could not see to write smaller. He was a pious man, and not one for heroics. Before the victory he had written a letter which Nelson did not receive until after the Nile: 'My dear Hor. I can never reflect upon the active part you are engaged in, upon the stage of life, without considering the many, that are your fellow travellers, unnoticed, some without abilities, others without being ever called forth, to any conspicuous actions, according to the poet's remark, in the village churchyard. Here, many a Hambden lies. [You] will, one day, be rewarded with unfailing laurels. You must increase, I am decreasing, waning away . . .'[38]

It is a letter whose sentiments were unlikely to be congenial to Nelson, whose appetite was always for the great stage of life, and already had his laurels. There were always those who were willing to set that stage for him. In the Commons on 11 December 1798 the young George Canning – then under secretary for foreign affairs, later to be foreign secretary and briefly prime minister – made a speech in which he said that though he still conceived it to be the paramount duty of a British member of parliament to consider what was good for Great Britain, yet he was against making a separate peace, considering that Britain's involvement in Europe was necessary. 'I do not envy the feelings of that man, who can look without emotion at Italy – plundered, insulted, trampled upon, exhausted, covered with ridicule, and horror, and devastation – who can look at all this, and be at a loss to guess what is meant by the deliverance of Europe.' His allusion was probably to the last sentence of the king's speech the month before, which said that the blow given at Aboukir to the power and influence of France, had afforded an opening which, if improved by suitable exertions on the part of other powers, might lead to the general deliverance of Europe. His may even have been the ministerial hand that wrote the king's speech.

As to Nelson, Canning made his own feelings plain in a note to Windham: 'Nelson only a baron – because under Ld St V's orders. Bad reason.'[39]

CHAPTER SIXTEEN

Fiddlers, Poets, Whores, and Scoundrels

FOR MORE THAN TWO weeks after the battle of the Nile the ruins of the French fleet lay in Aboukir bay, surrounded by the ships of Nelson's squadron, some in a scarcely better state. French boats came out from Alexandria under flags of truce to take off the sick and wounded prisoners. Nine of Nelson's own ships had suffered so badly that they had only two sound masts between them. His flagship, the *Vanguard*, was a wreck. Troubridge's *Culloden*, when she was scraped off her sandbank, was badly hurt in the hull and had lost her rudder. The shore of the bay, for ten miles, was covered with wreckage. To get a few nails or iron hoops, wandering Arabs on the beach were burning masts, gun carriages, and fragments of ships' boats.[1] The six soundest ships of the British squadron, and the six least battered of the French prizes, were patched and sent down the Mediterranean to Gibraltar under the command of Saumarez. The worst mauled of the French prizes – *L'Heureux, Le Mercure, Le Guerrier,* and *La Sérieuse* – were set on fire and blown up. Then Nelson in the *Vanguard*, with the crippled *Culloden* and one other ship of the line, left Aboukir for Naples. Two days out from Alexandria the clothes and belongings of the officers and men killed were sold at the mast, the proceeds to go to their families.[2] *Culloden* sailed so heavily, with a sail round her hull to stop her leaks, that all the ships were held back.[3] Nelson hoped that it might be soon, god grant, that the French army in Egypt would be destroyed by plague, pestilence, famine, battle, murder, and Mamelukes.[4]

The next two years were disastrous for Nelson. His passion for duty was by degrees subverted by a 'sacred promise' to protect the 'sacred persons' of the royal family of Naples.[5] He all but destroyed his reputation. He took a wrong course. But this wrong course could at first be justified by his admiralty orders, which were impossibly wide, adjuring him 'in every possible situation, to give the most cordial and unlimited support and protection to his majesty's allies'. After that, event followed event, and entangled him.[6] In the beginning he had not wanted to go to Naples at all. He could have taken the prizes to Gibraltar himself, but chose to stay with *Vanguard* and *Culloden*, which needed repairs that could be made only at Naples. Even as he set out, he wrote to St Vincent that his intention was to rejoin him, and then go on to England.[7] He was also distraught. Josiah Nisbet was not, as his mother had been told in England, spoken well of in the fleet, and St Vincent, in a letter Nelson received after the battle, plainly told him so. Nelson had always done everything he could for his stepson, but his reply to St Vincent was in a tone he had never used before:

> That part of your letter relative to Nisbet has distressed me more than almost anything in this world, as probably his mother's life and my happiness is wrapt up in this youth, if he drinks it is a vice not only lately learnt but which he could not have been taught by me, as to his company I can say nothing about it except that till you had the goodness to promote him he never was in any company but mine. As a seaman he is I can assure you the best of his standing of any I have ever seen, I wish I had half as good I could then sleep which I have not done since I left you, and as I owe my life to him I cannot but be interested for his having a good frigate, which I hope you will manage to give him.[8]

Nelson was saying that Fanny's life and his own happiness were wrapped up in the boy, that he had not slept for the three months since he left St Vincent, and he was asking for a doubtful officer to be made post. When Clarke and M'Arthur wrote their biography, they suppressed that part of the letter – perhaps out of delicacy towards Nelson, perhaps because it showed Josiah in a bad light – and it has not been used since.

One reason for Nelson's state of mind was his wound in his forehead.

He complained of it more often than he ever complained of the loss of his eye or his arm. When he told St Vincent that his head was 'splitting', it took him three attempts to spell the word. He said he was always sick and that if there was no fracture he was severely shaken.[9] Writing ahead to Hamilton, he was not sure he would live to see Naples, and later, having recovered somewhat, that he did not expect to stay there more than four or five days.[10] The passage to Naples took Nelson's crippled ships more than a month. Half way his old malaria returned to weaken him further. He told St Vincent that his life was thought to be past hope, never expected to see his face again, and that if St Vincent went home, he would feel unfit to continue in his command.[11] He could not have known that St Vincent's thoughts had already turned to home, and that he had written to the king asking for the rangership of Greenwich park, a sinecure with which went a beautiful house, so that the remains of his days could be pleasingly passed amidst the scenes of his youth, for he went to school in Greenwich.[12]

Meanwhile Naples had received news of the victory by Capel in the *Mutine*. Some English residents pulled out to her in a boat, and through a telescope Capel and his lieutenant were seen gesturing to them, depicting the blowing up of some ships and the sinking of others. When the news spread, Queen Maria Carolina wrote to her most frequent correspondent, Emma Hamilton, that the British flag was the finest in the universe, hip hip hooray, and she was mad with joy.[13] Lady Hamilton then wrote ahead to Nelson, saying the queen had fainted, cried, walked frantic about the room, kissed and embraced every person near her exclaiming, 'Oh brave Nelson, oh victor, saviour of Italy.'[14] When the *Vanguard* was towed into Naples on 22 September, boats and bands came out to meet her. King Ferdinand was rowed out several miles in his barge to greet Nelson, clasped him by the hand, and called him *Nostro Liberatore*. On shore, the bands had learned to play *Rule Britannia* and *See the Conquering Hero Comes*. 'You will not, my lord, I trust,' Nelson wrote to Spencer, 'think that one spark of vanity induces me to mention the most distinguished reception that ever, I believe, fell to the lot of a human being ... If God knows my heart, it is amongst the most humble of the creation, full of thankfulness and gratitude.'[15] To Fanny, he guilelessly wrote that Sir William and Lady Hamilton had come out to meet him too, and that she flew up and fell into his arms more dead than alive. She was an honour to her sex and a proof, he said, that even reputation might be regained, but it required a great soul. If this were not enough, he was then tactless about Josiah, who was with him, saying Lady Hamilton could make more of the boy, with all his bluntness, than any female. He then ended: 'Should the king give me a peerage I believe I scarcely need state the propriety of your going to court. Don't mind the expense. Money is thrash.'[16]

Among those who went out to meet Nelson was Cornelia Knight, daughter of an admiral, friend of the Hamiltons, and dilettante writer. She went on board the *Vanguard* with the king, sat down to breakfast with him and Nelson, and noticed a little bird hopping about on the table. The bird had come on board the evening before the action at the Nile and had remained there ever since, and was petted and fed by all who came near it for the sailors regarded the arrival of a bird as an excellent omen. She said it flew away soon after the ship reached Naples.[17] Nelson stayed with the Hamiltons, who received him with soft pillows and baths of asses' milk. Hamilton thought the deep wound on Nelson's forehead would surely have proved fatal if he had been without his hat, which was torn to pieces.[18] The hat was famous, and the king had asked to see it as soon as he met Nelson in the bay.[19] On Nelson's fortieth birthday, which fell a week after his arrival, eight hundred people came to supper at the Hamiltons', 1,740 danced at a ball, and a column was erected, bearing on its pedestal the inscription, 'Veni, vidi, vici'. Every ribbon and button had Nelson on it, sonnets and songs abounded, and a new verse was added to *God Save the King*, which began:

> Join we great Nelson's name
> First on the roll of fame
> Him let us sing . . .[20]

By then Nelson had met the Marquis de Gallo, the Neapolitan foreign minister, and derided his ribbon, ring, and snuffbox.[21] He promptly wrote to St Vincent, saying: 'It is a country of fiddlers and poets, whores and scoundrels.' He trusted that in a week they would be back at sea.[22] He was not. Another honour came his way, this time in the form of a most glorious decoration which he loved; and then he formed an ambitious and grandiose idea which he could not resist, and of which he became the protagonist.

The decoration was an aigrette, or chelengk, from the grand signior or sultan of the Ottoman empire. Since the French invasion of Egypt, which was Turkish territory, Turkey had been an ally. The chelengk was a blaze of brilliants crowned with a vibrating plumage of thirteen fingers or sprigs in allusion to Nelson's thirteen ships at the Nile. It had been taken from one of the imperial turbans, was to be considered the equivalent of the highest order of chivalry in Christendom, and was believed never before to have been conferred on an infidel. The whole turned on its centre by means of clockwork, the diamonds catching the light as they turned. Nelson wore it in his hat.[23]

The idea that captured Nelson was even grander. It was that Naples should take upon itself the salvation of Italy, invade Rome, and expel the French. It was a project entirely congenial to Nelson, but its begetter was Sir William Hamilton, and a large part of the blame for its catastrophic result must rest with him. He believed Italy could be 'cleared of these ragamuffins in a month's time', and that Nelson was the hawk to do it.[24] From the moment of his arrival in Naples, Nelson had been impatient of the procrastination of an enervated court. He told Lady Hamilton that the French were preparing an army of robbers and everyone knew that Naples was next marked for plunder, so why not press on with the war rather than wait for it? He was astonished the army had not marched a month before. The queen thought as Nelson did, but the other ministers, except for Acton, were for putting off the evil day, and doing nothing. Nelson wrote to St Vincent that the strong language of an English admiral telling Neapolitans the plain truths about their miserable system might do good. The king was attentive, and the queen truly a daughter of Maria Theresa. He said he was writing opposite Lady Hamilton, and therefore St Vincent would not be surprised at his glorious jumble of a letter. 'Were your lordship in my place, I doubt much if you could write so well: our hearts and hands must be all in a flutter.'[25] This was no more than a taking up by Nelson of the flirtatious tone in which St Vincent had written to Emma earlier in the year. It was the tone St Vincent employed again when he wrote to Emma, soon after Nelson's letter, saying: 'Ten thousand most grateful thanks are due to your ladyship for restoring the health of our invaluable friend . . . Pray do not let your fascinating Neapolitan dames approach too near him, for he is made of flesh & blood & cannot resist their temptation.'[26] Nelson was not at the time infatuated with Emma.

He ended the letter in which he spoke of hands and hearts a'flutter by saying, 'Naples is a dangerous place, and we must keep clear of it.' Two days later he wrote to Spencer that unless the king called for his help, Naples would see his squadron no more. And at the end of the year, two months on, he asked to be recalled to England. For a long time afterwards, Emma Hamilton was no more than a lively woman whose spirit he admired, and whose opinions he was all too ready to credit. His description of Gallo, for instance, almost word for word the same as Emma's, in a letter to him a few months previously, before he ever met the man.[27] This showed little judgment on his part, but that was all. He was much more infatuated with the divinity of the queen, whom he called a great soul and a great *king*.[28]

Nelson's orders to give unlimited support to Naples were too wide for sense, but there was one caveat. He was to cooperate actively with the Austrian and Neapolitan armies 'in the event of war being renewed in Italy'. War had not been renewed. That did not stop Nelson trying to renew it. He dined with the king and queen, he met the Austrian General Mack who had been sent to lead a Neapolitan army if it were decided to send one, and he conspired to make war. He attended what the queen called a 'session', with her, the king, Acton, and Mack. It was called a session and not a council because Gallo would have had the right to a voice in a formal council, and he was for peace.[29] Nelson did not try to hide this politicking from his commander-in-chief. He wrote and told him all about it, but at no time did St Vincent even hint to Nelson that he was going too far. The king at length appeared ready to act. He declared that he would march in three days with 30,000 troops, but then did not. Nelson, at another session, told Ferdinand he had a choice: either to advance, trusting to God, *épée à la main*, or remain quiet and be kicked out of his kingdom.[30]

Nelson and Hamilton got their war. On 23 November the king, Mack, and 32,000 men marched northwards. Nelson sailed with a squadron and 5,000 men to Leghorn to help the grand duke of Tuscany preserve his dominions and to cut off the French as they retreated.[31] The Neapolitan army had its difficulties on the march. General Mack spoke no Italian. Many of the rank and file were convicts and had no boots. Ferdinand entered Rome on horseback on 29 November and, among some moderate pillaging by his army and the drowning of some Jews in the Tiber, took up residence in the Farnese Palace, and issued a proclamation inviting the pope to return to the city which was, thanks to the miraculous San Gennaro, the patron saint of Naples, held by his Sicilian majesty. The Neapolitans throughout maintained the fiction that they were still at peace with France, which infuriated Nelson.[32] Troubridge was told by a Neapolitan general he had taken to Leghorn that his *orders* were not to make war, and bluntly asked in return whether the taking of Rome itself from the French was not to be considered a hostile transaction.[33]

By 5 December, having left Troubridge at Leghorn, Nelson was back in Naples, having given the queen his sacred promise to return as expeditiously as possible.[34] That same day the French resolved the matter of war or no war by massing their forces, reoccupying Rome, and taking the abandoned Neapolitan artillery, tents, baggage, and ten thousand prisoners. The Neapolitans fled from Rome as the French marched in. Ferdinand, Mack, and the remains of the army retreated south. Nelson told Spencer that some had run the first thirty miles; the Neapolitan officers had not lost much honour for, god knew, they had little to lose, but they had lost all they had.[35] By 15 December the French were invading Naples from the north, the situation in the country was critical, and all the people in it, Nelson believed, were traitors or cowards. The king had returned quietly to his palace.[36]

Nelson at the time was far from well. He told his brother William that his health had so declined that he would probably never take his seat in the house of peers.[37] He also felt done down. Emma by then had told him he ought to have been Duke Nelson, Marquis Nile, Earl Alexandria, Viscount Pyramid, Baron Crocodile, and Prince Victory.[38] He knew by then that he had been given only a barony, but did not receive Spencer's congratulatory letter on this honour until he returned from Leghorn to Naples in December. In his reply – and he could be a cutting writer – he said: 'I receive as I ought what the goodness of our sovereign, and not my deserts, is pleased to bestow ...'[39] He said nothing more than that publicly, but Emma Hamilton later put it about that he was grieved and indignant; that he would not have minded if they had left him as he was, but thought he merited more than a barony.[40] He even suspected that his commander-in-chief was delaying his letters from England. 'Lord St Vincent,' he told Fanny, 'is in no hurry to oblige me *now*. I am got he fancies too near him in reputation. In short, I am the envied man ...'[41] This was the first sign of animus towards his commander-in-chief. But he still believed himself to be the instrument of God. This is clear in another letter he wrote on his return from Leghorn, to the Ottoman grand vizier, thanking him for the chelengk. In it he said, referring to the battle of the Nile: 'I prayed that, if our cause was just, I might be the happy instrument of His punishment against unbelievers of the supreme and only true God – that if it was unjust I might be killed. The almighty took the battle into his own hand, and with his power marked the victory as the most astonishing that ever was gained at sea: all glory be to God! Amen! Amen!'[42]

The almighty had not taken the advance on Rome into his own hand, the attack Nelson so strongly urged had rebounded on him, and he had to fulfil his promise to protect the persons of their Sicilian majesties. He wrote to the British minister at Constantinople: 'I have the charge of the Two Sicilies intrusted to me, and things are come to that pitch, that I do not know that the whole royal family, and 3,000 Neapolitan émigrés, will not be under the protection of the king's [George III's] flag tonight.'[43] He did not say by whom the charge of the kingdom had been entrusted to him, but obviously he believed he had been chosen. The king and queen feared not only the advancing French but also those among the Neapolitian nobility who had liberal leanings, or were suspected of having them, and were promptly labelled Jacobins. The king suspected and imprisoned his own minister of war. The queen, remembering the fate of her sister Marie Antoinette in France, was all for leaving Naples, and was encouraged in this by Lady Hamilton. The king havered. To leave had its dangers. The *lazzaroni*, the mass of the people, hated the French and would fight, and would be reluctant to let their king go. The royal family was fortunate in having a second capital to fly to, Palermo in Sicily. But how would a flying royal family be received there? The king once again havered. Nelson prepared. He had only the *Vanguard* at Naples, so he recalled the *Goliath* from Malta, and the *Culloden* and the rest of Troubridge's squadron from Leghorn. Neither he nor Hamilton would go to the palace for fear of being held hostage by Jacobins, so Emma became the go-between. She and the queen corresponded so frequently that their letters were not suspected. The queen wanted to escape not only with her life and those of her numerous family, but with much of the treasure of the kingdom.[44]

And she would not trust her own navy to take her. Two Neapolitan ships of the line lay in the bay, under the command of Caracciolo, but she preferred to go with Nelson. Caracciolo took this as an affront. Miss Knight, at dinner with him, thought she never saw a man look so utterly miserable; he ate nothing, and did not even unfold his napkin.[45] For a week, night after night, Emma helped to remove jewels and thirty-six barrels of gold from the palace to the embassy, marked them 'Stores for Nelson', and got them to the ships. 'By many such stratagems I got those treasures embark'd,' she said, 'and this point gain'd, the king's resolution of coming off was strengthened; the queen I was sure of.'[46] By 18 December the queen was sending pathetic notes to Emma. 'Here are three more coffers and a box ... it's some linen for all my children on board ...' She hoped it was all right to send such a lot; her tears flowed unceasingly; she did not think she would recover, but would sink into the grave. She sent a sample ticket she would give to those she specially wanted to accompany her on board. It was the size of a visiting card, showed three cherubs, and a tree overhanging a decorative tomb, and bore the inscription, in her own hand, 'Embarque je vous prie. M.C.'[47]

The *Vanguard*'s journal shows the bustle on board. 'Sailmakers making cots for the royal family. Painters painting the wardroom, and offices under the poop; getting ready for sea and getting off the valuable effects of her Sicilian majesty in the night time ... Smuggling on board the queen's diamonds &c.'[48] On 19 December Nelson told Acton to hurry up, and next day received this reply: 'As the money is not shipped yet and secured under your protection, their majesties have suspended until tomorrow night 21st their embarcation.'[49] Next day the mob was out in Naples. A messenger from the Austrian court was taken for a Jacobin, murdered, and his body dragged by the legs under the windows of the palace. The *lazzaroni* had got wind of the impending flight and had to be reassured by the king and queen's promises made from a palace balcony.[50] The queen then sent Emma yet another note in her eloquent French, written as she spoke it, carelessly and without punctuation or accents: 'Je suis dans l'etourdissement et desespoir ... je ne sais ou j'ai la tete ce soir j'enverrai quelques autres caisses ... et croyez moi la plus malheureuse des femmes mere et reine mais sincere amie – Charlotte.' She was bewildered and in despair, she didn't know what she was doing but would send some more luggage, and believe her the unhappiest of women, queens, and mothers but a sincere friend. On the back of this letter, Emma scribbled: 'God protect us this night.'[51]

That night they did get off, by a trick. Kelim Effendi, who had been sent by the Turkish sultan with Nelson's chelengk, had been staying at the Hamiltons' house, and Sir William gave a farewell supper for him, from which he and Nelson slipped away unsuspected and embarked the royal party. There is the spectacle of Nelson entering the palace by a secret passage and bringing out the royal family: that was Sir William Hamilton's version. Emma's account is that she herself conducted them through a subterranean passage to the boats waiting at the jetty, and that she and Nelson had previously explored a passage leading from the queen's chamber to the sea.[52] Three barges and a cutter, with their men armed with cutlasses, awaited the fugitives at the wharf. First, at half-past seven, came the king, queen, four princes, three princesses, Acton, and others. Two hours later came the king's confessor and his surgeon, various servants, nurses, a priest, two cooks, and a whole retinue of others. All these were taken on board the British ships. The rest, including lesser princes and marquises, were taken to Caracciolo's ship. The least fortunate, including cardinals and ambassadors of countries unfriendly to France, ended up in transport ships; Nelson had arranged that cardinals displaying their red stockings should instantly be received on board.[53] Hamilton said the *Vanguard* 'had richer cargo on board than was ever risked before in one bottom'.[54] Nelson valued it as two and a half million pounds sterling, four times his estimate of the value of *L'Orient*'s cargo. Ferdinand was taking with him not only the pictures and other treasures of his palace but the gold of the kingdom which he had confiscated to pay for the war.[55] The queen may have lost her head but the king kept his. Before he left he sent a message to his kennel-master ordering him to ship the royal dogs to Sicily, where they would be needed for hunting.[56]

The weather was so bad that the men of war and twenty transports could not get out of the bay for another day and night, and then on the passage it blew harder than Nelson had ever known since he went to sea. *Vanguard*'s topsails were blown to pieces, she laboured horribly, the passengers were prostrate with sea sickness and in fear of death, and the king's confessor broke an arm when he fell out of his bunk. On the morning of Christmas day Prince Albert, Maria Carolina's youngest child, aged six, died in Emma Hamilton's arms. Emma was splendid.

Nelson said he and the royal family were under an obligation to her. She provided them with her own beds and linen, became their slave, and did not sleep for the five nights they were on board.[57] Sir William was stoical. At the height of the storm he was found in his cabin with a loaded pistol in each hand, saying he was resolved not to die with the guggle guggle guggle of salt water in his throat.[58]

Vanguard anchored at Palermo at two the morning of Boxing day. Before daylight, Nelson himself took the queen and the princesses ashore. At nine in the morning the king landed to be received 'with loudest acclamations and apparent joy'.[59] He was looking forward to good hunting on the royal estates round Palermo.

CHAPTER SEVENTEEN

The Sicilifying of My Own Conscience

NELSON AT PALERMO IN the first month of 1799 was as near to despair as he ever came. He thought the loss of Naples a dream. He despised the wavering councillors of the king who held three cabinets a day and did nothing. He confidently expected to die soon, and yet in his impatience would say one day that he would go and retake Naples, and on the next that he had had enough of it all and wanted to return to England. But the king and queen refused to allow him to move, which meant he would not allow himself to move from them. Apart from all this, his pride was hurt by what he perceived as a slight from the admiralty. 'As a piece of my command,' he wrote, 'is lopped off by the great S.S.S. there can be no occasion for a Nelson.'[1]

S.S.S. was Captain Sir Sidney Smith, a knight grand cross of the order of the sword of Sweden and therefore referred to contemptuously as the Swedish knight, who had been sent out to Constantinople to show the flag to the Turks, Britain's new allies. Nelson had learned this only on the passage from Naples to Palermo. Smith was a post captain junior to several in Nelson's squadron, but he knew the Turks, was the brother of J. Spencer Smith, the minister at Constantinople, and, to add to the confusion, was made joint minister with him. He was given a new 80-gun ship of the line, more splendid than anything Nelson had, arrogated to himself a commodore's broad pendant, and flew the royal standard on state occasions. It was a piece of necessary theatre. He and his brother were co-signatories of the new anti-French alliance between Britain, Turkey, and Russia. Nelson thought this took from his own consequence and, referring to himself in the third person, stated that if it were necessary for any sea officer to sign the treaty, that sea officer should have been Nelson.[2]

'I do feel, for I am a man', he wrote to St Vincent, 'that it is impossible for me to serve in these seas with the squadron [S.S.S.'s ship and two others in the Levant] under a junior officer: – could I have thought it! – Is it to be borne? Pray grant me your permission to retire ...' St Vincent, who had himself objected to Smith's coming out, mollified Nelson, telling him to take Smith under his command but to mortify him as little as possible, and hoping the greatness of his mind would keep up the body and induce him to stay with the royal family which he had preserved from the fate of their late royal relations in France. Nelson went on and on complaining of Smith's 'parade and nonsense', and made himself very clear to Smith himself: 'Your situation at the Porte [part minister, part sea officer] makes it absolutely necessary I should know who writes to me – therefore, I must direct you, whenever you have ministerial affairs to communicate, that it is done jointly with your respectable brother, and not mix naval business with the other, for what may be very proper language for a representative of majesty, may be very subversive of that discipline and respect from the different ranks in our service. A representative may dictate to an admiral – a captain of a man of war would be censured for doing the same thing; therefore you will see then propriety of my steering clear between the two situations. I have sent you my orders, which your abilities as a sea officer will lead you to punctually execute.'[3]

A smaller irritation for Nelson at this time, though he did say it was one that half killed him, was Josiah. He wrote to Fanny with real grief that her son had nothing good about him and must soon be broken. He did not know that his appeal to St Vincent after the Nile had had its effect, and that St Vincent had already written to him that he had the 'inexpressible pleasure' of making Josiah, at the age of eighteen, post in the *Thalia*. Nelson wrote again to tell Fanny the news, saying he hoped Josiah would deserve it, but more had been done for him than for any young man in the service, and he had made the worst use of his advantages. St Vincent, in a private letter to Nelson, departed from the inexpressible pleasure of his official dispatch: 'I hope the *Thalia* will not be thrown away on Captain Nisbet, she being the finest frigate I have, and the best man'd.'[4]

Nelson frequently despaired of his health. Both to St Vincent, and to Davison in London, he wrote that he could quit life with a smile. To Lady Parker, wife of Sir Peter, he wrote: 'A few weeks will send me to that bourne from whence none return: but god's will be done ... You who remember me always laughing and gay, would hardly believe the change ...'[5] He told his friend Admiral Goodall that Palermo was detestable and all were unwell and full of sorrow. 'Soon, very soon, we must all be content with a plantation of six feet by two, and I probably shall possess this estate much sooner than is generally thought ...' This was a time for writing to old friends, and to Locker at Greenwich, an older friend even than the Parkers, the man who taught him that if he laid a Frenchman close he would beat him, he wrote, with the underlying sense that victory at the Nile had not achieved what it ought to have achieved, that revolutionary principles were now so prevalent that no monarchical government was sure of lasting ten years. It was in this state of mind that Nelson had his portrait painted, to send to the sultan of Turkey in thanks for the chelengk. The painter, Leonardo Guzzardi, is known for nothing else, but made a most accomplished portrait of a worn and wounded man. The right eyebrow lacks hair, where it was struck by the fragments of stone at Calvi which deprived him of the sight of that eye. His hat is pushed far back on the head to avoid the wound on his forehead sustained at the Nile, and the triangular scars of this wound are clear.[6]

Nelson at Palermo had become, as he put it, almost a secretary of state, constantly writing to St Petersburg, Constantinople, Vienna, Venice, Trieste, Smyrna, Florence, Leghorn, Minorca, and to St Vincent and Spencer. He told Minto everything was going to the devil, that the queen was out of favour and in despair, and Acton on the king's side, or rather the king on his. As a newcomer to Palermo noticed at the end of January, the king was enjoying excellent shooting, the court was attending masked balls, and Nelson feared that if nothing were done Sicily would be lost as well as Naples. This newcomer was Charles Lock, newly appointed consul general to Naples, who had just arrived from England.[7] His appointment to a Bourbon court was inept. He brought with him his wife Cecilia, who was not only a cousin of Charles James Fox but also stepsister of Lord Edward Fitzgerald, an

Irish patriot and martyr who had been shot by the British. The consul
and his wife were naturally taken for Jacobins.

The years 1798 and 1799 are a tragic period in the history of
Naples, and many Italians feel aggrieved that events of that time
are generally seen in England as no more than a backdrop to the
doings of an English admiral, English hero though he may be.[8] There
is some truth in this. What happened was complex. After the feckless
flight of king and court, Naples slid into anarchy. The nobility and
the small learned classes favoured a republic, but in no sense did they
want a popular revolution. The interest of the *lazzaroni* was rather
in plunder than in this form of government or that. The mob sacked
palaces, released prisoners from jails, seized and occupied the city's
castles, and murdered those suspected of Jacobin leanings. When the
French came, these same *lazzaroni* fought bitterly, killing a thousand
Frenchmen and losing four thousand of their own number before the
city fell. The French general then declared a puppet Parthenopean
republic, Parthenope being the ancient name of the city, and appointed
a government of lawyers, ecclesiastics, poets, orators, and professors of
ancient Greek, mathematics, and botany. Young people talked about
liberty and equality. A tree of liberty was raised. A newspaper of the
republic was published, the *Monitore*. Its editor, Eleanora Pimentel,
convinced that the populace (*plebe*) should be elevated to the people
(*popolo*), proposed that Punch and Judy shows should be persuaded to
represent republican subjects and sing patriotic songs.[9]

Nelson's entire instinct was to loath the republic, which he always
called not the Parthenopean but the Vesuvian. What he really wanted
to do was lay a Frenchman close. Detachments from his squadron
were blockading Malta and cruising off Alexandria hoping to get at
the French transports which still lay inside the harbour, but he was kept
at Palermo by his devotion to a queen who for her own safety beseeched
him to remain; the closest he could get to a Frenchman was to take the
islands in the bay of Naples. He acquired the written authority of the
king for this, and then sent Troubridge to do it. Troubridge's orders
were to blockade the city, seize the islands of Procida, Ischia, and
Capri, induce the loyal islanders to take up arms against the French,
and extirpate the rebels. These were the king's orders which Nelson
passed on with the advice that speedy rewards and quick punishments
were the foundation of good government.[10]

Troubridge proved himself a good extirpator. On his first day, at Procida, he found a priest who 'ought to have his head off', and put thirty-five prisoners in irons. On Ischia he heard a priest was preaching revolt, hunted him down with Swiss troops, and asked for a judge to try him and other miscreants on the spot, saying eight or ten should be hanged. Having been sent his judge, Troubridge thought him the poorest creature he ever saw. '[He] talks of it being necessary to have a bishop to degrade the priests, before he can execute them. I told him to hang them first, and if he did not think the degradation of hanging sufficient I would piss on the d—d jacobins carcass, and recommended him to punish the principal traitors the moment he passed sentence, no mass, no confession but immediate death, hell was the proper place for them.' He heard that on the mainland there was a royalist called the Great Divil, alias the Angel, whose 'jolly party' had cut to pieces some women and their escort who had tried to leave Naples for Rome. 'I sincerely hope it is true, if we could muster a few thousand good soldiers, what a glorious massacre we should have . . .'[11]

Troubridge flourished. One of the king's loyal subjects sent him the head of a Jacobin, which he apologised for not sending on to Nelson since the weather was very hot. He fell out with a royalist general, kicked him out of his ship for refusing to land his men, and said the king would never do well until he hanged half his officers. He had, however, declined to furnish the judge with a hangman since he saw the drift: the Neapolitans wanted to throw all the odium on the English. By then Troubridge was having some trouble with the Swiss guards sent from Palermo, who seditiously murmured at the high cost of food. He sentenced them to death, drew them up in a square with their eyes bound, but then remitted the sentence at the last moment and sent some to the galleys. 'One of them', he wrote, 'was almost gone, before it was finished. I trust it will have a good effect.' Troubridge had also picked up news of Caracciolo, whom he knew well from Naples the previous year. He had crossed with the royal family to Palermo, but had been allowed to return to Naples to prevent his property being seized by the republicans. Troubridge first heard that he had been obliged to mount guard at the palace as a common soldier. Then, although he intercepted a letter signed by Caracciolo as head of the republican marine, he was assured by Neapolitan sailors that he had been forced to act as he had. Late in May, Nelson, though thinking

Caracciolo at heart no Jacobin, wrote to Spencer that he had been fool enough to quit his master when he thought the case desperate. Then Caracciolo's gunboats fired on a royalist frigate in the bay, and it was evident he had changed sides.[12]

After Troubridge was recalled to Palermo in the middle of May the command in the bay of Naples devolved on Captain Edward Foote, of the frigate *Seahorse*, to whom Nelson wrote on 6 June: 'Your news of the hanging of thirteen jacobins [at Procida] gave us great pleasure: and the three priests [sent to Palermo to be degraded] I hope return in the *Aurora*, to dangle on the tree best adapted to their weight of sins.' Nelson also wanted to shoot the general whom Troubridge had ejected from his ship. '*I am mad*,' he told Acton. 'Lay me at the feet of their majesties; tell me how I can best serve them. Only degrade this HOG and my life is at their disposal ...' He even wanted to hang Baron Thugut, chancellor of Austria, accusing him of 'caballing' against Ferdinand and of being a traitor to Europe. He seriously wrote as much to his friend Minto, who had recently become British minister in Vienna, saying this advice came from a seaman who spoke the truth and shamed the devil.[13]

From Palermo the king had sent out two men who might help restore the lost part of his kingdom. One was the Chevalier Antonio Micheroux, who had been Neapolitan minister in Venice. He was sent to hurry up the Russians who had promised to send 12,000 troops; he did procure some Russians and stayed with them until they eventually appeared in Naples. The other man sent out was Cardinal Fabrizio Ruffo. Nelson, who distrusted him from the beginning, called him a swelled-up priest.[14] He was never a priest but had been treasurer and minister of war to Pope Pius VI, who made him cardinal deacon, and his family owned vast estates in Calabria. The king sent him there in February, giving him no soldiers but a commission styling him his *alter ego*, and powers of life and death. Ruffo was a feudal viceroy. He exhorted bishops and priests to preach a crusade, offered exemption from taxes on earth and eternal rewards in heaven, his followers scented loot, and in this way he amassed an army of peasants, brigands, and pillagers as he went, from Bagnara in the deep south, to Matera, to Avellino, to Nola, gaining strength all the while. It was a good time to counter-attack, since Austria had at last declared war on France, and Austrian and Russian successes in northern Italy had compelled the French to withdraw most of their forces from Rome and Naples. By mid-June, Ruffo's Christian Army of the Holy Faith, as it was known, straggled in from the south and east and reached the gates of Naples. The French had left the Parthenopean republic to its own devices, leaving only a garrison of five hundred at the fort of St Elmo, which dominated the city. The remnants of the republicans had taken refuge in two castles by the waterfront, the Nuovo and Uovo. Ruffo's men wore in their caps a white cross and the red cockade of the Bourbons, but they were not an army but a holy mob, whom the cardinal admitted he could not govern or suppress. He wrote to Acton: 'They have dragged here and shot at least fifty in my presence. They have also wounded at least two hundred, whom they also brought here naked. Seeing that I was horrified by such a spectacle they comforted me, saying that the dead were really prominent scoundrels and that the wounded were bitter enemies of the human race.' He said that on the pretence of hunting Jacobins, this mob and eighty cursed Turks were robbing and plundering, all the time shouting, 'Long live the king'.[15] The Turks were there to fulfil a promise from the Sublime Porte to help restore Ferdinand. Russia, having promised 12,000 soldiers, had sent four hundred, but they were easily the best disciplined troops in the city. That was the scene in Naples. A Calabrian rabble led by a cardinal, Turks led by no one, a Neapolitian royalist mob motivated by greed and bloodlust, and a regiment of Russians led by an Irish mercenary called Baillie and accompanied by Micheroux, a Neapolitan diplomat with a French name. Out in the bay were the remains of the royal Neapolitan fleet, commanded by a German called Thurn. Also out in the bay was Captain Foote who, although willing to see a few Jacobins and priests hanged, was urging clemency. 'With all submission to the better judgment of my superiors,' he wrote to Nelson, 'I beg leave to recommend the offer of a free pardon, because when throwing dice for a kingdom, personal animosities, jealousies and every trifling object should be disregarded.'[16]

But back in Palermo the queen said a massacre would not cause her the slightest grief, and Acton remarked that the cardinal seemed to be in a disagreeable situation and that his majesty would accept the kind offer of Lord Nelson to present himself before Naples.[17] Nelson, then, had made the *offer*. He had long wanted to get at the Naples insurgents, but had been held back by the appearance in the Mediterranean of the

French fleet from Brest which had evaded the blockade of that port and which, it was feared, might join with a Spanish fleet from Carthagena. This combined fleet might then descend on Minorca. Or it might go to Malta, go on to Alexandria, take off the stranded French army, and then attack Sicily or Naples. All was uncertainty, and at this point, early in June, St Vincent went home ill, leaving the Mediterranean command to Lord Keith. Nelson decided to run the risk of leaving Sicily undefended for a brief period – he thought eight days would do it – and sailed to Naples for two reasons – because he considered the best defence of the Two Sicilies would be to place himself alongside the French if they were there, and also to restore the king to his throne.[18] So on 21 June he sailed from Palermo, with Sir William and Lady Hamilton, the queen having told Emma that all they needed was 'a second Aboukir'.[19] On 24 June Nelson appeared with his entire squadron in the bay of Naples.

In the ten days before his arrival the rebels in the Nuovo and Uovo castles had begun to negotiate terms with Ruffo. Perhaps they were encouraged by the surrender of the republican garrison at Castellamare, on the bay twenty miles southeast of the city. There the rebels had handed over the castle to Foote in exchange for the protection of the British flag, and he honoured this agreement.[20] The castles at Naples then began to treat for terms, and an armistice was agreed while the talks went on. Ruffo told Foote the castles showed reluctance to surrender to an ecclesiastic but might yield to him. 'The conditions are simple and plain enough', he wrote. 'It is granted to the French to be carried back by sea to France ... and those who are not French are allowed the liberty of following them, and to embark with their effects, but at their own expense. There is the whole of the matter.'[21] Micheroux and Baillie, who were in charge of the Russian troops, the only disciplined force in the city, received a draft capitulation from the castles and took it to Ruffo, who to their surprise signed it as it was. Micheroux later said the terms were generous, but he was inclined to compromise in order to save a beautiful city from horrible disasters. In any case, the French squadron at loose in the Mediterranean might appear in the bay at any time, so it was prudent to take the surrender while it was offered.[22] He told Ruffo that the rebels wanted the English to act as guarantors of the convention, and sent it to Foote, who signed it at about midnight on 22 June, though with a formal protest against anything that might be contrary to the rights of his Britannic majesty.[23] He later explained that this protest had nothing to do with the substance of the treaty, but was made solely because he had to sign last, under the names of the Turkish and Russian commanders, which might not be proper as he was acting as the representative of his king.[24] The terms were indeed generous. The castles would be delivered up to the Neapolitan, English, Russian, and Turkish commanders; the rebel garrisons should march out with the honours of war, their persons and property would be respected and guaranteed, and they should either embark on the ships (polaccas) prepared to take them to Toulon or stay at Naples without being molested.[25] Foote instructed the captain of the sloop *Bulldog* to take under his protection the polaccas to carry the Neapolitan republicans destined for Toulon, and to get a proper receipt for them on arrival.[26] The treaty was complete. Then Nelson arrived.

While he was still forty miles from Naples he received reports, at sea, that an armistice of twenty-one days had been granted to the French and the rebels; that if they were not relieved by their friends within that time they should be allowed to evacuate Naples in this triumphant manner. The reports were wrong. There had been a much shorter armistice, which had since been succeeded by the treaty. This confusion between armistice and treaty is at first understandable, but Nelson persisted in it. And having received these false reports at sea, he wrote an 'Opinion', addressed to no one and apparently a memorandum to himself. 'I fancy,' he wrote, 'the question need not be asked whether, if the French fleet arrived this day in the bay of Naples, whether the French and rebels would adhere one moment to the armistice? "No!" the French admiral would say, "I am not come here to look on but to act." And so says the British admiral; and declares on his honour that the arrival of either fleet, British or French, destroys the compact . . .' As to rebels and traitors, they must instantly throw themselves on the clemency of their sovereign, for no other terms would be allowed them.[27]

This would have been fair enough if there had been only an armistice. But Nelson learned the true position when he entered the bay and called Foote on board his flagship, the *Foudroyant.* It was 24 June, a Monday. Foote told him he had signed a formal treaty, a capitulation. He explained, reasonably, that he had considered the cardinal knew the king's mind. Nelson at once made a signal to annul what he called the

Eighteenth-century Naples. Centre top is fort St Elmo (23), occupied in June 1799 by the French garrison. The Neapolitan rebels embarked from the forts of Uovo (11, left foreground) and Nuovo (4, centre foreground). The royal palace (1) is to the left of Nuovo. Galleys and a polacca lie in the inner harbour. Engraving by Guiseppe Pietrasante.

truce, and Hamilton at once wrote to Acton in Palermo. 'Here we are', he said, and recounted that Nelson highly disapproved of the shameful capitulation – in his letter Hamilton did call it a capitulation – which Ruffo had granted, and that Nelson had commissioned him to tell the cardinal so, and that he must be ready at daybreak to cooperate with the British fleet in 'completing the business'.[28]

What happened that day and on the succeeding few days has to be patched together from as many as six sources – from the letters of the protagonists, some written at the time and others two or three weeks later; from reports written to exculpate the writer or gratify the recipient; from the journals of observers who could say what they heard and saw but knew nothing of what went on in the minds of the protagonists; and from recollections published many years later. A few things are certain, some are probable, and some unlikely, but together they paint a picture. The matter has to be gone into in detail, because at the heart of it is the question of Nelson's good or bad faith.

The log of the *Foudroyant* records that many officers came on board that first afternoon. There also came on board the Hon. John Rushout, a friend of the Hamiltons, who had been in Naples during the days of the republic. There is a question how much reliance can be placed on his evidence, because he gave it long after the event, but it is consistent with what is known from other sources. He described Nelson on the *Foudroyant* as being in a great passion, which Hamilton tried to assuage. He said Nelson told him to go ashore and tell them he would batter down the city the next day, a message he asked to be excused from delivering, and that Hamilton then entreated him not to mention what he had seen. This is consistent with Hamilton's letters of the period, in which he several times takes credit for cooling Nelson down, and for stemming 'the torrent of his impetuosity'.[29] Here was Nelson being as hasty as he had some years before told an Old Bailey judge he was. And battering down a town was custom and practice with him; he had threatened to batter down Grand Turk, Bastia, and Santa Cruz, Tenerife. It was a phrase he used. Besides which, battering was what his captains, Troubridge and Ball, were asking Ruffo to do that evening. They took him a copy of the 'Opinion' which Nelson had written at sea. He rejected it. He referred to the rebels as patriots, which Nelson, when he heard, considered a prostitution of the word. He said Nelson could break the agreement if he wished; he was tired of the situation.

Troubridge then asked the plain question: 'If Lord Nelson breaks the armistice, will your eminence assist him in his attacks on the castles?' To which Ruffo answered: 'I will neither assist him with men or guns.' The discussion was bitter on both sides and nothing was agreed about the rebels.[30] But one other significant event did take place that day, if we take Emma Hamilton's word for it, because no one else reports it. She says that the chief of the *lazzaroni*, one Pali, an old friend, came to her and said he had 90,000 men 'ready at the holding up of his finger', but that only twenty were armed; and that Nelson gave them a large supply of arms. The figure of 90,000 can be shrugged off as exaggeration, but for Nelson to give the man weapons would have been extraordinary.[31]

Before we go on, it is best to make clear which of the actors in the drama was writing to whom, and with what authority. In Palermo there were the king, queen, and Acton; at Naples Nelson, Sir William Hamilton, and Lady Hamilton. Depending on the weather, a letter took two to three days either way. Since the flight to Palermo, the queen's influence had diminished, the king having blamed her for encouraging the rash attack on Rome. The real power now lay with the king, but the queen, by virtue of a clause in her marriage settlement, remained by right a member of his council. Whether Acton was on the king's side or the king on Acton's, it was always Acton who wrote on their behalf, and always to Hamilton, in English; and Hamilton replied to Acton. The queen wrote to Emma, in French, often asking her to convey this or that to Nelson: before the *Foudroyant* left Palermo she asked Emma to act as her interpreter to him.[32] Emma considered she had been sent as the queen's 'deputy', because she spoke the Neapolitan dialect and was very popular; every night she sent a messenger to Palermo with all the news, and the queen gave her orders the same way. In three weeks of June and July 1799, Emma wrote at least twenty-two letters to the queen.[33] Nelson required a translator for everything. He had no Italian and little French, and the negotiations were in those languages. Emma's role of interpreter was important, and very likely persuasive, but there is little to show that she was already his mistress. It has often been asserted that she was; one important piece of evidence adduced has been an explicit letter from Nelson to her which, if it had been written at that time, would settle the matter. But it is undated, and although it has been attributed to 1799, internal evidence shows beyond a doubt that it

was written in 1800. We shall come to it later. The important point is
that she did not, at Naples in June 1799, have a mistress's power over
him. He admired her. She had influence with him, which some believed
to be great, since several petitions to him were directed through her,
but his actions cannot be extenuated by an infatuation with her.

The day after Nelson's arrival, Tuesday 25 June, he wrote to his
second in command in the bay, Rear-Admiral Duckworth, saying that
he and the cardinal had begun their career by a complete difference
of opinion. 'He will send the rebels to Toulon – I say they shall not
go. He thinks one house in Naples [which might be destroyed if the
fighting continued] more to be prized than his sovereign's honour.'
He ordered his ships to be anchored not more than two-thirds of a
cable from each other, and brought in the gunboats from Procida.[34]
The British squadron was anchored in close line of battle from the
Arsenal towards Portici. There were nineteen ships of the line, half as
many again as Nelson had at the Nile. De Nicola, a resident of the city
who kept a journal, recorded this, calling it a magnificent spectacle;
but it was all over the city that the terms of the capitulation were not
published because the king would not treat with rebels. The question,
wrote De Nicola, was now one of saving the city from the injury which
the despair of the rebels might inflict upon it.[35] Micheroux suggested
that he and Ruffo should meet Nelson personally. This was agreed.

So came about the famous meeting on board the *Foudroyant* between
Nelson, Ruffo, and the two Hamiltons. Ruffo was saluted with thirteen
guns, but there the courtesies ended. Nelson refused to deal with
Micheroux at all, and only Ruffo was admitted to the great cabin.
Nelson and Hamilton mention the interview briefly in their accounts,
neither saying Emma was there. Hamilton reports that the cardinal said
he had acted as he had to prevent the capital becoming a heap of stones.
Another account, inspired if not dictated by Emma, reports the meeting
at much greater length and more vividly, perhaps because of the large
part it shows her to have played. The dispute ran very high. Hamilton
interpreted between Nelson and Ruffo until after two hours he was
exhausted. Emma then took over, and Nelson continued pacing the
cabin. 'The pleasingly persuasive voice of her ladyship, delivering the
manly sentiments of his lordship, made no impression on the cardinal.
He would not submit to reason, nor his lordship to anything else.'
Nelson suddenly put an end to the argument, saying that since he

found an admiral was no match for a cardinal in talking, he would
write. The cardinal retired in disgust.[36] What Nelson wrote was brief
the treaty – and he did here call it a treaty – could not be carried into
execution without the approbation of his Sicilian majesty.

Then the allied commanders, Baillie for the Russians, Achmet fo
the Turks, and Micheroux, made a strong protest to Nelson: 'Tha
the treaty of capitulation of the castles of Naples was useful, necessary
and honourable ... seeing that the deadly civil and national war wa
ended by that treaty without further bloodshed, and that it facilitated
the expulsion of the common alien enemy from the kingdom. That a
it had been formally entered into by the representatives of the said
powers, an abominable outrage would be committed against public
honour if it were to be violated; and, beseeching Nelson to recognise
it, they protested their fixed determination to execute it religiously
holding responsible before god and the world whoever should dare to
impede its execution.'[37]

Nelson in the meantime had sent to the republicans in the castles
of Uovo and Nuovo a statement that he would not permit them to
leave those places or embark. The Russian troops, whose presence
the rebels found reassuring, were withdrawn from outside the Uovo
Some rebels who were with the French in the fort of St Elmo
suspecting Nelson would break the treaty, proposed to the French
commandant that he should hang the hostages whom Micheroux
had left there as a guarantee that the terms would be honoured
The agreement had been that these hostages should remain with the
French garrison until the polaccas carrying the Neapolitan republicans
reached Toulon. One of the hostages was a cousin of the Chevalier
Micheroux, so he also had a personal reason for wishing the capitulation
to be carried into effect.[38] That evening Ruffo sent a note to Massa
the commandant at Nuovo, saying that though he and the other
allies regarded the treaty as sacred and inviolable, Nelson refused
to recognise it; he suggested that the rebels there should walk out
into the city. This would have been dangerous with the royalist mob
still roaming round, but that evening a trumpeter went round the
city warning the public against molesting anyone leaving the castles
on pain of being shot.[39] Massa refused the offer and insisted on the
performance of the original terms. All day there had been boats
and music in the bay, and crowds shouting 'Viva Il Re'. After dusk

much of the city was illuminated, but Naples was a dangerous place that night.

Early next morning, Wednesday, there was a general panic at a rumour that the forts would be attacked. Thousands of people streamed out of the city to Portici and other places on the sea shore, for fear of being caught in the middle of a bombardment.[40] Then came a turnaround. Nelson, after what Hamilton called cool reflection, authorised him to write to Ruffo saying Nelson was resolved to do nothing which might break the armistice the cardinal had granted to the castles.[41] The word armistice was again being used. The cardinal seems to have asked for some confirmation of this sudden change of mind, because Nelson himself then wrote to Ruffo, saying, '... I will not on any consideration break the armistice entered into by you, I hope your excellency will be satisfied that I am supporting your idea'.[42] This message was conveyed by Troubridge and Ball.[43] Micheroux said he never knew what induced Nelson suddenly to change his mind, but at about ten in the morning the cardinal gave him orders to replace the Russians (under the command of Baillie) and, to reassure the rebels, sent him the documents from Nelson, presumably Hamilton's letter and Nelson's.[44] This is corroborated by Rushout, who said he was at breakfast when the commander of the Russian forces, whose name he thought was Baillie, came in and said Nelson was now quiet and that he had been ordered to carry the capitulation into execution, at which all rejoiced.[45] At Uovo the rebels were gathered together and asked how many wanted to go to Toulon and how many to go free into the city; ninety-five chose Toulon and thirty-four to stay in Naples. Micheroux brought the Russians back to Uovo. He had Nelson's papers with him, but the rebels knew him and relied on his word alone, so he did not need to show them. From six to half-past eight in the evening all those from Uovo and Nuovo who wanted to go to Toulon embarked on the polaccas, and five hundred English marines occupied the forts.[46] Hamilton and Nelson watched from a boat as the marines landed. When they took the castles a *feu de joie* went up over the city. The republican flags were taken to the cabin of the *Foudroyant*, and in the city the British and Neapolitan flags were displayed in many windows. 'In short,' said Hamilton, 'I am now in the greatest hopes that Lord Nelson's coming here will be of infinite service to their Sicilian majesties. A little of my phlegm was necessary between the cardinal and Lord Nelson or all would have blown up the very first day and the cardinal has written to thank me and Lady Hamilton.'[47]

With the republicans now in the polaccas in the bay, let us turn to the trial and execution of Caracciolo. The classic account is Clarke and M'Arthur's, which says a price had been put on Caracciolo's head, that he was found in the mountains, and brought on board the *Foudroyant* in a wretched state, disguised as a peasant and with his arms bound; he appeared to be about seventy (he was forty-seven) Hardy, Nelson's flag captain, who knew Caracciolo well, ordered his fetters to be taken off and offered him refreshment, which he declined Nelson immediately ordered Count Thurn, the senior Neapolitan sea officer in the bay, to assemble a court of five other Neapolitan officers and try Caracciolo on the charge of firing on Thurn's frigate, the *Minerva*.

The best witness is Hamilton, who mentions Caracciolo in four letters to Acton, two of which he wrote while the court martial was in progress. Two days before Caracciolo was brought on board Nelson and Hamilton already knew he had been taken. Hamilton had written: 'Caracciolo and twelve of the most infamous rebels are this day to be sent to Lord Nelson. If my opinion is relished they should be sent directly to be tried by the judge at Procida ... Caracciolo will probably be seen hanging at the yard arm of the *Minerva*, Neapolitan frigate, from daybreak to sunset, for such an example is necessary ...'[48] Then, the place for the trial having been settled on as the flagship, he wrote again: 'Such a sight we have seen this morning! Caracciolo with a long beard, pale and half dead, and never looking up, brought bound on board this ship, where he now is with ... other villainous traitors .. It is shocking to be sure, but I that knew their ingratitude and crimes, felt less than many of the spectators.' Then at the end of his letter he wrote: 'P S – Caracciolo's trial is now going on, by officers of his Sicilian majesty's marine. If condemned, as I suppose, the execution will soon follow. He seems half dead already with fatigue – wanted to be tried by British officers.'[49] Later, just after midday, he wrote another letter: 'I have just time to add that Caracciolo has been condemned by a majority of the court martial, and Lord Nelson has ordered him for execution this afternoon at 5 o'clock at the foremast yard arm of the *Minerva*, and his body thrown into the sea. Thurn represented it was usual to give 24 hours for the care of the soul. Lord Nelson's orders remain the same, although I wished to acquiesce with Thurn's opinion. All is for the best . . .'[50]

Nelson was commander of the British and Neapolitan fleets, and so had the authority to act as he did. But he had tried Caracciolo with the greatest of haste, on board a British ship. He and the other officers knew Caracciolo well, had fought alongside him, and had been entertained on board his ship. Caracciolo was one of those who went out into the bay with the king to welcome Nelson the day he came to Naples after the Nile. Yet Nelson showed him not the slightest civility or humanity. Thurn, the president of the court, was the man whose ship Caracciolo was charged with firing on, and was besides his personal enemy. Caracciolo was undoubtedly guilty. It was public knowledge that he had fired on the *Minerva*, but there were no witnesses at the trial. The sentence of death was not unanimous, but by a majority. Even at the request of Thurn, Nelson refused a day for Caracciolo to prepare himself: it was all of a piece with his willingness to hang mutineers on Christmas day. And to the death sentence of the court Nelson added his own touch, that the body was to be thrown into the sea, that is to say without Christian burial, just as Troubridge at Procida had wanted his rebels hanged without time for mass. After Nelson had signed his death warrant, Caracciolo twice asked the lieutenant who had been placed in charge of him to intercede with Nelson, first asking for a new trial, and then that he might be shot since the disgrace of hanging was dreadful to him. Nelson refused both requests.[51]

The trial took place from ten to twelve in the morning, in the wardroom of the *Foudroyant*, which is said to have been open to any officer. There was no transcript, which is strange because at all British naval courts martial minutes were taken, sometimes fifty pages and more long, and sent to the admiralty. There are however three accounts of the proceedings. The first, short and formal, is by Thurn. He said that Caracciolo in his defence had stated that he had served the republicans because they had threatened to shoot him if he did not, and that though he had fired on Neapolitan troops he did so believing them to be rebels; he admitted that he had given written orders to oppose the king. The second and third accounts, both much fuller, were not published until forty years later, and both contain assertions that cannot be true. One is familiar, and has often been quoted, and if that is worth giving, so is the other.

The familiar account is by G. S. Parsons, who was signal midshipman on the flagship. In 1843, as a retired lieutenant, he published his reminiscences. Some of them are very lively – as when at a royal ball in Palermo a group of midshipmen armed with their ceremonial dress-dirks charged the royal Neapolitan footguards and scattered them. Parsons, though it appears he knew no Italian, gives the fullest account of Caracciolo's defence. He said he had not deserted his king; the king rather had deserted him and all his subjects, collecting everything that could be converted into specie into five hundred casks and fleeing with it to Palermo to live in luxury, after which for lack of pay the army was then disbanded and the French occupied Naples. Who was then the traitor, the king or himself? He asserted that his destruction was predetermined, that the court was anything but a court of justice, and that his blood would be on the heads of its members and of their children. Parsons describes the hanging, with seamen clustered like bees on the rigging to watch, consoling themselves that it was only an Italian prince who was hanging, 'a person of very light estimation compared with the lowest man in a British ship'.[52]

The unfamiliar account is by the same Mr Rushout who reported that Nelson wanted to batter down the city. He became Lord Northwick in 1800, when he inherited that title, and made his statement in 1846, when he was seventy-six. He was not senile. He lived for another thirteen years. What he said was taken down by Antonio Panizzi, then chief keeper of printed books at the British Museum.[53] The statement does reflect badly on Nelson, and Panizzi was an Italian patriot, who would naturally have sympathised with the Parthenopean republic. But against that, Rushout had always been an admirer of Emma Hamilton, whom he first met in 1792. He was grateful for her kindnesses to him, praised her warmth and accomplishments, and possessed two paintings of her, one of her as a young girl by Romney and the other an enamel after Vigée LeBrun's depiction of her as a bacchante.[54] He deposed that Nelson had asked him to be present at the court martial because neither he nor anyone else aboard spoke Italian. He went in, bowing to Count Thurn but not to the other Neapolitan officers, who did not mix in good society. Thurn frowned and ordered the room to be cleared. Rushout made himself known, but Thurn repeated his order for strangers to withdraw. When the court was opened again, Rushout learned that two officers apart from Thurn had been for executing Caracciolo, and two

NELSON
THE YOUNG
SEA OFFICER

This portrait, by Francis Rigaud,
shows Nelson in the uniform of
a post captain, but it was begun in
1777 when he was a lieutenant of
eighteen. He first saw the portrait
four years later in 1781, when he was
invalided home from the Caribbean,
and told the artist to 'add beauty'.
Rigaud changed the uniform, and
added the fort of San Juan, Nicaragua,
in the right backround, but left the
features as those of the fresh young
man he had originally begun to paint.

Right:
Boreas *at Antigua*
in 1787, with
four other ships of
Nelson's squadron,
on the day when
William Clark,
seaman, was con-
demned to death
for desertion. He
was later pardoned.

H.M.S. SOLEBAY
Captain Holloway
H.M.S. MAIDSTONE
Captain Saurine
H.M.S. RATTLER
Captain Collingwood

H.M.S. BOREAS
CAPTAIN HORATIO NELSON
The Sentencing of Able Seaman William Clark
English Harbour, Antigua, B.W.I.
16th April, ½ past 11, 1787.

H.M.S. PEGASUS
Captain H.R.H. Prince William Henry

The West Indies
AND AFTER

Above: a watercolour of Nelson painted by his friend Cuthbert Collingwood at Antigua in 1784, the year before he met his future wife Frances Nisbet.

Right: a pencil sketch of Frances Nelson done by Daniel Orme in 1798.

Chatham royal dockyard, where Victory *was built. It was there that Nelson joined the* Agamemnon *in 1793, at the start of the French wars.*

The capture of the Ça Ira, a French 80-gun third rate, in Hotham's action of March 1795, the first fleet action in which Nelson fought. His ship, Agamemnon, 64, is shown on the right raking the dismasted Ça Ira, which later struck her colours. Painting by Nicholas Pocock.

EARLY YEARS
IN THE
MEDITERRANEAN

Nelson commissioned this
miniature in oils from an
unknown artist at Leghorn
in 1794, and sent it home for
Fanny. He did not think it a
strong likeness. Fanny liked it better.
She lent it to be engraved after the Nile,
and then kept it for the rest of her life.

The romantic hero
Nelson after he lost his right arm at Santa Cruz, which is shown burning in the backround. Mezzotint by W. S. Barnard, May 1798, after Lemuel Abbott.

The caricature
The Hero of the Nile, wearing the chelengk and scarlet pelisse given to him by the Turkish sultan. Coloured etching by James Gillray, December 1798.

The battle of the Nile *A spirited but inaccurate engraving published by Edward Thompson in October 1798, when news of the victory reached London. The fort of Aboukir was more than a mile away and played no part in the action, and Bruey's flagship, L'Orient, blew up in darkness, late at night.*

NAPLES, and the two women who changed Nelson's life

Left: Portrait by Leonardo Guzzardi which Nelson commissioned at Palermo in 1799 to send to the Turkish sultan in thanks for the chelengk, which he wears. His hat is pushed back on his forehead so as not to irritate the wound he received at the Nile, and his hand indicates a scene of that battle.

Below: Emma Hamilton in two of her classical Attitudes, engraved in 1794, after Frederick Rehberg.

Below left: Maria Carolina, Queen of Naples, daughter of Empress Maria Teresa, and sister of Marie Antoinette.

'LIKE THE PRINCE OF AN OPERA'

Right: On the overland journey home from the Mediterranean to England in 1800, Nelson was painted in pastels by J-H. Schmidt, court artist at Dresden. He displays the two gold medals of St Vincent and the Nile, and, strangely, wears the stars of his Turkish and Sicilian orders above that of his British order of the Bath.

Below: Isaac Cruikshank published 'Smoking Attitudes' two weeks after the lovers' return to London. Emma says: 'Pho, the old man's (Hamilton's) pipe is always out, but yours burns with full vigour.' And Nelson replies: 'Yes yes I'll give you such a smoke. I'll pour a whole broadside into you.'

Emma, also by Schmidt. Nelson had this picture in his cabin at Copenhagen and called it his Guardian Angel.

The Füger portrait

This, the most penetrating study of Nelson, and the only one in civilian clothes, was painted in Vienna in 1800 by the Austrian court painter and miniaturist, Heinrich Friedrich Füger, on a commission from Nelson himself. Füger kept this canvas for himself and delivered to his client a version with the features slightly less severe, showing him in gold-braided full-dress uniform with all his medals and orders, and against a brighter backround, yellow rather than grey. Neither Nelson nor Emma ever mentioned either version, and this one was not shown in England until 1859.

The Nelson Touch

Nelson explaining his plan of attack before Trafalgar. 'It was,' he wrote, 'like an electric shock, some shed tears, all approved, it was new, it was simple ... ' Collingwood, his second in command, is on Nelson's right, and among the captains are Hardy, Berry and Fremantle. This engraving by W. M. Craig was published on the day of Nelson's funeral.

"NELSON"
Cast from Nature after his death
on board the "VICTORY."

Above: a reputed death mask, said to have been made on board Victory.

Left: The Death of Nelson. Gillray's cartoon shows Emma as Britannia, George III as Capt. Hardy, and the Duke of Clarence as a kneeling seaman.

State funeral in St Paul's. Captured Spanish and French ensigns hang to left and right. Engraving after Augustus Pugin.

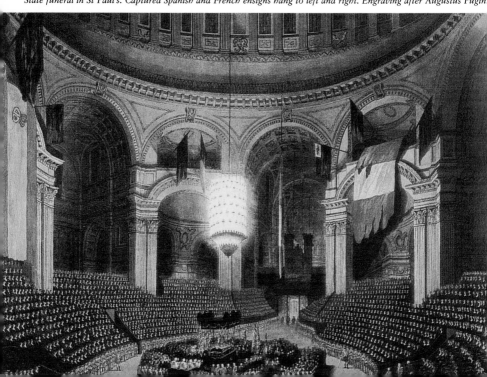

for respiting him until the king's pleasure was known. That afternoon Rushout and some officers were pacing the deck, waiting for dinner, when Caracciolo came up from below to be transferred to the Italian frigate. He threw himself into an almost kneeling position and said: 'Sono condamnato injustamente', or something of that sort. Rushout said he dined with Nelson that day, when all his most distinguished officers spoke openly and strongly against the execution. Nelson was agitated and threatened some of them for their interference. When the gun announcing the execution was heard, Emma Hamilton rose with a glass in her hand and thanked God for the death of a traitor. Rushout also said that he had previously helped Foote arrange the terms for the rebels, and that when Ferdinand did eventually come to Naples he said he would have spared Caracciolo's life.

Let us return to the rebels who on Wednesday had left the castles and embarked on the polaccas to go to Toulon. The following day, 27 June, Nelson wrote to the lords of the admiralty congratulating them on the possession of the city of Naples, although, he said, the French were still in St Elmo. The moment the city was a little quieted he would bring guns against that fort. He was about to send Troubridge to cut down the tree of anarchy and burn it before the king's palace.[55] Hamilton, writing to Acton that same morning, called it the tree of abomination which they were cutting down, and said – and this is the first intimation of anything like this – that the rebels on board the polaccas could not stir without a passport from Nelson. And then he wrote this sentence: 'However, we shall now act perfectly in concert with the cardinal, tho' we think the same as we did at first as to the treaty his excellency made before our arrival. If one cannot do exactly what one would wish, one must make the best of a bad bargain and that Lord Nelson is doing . . .'[56] In other words, they were stringing the cardinal along.

That same day De Nicola wrote in his diary about the amusement the mob had given itself shooting at the tree while it was still burning, and then reported a rumour that if the French in St Elmo fired on the city, one of the French prisoners on board the English ships would be killed for every shot. This seems the wildest of rumours, but Hamilton did write to Acton saying it was a good thing the principal rebels were in their power in the polaccas, 'for we may cut off a head for every ball the French fire'.[57]

On Friday, 28 June, letters arrived from Acton and the queen in Palermo. Acton wrote that Ruffo had exceeded his orders, that no terms were to be allowed to the 'scoundrels in the castles [and] all the people of their ridiculous government', and that the cardinal should do whatever Nelson thought proper.[58] All trust in the cardinal was at an end, he was even suspected of being a Jacobin, and the king recommended his capital to the brave and loyal Nelson. The queen wrote to Emma that the rebels were entirely at the mercy of their offended, betrayed, but merciful king; that the women were to be treated in the same way as the men, without pity; and finally that she recommended Nelson to treat Naples as if it were a rebellious Irish town.[59] De Nicola wrote in his diary that the English admiral was in a rage, and that the English fleet had manoeuvred nearer the polaccas to prevent anyone from leaving. 'The criminals', wrote Hamilton, 'will remain at the mercy of his Sicilian majesty in the midst of our fleet. Lord Nelson's manner of acting must be as his conscience and honour dictate, and I believe his determination will be found best at last ... Tomorrow we attack the castle of St Elmo. God prosper the cause. The die is cast; we must abide by it as well as we can.'[60]

Two days later, on 30 June, Hamilton received from Acton two letters which he was to make use of if necessary. The first was for Ruffo, unsealed so that Hamilton and Nelson could read it, and ordered the cardinal to Palermo to explain himself. The second was for Nelson, giving him powers to arrest the cardinal if he refused to obey this order.[61] Hamilton replied that he and Nelson thought there was no occasion to come to extremities with the cardinal, though he was protecting 'some of the most conspicuous of noble jacobin families'. They thought it best to 'keep smooth' with him. As Hamilton told Acton: 'The cardinal dines with Lord Nelson today, but we keep it a profound secret, that we have any letters, from his eminency – so that your excellency understands all those packets lay dormant in Lord Nelson's writing box, and will do so unless there should be a necessity of making use of them ...'[62] Nelson said in two letters, to the king and to Acton, that it had been a 'toss-up' whether he arrested the cardinal or not, and that he hoped the most notorious rebels he had in irons in the fleet would meet the same fate as Caracciolo.[63] Thus Hamilton and Nelson played a double game with the cardinal.

In the city the pillage and massacres continued. De Nicola, who was a sober observer, wrote in his diary that on 1 July the mob burned the bodies of two Jacobins and ate the roasted flesh.[64] The bombardment of St Elmo commenced. From the prisoners on board the polaccas, those who had held any office in the republic continued to be searched out and taken to the ships of Nelson's squadron. Captain Foote was sent to Palermo in the frigate *Seahorse* to bring the king to Naples. The king preferred to make the passage in a Neapolitan frigate, so as not to hurt the feelings of those Neapolitan sea officers who had remained loyal to him. Foote took the opportunity to remind Acton that he had given his word to the rebels at Castelamarre that they should go free, and this was agreed, although Acton had earlier thought of exiling them to Africa.[65] From Naples, Emma Hamilton sent the queen lists of Jacobins, making additions in her own hand. One name she added was that of Domenico Cirillo, her friend for many years, and her physician and the queen's.[66] Cirillo was perhaps the best known of all the Neapolitan Jacobins: he had been professor of botany at the University of Naples, was a friend of Linnaeus, and had been elected a fellow of the Royal Society in London before he was thirty. On the back of one of the queen's letters, fulsomely thanking her for sending three such lists, Emma wrote: 'This from my friend whom I love & adore yes I will serve her with my whole heart & soul my blood if necessary shall flow for her Emma will prove to Maria Carolina that an humble born Englishwoman can serve with zeal & a true soul even at the risk of her life.'[67] From the polaccas, Cirillo wrote to Emma, saying that he had lost everything, and asking her in the name of God to intercede for him. She had already denounced him, and he hanged. Pitiful letters came to her, addressing her as 'Signora excellentissima', 'Bella milady', 'Excellenza', all begging for help. One, signed simply Giuseppe, began: 'Cara amica: sono in una terribile agitazione . . .' Nelson was irritated that her time was taken up with 'excuses from rebels, jacobins, and fools'. One appeal Emma did respond to was from John Jolly, a marine sentenced to death for drunkenly striking and threatening to shoot an officer. He addressed her, he said, from the first step to the grave, condemned after a fair trial, but she could save him for he knew her delight in doing good. 'Oh, madam . . . This is a letter from the dead to the living. You may be now the giver of life. The brave are always good. Lord Nelson will pardon, if you apply for mercy.' Nelson did pardon the man.[68]

Ferdinand at last arrived in Naples on 10 July, and the following day saw his royal standard raised on the fort of St Elmo, which had just surrendered. He did not set foot ashore in the month he stayed, holding his levees on the quarterdeck of the *Foudroyant*. He occupied the great cabin all but for one room where Emma received his lady visitors. 'He calls me his grande maitresse,' Emma wrote to a former lover. 'I was near taking him at his word.'[69] Two days after the king's arrival the corpse of Caracciolo is supposed to have risen from the bay to accost him. This has been stated as fact ever since Clarke and M'Arthur told the story, which was later elaborated by Parsons, but it has been so dressed up that it sounds more like legend. One French source even has the corpse swimming towards the shore.[70] The usual story is that the body was sighted from the *Foudroyant*, which was standing out to sea; that Hamilton tactfully told the king that Caracciolo could not rest until he came and implored his majesty's pardon; and that with the king's permission the body was allowed a Christian burial. Clarke said Captain Hardy told him the body had floated in spite of the 250 pounds of shot attached to it. Parsons, writing forty-four years later, gives details of Caracciolo's grey hair streaming in a light breeze and his eyes staring from their sockets, but he says it was a priest who had the adroitness to tell the king the tale about forgiveness sought. One strange thing is that this memorable incident is not mentioned by Harrison, who wrote three years before Clarke and M'Arthur and, was, moreover, retailing Emma Hamilton's own account of events. It is a good story. But even if it were true, the body would have been in the sea for two weeks, and unrecognisable.

From the other end of the Mediterranean, Keith wrote to Nelson to tell those Neapolitans not to be too sanguinary, since cowards were always cruel.[71] But the executions of those taken from the polaccas and the British men of war had already started in the squalid piazza Mercato. And the queen, who had been left behind in Palermo, had her own way with Jacobins. 'The two Vesuvians, being rebels, I have had burnt by the hands of the executioner at the four quarters, and the ashes thrown into the sea to produce an effect. We begin to feel the heat very much.'[72]

On 1 August, the first anniversary of the Nile, the British squadron and Sicilian ships in the bay were lit up, and when at dinner on the *Foudroyant* the king proposed Nelson's health a twenty-one gun salute was fired from the castles and from the ships. 'Amongst others,'

Nelson wrote to his wife, 'a large vessel was fitted out like a roman galley. On the oars were fixed lamps and in the centre was erected a rostral column with my name, at the stern elevated were two angels supporting my picture. More than 2,000 variegated lamps were fixed round the vessel, an orchestra was fitted up and filled with the very best musicians and singers. The piece of music was in great measure my praises, describing their distress, but Nelson comes, the invincible Nelson, and we are safe and happy again.'[73]

How does Nelson come out of all this?

He had the power, as commander-in-chief of the Neapolitan fleet, to court-martial Caracciolo once the man was in his grasp. But nothing suggests he had any authority to hunt him down ashore, as he was hunted. Hamilton's cold letter to Acton shows Nelson knew he would be brought aboard. But if it is assumed that Caracciolo came lawfully into his hands, what of the conduct of the trial and the manner of the execution? As Hamilton's letters again show, he expected Caracciolo to be tried and hanged the same day. Hardy treated the prisoner decently, having him unbound and offering him refreshment. Nelson tried him instantly, signed his death warrant, refused to shoot rather than hang him, and carried out the execution that day, not even waiting until the pleasure of the king, in whose name he was acting, could be known. He also added to Caracciolo's sentence the ignominy of his body being thrown into the sea, for which he had no authority whatever. It was hasty, pitiless, and unnecessary.

Nelson's treatment of Caracciolo is distasteful. His conduct towards the rebels in the castles is a graver matter. First he denied there was a treaty, calling it an armistice. When he learned from Foote that it was a treaty, he annulled it, or rather broke it, even though it had been entered into by all the allied powers, even though the rebels had insisted on a British signature because they trusted it, even though it had been signed by the officer he had left in command of the British ships in the bay. And even though, when he left Foote in command, he had written to him: 'I need not pretend to point out what your local situation enables you so much better to judge than myself.'[74] Nelson's breaking of the treaty was politically inept. If he had waited while Ruffo let the rebels go, nothing would have been lost. Nelson wanted to finish the business himself, by battering down the town, and achieved nothing except to keep the city in chaos for two more days while the rebels remained in the castles. Ruffo was no angel, but he was subtler. He knew the Neapolitans as Nelson did not, and was acting more sanely in wanting to get the republicans quietly out of the city. They were no danger to the state except as martyrs. He had, as it turned out, no power to treat with rebels as he had done. His original commission had given him the power of a viceroy, but the king did later tell him to give no terms to rebels.[75] This, however, was a matter between Ruffo and the king, and did not affect the validity of a treaty entered into by Naples, Russia, Turkey, and Great Britain, and a treaty which, as was admitted even by Hamilton, had in some measure been put into effect before Nelson arrived.[76]

But Nelson first declared the treaty null and then, two days later, on the morning of 26 June, suddenly stated that he was resolved to do nothing which might break it. The rebels thereupon came out of the castles and embarked on the polaccas in which, far from being taken to Toulon, they were imprisoned. Ninety-nine of them were later hanged. The question is, were they tricked into coming out of the castles, and, if so, by whom?[77]

Nelson always maintained that the rebels came out to throw themselves on the mercy of the king. He told Keith so. To Spencer he wrote that 'the rebels came out of the castles with this knowledge . . .'[78] It is unlikely that they came out to be hanged, and there is a mass of evidence, much of it still lying in Nelson's papers, that they believed, and continued to believe, that they had embarked to go to Toulon. There were, in all, about 180 petitions from the rebels to Nelson or Hamilton. On 29 June, Giuseppe Albanese wrote from the polaccas to Ruffo, Micheroux, and Baillie saying the weather had been favourable for departure for two days but no victuals had been taken on board for the passage, that he had seen with great grief a search made on board the vessels for Cirillo, Piatti, and other republicans, who had been taken on board the English ships, and that the whole garrison looked to Ruffo and the others for an explanation and for the execution of the treaty.[79] In early July, Don Mario Pagano, a professor of law aboard one of the polaccas, making the best of his situation, cheerfully remarked that in exile at Toulon he would set up a fencing school, and share the profits with his fellow exiles.[80] On 3 July Placido Moreno complained to Nelson from polacca No. 6 that a visitor had gone through his luggage looking for money, thrown his and his wife's clothes into the filthy hold, and taken his pair of English pistols. When he embarked he had been promised that his property would not be touched, and he asked for the restitution of the pistols, giving his word of honour he would not use them but lock them at the bottom of his trunk.[81] A man who hopes the English admiral will give him back his pistols is not a man who has surrendered with the prospect of being hanged. On 9 July, L'Aurore, former commandant of Nuovo, wrote from the *Zealous* reminding Nelson with the deepest respect that it had been agreed that he and his garrison should be taken to Toulon, that he was ill and his property had been pillaged, and asking to be sent to Toulon.[82] And so on.

There are many other petitions – from Ricciardi and Davanzati, and from Landini who asks to see Nelson for a few minutes – but one more will speak for them all. It is addressed to Nelson by those on board *La Stabia*, unsigned and undated, but evidently written towards the end of July when it must have been only too evident what was happening. The petition is in two columns, in French on the left and Italian on the right. It is written on behalf of many, and asks Nelson, before he leaves their shores to gain new victories, to listen to those who will be in the deepest misery if he closes his heart to the noble and generous feelings which distinguish his illustrious nation. They say they have been the victims of a seduction. They have previously sent him several petitions, but do not know whether he received them. 'Will the invincible Nelson be generous no longer? All Europe has its eyes on you ... Add to your triumphs the sweet satisfaction of holding out a helping hand to us unfortunates who will never cease from praying to heaven for the happiness of one of the greatest heroes of Great Britain.'[83]

So there can be no doubt that the rebels were brought out of the castles by deceit, but who deceived them? Ruffo may have had a hand in it. When, on 26 June, Troubridge and Ball took to him Nelson's declaration that he would not on any consideration break the armistice it must have seemed an extraordinary change of mind, and one source – the cardinal's secretary writing thirty-seven years later – says Ruffo suspected bad faith but was unwilling to argue and sent Micheroux to arrange the evacuation of the castles.[84] Perhaps Ruffo did have his suspicions. But even if he did, and was prepared to wash his hands of the matter, the bad faith he suspected still had to have come from Nelson and Hamilton. Nelson was implacable. He may very well have convinced himself that any action was honourable which saved what he saw as the king's honour. He was not the king's viceroy, as Ruffo was, and until he received Acton's letter on 28 June he did not have the power to overrule Ruffo, but he did have previous written powers from the king 'to extirpate, as is urgent, that nest of malefactors ... [by] every means that may best tend to attain that necessary end'.[85] But, as he told Fanny early in their acquaintance, he could not wear two faces. Common tact was beyond him, let alone finesse. Finesse was not beyond Hamilton. It was Hamilton's business. And it as well here to consider the comparative positions of admiral and ambassador. The squadron was Nelson's. But as he himself had firmly stated earlier that year to Sidney Smith, a representative – the king's minister or ambassador – could indeed dictate to an admiral.[86] Hamilton was the political master, though he was too wise to make that clear to Nelson in as many words. As Hamilton eventually reported in his dispatch to the foreign secretary: 'We contrived to keep everything going on decently, by supporting the king's vicar general [Ruffo] until we had answers from their Sicilian majesties at Palermo, to whom we had painted exactly the state of affairs, and the confusion at Naples, preventing at the same time his eminency from doing any essential mischief ...'[87] And then there are his more freely written letters to Charles Greville, his nephew and heir. 'Nothing but my phlegm could have prevented an open rupture on the first meeting between Cardinal Ruffo and Lord Nelson ... We have had the glory of stepping between the king & his subjects to the utility of both. In short, the king's fleet & a little good management & temper has placed their Sicn. Majesties once more on their throne of Naples.'[88] And again, in a later letter to his nephew: 'The king has thank'd often Emma and me seeing that without us the Two Sicilies would probably have been lost again ... I admire Lord Nelson more every day – but it requires some temper to stem the torrent of his impetuosity, even against his best friends, & in that respect he is just enough to own that I have been of infinite use to him. In short Ld Nelson & I with Emma are the *tria juncta in uno* that have carried on affairs to this happy crisis.'[89]

But in the end Hamilton's finessing did him and Nelson and the interests of Britain no good. For Nelson to have annulled the treaty left a bad taste. But for him *first* to annul a treaty and *then* take advantage of it to lure the rebels on to the polaccas, where he imprisoned them, and indeed to have made his own ships prisons for the principal republicans, was indefensible both morally and in law. Talking all the time about honour, he shamed himself by dishonouring what he called a shameful treaty. Hamilton's finessing brought an end to his own career, which he had thought it would crown, and irretrievably damaged Nelson's reputation. The British government recalled Hamilton and treated him with courteous contempt. Nelson was too valuable to dispense with. He ever after asserted the right and justice of what he had done, even telling the Duke of Clarence that he had done it with god's blessing.[90] He did once, four years later, in a letter about the cost of the dukedom of Bronte which Ferdinand gave him, admit the consequences to himself of what he had done, though not its injustice. 'I paid more attention to another sovereign than my own; therefore the king of Naples' gift of Bronte to me, if it is not now settled to my advantage, and to be permanent, has cost me a fortune, and a great deal of favour which I might have enjoyed, and jealousy which I should have avoided. I repine not on these accounts. I did my duty to the Sicilifying of my own conscience, and I am easy.'[91]

In the bay of Naples, what did the officers and men of the English squadron think of what they saw? They knew nothing of the politicking between Ruffo, Nelson, and Hamilton. But in a Neapolitan high summer, without proper food or shelter, the republicans and their families were crammed into polaccas close to British ships, some of them for a month, in full view. Midshipman Parsons, writing many years later, still remembered young Italian women, whose families had been murdered, lying prostrate on the decks. Parsons is not to be trusted for dates or details, but he probably is when he remembers, he s sorry to say, how these women were treated on the polaccas.[92] Later, at Copenhagen, when it served his purpose, Nelson protested that when the Danes became his prisoners, he became their protector.[93] This did not occur to him at Naples. His treatment of prisoners there was all of a piece with the manner in which he ordered Troubridge to deal with the garrison at Capua: '... as degrading terms as it is in your power to give them – no covered wagons, no protection to rebels.'[94] And there is the evidence of Charles Lock, the new British consul at Naples. He arrived in Naples on 3 or 4 July, rather aggrieved that Hamilton had not even told him two weeks before that he was going o Naples on Nelson's flagship. Lock was not an admirable man. He had hoped to make £4,000 a year out of victualling the squadron, but Nelson's captains and their pursers preferred to do it themselves. Lock thought Emma Hamilton grasping and vulgar, and later in the year fell out badly with Nelson. But in July, when that dispute was in the future, he wrote home to his father: 'You will hear with grief of the infraction of the articles convented with the Neapolitan jacobins and of the stab our English honour has received in being employed to decoy these people, who relied upon our faith, into the most deplorable situation . . . but *the sentiment of abhorrence expressed by the whole fleet* will I hope exonerate the nation from an imputation so disgraceful. And charge it where it should lie, on the shoulders of *one or two.*'[95]

Some of the fleet did share such feelings even if few expressed them. One of the most remarkable of all the petitions sent to Nelson and Emma Hamilton is from the officers of the *Leviathan*. Having sought in vain some means of alleviating the miseries of the unfortunate family of Piatti, whom they had on board, they unanimously asked Emma to intercede with the king. They hoped that, with the help of her benevolence, the Piattis might have the good fortune to experience the king's pardon. This petition was signed by the first lieutenant, all six other lieutenants, the master, and the surgeon, virtually the entire wardroom. And the *Leviathan* was the flagship of Rear-Admiral Duckworth, Nelson's second in command.[96]

The officers' hopes were not fulfilled. The bankers Domenico and Antonio Piatti, father and son, were hanged on 20 August in the Piazza del Mercato in company with a bishop and Eleanora Pimentel who had had such faith in the politically educative value of Punch and Judy shows.[97]

The Naples business was not finished. It followed Nelson for the rest of his life, and beyond. Charles James Fox, as we shall see, took the matter up, and Captain Foote persisted in a stubborn defence of the treaty he had concluded. Nelson's conduct has remained a matter of controversy. Broadly, Italian and French writers have unanimously condemned Nelson, or Nelson and Hamilton. The severest Italian critic says flatly that the queen behaved like a tigress and Nelson like a pirate.[98] The French, from Lamartine and Alexandre Dumas the elder, have said Nelson shamed his country. Some English authorities have held that Nelson was blameless. As many others, from Southey onward, have impugned his honour. Perhaps the most disinterested analysis is by a German, Hermann Hueffer, who concludes by asking from which point of view – legal, moral, or political – the conduct of the British in Naples is most to be condemned. A survey of these conflicting opinions and some details of the vast literature are in Appendix A.

The controversy continues. In January 1999, in a three day conference at Naples on the bicentenary of the Parthenopean republic, Professor Gerardo Marotta, director of the institute of philosophical studies in Naples, said Nelson had shamefully reneged on his promises, and Professor Gieseppe Galasso that Nelson's actions had left an indelible stain on his reputation. Professor Antonio Gargano, on BBC radio, called Nelson a war criminal. At a seminar on 11 September 1999 at the Royal Naval Museum, Portsmouth, Dott. Carlo Knight, from Naples, argued that Nelson could be pitiless but was straight, and had been misled by Hamilton, in 'an eighteenth century minuet', into acting as he did. In the same year the novelist Barry Unsworth, who won the Booker prize with a previous work, published *Losing Nelson*, in which the narrator, an admirer of Nelson intent on writing a biography which would exonerate his hero, gradually loses his faith in Nelson and with it his own reason, and goes mad in Naples after visiting the castles of Uovo and Nuovo.

CHAPTER EIGHTEEN

Inactive at a Foreign Court

FERDINAND DID NOT FEEL safe in Naples, reconquered though it was, and returned to Sicily. While the junta at Naples got on with hanging one hundred and twenty of the Parthenopean republicans, ninety-nine of them from among those detained in the polaccas or in British ships, Nelson in Palermo received from the grateful king, in thanks for the restoration of his kingdom, a sword and a dukedom.[1] The sword, with a jewelled hilt worth four thousand guineas, was that given to the king by his father, traditionally with the following words: 'With this sword I conquered the kingdom which I now resign to thee. It ought in future to be possessed by the first defender of the same; or by him who shall restore it to thee, in case it should ever be lost.'[2] The kingdom had been lost, Nelson had restored it, so the sword was his. The dukedom was that of Bronte, which Ferdinand invented for the occasion. Bronte, in Greek, means thunder. The domain was on the outskirts of Etna and supposed to yield £3,000 a year, but it was in ruins and Nelson in his lifetime got nothing. Emma's story was that Nelson protested against receiving any reward, resolutely demurred for two or three days, and consented only when she had begged him on her knees to accept. She was herself rewarded with two coach loads of costly dresses and a miniature of the queen set in diamonds and inscribed *Eterna Gratitudine*.[3] Nelson settled the succession to the dukedom first on his father, then on Maurice, then on William and his children, then on Susannah and hers, then on Catherine and hers. The East India Company, in gratitude for the Nile, presented him with

£10,000. He was, as always, generous with money, and gave £500 to his father and to each of his brothers and sisters.[4]

He was in trouble with the admiralty and with his commander-in-chief. Keith, who had unexpectedly taken over the command in May, was irritated that Nelson, at the other end of the Mediterranean, should have 'a distinct detachment of half the fleet'.[5] Fearing for Minorca, he ordered Nelson to send as many ships as he could spare. Nelson replied that he would do so as soon as Naples was secure, and sent nothing. Troubridge was still busy reducing the last French garrisons of Capua and Gaeta, the first some miles inland and the second on the coast forty miles north of Naples, employing marines and seamen from the fleet. To Spencer, the same day, Nelson wrote: 'I will not part with a single ship ... I am fully aware of the act I have committed; but, sensible of my loyal intentions, I am prepared for any fate which may await my disobedience. I have done what I thought right ...' It is a perilous thing for a rear-admiral to say 'I will not' to a first lord, which Nelson well knew, since he wrote to the Duke of Clarence that though a military tribunal might think him criminal, the world would approve his conduct. Keith wrote again, this time ordering Nelson to send the greater part of his force. Nelson again replied: 'I think it right not to obey your lordship's orders ... I have no scruple in deciding that it is better to save the kingdom of Naples and risk Minorca ...' In a private letter he went so far as to tell Keith that he declined touching on the subject. Yet a third time Keith wrote, saying that he was leaving the Mediterranean in pursuit of the French fleet, even towards Ireland, and again requiring and directing Nelson to send the greater part of his fleet to Minorca. Nelson still did not go himself, but sent Duckworth with four ships of the line, all undermanned because their marines were ashore storming French forts.[6]

Then he wrote personally to Spencer and in a style which, had he not been the victor of the Nile, would have sunk him. 'My dear lord, I certainly, from only having a left hand, cannot enter into the details which may explain the motives which actuate my conduct ... My principle, my dear lord, is, to assist in driving the French to the devil, and in restoring peace and happiness to mankind.' He went on cordially to congratulate the first lord on the arrival at Cadiz of the combined French and Spanish fleet for which Keith had been unsuccessfully quartering the Mediterranean; 'for [he wrote] having escaped the vigilance of Lord Keith, I was fearful they would get to Brest'.[7] The combined fleet was no longer at large. It had evaded Keith as the French fleet had evaded Nelson for so long in 1798. Nelson in the end found his enemy. Keith did not have that good fortune. For Nelson to disobey orders while writing about restoring happiness to mankind was bad enough; for him then to remark on the enemy's 'having escaped Keith's vigilance' was disloyal and ungenerous. He used that phrase in letters to Spencer at the admiralty, to Sidney Smith in the Levant, and to Ball at Malta. To Hamilton he expressed himself as enraged at the escape.[8] To Davison he wrote that he had restored a faithful ally by breach of orders while Keith had lost a fleet by strict obedience to his.[9]

Before Nelson's disobedience to Keith's orders was known in London, Spencer had written saying the repossession of Naples gave the most sincere pleasure to everyone, to no one more than himself. There was a sting in the tail, since Spencer hoped Nelson would now be 'set at liberty to attend to some other points where the assistance of the fleet will probably be very essential to the cause of his majesty and his allies'.[10] It was not until 20 September that Nelson received another two letters from an admiralty board which had received both his later dispatches and Keith's. The first stated that their lordships approved of his having gone into the bay of Naples to restore the king, but told him not to send seamen ashore again as part of any army, and that their lordships saw no sufficient reason for his disobeying Keith's orders and having left Minorca exposed. There was also a separate letter making him acting commander-in-chief in Keith's absence. In reply to their lordships, Nelson observed the rebuke 'with great pain', and then, in a private letter to Spencer, went on to write in his most outrageous style. He said common sense had told him Minorca could be in no danger by his breach of orders. 'And, my dear lord, I only wish that I could have been placed in Lord Keith's situation ... I would have broke the orders like a piece of glass: in that case, the whole marine of the French would have been annihilated ... although I regret to say it, I do not believe any sea officer knows the sea and land business of the Mediterranean better than myself.'[11]

Although he was now acting commander-in-chief, Nelson felt got at in several ways. Before Keith left, he had declined Nelson's request for St Vincent's flagship, the new *Ville de Paris*, on the grounds that she was too large for detached service. Nelson then hoped he would be sent the *San Josef*, the Spanish prize he had taken at St Vincent, but did not get her either.[12] He asked Spencer to make Maurice a commissioner of the navy, but nothing came of that. And he had fallen out publicly, on his own quarterdeck, with Charles Lock, who had as good as accused his captains and pursers of profiteering and asserted that the fleet would be better served by contracts for beef and wine, that is to say by Lock's own contracts. This dispute reached the victualling board in London, to whom Nelson wrote a scornful letter: 'I defy any insinuations against my honour. Nelson is as far above doing a scandalous or mean action as the heavens are above the earth.'[13] The affair was dropped.

Lock was also writing home about the prisoners in the polaccas. 'Many of these victims to their confidence in us have already been executed. The government is burdened with upwards of 10,000 prisoners ... To be sure, they die very fast, in the unwholesome prisons they are confined in, heaped upon one another ...'[14] Captain Foote, the frigate captain who had signed the treaty Nelson had annulled, had not let the matter drop either. He put his case to Keith, sending him a copy of the long account of the negotiations which Nelson had demanded, and added a commentary. 'It will give your lordship some idea of my situation when almost left alone for five weeks in Naples bay ... I had much more reason to expect the arrival of a French than an English squadron from all the intelligence received & on the morning of the day Lord Nelson arrived, I got a letter from him written only four days before off Maritimo, in which his lordship did not give me the least hope of seeing him, or any English ships. [He said here that Nelson would not abide by the terms made.] I shall only observe that I feel perfectly easy as to my own conduct, and ready to justify it in any way whatever ... There is a wide difference between treating when your force consists of a few small ships and brigs, and when you are backed by 17 sail of the line!' Keith sent this letter, without written comment, to the admiralty.[15] Foote was brought home.

In September, Troubridge took Civita Vecchia and was offered the surrender of Rome. Thus, said Captain William Hoste, who was there, was the whole Roman state, once mistress of the world, taken by three hundred Englishmen: how times had changed since Julius Caesar. And thus, wrote Nelson in a letter to the new pope, Pius VII, was a prophecy fulfilled that a friar had made to him after the Nile, that he should do a greater thing, and take Rome with his ships.[16] In the fall and winter of 1799–1800 Nelson disposed his fleet round the Mediterranean, from Constantinople in the east to Gibraltar in the west, guarding Minorca and Naples, and blockading Malta. For himself, he stayed four months at Palermo with the Hamiltons and the queen, who implored him to stay. She at this time was in correspondence with the marquis de Gallo in Vienna, the man whom Nelson so despised, about the most pressing matters of state, which in her estimation were the dynastic marriages of her sons and daughters. If she could get the children settled, she wrote, she would die content. Italy was being carved up. Perhaps Leopold, the crown prince, could marry a Russian princess and have Tuscany. Mimi [Clementina] could marry the son of the archduke of Milan, whom Ferdinand could then name captain-general of Sicily, and Gallo could be his minister. As for Amelie, the wife of the grand duke Constantine was about to die, so Amelie could marry him. For Antoinette the queen wanted Spain, or in default of that she could marry the son of the elector of Bavaria. She did not mention Naples, so recently recovered and at such a cost.[17]

By then Nelson was besotted with Emma. He shared a house with the Hamiltons. Lord Elgin, passing through Palermo on the way to take up his post as the new ambassador to the Turkish Empire at the Porte, found Nelson prematurely aged and with a film over both eyes. In the young Lady Elgin's opinion, there was never a man turned so 'vain-glorious' as Nelson; he seemed quite dying and yet as if he had no other thought but Emma, who completely managed him. But she thought Emma handsome: 'My father would say, "There's a fine woman for you, good flesh and blood." She is indeed a whapper.'[18] The same Mr Rushout whom Nelson had asked to convey a message that he would batter down Naples, had returned with the royal party to Palermo, and observed that gaming went on half the night. Nelson sat with large parcels of gold before him and generally went to sleep, Emma taking from the heap without counting, and playing with his money, up to £500 a night.[19] It got so bad that Troubridge wrote warning Emma what was being said, and asking her not to gamble any more; she promised him not to. He also told her he trusted nothing at the Sicilian court. He had paid £500 out of his own purse for spies, intelligence, wood, cart-hire, horse-feed and a thousand other things, and the court had never offered to repay. He thought Acton duplicitous. When the queen, through Emma, offered him a pension, he replied that he well knew there was no intention of doing anything: if the queen had any power, a small lump sum given at once would content him.[20] He saw clearly what Nelson never brought himself to see.

The rumours were spreading to England. Lady Hamilton's 'admiral attitudes' were spoken of. *The Times*, reporting that Keith was returning to the Mediterranean and that Nelson would then come home, said: 'Heroes and conquerors are subdued in their turn. Mark Antony followed Cleopatra into the Nile, when he should have fought with Octavius! and laid down his laurels and power, to sail down the Cydnus with her in the dress, the character, and the *attitudes* of Venus.'[21] The day after this paragraph appeared, Admiral Goodall, a friend since Toulon in 1793, wrote to Nelson from London, making not a classical but a medieval allusion, saying Nelson was being called Rinaldo in the arms of Armida, and that it required a brother knight to draw him from the enchantress. 'To be sure,' he wrote, "'tis a very pleasant attraction, to which I am very sensible myself. But my maxim has always been – *Cupidus voluptatum, cupidior gloriae.* [Eager for pleasure, more eager for glory.]'[22]

Some more glory had come Nelson's way, in the form of a diamond star from the Turkish sultan which he was tactless enough to tell Spencer he wore above the star of the Bath.[23] Spencer was indulgent of Nelson, but never congratulated him on his dukedom, his sword, or his diamond star. And Nelson was thin-skinned. To Duckworth he asserted that he felt superior to the smiles or frowns of any board, but the very next day wrote imploringly to Spencer: 'Do not my dear lord, let the admiralty write harshly to me – my generous soul cannot bear it, being conscious it is entirely unmerited . . .' Three days after that he was asking the British minister at Turin to 'pity the sorrows of a blind and (in constitution) old man'.[24] Nelson, in an apparently dying state at Palermo, was becoming impossible to deal with, and yet he bitterly resented it when Keith was sent back to take over the command in the new year.

In October, at the request of John M'Arthur, then joint editor of *The Naval Chronicle*, Nelson wrote a sketch of his life.[25] It was a plain and vivid narrative, though shot through with contrasting strains of modesty and bombast. In the Leewards, in the dispute over trade with the Americans, he said his conscious rectitude bore him through. The wound he received at Tenerife he described only as 'some unlucky management of my arm'. Then he ended, after mentioning that he had placed the King of Naples back on his throne, with these ringing words: 'Without having any inheritance, or having been fortunate in prize money, I have received all the honours of my profession, been created a peer of Great Britain, and I may say to the reader: GO THOU AND DO LIKEWISE.' In the middle of the sketch he included this sentence: 'And in March [1787] I married Frances Herbert Nisbet, widow of Dr Nisbet, of the island of Nevis; by whom I have no children.' He was prepared to make public his disappointment at his childlessness at a time when his wife had not seen him for two years, and he was at Palermo with Emma Hamilton.

At home, in Bath and London, Fanny dined with St Vincent, and saw a great deal of Lady Berry and of Sir Peter and Lady Parker. 'We have agreed to go and see the famous French milliner. Lady P declares they will put me in a sack and send me to Bonaparte.' She reported the gossip. Everyone in the West Indies who had seen the hem of Nelson's garment now claimed his acquaintance. Admiral Dickson was going to marry a girl of eighteen and was surely out of his senses. She asked four times to come out to the Mediterranean, saying her doctor had ordered her to Lisbon and that the comptroller of the navy had offered her a passage to the Mediterranean, but she would not come out without Nelson's leave. She had had a new chariot and harness made for Nelson, at a cost of £352. She had persuaded Sir William Beechey to paint Nelson's father: at first he said he never went out except to the royal family, but when Fanny told him who the sitter was, he said, 'My god, I would go to York to do it'.[26] The old man himself wrote out to the Mediterranean, saying that, in Fanny, Nelson had given him another daughter. 'Lady Nelson's kindness, as a friend, a nurse, and a daughter, I want words to express.'[27]

To Fanny's hints that she should come out Nelson did not reply, but he had told her the previous April that if any advice had carried her out to a 'wandering sailor', he could *only* have struck his flag and carried her back again, for it would have been impossible to set up an establishment at either Naples or Palermo.[28] He asked her to send out some of the caricatures done of him after the Nile. He was again pestered by his brothers. William complained that all he had got from the lord chancellor was a small living which would clear £120 a year,

and then that the previous week *two* deaneries and *two* prebendal stalls
were disposed of, but that the name of Nelson was not even thought of
by Mr Pitt.²⁹ Maurice wrote that he was most severely mortified that
neither Spencer nor Pitt took notice of *him*, and that he must repine in
silence: he then went on at length about a deal to be done to buy him a
job at the victualling board.³⁰ Nelson then took what he called a very
strong line with Spencer and 'told him such truths', writing that he
could not but recollect that in the war he had taken nineteen ships of the
line and four admirals, that he had set his heart on Maurice becoming
a commissioner of the navy, but that he had completely failed in all
his applications for his friends. Spencer was short: 'After the marked
attention which I have ever shown to your *élèves* and followers ... I
do not think I had any reason to expect the kind of hint you throw
out on the subject of interest ...'³¹

In January 1800 Keith was at Leghorn, and summoned Nelson there.
'I am come here,' Nelson wrote to Fanny, 'to pay homage to him. Now
I have only to obey and god only knows on what service he will order
me ... god bless you and believe me your ever affectionate Bronte
Nelson.'³² Keith and Nelson settled the details of the Leghorn blockade,
and then on 25 January sailed together for Palermo. The passage took
eight days, during which Nelson wrote Emma a letter quite different
in tone from that to Fanny.

> Wednesday 29ᵗʰ Jany [1800]
> Separated from all I hold dear in this World what is the use of living
> if indeed such an existence can be called so ... no separation no time
> my only beloved Emma can alter my love and affection for you, it
> is founded on the truest principles of honor, and it only remains for
> us to regret which I do with the bitterest anguish that there are any
> obstacles to our being united in the closest ties of this Worlds rigid
> rules, as we are in those of real love. Continue only to love your
> faithful Nelson as he loves his Emma, you are my guide I submit
> to you, let me find all my fond heart hopes and wishes with the
> risk of my life as I have been faithful to my word never to partake
> of any amusem[en]t or to sleep on shore, Thursday Jany 30ᵗʰ: We
> have been six days from Leghorn and no prospect of our making
> a passage to Palermo, to me it is worse than death, I can neither
> eat nor sleep for thinking of you my dearest love, I never touch

even pudding you know the reason, no I would starve sooner, my only hope is to find you have equally kept your promises to me, for I never made you a promise that I did not as strictly keep as if made in the presence of heaven, but I rest perfectly confident of the reallity of your love and that you would die sooner than be false in the smallest thing to your own faithful Nelson who lives only for his Emma, friday I shall run mad we have had a gale of wind that is nothing but I am 20 leagues farther from you than yesterday noon, was I master notwithstanding the weather I would have been 20 leagues nearer but my Commander In Chief knows not what I feel by absence, last night I did nothing but dream of you altho' I woke 20 times in the night, in one of my dreams I thought I was at a large table you was not present, sitting between a Princess who I detest and another, they both tried to seduce me and the first wanted to take those liberties with me which no Woman in this World but yourself ever did, the consequence was I knocked her down and in the moment of bustle you came in and taking me to your embrace wispered I love nothing but you my Nelson, I kissed you fervently and we enjoy'd the height of love, Ah Emma I pour out my soul to you. If you love any thing but me you love those who feel not like your N. Sunday [2 February] noon fair wind which makes me a little better in hopes of seeing you to morrow, just 138 miles distant, and I trust to find you like myself, for no love is like mine towards you.[33]

This is the letter which has been attributed to 1799, but that cannot be so. It was in 1800 that Keith came out to supersede Nelson and relieve him of his acting command and that Nelson made this passage from Leghorn to Palermo on the dates stated. Palermo was not to Keith's Scottish taste. He stayed with the Hamiltons, and became tired of their balls and operas and of the court. As he told his sister: 'The king, queen, and the family have passed the day with me [on board his flagship] and seemed content – so am I that they are gone.'[34]

In mid-February, Nelson with a squadron of three ships took the *Généreux*, one of the only two French ships of the line which escaped him at the Nile. That evening he wrote to Emma: 'I have got her, Le Genereux – thank god – 12 out of 13, only the Guillaume tell

Facsimile of part of letter from Nelson to Emma Hamilton, January 1800, in which he recounts to her his erotic dream. By kind permission of Mr and Mrs Harry Spiro, New York.

remaining – I am after the others – I have not suffered the French admiral to contaminate the Foudroyant by setting his foot in it.'[35] Writing to Minto in Vienna about the *Généreux*, Nelson said no one had taken more pains than Minto to make him noticed in the world, and this was true.[36] This gives all the more force to what Minto then wrote of Nelson: 'I hope he will not [go home] for his own sake, and he will at least, I hope, take Malta first. He does not seem at all conscious of the sort of discredit he has fallen into . . . But it is hard to condemn and use ill a hero, as he is in his own element, for being foolish about a woman who has art enough to make fools of many wiser than an admiral.'[37]

Nelson would not stay for Malta. From Palermo he wrote to tell Keith he had nearly died two days before from the swelling of some vessels of the heart. He knew anxiety was the cause. It had first happened when he had missed the French fleet in 1798. 'More people, perhaps, die of broken hearts, than we are aware of.'[38] Then at the end of March three ships of his squadron took the *Guillaume Tell*, the last of the French survivors from the Nile. She struck to his friend Berry, whose note to Nelson – scrawled, blotted, and water-stained – says that the *Foudroyant*'s lower masts and main topmast are still standing, but with every roll he expects them to go over the side; he is hurt in the foot and has forty men wounded, 'besides the killed, which you shall know hereafter'. He asks Nelson to send this to his wife, and finishes: 'Within hail before I fired.' Nelson's letter to the admiralty was no less dramatic. 'Thus owing to my brave friends is the entire capture and destruction of the French Mediterranean fleet to be attributed and my orders from the great Earl of St Vincent fulfill'd ... My task is done, my health is finished, and probably my retreat for ever fixed, unless another French fleet should be placed for me to look after.'[39]

Meanwhile there was trouble for Nelson at home. Buonaparte had escaped from the Levant, returned to France, overthrown the Directory, and established himself as first consul. This would have come as no great surprise to Nelson, who after the Nile had intercepted a packet of letters from Buonaparte which made it clear he would 'strive to be the Washington of France'.[40] Once established as first consul, Buonaparte made overtures for peace, but on terms not acceptable to the British government. Fox rarely attended Parliament, but he did speak in the Commons debate on the government's rejection of the terms offered. After the government had put its case, he rose to reply. He said he knew it was late, four in the morning, and that the house exhausted, but then he spoke for the better part of an hour. He believed the people wanted peace. Was war to be eternal? Who were our allies? Russia, he supposed. The Emperor of Russia had declared himself grand master of the knights of Malta; the king of England might with as much propriety declare himself head of the order of Chartreuse monks. Was the war to continue until the house of Bourbon had been re-established in France? We could as safely treat with Buonaparte. Where the power essentially resided, there we ought to go for peace. He hoped we were now convinced that a republican government, like that of America, might exist without danger to other established monarchies. Near the end of his long speech he came to the restoration of another Bourbon monarch, the king of Naples, and referred to the events of the previous June and July.

'I wish,' said Fox, 'that the atrocities of which we hear so much, and which I abhor as much as any man, were indeed unexampled. I fear that they do not belong exclusively to the French ... Naples for instance has been what is called "delivered", and yet, if I am rightly informed, it has been stained and polluted by murders so ferocious, and by cruelties of every kind so abhorrent, that the heart shudders at the recital. It has been said not only that the miserable victims of the rage and brutality of the fanatics were savagely murdered, but that in many instances their flesh was eaten and devoured by the cannibals who are the advocates and the instruments of social order. Nay, England is not totally exempt from reproach if the rumours which are circulated be true. I will mention a fact, to give ministers the opportunity, if it be false, of wiping away the stain that must otherwise fix upon the British name. It is said that a party of the republican inhabitants of Naples took shelter in the fortress of the castle de Uovo. They were besieged by a detachment from the royal army, to whom they refused to surrender, but demanded that a British officer should be brought forward, and to him they capitulated. They made terms with him under the sanction of the British name. It was agreed that their persons and property should be safe, and that they should be conveyed to Toulon. They were accordingly put aboard a vessel, but before they sailed their property was confiscated, numbers of them were taken out, thrown into dungeons, and some of them, I understand, notwithstanding the British guarantee, actually executed.'

This is from the parliamentary report. It is not verbatim. *The Morning Chronicle*'s report of the speech is twice as long. Both the *Chronicle* and the *Whitehall Evening Post* add that Fox asked ministers to investigate.[41] No report mentions the name of Nelson. There was no reply to Fox's speech. The vote was taken immediately afterwards, giving the government a majority of 265 to 64. Fox's informant was probably Charles Lock, whose wife Cecilia was Fox's first cousin.

Before Keith arrived back in England the previous year he had received Foote's report, and is known to have had his doubts about Nelson's conduct.[42] When Foote returned to England in 1800 he found that the transactions at Naples had become a topic of common conversation. He intended to ask for a public inquiry, but was told by a naval member of the admiralty that this would injure the interests of his country and would attach him to a political party; for which, said Foote, there seemed good grounds after Fox's speech. Foote's first interest was to clear his own name, since the treaty Nelson annulled was signed by him. But he went further than that. He believed it was only too true that the garrisons of Uovo and Nuovo had been taken out of the castles under the pretence of putting the capitulation he had signed into execution. Nelson was fortunate Fox did not directly name him. He was fortunate that Fox's speech was made in the early hours of the morning, and that the reference to cannibalism was likely to detract from its credibility. He was fortunate that the speech was made by Fox and not by some more moderate member with whom Foote would have felt able to associate himself. What Foote believed is summed up by a note he pencilled on the back of one of the documents he collected to support his case: 'It is unreasonable to require me to sacrifice myself at the shrine of Lord Nelson.'[43] But in 1800, out of a combination of patriotism and prudence, he kept his peace.

When he heard of Fox's speech, Nelson was enraged, writing to Davison that Fox had used language unbecoming an English gentleman, who ought always to suppose that his majesty's officers would act with honour. He called the treaty infamous, and said he had sent in his note 'on which the rebels had come out of the castles, *as they ought*, and as I hope all who are false to their king and country will, *to be hanged*, or otherwise disposed of . . .' He said nothing had been promised by a British officer which his Sicilian majesty had not complied with – which was manifestly untrue. He sent written observations which he asked to be sent to George Rose, secretary to the treasury.[44] Rose did nothing publicly. The same day, Nelson wrote another letter to Davison which began the long dispute over prize money with his old chief St Vincent, for ships taken in the Mediterranean after St Vincent's departure, saying that the earl's claim, if persisted in, would be a dishonourable act.[45] Nelson was quarrelling with everyone.

And in the Mediterranean in 1800 there was another treaty with which he disagreed. The Turks, in order to get rid of the French whom they could not themselves expel from their territories, had signed a convention under which the army would be allowed to return to France. The British government did not like this and was not a party, but did not wish to offend an ally. Nelson saw the treaty as undoing his victory at the Nile, and wished all the French to perish in Egypt to give a great lesson to the world of the justice of almighty god.[46]

As it was 16,000 French would be freed to fight against England. But the British government decided to honour the treaty. Keith told the admiralty he had sent Nelson the secret admiralty order to act 'with all possible earnestness for the personal protection of those [French] who, on the faith of a sacred convention, may be said to have entrusted their lives to the honour of their adversaries'.[47] To Lord Elgin, the new minister at Constantinople whom he had recently met at Palermo, Nelson wrote: 'And was I commander in chief, even when the thing was done, I should have refused to ratify any consent or approbation ... I never should for a moment have forgot my text – that at all risk of giving offence, *not one Frenchman should be allowed to quit Egypt.*'[48] As it happened, new fighting broke out between the French and the Turks, and the treaty was superseded. But what is important is Nelson's stated attitude towards a completed treaty. 'Even when the thing was done' – as it had been the year before in Naples – he would have refused to ratify it.

At Palermo, Acton married his niece in two ceremonies, one Roman Catholic in the presence of the king and queen and the other Anglican, conducted by Nelson's chaplain at Hamilton's house. As Nelson told his friend Goodall, the girl was only thirteen, '... so you hear it is never too late to do well. He is only sixty-seven'.[49] Nelson was only forty-one. And Hamilton had been recalled. He did not know of it until his successor, Arthur Paget, son of Lord Uxbridge, was reported to be on his way out. But Grenville had dismissed Hamilton on the previous Christmas eve: his letter, and Hamilton's eventual reply when he received it late in March, constitute a tiny minuet of courteous insolence. Grenville wrote that the present situation of affairs in Italy appeared to offer an opportunity for Hamilton to avail himself of his majesty's gracious permission to return to England after the very laborious duties in which he had lately been engaged. Hamilton in reply begged his lordship to lay him at his majesty's feet and return humble thanks for his gracious permission, and that the approbation of his majesty, and of Grenville, would be to him the greatest consolation he had ever experienced in the whole course of his life.[50] Then it was Nelson's turn to be the subject of compliments from London. Admiral William Young, a lord of the admiralty, wrote to Keith that he was grieved that a man who on other occasions had done so well, should have exposed himself to ridicule and censure.[51] Then Spencer wrote the silkiest letter to Nelson. He should much prefer Nelson to remain to complete the reduction of Malta. 'But if, unfortunately, these agreeable events are to be prevented by your having too much exhausted yourself in the service ... I am quite clear, and I believe I am joined in opinion by all your friends here, that you will be more likely to recover your health and strength in England than in an inactive situation at a foreign court, however pleasing the respect and gratitude shown to you for your services may be ...'[52]

Before he could receive this, Nelson had taken the Hamiltons on a cruise of five weeks in the *Foudroyant*, first to Syracuse for two days sightseeing among Roman remains, and then to Malta, where they lay anchored for two weeks. This, for the active Nelson, was an extraordinary inactivity. He hoped to see the French garrison at Valletta surrender while he was there, but it did not. But it was a triumphal cruise. Nelson's great cabin was decorated with a tricolour wooden plume from the figurehead of the *Guillaume Tell*, four muskets taken from the *San Josef* which Nelson had taken at St Vincent, and the flagstaff of *L'Orient*, which had blown up at the Nile.[53] And Emperor Paul of all the Russias, having proclaimed himself grand master of the nominally restored order of St John of Jerusalem, which Buonaparte had abolished, had agreed to Nelson's suggestion that Lady Hamilton should become a member of the order. She was made a *dame petite croix*, and wore the enamel cross round her neck. This is the voyage which, a year later, in the Baltic, Nelson remembered for its 'days of ease and nights of pleasure'. Whatever Hamilton saw he chose not to notice, as he continued not to notice, and we cannot know why. He was sixty-nine, though an active man. He was also a diplomat by nature, Nelson was his honoured friend, and he had nothing to gain from a falling out. Perhaps he tacitly recognised that he had after all received Emma in the first place from his nephew, and that Nelson now received her in his turn. Such things can only be speculation. What is almost certain, from the date of the birth, is that Nelson's child by Emma was conceived on that cruise.[54]

Back in Palermo, Nelson received his last honour from Ferdinand. The order of St Ferdinand and Merit was, like the dukedom of Bronte, invented for the occasion; it gave him the privilege of keeping his hat on in the royal presence.[55] He replied to Spencer's letter about an inactive situation at a foreign court, saying it gave him much pain. 'But I trust,' he said, 'that you and all my friends will believe that mine cannot be an inactive life, although it may not carry all the outward parade of *much ado about nothing.*' But the next few months were just such a parade. Ferdinand, he said, had placed the queen and her children absolutely under his care, and he would feel himself a beast if he should have a thought for anything but their comfort.[56] He was as good as his word, but catering to Maria Carolina's all-demanding foibles was not the first business of a British admiral.

Nelson began his journey home, sailing for Leghorn, taking with him the queen and her children, Sir William and Lady Hamilton, and Miss Knight. The plan was that at Leghorn the queen should continue overland to Vienna, where another of her daughters was empress, and that Nelson and the others should go home to England by sea. They arrived in Leghorn at a bad time. In mid-June, Buonaparte won the battle of Marengo and was once again in a fair way to conquer Italy. Keith had to evacuate Genoa, and wrote ordering Nelson there with every ship he had.[57] Nelson did not come. He was at Leghorn. From there, Hamilton wrote asking Keith for a ship in which he, Emma, and Nelson could go home together, explaining that his pictures and antiquities had been put on board the *Foudroyant.* Keith was in a trying situation. The French were advancing. He needed every ship. He had a junior flag officer at Leghorn, sixty miles away, who had two ships of the line, a queen, and Lady Hamilton with him. Keith wrote telling him the *Foudroyant* could not leave the Mediterranean, that if he wanted to go to England by land he could strike his flag at Leghorn and do so, that if he wanted to go by sea he could take a troop ship from Minorca, but that if he wanted to stay he should take upon himself the duties of senior officer at that island.[58] While he waited for Nelson to make up his mind, he told the admiralty that the queen 'and a great train' had arrived at Leghorn.[59] She had fifty followers, the crown prince, and three daughters. She had been over-modest in her letter to Gallo about their marriage prospects. Nelson was lugging four queens about with him, the queen of Naples, and three princesses who would become queens of France (Amelie), Spain (Antoinette), and Sardinia (Clementina.)[60] Two of these were most likely the princesses who tried to seduce Nelson in his erotic dream. Emma, as she had done in the flight from Naples, was acting as removal agent for the royal treasure – 'Here,' said Maria Carolina in a note to her, 'are all the jewels of an unfortunate family, a packet of our personal things, a little plate, and a box of the linen and the clothes ... A thousand compliments to our liberator.'[61] But she could not decide whether she wanted to go on to Vienna as she had planned, or go back to Palermo for fear of running into the advancing French if she went on. For eleven days she dithered, with Nelson in attendance.[62] It was within Keith's power, pressed as he was, to give his junior admiral a straight order to get back to his duty. He had a discretionary order from the admiralty to let him go home, and therefore a discretionary power to keep him.[63] Perhaps he was glad to get rid of him. He was irritated by Nelson his subordinate, but at the same time apprehensive of Nelson the hero of the Nile. As he wrote to Downing Street later, when he was asking for a special remainder of his barony, he did not mean to compare himself with other sea officers – he did not name them but from the context they were St Vincent and Nelson – yet though he had 'not had the good fortune of obtaining any brilliant victory', his services had been long, constant, and severe.[64]

He decided to tolerate and humour Nelson, but only just. 'I must go to Leghorn,' he exclaimed, 'to be bored by Lord Nelson for permission to take the queen to Palermo and the prince and princesses to all parts of the globe. To every request I have said my duty to the nation forbids it, god knows it is true.' But he let him go home overland with the queen. Nelson was halfway home by the time Keith received the following note from Spencer: 'Private. I hope it will not be long before Lord Nelson arrives in this part of the world. His further stay in the Mediterranean cannot I am sure contribute either to the public advantage or to his own.'[65] Keith had used his discretion well.

Nelson at Leghorn was not admired. Major General John Moore was also there at the time, having arrived from Minorca with Abercromby, his chief, too late to land his troops in the defence of Genoa. Moore and Nelson had disliked each other on Elba in 1793. Now, at Leghorn, Moore wrote that Nelson was covered with stars, ribbons, and medals, more like the prince of an opera than the conqueror of the Nile.[66] When Lord Keith refused her the *Foudroyant*, the queen wept, but he remained unmoved, and told her Lady Hamilton had had the command of the fleet long enough.[67] At last the queen got off, travelling to Vienna by way of Florence and Ancona and then across the Adriatic to Trieste, and Nelson and the Hamiltons went with her. Nelson had always intended to go home by sea, taking the Hamiltons with him,

and even without a ship of the line he could have done so in some
comfort and at no expense. Keith at Leghorn refused the queen a ship
of the line. Abercromby, commander-in-chief of the British army in the
Mediterranean, refused the queen's request to undertake the defence of
the kingdom of Naples, saying it would sacrifice a corps which could
be used to better purpose.[68] Nelson was able to refuse her nothing
and started off on an overland journey which would take five times
as long and cost him a small fortune, all because he had promised
to protect the queen he thought great. He was not even in charge
Prince Belmonte, one of the queen's favourites, directed the march. Sir
William was ill and said he would die by the way. But in consonance
with Maria Carolina's wishes Emma had discovered that she hated the
sea, and that anyway she would like to visit the courts of Germany. The
first was nonsense: Emma was an excellent sailor. The second rings
true. So Maria Carolina, with fourteen carriages and three baggage
wagons, and with Nelson and the rest in her train, straggled across
Italy. A wheel came off Nelson's carriage, hurting the two Hamiltons.
The queen left them and pushed on ahead. At Ancona the whole party
had to wait three weeks until a passage to Trieste was arranged in
two Russian frigates. Miss Knight said their party was very helpless
and that poor Lord Nelson's only comfort was in talking about the
Foudroyant, whatever was done to turn the conversation.[69] Very likely
it was true. Nelson, having struck his flag at Leghorn, was now in
command of nothing. When he left the *Foudroyant* he had received this
letter from his barge's crew: 'It is with extreme grief that we find you
are about to leave us. We have been along with you (though not in
the same ship) in every engagement your lordship has been in, both
by sea and land ... My lord, pardon the rude style of seamen, who
are but little acquainted with writing, and believe us to be, my lord,
your ever humble and obedient servants.' These men would have seen
much more of him than his other people, and were also among the few
who had been rewarded by the Neapolitan court. When Ferdinand was
brought off from Naples and landed at Palermo at Christmas 1798, he
had not only promised but paid one hundred ounces of silver (three
months' pay for every man) to the three barges' crews who took him
and his treasure out to the British ships in the bay.[70]

At Vienna the queen was delivered to her daughter the empress.
Nelson was applauded in the street, and people brought their children

to touch him. Lady Minto said he was a gig from ribands, stars, and orders, and that Emma and she led him about like a keeper with a bear.[71] Emma was said by one unforgiving Englishwoman to be colossal, with her waist positively between her shoulders.[72] Nelson on the other hand was described by a Lutheran pastor as one of the most insignificant figures he ever saw, who could not have weighed more than seventy pounds, but whose steady eye revealed the conqueror's great soul.[73] Emma must have been twice his size.

They were presented to the emperor and empress. For four days they were entertained by Prince Esterhazy at the palace of Eisenstadt where a hundred grenadiers waited at table, and were entertained to a concert at which Haydn conducted his *Creation* oratorio and set to music one of Miss Knight's effusions on the battle of the Nile, the last two lines of which went: 'The solid pyramids confess the shock/ And their firm bases to their centre rock.'[74] While Nelson and the Hamiltons were still at Vienna, two ominous paragraphs appeared in the London newspapers. One, in *The Morning Chronicle*, demanded that Nelson and the Hamiltons should be called to account when they reached home. 'There is indeed a terrible scene to be unfolded of what has passed in Naples these last twelve months. We can assert, from the best information, that the British name has suffered a reproach on the continent by the transactions at Naples.' This appeared on 11 September, the day that Luisa Sanfelice, who had been condemned by the junta but was reprieved because she pleaded pregnancy, became the last of the Neapolitan rebels to be hanged in the Mercato, fourteen months after the first executions. The second paragraph, in *The Morning Post*, said: 'The German state painter, we are assured, is drawing Lady Hamilton and Lord Nelson at full length together. An Irish correspondent hopes the artist will have the delicacy to put Sir William between them.' The painter was probably Heinrich Fuger, who made two portraits of Nelson, one with all decorations and one in civilian clothes. Everyone who saw Nelson at this time commented ironically on his stars and orders, but Fuger's portrait out of uniform is the one which gives the best idea of the great soul which the Lutheran pastor saw.[75]

At Dresden, Nelson and his party met Hugh Elliot, the British minister there and the brother of Lord Minto. He called Nelson and Emma 'Antony and Moll Cleopatra'. While they were in the city,

Nelson had two more portraits done of himself and Emma, in pastel, by Johann Schmidt.[76] His is a haunting image, hers a representation of a still beautiful woman, whatever her bulk. It is the picture of her he liked best, and kept in his cabin in the *Victory*. From Dresden the whole party, with coach, baggage, and eleven servants, embarked on two specially fitted up gondolas, and sailed up the Elbe, by way of Magdeburg, to Hamburg. There a wine merchant offered Nelson as a gift six dozen bottles of Rhenish wine, vintage 1625, declaring he would be honoured if his wine could flow in the heart's blood of the immortal hero. Nelson accepted half a dozen bottles, saying he hoped to have half a dozen victories yet and would drink a bottle after each. He did drink one after Copenhagen.[77]

Then they went home. The frigate he had expected to meet him did not come. He and his party took the Yarmouth packet. Nelson was in eclipse, and this was reflected in a ponderous biographical notice which appeared at the time in *The Naval Chronicle*.[78] It gave a priced list of all the 'presents' Nelson had received – the pension of £2,000 a year, the £10,000 from the East India Company, the aigrette from the grand signior valued at £2,000 and a pelisse from the same at £1,000, the emperor of Russia's diamond box at £2,500, the dukedom of Bronte at £3,000 a year, gold headed sword and cane (unpriced), freedoms of cities, and so on. And it said: 'In whatever light we consider the character of this illustrious mariner, its brilliancy dazzles the eye with an endless variety ... Yet whilst we draw such conclusion we must remark, that LORD NELSON'S SEVEREST TRIAL IS YET TO COME! His present elevation has drawn upon him the eyes of all men; and those of envy ever wakeful will steadily observe whether the great conqueror [Nelson] of the modern hydra [Buonaparte], excels the demigod of Greece [Hercules], by rising superior to the delusive snares of prosperity.' His character in the humble and private walks of life, and in his professional one, would excite equal admiration. 'They [both sides of Nelson's character] will bear to be considered as the sun; in which brightness will hide the blemishes: and whenever petulance, ignorance, pride, malice, malignity, or envy interpose to cloud or sully his frame, I will take upon me to pronounce, that THE ECLIPSE WILL NOT LAST LONG.'

It was altogether a backhanded compliment.

CHAPTER NINETEEN

The Homecoming

WHEN NELSON AND THE Hamiltons arrived back in England they were uneasy and beset with doubts. Nelson was infatuated with Emma but unsure of her. She was just as unsure what to do for the best. She was six months pregnant, had lost her dominant position at the court of Naples, and knew she would not be received at the court of St James. Any position she might hold in London society would owe itself to Hamilton, but he had lost his ambassadorship, was overdrawn £7,000 at his banker's, and was even uncertain of a decent pension. The cost of the unwanted overland journey from Leghorn had been high, £3,431, and had been paid by Nelson.[1] That was seven years' pay for a rear-admiral. And Nelson was unsure of himself with Emma, with his wife, with the admiralty, and with St Vincent who, he was convinced, was robbing him.

He had not already decided to break with Fanny. Miss Knight, on the journey across Europe, had remarked that when they were at Leghorn he hoped he and Fanny would often dine with the Hamiltons, and that afterwards, when they went on to their musical parties, he and Fanny would go to bed. Even at Hamburg he bought a magnificent lace trimming for a court dress for his wife.[2] And at Leghorn he had written to Fanny in a way that showed some intimacy still existed between them: 'My health at times is better but a quiet mind and to give content is necessary for me . . . I could say much but it would only distress me and be useless.'[3] Fanny must have sent letters to wait for him at Yarmouth, because he wrote to her from there saying: 'Sir [William] and Lady Hamilton beg their best regards and will accept your offer of a bed.'⁴ So the party, on its way from Yarmouth to London, would stay the night with Lady Nelson at Round Wood near Ipswich. Obviously no break was intended.

At Yarmouth, the citizens took the horses from the shafts and pulled Nelson's carriage. After fireworks and bonfires the party left the next day and did go to Round Wood, which they found empty. Letters had crossed, there was some misunderstanding, and Fanny had after all gone on to London to wait as Nelson had previously asked her. On Sunday 9 November, the day of the worst storm in London since 1703, Nelson and his party arrived at St Nerot's hotel in St James's. Hamilton was thin, Emma looked charming and a very fine woman, and Nelson wore full dress uniform with all stars and orders to meet his wife and father who, as the *Morning Post* put it with something of an edge, 'had been some time awaiting his arrival'.⁵ The Nelsons and the Hamiltons dined together, and then Nelson went in a chariot to meet Spencer at the admiralty. This was the start of a period during which Nelson was greeted with a mixture of ceremony, adulation, and derision.

Next morning he visited the foreign office, the admiralty in Whitehall, and the navy office at Somerset House, and was mobbed in the Strand. In the afternoon he took part in the Lord Mayor's show, and once again the horses were taken from the shafts of his coach and the people drew him to Guildhall. On the way round St Paul's churchyard and Cheapside, women waved their handkerchiefs from the windows and persuaded him to put his hand out of the carriage so that they could kiss it. He was presented by the City of London with a gold-handled sword decorated with the figure of a crocodile to celebrate the Nile, the city chamberlain saying that the shores which had beheld the destruction of the Persian by the Greeks now resounded with the echo of British thunder. In *The Whitehall Evening Post* Lady Nelson was described as wearing a white gown and violet satin head dress, her features handsome and her appearance elegant. *The Morning Post* said Emma had changed in complexion since she was described as a rock of alabaster streaked with veins of celestial hue, and that she had got a tawny tinge in Italy. *The Morning Herald* described her figure as 'on the wane from too great a propensity to the *en bon point*', and then remarked, 'Such after ransacking Herculaneum and Pompeii for thirty-eight years is the chief curiosity with which that celebrated antiquarian Sir William Hamilton has returned to his native country.'[6] Nelson's return provided the most titillating news of the season.

On Wednesday came the king's levee. Hamilton went as the retiring ambassador to Naples, and handed the king a letter Emma had brought from the queen of Naples to queen Charlotte. It did her no good.[7] And Nelson complained that when he made his bow he was coldly received, the king asking whether he had recovered his health and turning away without waiting for an answer, and talking with some general for half an hour.[8] The king's coldness is usually attributed to Nelson's having appeared in his full blaze of foreign orders, but he had twice sought the advice of Garter king of arms on the etiquette, asking where he should wear the sultan's aigrette and star, and where the king of Naples's orders, and indeed whether he could wear the star of the Bath at home, not having been formally inducted into the order. He wore it abroad, but was he to cut it off his coat when he came to England?[9] One possible reason is that the king was unwell: he was close to one of his periodic fits of apparent madness, and there was talk of a regency. That afternoon, still smarting from the snub, Nelson took Fanny to dinner with the Spencers, as he had before he left for the Mediterranean nearly three years before. 'Such a contrast I never beheld,' said Lady Spencer, or at any rate these are the words put into her mouth some years later.[10] 'After dinner Lady Nelson, who sat opposite to her husband (by the way he never spoke during dinner and looked blacker than all the devils), perhaps injudiciously, but with a good intention, peeled some walnuts and offered them to him in a glass. As she handed it across the table Nelson pushed it away from him, but so roughly that the glass broke against one of the dishes. There was an awkward pause; and then Lady Nelson burst into tears. When we retired to the drawing room she told me how she was situated.'

More triumphs followed. Nelson was fêted at a dinner in honour of the Hero of the Nile given by Davison and attended by the prime minister and three members of the cabinet, but the newspapers were full of suggestive paragraphs. The opposition *Morning Chronicle* placed a story about Lady Hamilton as one of the queen of Naples's maids of honour next to one about literary ladies being 'in the straw' and 'laid in sheets' – the allusion being to a new method of making paper from straw. A reference to the new Adultery Bill before Parliament was put next to one about Nelson at Covent Garden sitting between Lady Hamilton

and Lady Nelson. Next day the paper was at it again, saying it was
interesting that the bill should be suspended 'in the present state of
affairs'.[11]

On the very day Nelson took his seat in the House of Lords for the
first time, a coloured caricature by Cruikshank went on sale. It was
entitled 'A Mansion House Treat, or Smoking Attitudes', and showed
the lord mayor, Sir William Hamilton, Pitt, Emma, and Nelson all
smoking pipes. Hamilton cannot get his pipe lit. Emma, seen in profile
in a muslin gown and in a position immediately recognisable from her
famous Attitudes, is exclaiming: 'Pho the old man's pipe is always out,
but yours burns with full vigour.' To which Nelson, smoking a pipe
which stretches down to the ground, with a phallic tip, replies: 'Yes
yes I'll give you such a smoke I'll pour a whole broad side into you.'[12]

Nelson's father could not read all this in the newspapers because of
his short sightedness. Fanny could. Three times the Hamiltons and
the Nelsons went to the theatre together, to Covent Garden, the
Haymarket, and Drury Lane. He wore all his stars, and whenever he
rose between acts the audience saluted him and he bowed. On the third
evening, at Drury Lane, according to which account is believed, Lady
Nelson either just fainted, or she shrieked and fainted and the house
was thrown into confusion; either she recovered enough to return to
her seat or she was helped from the theatre by Emma and by Nelson's
father. Nelson in any case stayed to the end for 'God Save the King'
and 'Nelson of the Nile', which was encored.[13]

And by some ill luck, while Nelson, Emma, and Sir William were in
town, the case of *Hoare v Williams* came before the court of King's Bench.
It filled columns of newspaper space. Mr Hoare had a wife, Elizabeth,
who was twenty-three, pure of mind, and beautiful of person. She eloped
with Williams, an officer in the army, whom Mr Hoare sued for £20,000
damages for criminal conversation – adultery. Counsel for Hoare said
the husband had even hired a post chaise for his wife to elope in and
was thus surrendering his wife, *in transitu*, into the arms of an adulterer.
The judge said he remembered a case where a man had put two pillows
in the bed, one for his wife and another for the adulterer, and the judge
in that case had held that some small damages might lie. They lived,
said the judge, in distempered times, when it became necessary to
inculcate more strictly the duties of religion and morality. But still,
the husband had known, at the time his wife left him, that she would

go with the defendant, so he could not come to the court for damages. The complaisant husband got nothing.[14] The newspapers returned to debating whether Emma would be received at court. She never was.

While all this was going on in London, Lord St Vincent, in the west country, wrote to his friend Nepean at the admiralty, about Nelson. Nepean was secretary to the admiralty, but he had once, twenty years before, been St Vincent's purser and secretary. St Vincent, who knew Nelson's strengths and weaknesses, often wrote to Nepean informally and indiscreetly. 'I have no doubt,' he wrote, 'he is pledged to getting Lady Hamilton received at St James's and everywhere, and that he will make a great *brouillerie* about it ... [Spencer] cannot give him a separate command, for he cannot bear confinement to any object; he is a partisan; his ship always in the most dreadful order, and never can become an officer for to be placed where I am.'[15] St Vincent was then commander-in-chief of the Channel fleet, which he ran in his irascible way, complaining to Nepean that the fleet was 'loaded with delinquents', abounded in worthless and continually drunken lieutenants and boatswains, and that one of the captains he had been sent, Tom Bowen, was 'near an idiot' and one of the poorest of God's creatures. Here he shot himself in the foot, since he had himself, at the request of Emma Hamilton, made Tom Bowen post two years before.[16] But St Vincent and Nelson had always got on, so Nelson was to be sent to the Channel fleet under him. There was now, though, the matter of prize money between them. This had arisen in late 1799 when Nelson was acting commander-in-chief of the Mediterranean during the absence of both Keith and St Vincent. Four Spanish frigates were taken and the senior admiral would normally receive one-eighth of their value. But the question was whether St Vincent, who had gone home ill, still held the nominal command and should therefore take the money. St Vincent at the time told Nepean he had not dreamed of 'a share in the lottery ticket of the four frigates'.[17] Nelson had never been lucky with prizes. One of the lieutenants who was made at the same time as he was, back in 1777, two years later gained £30,000 in prize money, 900 years' pay, when he was in command of a cutter.[18] Duckworth, who had been Nelson's second at Naples, had then gone to blockade Cadiz and was said to have made £75,000.[19] The only time Nelson openly chased prize money was at Tenerife. He was not greedy, but he did claim the four Spanish frigates as his, and in 1800 and 1801 the case was with the lawyers, who sharpened both parties' sense of grievance. The prize money at stake amounted to £13,000. St Vincent wrote to Nelson assuring him that, god forbid, he would never deprive him of a farthing, but only making things worse by saying Nelson's command never extended to Gibraltar, let alone to Finisterre where the ships had been taken.[20] There was a chill between the two men.

Meantime business had to go on. St Vincent wrote again to propose the *San Josef* for Nelson. This was kind. She was the Spanish ship Nelson had taken at the battle of St Vincent and had later included in his coat of arms. The earl had even let the Plymouth dockyard think she would be his own flagship, so that she would be the better fitted out for Nelson. But St Vincent wrote with a natural asperity, and he began his letter making this generous offer with the words: 'Now that your ceremonies and presentations are nearly run through . . .'[21]

Nelson, whose ceremonies in London continued, was dined by the East India Company, painted by Beechey and Hoppner, and sculpted by the Hon. Anne Damer, daughter of a field marshal. She made a massive marble bust, twice life size, for the City of London. *The Morning Post*, in its fashion column, reported his daily sittings to the 'fair artist', and then, with the sexual innuendo which followed Nelson round, announced that a part of the nose had broken off which it was feared 'would spoil the whole of the capital performance'.[22] Nelson's dukedom was also mocked. 'Lord Nelson', said *The Morning Herald*, 'has entirely dropped the title of BRONTI, conferred him by the king of Naples. His lordship, no doubt, very properly considers that a brave English seaman can derive no very great degree of credit from an *Italian name*.' Nelson thought nothing of the sort. Lord Grenville at the foreign office had received a request from Castelcica, the Sicilian ambassador in London, asking him to obtain the king's permission for Nelson to use the title, and also making it clear that Ferdinand had given Nelson extraordinary powers to name his own successor to the dukedom, who could be 'any person he wishes, even outside his family, and that whether or not he has heirs of the body'.[23] He had already named his father and brothers as his next heirs, but could have named the coxswain of his barge.

Nelson was living in style. He had taken a house just off Piccadilly which was filled with servants, where his father, who had stayed in town, was uncomfortable. 'The suite of nobility is long', he wrote to his daughter Catherine. 'Your bro. is so constantly on the wing that I can but get a short glimpse myself.'[24] At Christmas, Nelson left Fanny behind and went off with the Hamiltons to Fonthill, near Salisbury, to the 1,700 acres and vast Gothic mansion of William Beckford. Mr Beckford was *nouveau riche*, bisexual, and ambitious. He had cultivated Hamilton, and hoped to get a title by him. The idea was that Hamilton, for his services at Naples, should accept a peerage rather than a pension, that he should somehow get Beckford named in the succession as his heir, and that in return Beckford would pay a pension to Hamilton for life and afterwards to Emma. This gave Emma the prospect of becoming a peeress, in which case Nelson could be the less sure of her. Peerages were jobbed, though hardly in that manner, but Beckford took the business seriously, and the idea was not abandoned until July 1802.[25]

After Christmas, Nelson returned to London. He had been fêted and feasted. He had been ridiculed and caricatured. He was above all a hero, and as such he was used by the government on the last day of the year, when he was present at the king's speech from the throne. It amounted to a threat to Russia, which with Denmark, Sweden, and Prussia was in the process of forming an armed neutrality of the north. The essence was that this armed neutrality would seriously hinder the British blockade of France, and Britain could not tolerate this. At the ceremony in the House of Lords the king was supported by two peers. One was Hood and the other Nelson. He was the newest of peers, still among the more junior admirals, and in no good odour with the king, but he and Hood served very well as symbols, to show the northern powers that Britain had a navy. And St Vincent had just reminded Spencer, the first lord, of the proper uses of Nelson. 'I always', he said, 'had the *San Josef* in view for my friend Nelson, who seems most highly flattered by it: all the fear I have about him is, that he will tire of being attached to a great fleet, and want to be carrying on a predatory war, which is his *métier* . . .'[26] So it was, and he would soon have a chance to prove it once again.

Meantime his situation with Fanny was impossible, and hers with him. One account has him wandering at night through the streets of London, in despair, from Piccadilly as far east as the city, the Fleet market, and Blackfriars Bridge, and then arriving exhausted at four in the morning at the Hamiltons' house in Grosvenor Square, where he threw himself on their bed. That is a walk of at least six miles. The account is Emma Hamilton's.[27] She, of all those who wrote about Nelson's state of mind at that time, knew him best. She also showed herself, in her letters later that year, to be a malicious liar. But there is likely to be some truth in what she says here. It is in part, and certainly in tone, corroborated by a letter Nelson wrote to her on the morning of 3 January. He was about to set off for the funeral of Captain Locker, with whom he had gone to the West Indies twenty years before, and corresponded with ever since. He wrote: 'My dear Lady Hamilton, it is now six o'clock and I dread the fatigue of this day being not in the best spirits, and believe me when I say that I regret that I am not the person attended *upon* at this funeral, for although I have had my days of glory, yet I find this world so full of jealousy & envy that I see but a very faint gleam of future comfort. I shall come to Grosvenor Square on my return from this melancholy procession & hope to find in the smiles of my friends some alleviation for the cold looks and cruel words of my enemies. May god bless you my dear lady and believe me ever your unalterable Nelson. Saturday morn.'[28]

By early January it was settled that a fleet would go to the Baltic, and Nelson knew from Spencer that he would probably go with it. This should have been assurance enough, but at the same time he was uneasy about the way he had left the Mediterranean, and wrote a formal letter to their lordships of the admiralty requesting that they would not consider his 'necessary coming from Italy as a dereliction of the service, but only a remove from the Mediterranean to the Channel fleet', and asking for his full pay en route.[29] This was refused. In the middle of the month, he travelled to Plymouth to take possession of the *San Josef*. The break with Fanny had already come. William Haslewood, Nelson's solicitor, was at breakfast with them one morning when Nelson mentioned something Emma had done, at which Fanny rose, saying she was sick of hearing about dear Lady Hamilton, left the room, and drove from the house. Haslewood was anxious to portray Nelson as the offended party, and was emphatic that Fanny made no overture towards a reconciliation.[30] He was wrong. He just did not know. She did, as we shall see, make several attempts, and even at this time behaved warmly towards her husband. After the first payment of his quarterly allowance to her, of £400, was made on 13 January, she wrote addressing him as her dearest husband, thanking him for his generosity, and saying that, had he left it to her to decide the amount, she could not in conscience have asked for so much. 'Accept my warmest, my most affectionate and grateful thanks. I could say more but my heart is too full. Be assured that every wish, every desire of mine is to please the man whose affection constitutes my happiness.'[31] Mrs Berry, her close friend, later said that in temper, person, and mind, Fanny was everything Nelson could have wished, and that they never had a quarrel. But the siren had sung and cast her spell about Nelson, and he was too guileless to see the danger.[32]

On his way to Plymouth, Nelson visited St Vincent at Tor abbey, near Torquay, where he was spending the winter ashore. Neither mentioned prize money. While they were together a letter arrived announcing the appointment of Admiral Sir Hyde Parker to the North Sea command and therefore to the command of the Baltic fleet. Both had expected this.[33] They then talked about the best way of destroying the Danes. That was how Nelson saw it. St Vincent put it differently in two letters he wrote the next day. In the first, to his friend Nepean, he said: 'Nelson was very low ... appeared and acted as if he had done me an injury, and felt apprehensive that I was acquainted with it. Poor man, he is devoured with vanity, weakness, and folly; was strung with ribbons, medals, etc, and yet pretended that he wished to avoid the honour and ceremonies he everywhere met with upon the road.'[34] To Mr Kaye, his man of business in the prize case, he wrote more sharply, saying Davison, Nelson's prize agent, had behaved in such an indecent manner that he suspected there was a serpent lurking somewhere, perhaps Lord Hood who had been an adviser throughout, determined to create a rupture between him and Nelson. 'I could discover by the manner of Lord Nelson, when he was here, that he felt he had injured me, but we parted good friends, and as he owes all the fame, titles, badges, and distinctions he wears [to] my patronage and protection, and I still continue kind to him in the extreme, I hardly think it possible he can break with me.'[35]

The two men continued in their public cordiality and private misgivings. Nelson, on board the *San Josef*, wrote to St Vincent that she was the finest ship in the world and worked like a cutter, and that he hoped soon to get rid of all her women, dogs, and pigeons and get under sail for Torbay.[36] St Vincent rejoiced in the hope of seeing Nelson again, thanked him for wishing him a happy sixty-sixth birthday, and advised him to give a little personal attention to the ladies of Plymouth: 'You know how to tickle them.' To Davison, Nelson wrote that St Vincent overwhelmed him with civilities, but that he would not spare the earl an inch point of law, and was prepared with a broadside as strong as any he could send.[37]

At the Hamiltons' house, Emma was near giving birth. She had Nelson's child at the end of January, and the baby was immediately put out to nurse with a Mrs Gibson, about a mile away. Nelson first heard of the birth on 1 February while he was in the *San Josef* at Torbay. He wrote wildly to Emma that he was mad with joy, prayed, and raved about her. Or rather, he wrote that a young man who was Mrs Thompson's friend, and was at his elbow, did all these things. They had settled on this code. A Mrs Thompson in London had had a baby and was being looked after by Emma, while Mrs Thompson's friend, the father, was at Torbay being looked after by Nelson. The friend swore before heaven he would marry Mrs Thompson as soon as possible, which he fervently prayed might be soon. He wished the child to be called Emma, but was overruled by Mrs Thompson who called her Horatia. The friend gave Lord Nelson £100 to send to Emma so that she might distribute that sum among those who had been useful to Mrs Thompson 'on the late occasion'. And the child's parents, when she was christened, should be given in the register as Johem and Morata Etnorb, which, as Nelson explained, would be Bronte backwards and an anagram of Emma and Horatio, who were the parents' friends.[38] There has been speculation that Emma had borne twins, had kept Horatia, and put the other in a foundling hospital. The evidence for this is one line in one letter of Nelson's, written three weeks after the birth, in which he looks forward to seeing Emma again, and writes: 'I daresay twins will again be the fruit of this meeting.'[39] Of this letter we have only a transcript; the original was sold at auction in 1897 and its whereabouts are unknown. A simple error in transcription of the word 'twins' or 'again' could explain matters. It could even be a joke: this was one of the letters in which Nelson was writing on behalf of Thompson. But twins are inherently unlikely. Nothing in any other of Nelson's many letters to Emma after the birth mentions a twin. Nor does it make sense to argue that she kept it from him. A child strengthened Emma's hold on him, and he would have been more delighted with two than one. She could as easily have put two children out to nurse as one. As to the foundling hospital, it was the custom for ladies of fashion to stand as godmother to foundlings, and Horatia, when she grew up, remembered that Emma had stood as godmother to such a child.[40]

Nelson's letters went on and on, sometimes three a day, and they soon became the letters of a man who was not only delighted, and infatuated, but also afraid. We have none of Emma's letters to Nelson; he burned them, though he said it went to his heart to do so.[41] But we can get some idea of the style in which she may have written from a later letter to Davison in which she expressed her view of Fanny:

The apoticarys widow, the Creole with her Heart Black as Her feind like looking face was never destined for a Nelson for so noble minded a Creature. She never loved Him for Himself. She loved her poor dirty Escalopes [Aesculapius, referring to Fanny's first husband, Dr Nisbet] if she had love, and the 2 dirty negatives made that dirty affirmative that is a disgrace to the Human Species [Josiah]. She then starving took in an evil hour our Hero she made him unhappy she disunited Him from His family she wanted to *raise up* Her own vile spue at the expence and total abolation of the family which shall be immortalized for having given birth to the Saviour of his Country. When He came home *maimed lame* and covered with Glory She put in derision His Honnerable wounds She raised a clamour against him because He had seen a more lovely a more virtuous woman who had served with him in a foreign country and who had her heart and senses open to his Glory to His greatness and His virtues. If he had lived with this daemon this blaster of His fame and reputation He must have fallen under it and His Country would have lost their greatest ornament – No, let him live yet to gain more victory and to be blessed with his idolising Emma.[42]

Whatever Emma wrote to Nelson at Torbay, it was such that within a week he was saying he had never been so miserable as at that moment, and that he feared she would not be true to him.[43] 'I am alone with your letters, except the cruel one, that is burnt, and I have scratched out all the scolding words, and have read them 40 times over . . . again I intreat you never to scold me, for I have never deserved it from you, you know.' Very occasionally he answered back: 'Suppose I did say that the west country women wore black stockings, what is it more than if you was to say what puppies all the present young men are? You cannot help your eyes, and god knows I cannot see much.'[44] Within five days of the birth, Nelson was in anguish at the prospect of Sir William Hamilton asking the Prince of Wales to dinner, not alone but in company, because he feared the prince might seduce Emma. His objections were many and repeated. It would be highly improper; Sir William thought of a regency as certain and therefore thought she would sell better; the prince would be next to her and telling her soft things; he would put his foot near hers; he would want to have her alone; don't let him touch; do not let the unprincipled liar come, god blast him; surely Sir William must be mad to give his wife the reputation of whore to the prince; she was at auction – by god, his blood boiled. For his part, Nelson assured Emma that he might in his present state be trusted with fifty virgins naked in a dark room.[45] He went on like this, in letter after long distracted letter, until Hamilton himself replied to Nelson: 'Whether Emma will be able to write to you today is a question, as she has got one of her terrible sick headaches. Among other things that vex her is that we have been drawn in to be under the absolute necessity of giving a dinner to the Prince of Wales on Sunday next. He asked it himself having expressed his strong desire of hearing Banti's [Italian opera soprano] and Emma's voices together. I am well aware of the danger that would attend the prince's frequenting our house, not that I fear that Emma could ever be induced to act contrary to the prudent conduct she has hitherto pursued, but the world is so ill natured that the worst construction is put upon the most innocent actions ... Emma would really have gone to any lengths to have avoided Sunday's dinner, but I thought it would not be prudent to break with the prince who really has shown the greatest civility to us ... and she has at last acquiesced to my opinion. I have been thus explicit as I know your lordship's way of thinking and your very kind attachment to us and to everything that concerns us.'[46]

Now it was common talk that Nelson and Emma were lovers. Anyone who could read a newspaper knew that. Cruikshank's print could not have been more explicit and was on public sale. Emma's pregnancy had been hinted at by several references to her embonpoint. And Hamilton could not have been unaware of Emma's having given birth in his own house, but this letter is his only written acknowledgment of her and Nelson's attachment. Why, unless he knew of the attachment and was complaisant, and moreover knew of Nelson's jealousy and was anxious to appease it, should Hamilton have thought it mattered to Nelson whether or not he had the Prince of Wales to dine at his house? The letter is a masterpiece of diplomacy, saying nothing and yet everything. When Nelson was not reading Emma's letters forty times over and scratching out the scolding words he was writing to her in this vein:

'It setts me on fire, even the thoughts much more than would be the reality. I am sure my love & desires are all to you, and if any woman were to come to me, even as I am at this moment from thinking of you, I hope it might rot off if I would touch her even with my hand . . .'[47] This is innocent enough, and so is Nelson's description of Horatia as their 'true love-begotten child', and of Emma as his own dear wife, for such, he said, she was in his eyes and in the face of heaven.[48] But this meant that he had to be rid of Fanny. 'That person', he told Emma, 'has her separate maintenance.' It was widely known that they had separated. The former Betsy Wynne, who had married Captain Fremantle and knew Nelson from Corsica and Tenerife, wrote in her diary: 'Lady Nelson is sueing . . . I have no patience with her husband, at his age and such a cripple to play the fool with Lady Hamilton.'[49] Fanny had no need to sue. Nelson, as generous in making gifts of his own money as he always was, had already arranged with his solicitors to pay her £1,600 a year, half his income. Then, early in March, he wrote a last letter to her, addressed to Brighton:

> Josiah is to have another ship and to go abroad if the Thalia cannot soon be got ready. I have done *all* for him and he may again as he has often done before wish me to break my neck, and be abetted in it by his friends who are likewise my enemies, but I have done my duty as an honest generous man and I neither want or wish for any body to care what become of me, whether I return or am left dead in the Baltic, seeing I have done all in my power for you. And if dead, you will find I have done the same, therefore my only wish is to be left to myself and wishing you every happiness, believe that I am your affectionate Nelson & Bronte.[50]

Fanny wrote across it: 'This is my Lord Nelson's letter of dismissal, which so astonished me that I immediately sent it to Mr Maurice Nelson who was sincerely attached to me for his advice. He desired me not to take the least note of it, as his brother seemed to have forgot himself.'

Nisbet did not get the *Thalia*. He had quarrelled with his first lieutenant and with his master in the Mediterranean the previous year, calling the master a damned rascal and recommending him to jump overboard. He had also got into a brawl at the theatre in Leghorn. Duckworth tactfully sent him home to avoid a court martial, and he

never held another command. But Nelson, in spite of his low opinion
of his stepson, did try three times, that March and April, to get him a
ship. The admiralty would not stand it.[51]

But he had done with Fanny. Most of his family dropped her as
well, and quickly took to Lady Hamilton. The first and most eager
was The Revd William Nelson, who, travelling down to Plymouth to
his brother's ship, wrote her these lines: 'Your image and voice are
constantly before my imagination, and I can think of nothing else . . . It
is no wonder that my good, my great, my virtuous, my beloved brother
should be so attached to your ladyship after so long a friendship, when
I feel so much after a short acquaintance. May it continue unabated to
the latest period of our lives.'[52] Mrs William Nelson fell as easily. Emma
called her 'mia cara amica' and told her their souls were congenial, and
they were soon abusing Tom Tit, their name for Fanny, and exchanging
extravagant praise of Great Jove, who was Nelson.[53] Catherine also
conceived an antipathy for Fanny. Susannah Bolton, Nelson's eldest
sister, did at first remain sympathetic. 'Will you', she wrote to Fanny,
'excuse what I am going to say? I wish you had continued in town a
little longer, as I have heard my brother regretted he had not a house he
could call his own when he returned. Do whenever you hear he is likely
to return, have a house to receive him. If you absent yourself entirely
from him there can be no reconciliation . . . Your conduct as he *justly*
says is *exemplary* in regard to him and he has not an unfeeling heart . . .
I hope in god one day I shall have the pleasure of seeing you together as
happy as ever, he certainly as far as I hear is not a happy man.'[54] When
Fanny replied that she did not wish Susannah to take too much notice
of her for fear it might injure her with Nelson, she replied: 'I assure you
I have a pride, as well as himself, in doing what is right . . .'[55]

More than anyone else, Nelson's father was anxious for Fanny. He
thought of her as a daughter, she had not written since she left London,
and he was anxious about her. 'How long do you think of remaining
at Brighton? Can I contribute anything to the further increase of your
comfort . . . Have you taken or do you think of taking a house in London?
Can I be of any use in these things? Believe me curiosity does [not]
excite me to make such enquiries but a sincere wish to prove that I am
truly yours most affectionately, Edmund Nelson.'[56] For the rest of his
life, another year, she cared as best she could for the old rector's ease
of mind and body, while Nelson as steadily neglected his father.

CHAPTER TWENTY

Champion of England in the North

BY FEBRUARY 1801 NELSON was ready to be off, as he told Emma, 'to be the champion of England in the north'.[1] He had a new first lord to answer to. Pitt had resigned on the issue of Catholic emancipation, nothing to do with the war, and was succeeded as prime minister by Henry Addington. St Vincent became first lord, taking Troubridge with him as one of the new lords of the admiralty. This increase in St Vincent's power led Nelson to suppose that he would lose his prize case, having only justice and honour on his side while his chief had 'partiality, power, money, and rascality' on his.[2] As to the Baltic, Nelson's aim was 'strike quick, and home', but Hyde Parker, his commander-in-chief, possessed no such urgency.[3] Parker, who was no relation of Sir Peter Parker, had been knighted in the American war for forcing a difficult passage up the North River, at New York, and had been commander-in-chief in the West Indies, where he had made a fortune in prizes. He was very much senior to Nelson, who in January 1801, when he was promoted vice-admiral of the blue, was still only eighty-third on the list of flag officers. Hyde Parker was sixty-one, and he had just married a girl of eighteen, which amused the newspapers, *The Morning Post* calling the poor girl the admiral's '*sheet* anchor'.[4]

After three days' leave in London, during which Nelson saw Horatia for the first time, he returned to his ship still in a turmoil, writing to Emma one day that she was his dear wife and the next that if she admitted the prince into her company he would consider Nelson

rejected, and would rather see the end of the world that week.[5] Then
he joined Parker at Yarmouth on 6 March. Parker delayed. Nelson
dropped Troubridge a hint that his commander-in-chief preferred lying
in bed with his new wife, a direct order to sail was given, and the fleet
of sixteen ships of the line weighed anchor on 12 March. It was twelve
days before they were off Elsinore, and on the passage Nelson had
another dream about Emma: 'I dreamt last night that I beat you with
a stick on account of that fellow & then attempted to throw over your
head a tub of boiling hot water, you may believe I woke in an agony
and that my feelings cannot be very comfortable . . .' He complained to
her that he was sorry to be sent on such an expedition, that everyone
hated him, and that Parker had told him nothing.[6] He had heard that
a minister was to be sent ashore to negotiate with the Danes, of which
he disapproved, writing to Davison that he would anchor the fleet
outside Copenhagen, and then a Danish minister would think twice
about war with England, when the next moment he would probably
see his master's fleet in flames and his capital in ruins.[7]

Parker's orders, which he did not show Nelson, were to deal with
Denmark first, then the Russian ports, and then Sweden. Nelson had
always believed that Russia was the trunk and the other powers merely
the branches of the northern alliance, and off Elsinore he wrote Parker
a letter of grand strategy, in the tone of a lecture. They should not lose
a moment in attacking. The safety and honour of the country rested
with Parker, whether it should be degraded in the eyes of Europe or
raise its head higher. He recommended an attack on both Copenhagen
and on the Russians, more or less at the same time. 'Would it not
be possible . . . to detach ten ships of three and two decks, with one
bomb[ship] and two fire ships, to Revel [now Talinn], to destroy
the Russian squadron at that place? I do not see the great risk of
such a detachment, and with the remainder to attempt the business at
Copenhagen. The measure may be thought bold, but I am of opinion
the boldest measures are the safest . . .'[8] Parker did not take his advice.
When the Danes rejected the terms offered by the diplomats, the fleet
was lying off Elsinore. Another week was wasted while Parker dithered
over whether to attack Copenhagen from the north or the south, and
it was 1 April before the British fleet anchored six miles north of the
city. It had taken Parker three weeks to get there from Yarmouth.

What followed the next day was the bloodiest and closest-run of

Nelson's battles, but it was in no sense a fleet engagement. It was a battle between the assembled and stationary defences of Copenhagen and a British squadron manoeuvring in two deep channels with a great shoal between. The Danish defences were the two Trekroner forts at the north of the city, other shore batteries, and eighteen assorted men of war – masted and without masts, rigged and unrigged, hulks, floating batteries, and an old Indiaman – anchored north to south parallel with the shore, forming a line a mile and a half long.[9] Since the whole British fleet could not manoeuvre in such narrow passages, Nelson offered to go in with a squadron. Parker gave him ten ships of the line, two fifties, seven frigates, and nine bombs and fireships. Parker, lying north of the city, kept eight ships of the line with him, and took no part in the action.

The battle began at ten o'clock on 2 April. The casualties were heavy, particularly on the floating batteries whose crews, as they fell, were replaced by volunteers from the city. By one in the afternoon the *Bellona* and *Russell*, of the British ships of the line, were aground and flying distress signals, and *Agamemnon* was unable to work herself into the line. The British frigates took a terrible battering. The line was obscured by smoke. It was then that Parker, three miles off, made signal number 39, *Discontinue the action.* Nelson, on board the *Elephant*, acknowledged the signal and disobeyed it, keeping his own signal for close action flying. The battle continued. The *Dannebrog*, 62 guns, a dismasted two decker, drifted in flames. Some of the Danish floating batteries fell silent. Others struck or were understood to have struck, yet when boats from the English ships tried to take these batteries, they were fired on. Nelson then sent ashore a letter proposing a truce.

It was in his own hand and addressed to 'The Brothers of English Men, the Danes', and it read: 'Lord Nelson has directions to spare Denmark when no longer resisting but if the firing is continued on the part of Denmark Lord Nelson will be obliged to set on fire the floating batteries he has taken, without having the power of saving the Brave Danes who have defended them.'[10] Nelson folded the paper and asked for sealing wax. A man was sent for some, but was killed. He gave the order to send another messenger, at which someone pointed out that there were wafers, paper seals, on his table. He insisted on sending a second man for sealing wax, and then sealed the letter, taking care to make a perfect impression. When he was asked why he took such

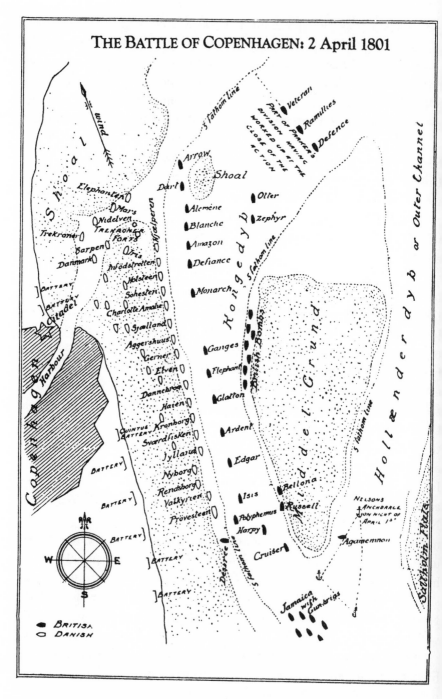

THE BATTLE OF COPENHAGEN: 2 April 1801

From Clowes's Royal Navy: a History, *vol IV, 1899.*

rouble, he said that a wafer would have suggested he had a pressing eason for being in a hurry. The wax told no such tale.[11]

The letter was sent ashore under a flag of truce. Frederick, the young Danish prince regent, sent Adjutant General Hans Lindholm to ask Nelson's reasons for requesting a truce. Nelson boldly replied in writing hat his object was humanity; he consented that hostilities should cease until he had taken his prisoners out of the prizes, and would land all he wounded Danes and burn or remove his prizes.[12] He then referred Lindholm to Parker for a conference on details. Parker was three miles off, and it was a long row up to him. A twenty-four-hour truce was concluded. The Danish wounded were landed. When Nelson began to withdraw his ships from the channel, the *Defiance* and *Elephant* ran aground, the *Ganges* ran on board the *Monarch*, and the *Russell, Bellona* and *Agamemnon*, which had been stuck fast all day, were not released until late that night or the next day. The British casualties were three hundred and fifty dead and almost a thousand wounded. The Danish losses, killed and wounded, were put at anywhere between 1,800 and 5,000.[13] That evening Nelson wrote to Emma: 'That same deity who has on many occasions protected Nelson has once again crowned his endeavours with compleat success.' Then, after such a day, he reverted to his old jealousy: 'I could not wish to consider you as my friend if you kept such scandalous company as the P— W— how Sir Wm can bear to associate with such wretches I cannot think.'[14] Next day, 3 April, at Parker's request, Nelson went ashore to meet the crown prince. He landed from his barge and walked to the Amelienborg palace. One account says that a strong guard was needed to keep off the mob.[15] Nelson saw things differently. 'I was received in the most flattering manner by all ranks,' he wrote to Davison, 'and the crowd was, as is usual, with me. No wonder I am spoilt. All my astonishment is that my head was not turned.' Plainly it was, since he told Emma that 'even the stairs of the palace were crowded, huzzaing & saying god bless Lord Nelson'.[16] Whether or not this was likely in a city full of the dead and wounded of the battle, it was what he brought himself to believe.

Nelson talked for two hours with the prince who was attended only by Lindholm. The prince's English was excellent. No minister was present. We have only Nelson's account of this meeting, which he wrote directly to Addington. He and the prince started with courtesies, Nelson saying it was the greatest affliction to every man in England

that Denmark had fired on the English flag and become leagued with
her enemies. The prince objected that Parker had declared war on
Denmark, and asked why the British fleet had come into the Baltic
'To crush a most formidable and unprovoked coalition against Great
Britain', said Nelson. The prince replied that his uncle, George III
had been deceived, and that nothing would ever make him take a
part against Britain; to which Nelson replied that there could be no
doubt of the hostility of Denmark, for if her fleet had been joined with
Sweden's and Russia's they would have menaced the coast of England
and probably have joined the French. He asked for a total suspension
of Denmark's treaties with Russia while the negotiations were going
on. The prince thanked Nelson for his open conversation, and said he
must call a council.[17] Nelson went back to his ship and wrote to Emma:
'The prince seemed to quake ... and if they have not had enough we
must try and get at their arsenal and city that will sicken them if they
have not had enough.' He went on to tell her that two portraits of her
hung in his cabin, including the one done at Dresden (which showed
her wearing the cross of Malta he had procured for her from the mad
czar of Russia whose devoted enemy he had since become). He called
them his guardian angels.[18]

Over the next few days, while negotiations continued, the prizes
were burned, the British fleet refitted, and bomb ships brought up
so that they could bombard the city if talks broke down. Nelson
wrote constantly to Emma, once giving her the numbers of four
tickets he had in the lottery and asking her to check to see if he
had been lucky.[19] On 8 April Nelson went back to the palace again,
this time with Lieutenant Colonel the Hon. William Stewart, who was
in command of the troops in the fleet. They acted as joint negotiators.
The Danes were afraid of Russian reprisals if Denmark left the northern
alliance, and the British offered to leave a fleet in the Baltic for their
protection. At one point the talks stuck, one Danish delegate remarked
to another in French that they might have to renew hostilities, at which
Nelson, who had understood, said: 'Tell him that we are ready; ready
to bombard this night.' They then went up a grand staircase to dinner,
the prince leading the way. Nelson, looking around him, whispered to
Stewart: 'Though I have only one eye, I see all this will burn very
well.' An armistice was agreed, which the next day was signed by
Nelson and Stewart, and ratified by Parker.[20] Nelson again wrote

lirectly to Addington, briskly listing the heads of the negotiations. 1st We had beat the Danes. 2nd We wish to make them feel that we are their real friends, therefore have spared their town, which we can always set on fire; and I do not think if we burnt Copenhagen it would have the effect of attaching them to us; on the contrary they would hate us. 3rd They understand perfectly that we are at war with them or their treaty or armed neutrality made last year. 4th We have made them suspend the operations of that treaty. 5th It has given our fleet free scope to act against Russia and Sweden.' Nelson was riding high. After the armistice was signed, and while he still lay off Copenhagen, he wrote Lindholm an extravagant letter congratulating Europe on the death of the Russian emperor Paul – the news of whose murder by his courtiers having come a little too late, since the same news earlier night have so weakened the alliance that the battle of Copenhagen would have been unnecessary. Admirals second in command of fleets lid not usually congratulate continents. Nelson did, and then he asked Lindholm to accept a Nile medal and a short account of his life, which t might not be amiss for Danish youths to study.[21] At the same time he wrote to Emma saying that if the government did not approve of his humane conduct he begged them to allow him to retire under the shade of a chestnut tree at Bronte where the din of war would not reach his ears, and where he could give his advice (if asked) to enable Ferdinand, his *benefactor*, to be more than ever respected in the Mediterranean.[22] He did not yet know that his Neapolitan benefactor had signed an armistice with France which excluded British ships from his ports, and that Maria Carolina had settled in Austria.[23]

The two most contentious matters of the battle are Parker's signal and Nelson's truce, and in both the first hand evidence of Colonel Stewart is essential. On the day of the battle he was with Nelson in the *Elephant*.

Parker did make a signal to leave off action. Nelson did disobey it. Apart from anything else, he *could* not have obeyed Parker's signal because he could not have got his ships out. It has been argued that the signal was discretionary, but that cannot be so. If the signal had been for Nelson alone, which might conceivably have allowed him a discretion, it would have been flown, according to the signal regulations, under a red pendant. But it was not. It was a general signal to all ships that saw it, and indeed Nelson's frigates, which were nearer to Parker, did

obey it, as they were bound to.[24] The matter is clinched by a private
letter from Vice-Admiral William Young, a lord of the admiralty, to
Keith in the Mediterranean, saying that Parker had been recalled. 'He
[Parker] complains of Nelson having disobeyed his signals ... to call
the ships off, which I understand could not have been obeyed without
exposing the whole to certain destruction ...'[25] Neither Nelson nor
Parker had mentioned the signal in their official dispatches home
and it was unwise of Parker to complain privately. Parker's motive
has never been established. He may simply have thought the Danish
fire too heavy for Nelson's squadron to bear, but he was really too far
away to know.

Parker's signal and Nelson's disobedience are established. A quite
separate matter is the legend of the telescope and the blind eye, and
that is a fairy tale. Colonel Stewart was with Nelson on his quarterdeck
and in a letter home he gave a detailed description of the action, 1,700
words long. Five hours had passed in one incessant roar of cannon.
He thought the battle hazardous, the fleet intrepid, and Nelson 'most
grand'. He had never so admired any officer. He scorned the 'croakers' –
and he said there were many – who thought the victory had been bought
infinitely too dearly. Nelson was a man who attracted admiration, and
Stewart was one of nature's admirers. As he had been with Colonel
Drinkwater at St Vincent, so Nelson was lucky with Colonel Stewart
at Copenhagen. Stewart was writing to his friend Sir William Clinton
who was *aide-de-camp* to the Duke of York, and the duke was the king's
second and favourite son and commander-in-chief of the British army.
So Nelson's actions that day were made known, in glowing terms,
in the highest quarters.[26] And so far as the legend of the blind eye
is concerned, what Stewart did not write is most significant. Several
times, and at length, he quoted Nelson's remarks on those fellows the
Danes and on the timid pilots who had been afraid to anchor nearer the
hulks and the batteries for fear of running ashore, but when he came to
the signal to leave off action, he reported it to Clinton simply. 'This is
a fact,' he wrote, '& is a source of much conversation in our fleet now.'
He said Nelson did not answer it, but expressed his astonishment, and
kept the signal for close action flying. That is the unembroidered story.
No telescope, no blind eye, no exclamation of 'I really do not see the
signal'. If the drama with the telescope had taken place, or if Nelson
had said anything like those words, Stewart could not have resisted

recounting the tale, but in a letter of six closely-written pages he said nothing about it. Stewart also kept a handwritten journal, which reads as though he wrote it up immediately after he got home from the Baltic, in which he again said that Nelson did not repeat signal number 39 but on the contrary said he was determined 'to give it to them till they should be sick of it ...'[27] Again, there was no telescope or blind eye. The blind eye first appeared in Harrison's biography of 1806, on the authority of Mr Furgusson, surgeon of the *Elephant*, who added snatches of conversation. Now the last place a surgeon would be in action was the quarterdeck. His place was below with the wounded, so what he said has to be regarded with scepticism. But his account ran like this: when Nelson was told Parker was flying number 39 he exclaimed: 'Then damn the signal; take no notice of it, and hoist mine for closer battle: that is the way I answer such signals ... Now, nail mine to the mast!' Then, turning to Captain Foley, he said, 'Foley, you know I have lost an eye, and have a right to be blind when I like; and, damn me if I'll see that signal!'[28] So now we have a blind eye and a flag nailed to the mast, but still no telescope. The legend did not begin to emerge in all its fullness until Clarke and M'Arthur's hagiography of 1809, which gave an account 'by an officer who was with Lord Nelson'. This officer wrote that Nelson was pacing the quarterdeck when a shot hit the main mast and knocked a few splinters among them, at which Nelson said it was warm work but he would not be anywhere else for thousands. When Parker made signal number 39, the signal lieutenant told Nelson, who continued pacing. When the lieutenant asked him if he should repeat it, he said, 'No, acknowledge it'. As the man turned away, Nelson called after him, asking if number 16, for close action, was still hoisted [on the *Elephant*]. The lieutenant said it was, and Nelson told him to keep it so. He then walked the deck much agitated, moving the stump of his right arm, saying, 'Leave off action? Damn me if I do.' Nelson then, with what the observing officer called an archness peculiar to his character, put the glass to his blind eye and exclaimed, 'I really do not see the signal.'[29] The telescope had appeared. The legend reached its apotheosis four years later in Southey's life of 1813, which brought together the signal nailed to the mast, the immortal quotation, 'I really do not see the signal', the blind eye, *and* the telescope, and so it has lived on ever since, with some unwitting assistance from Nicolas in the 1840s. He found the manuscript from which Clarke and M'Arthur

had taken their account, and restored the first paragraphs, which had
been cut. This restoration revealed that their source had been none
other than Colonel Stewart. Nicolas was scrupulous, and his reputation
gave credibility to the story, though all he did was reprint it, with
acknowledgement, from Clark and M'Arthur, of whose work he had a
low opinion. Stewart, then, had written three accounts. The first was in
his letter written at the time to Sir William Clinton. The second was in
his contemporary manuscript journal. In his third version, which seems
to have been written specially for Clarke and M'Arthur (who invited
many people to contribute their reminiscences), Stewart added to his
own two earlier versions the details which had appeared three years
before in Harrison's biography, and then also added the telescope.[30]
Legends are created like that.

So much for the signal. The second and more important question
is that of the truce. Nelson always insisted that his reason for asking
for a truce was humanity. That was not his principal reason, let
alone the whole. Stewart, who was with him at the time, said in his
letter to Clinton that the truce was 'a masterpiece of policy' because,
victorious though they were, the narrowness of the channel and the
commanding batteries on shore had left six British ships aground. 'Lord
Nelson then *commanded* a cessation of hostilities, and by prolonging it
under one pretext or another, in four and twenty hours after got our
crippled ships off the shoals, and from under the guns of the enemy's
batteries . . .' He used the word 'pretext'. He also said that without the
truce the *Elephant* and *Defiance*, at the north end of the British line,
would certainly have suffered severely, if they had not been destroyed,
and that the Trekroner fort at the north of the line, although too far
away to do serious damage to most of the squadron, was hurting the
Monarch, whose loss in men that day exceeded that of any ship of the
line in the war.[31]

Stewart, then, said nothing about humanity, did not observe any
such feeling in Nelson, and did not mention it among the reasons he put
forward to explain Nelson's 'policy'. Nelson, moreover, had throughout
acted deliberately – demanding sealing wax so as not to appear hurried,
and consulting his captains. Before the boat offering the truce returned,
he asked Fremantle and Foley whether the British ships least damaged
could be advanced to that part of the Danish line not yet damaged, and
they replied that, on the contrary, they were in favour of moving the

ships, while the wind held fair, from their present intricate channel. So, said Stewart, Nelson knew how to act when Lindholm came on board to ask his reason for the proposed truce.[32]

And so far as Nelson's motive was humanity, it was humanity with a threat: if the Danish firing did not cease he would be obliged to set the floating batteries on fire, without being able to save the men in them. He would burn the men along with the batteries. In the letter he wrote to Emma that night he was almost candid: 'I sent a flag of truce on shore with a kind note which instantly brought off the adjutant general of H.R.H.'s with a civil message wishing to know the precise meaning of my flag of truce and to say that the fire of the state of Denmark was stopped and that the officer would agree to my cessation of hostilities, this was not very inconvenient to me as the *Elephant* had been on shore opposite a 74 and two or three floating batteries.'[33]

The matter is settled by two letters Fremantle wrote, one to his wife Betsy and the other to his patron the Marquis of Buckingham. Fremantle had been with Nelson at Bastia and at Tenerife, and they were friends. To his wife Fremantle wrote: 'Every merit is due to Lord Nelson for his policy as well as bravery on this occasion ... He hailed and desired I would come on board ... he was sending an officer with a flag of truce on shore to tell the prince that if they did not cease firing from the batteries he should be under the necessity of burning all the ships with the people in them. This produced a cessation to the very severe battle, which was certainly as convenient for us and the enemy, as we had several ships on shore and most of the ships engaged so completely crippled that it was with difficulty they could sail out.' To Buckingham he wrote on the same day: 'He put into my hand a letter which he meant to send immediately to the prince threatening to burn every ship captured if the batteries did not cease firing. At this time he was aware that our ships were cut to pieces, and that it would be difficult to get them out.'[34]

Fischer, the Danish commodore, later stung Nelson by writing to the crown prince that 'this hero, in the middle and very heat of the battle, sent a flag of truce on shore'. This brought from Nelson the statement that it was not from fear of fighting that he negotiated but, again, from humanity.[35] No one ever said Nelson acted out of fear. But after Fischer's statement appeared in the London newspapers, questions were asked. *The Morning Chronicle* said that although it had previously ascribed Nelson's proposal for a truce to the most refined humanity, it now appeared to be not so much a measure of humanity as a *ruse de guerre*, to get his ships out, and the editors were not quite sure whether it was a justifiable one.[36] When news of this reached him, Nelson wrote yet another letter to Addington, on 8 May, to vindicate himself. Now these letters of Nelson's to Addington are strange. Junior admirals, when in the company of their commanders-in-chief as Nelson was, did not usually write direct to the prime minister, but Nelson did so – he said at Addington's own request.[37] On the evening of his first meeting with the crown prince he wrote both to Addington and to Emma, adding to Emma's letter his observation that the prince had seemed to quake.[38] After the second meeting at the palace he did the same, writing to both his mistress and the prime minister, and he did the same a third time on 8 May when he wished to defend himself against the charge that he had asked for a truce out of policy.

'My dearest friend,' he began to Addington, 'as both my friends and enemies seem not to know why I sent on shore a flag of truce – the former, many of them, thought it was a *ruse de guerre* and not quite justifiable; the latter, I believe, attributed it to a desire to have no more fighting, and few, very few, to the cause that I felt, and which I trust in god I shall retain to the last moment, *humanity*, I know it must to the world be proved, and therefore I will suppose you all the world to me.' So in a letter repudiating the *Chronicle*'s accusation that the truce had been a *ruse de guerre*, he was admitting that many of his friends thought it was just that. He continued by saying that the Danish batteries, in firing at him, had been hitting the surrendered ships, as had the returning British fire, and that since four of these ships had got crowded together it was a massacre. 'This caused my note. It was a sight which no real man could have enjoyed. I felt when the Danes became my prisoners, I became their protector; and if that had not been sufficient reason, the moment of a complete victory was surely the proper time to make an opening with the nation we had been fighting with.'

This is remarkable. He was addressing the prime minister, whom he barely knew, as his dearest friend. This was the way he often began his letters to Emma. What happened on 8 May was that he wrote to Emma and Addington, as he had done before, but this time he made one letter do for both. He wrote to Emma first, in his own hand. He

hen sent a clerk's copy of this letter to Addington, and the clerk left
n the original salutation. The letters are identical, but Nelson added
wo passages to Emma's. The first reads: 'If after this either pretended
riends or open enemies say anything upon the subject, tell them they
e *damned.*' The word *damned* is underlined three times. Then at the
ottom of the next page he wrote: 'Get Mr East or some other able
nan to put these truths before the public. Envious men, & enemies
vish to hurt me, but truth will stand its ground & I feel as firm as
a rock.'[39]

Nelson protests too much. He had not, as he wrote, acted in a moment
of complete victory. He knew three of his ships were aground and that
Fremantle and Foley had just advised him to get the others out of the
channel while the wind was fair. He did have the advantage, but if his
ships remained aground that could disappear. It would soon get dark,
which would hamper him further. What he did was certainly a *ruse de
guerre*, and a very successful one. A bloody battle ending in a virtual
draw would have been useless to England. 'If we had not conquered on
that day,' as one lord of the admiralty put it, 'it would have been such a
triumph to the Danes and such a disgrace to our navy as we would not
easily have got the better of. A drawn battle would have been a victory
to Denmark.'[40] Nelson needed time, which a truce gave him. In the time
it took to go back and forth with a flag of truce, and the time it took
to remove the wounded Danes, and the time it took Lindholm to row
to Parker three miles away, Nelson was able to get out all but three
of his ships of the line. And all that time the fresh ships of Parker's
division were approaching: *Veteran, Ramilles,* and *Defence* were within
half a mile by early evening. He showed great nerve. When he was
asked by the Danes to put his reasons in writing, and said humanity,
he also wrote that he *consented* that hostilities should cease, when it was
the Danes' consent he was asking for. He wrote moreover that he would
ever esteem it the *greatest victory* he had ever gained. Thus he ensured
that if he gained a truce it would be considered a victory, for that is
what he had already called it. Nelson's actions at Copenhagen were a
brilliant exercise in *realpolitik.* What he could not achieve decisively
with cannonades he achieved with a truce. He offered a truce because
he needed it, and the Danes accepted because they needed it too. The
Danes recovered their wounded. Nelson recovered his ships, and that of
course won him the day. He had gulled the Danes, but he would not see

that because he had acted by instinct. A ruse was nothing new to war a
sea. It was commonplace for a man of war to approach an enemy unde
a false flag which she struck at the last moment, only then running
up her true colours. Winning was Nelson's genius, and he had won
But he also wanted to be seen to have won gallantly, and was grieved
when even his friends, as he tells us, did not see it that way.

The matter is neatly put, though in a way he may not have intended
by the American naval historian Captain A. T. Mahan, one of Nelson'
fiercest partisans and defenders. In his classic biography of 1899 he
writes as follows: 'As for the message sent, it simply insisted that the
Danes should cease firing; failing which, Nelson would resort to the
perfectly regular, warlike measure of burning their ships. As the ship
were beaten, this might not be humane; but between it and leaving
them under the guns of both parties, the question of humanity was
only one of degree. If Nelson could extort from the Danes a cessation
of hostilities by such a threat, he had a perfect right to do it, and his
claim that what he demanded was required by humanity, is at leas
colourable.' *Extort* and *colourable* are damning words, in what amount
to a damning defence.[41] There is one other thing: does not the man
who exploited such a ruse at Copenhagen, when his purpose was to
save his ships which were aground, reveal himself as the more likely
to have resorted to another ruse two years before, when his purpose
was to induce the republicans to leave their castles at Naples?

When news of the victory reached London on 15 April the Hamiltons
held a rout at their house in Piccadilly, attended by the dissolute Duke
of Queensberry, the Duke of Gordon, his son Lord William Gordon the
poetaster, the Neapolitan Duke of Noia, and Nathanial Wraxall, friend
of nabobs and gossip-about-town, who described it. Emma danced the
tarantella, first with Sir William who 'maintained the conflict' for
some minutes, then with Noia, who soon gave up, and then with
a Coptic maid, perfectly black, whom Nelson had brought her as a
present from Egypt. Wraxall explained that the two performers were
supposed to be nymph and satyr, or bacchante and fawn. 'It was', he
said, 'certainly not of a nature to be performed except before a select
company, from the screams, attitudes, starts, and embraces with which
it was intermingled.' One of the select company was the Revd William
Nelson who, with the victory, felt a bishop's mitre within his grasp.[42]

Next day, both houses of parliament conducted themselves in a way which soon afterwards looked absurd. Both passed votes of thanks to Hyde Parker and to Nelson, in that order. Lord Grenville called it a victory not equalled by any achieved before (this before any real details of the engagement were known) and praised the admiralty for its astonishing dispatch' (when the whole expedition had been a catalogue of delays).[43] But in the Commons, Charles Grey, a whig who a few years later became foreign secretary, remarked that this was perhaps the only war the country had fought, where the first information received by the House had been a motion for a vote of thanks for a victory. And that was the fact. The king's speech of the previous new year's eve had been a threat to Russia. Not until mid-January was it known that Denmark had joined the alliance, and ministers had told the Commons nothing about sending the fleet. Already it was a muted victory. No public offices were illuminated, and at the request of the lord mayor the money which, as the *Morning Herald* put it, would have been thus 'uselessly expended', was used to console the widows and orphans of the battle, £5,000 being subscribed in two days.[44] Illuminations had never been thought useless after any previous battle. And when Stewart returned to England three days after the votes of thanks, and the terms of the convention signed at Copenhagen were known, it became obvious that all that had been achieved was a fourteen week armistice. *The Morning Post* said it was plain the fleet had been unable to subdue the court of Denmark. *The Chronicle* pointed out that, with all the impression of a victory, Britain had not been able to detach Denmark from the confederacy.[45] It was becoming clear that Nelson, by whatever means, had won the battle, but that the crown prince had won the peace. The admiralty, having learned of Parker's signal to withdraw, recalled him and gave Nelson the Baltic command. St Vincent told the government that the merit of the attack rested solely with Nelson, and he was made a viscount.[46] Parker got nothing. His errors as a sea officer had been delay, and that signal. His political error had been not to lead the negotiations himself. Lady Malmesbury, a friend of the Mintos, put her finger on it when she said: 'I feel sorry for Sir Hyde; but no wise man would ever have gone with Nelson or over him, as he was sure to be in the background in every case.'[47] Parker wanted an inquiry, but Nelson thought his real friends would not: they respected and loved him, and he was not criminal but idle.[48] No medals were given to the captains, as they had been in all other actions, the City of London did not vote its thanks, as it always had before, first lieutenants were not promoted, and the prize money was small.[49]

Lord Spencer was in Bath when news of the victory came, and immediately told Fanny. She wrote to her husband: 'I cannot be silent in the general joy throughout the kingdom ... What my feelings are your own good heart will tell you. Let me beg, nay intreat you, to believe no wife ever felt greater satisfaction for a husband than I do. And to the best of my knowledge I have invariably done everything you desired. If I have omitted anything I am sorry for it.' She wrote that she was going to his sick father, and ended: 'What more can I do to convince you that I am truly your affectionate wife?' She received no reply but on 23 April Nelson wrote to Davison to tell Lady Nelson to leave him alone, without any enquiries: that was why he had made her a liberal allowance, and his mind was 'fixed as fate'. If Fanny had still had any chance, her letter had arrived at the wrong time. On the same day as his note to Davison, Nelson wrote to Emma: 'My dearest amiable friend, this day 12 months we sailed from Palermo on our tour to Malta. Ah! those were happy times, days of ease and nights of pleasure.'[50]

He so much wanted to be with her, that when he received the news that he was made commander-in-chief he was grief-stricken. With that news came letters from Emma, who was still writing sharply. 'For God's sake,' he replied, 'do not *scold* me I cannot bear it . . . I *am very ill* and any *unkindness* from you will kill me much sooner than any shot in Europe.'[5] Nelson's letters at this time are those of a man out of his mind. To quote parts of them, and in print, conveys little sense of what and how he wrote. He went on for page after page, repeating himself, with some words underlined two, three, or even five times, and others obliterated with heavy ink crosses. In this state of mind, and now that he was commander-in-chief, he did what he had wanted to do in the first place and went hunting for the Russian fleet at Revel. But the fleet, now that the ice had broken, had sailed north to Cronsdtadt three days before. It was just as well. The emperor Paul, whose ambitions had caused all the trouble, was dead, and the new emperor's intentions were more pacific. But still, from Revel, Nelson wrote to St Vincent that had the fleet still been there nothing could have saved one ship of them within two hours of his entering the bay. A single three decker moored at the mouth of the harbour could have raked the whole dock from end to end. As it was, he had to make do with a state reception by the governor. 'Hundreds come to look at Nelson,' he wrote to Emma, '*that is him, that is him*, in short 'tis the same as in Italy & Germany and I now feel that a good name is better than riches.'[52]

Then Nelson heard the news that his brother Maurice had died of a brain fever. He was forty-eight. He had been promoted chief clerk only a month before his death, and was proud to have achieved this in his own right.[53] Nelson's interest had never been able to get anything for him, though he had asked often enough. St Vincent, in his letter of condolence, said that he had been occupied in Maurice's advancement when he learned of his death. This was disingenuous of St Vincent who, two days before Maurice died, had decided *not* to make him a commissioner of the navy, but merely to remind Addington that Pitt had intended to place him on the board of customs.[54] Davison managed the funeral on behalf of the Revd Edmund Nelson. Maurice was the sixth of the rector's eight sons to die before him, and the third in adulthood. He asked that the ceremonies should be carried out in a 'most decent frugall manner', with the consent of the widow. Then, a few days later, he asked Davison whether he was sure his dear late son was ever legally married. It appeared he was not, but had lived for many years with a Mrs Sarah Ford, who had lost her sight and become a cripple. Nelson was generous. He told Davison to be liberal, for she should always be considered as Maurice's honoured wife. He wrote to her himself, as Mrs Maurice Nelson, saying that she must have whisky, a horse, and everything to keep her comfortable and cheerful. He paid her debts and gave her an annuity of £100.[55]

The new Russian emperor conveyed to Nelson his desire to return to an amicable alliance with Britain, and even said he would be delighted to receive the hero of the Nile at St Petersburg, provided he came in a single ship.[56] But Nelson was ill. He told St Vincent that he must have a little rest or go to heaven, and Emma that he had suffered a terrible spasm or heart stroke that nearly carried him off. With her he was more elaborately infatuated than ever. In June he wrote to her, 'my nails are so long, not cut since February, that I am afraid of their breaking, but I should have thought it a treason to have them cut, as long as there was a possibility of my returning for my old dear friend to do the job for me.'[57] He asked to be relieved, yet he still wanted to renew the war. In the middle of June, having received reports that the Danes were, naturally, masting and rigging their ships and taking guns on board, in defiance of the armistice, he wrote to St Vincent that Jacobins ruled in Denmark and talked about setting Copenhagen ablaze.'[58] He was recalled.

His father wrote, having heard he was coming home. He remembered how his son, more than twenty years before after the Nicaraguan campaign, when he had to give up the beautiful frigate *Janus*, had said that nothing but real necessity could drive him to give up a command. 'This is my dear son, a sad reflection to me who am already bereaved of my children. Step forth, then, and save your self today whilst it is still called today . . . to recover and preserve your private and publick good. Riches and honor are in one hand, and there are probable means yet left, to secure in the other length of days.'[59] There was a sting in this. He was quoting from the New Testament, and Nelson as a parson's son would have recognised the allusion. The full verse runs: 'But exhort one another dayly, while it is still called to day, least any of you be hardened through the deceitfulness of sinne.' The sin he alluded to was his son's separation from his wife, and his attachment to Emma.

CHAPTER TWENTY-ONE

Not Since the Armada Business

NELSON RETURNED TO ENGLAND at the beginning of July and went to the Hamiltons' house in Piccadilly. Then the three of them, together with William Nelson and his wife, and Edward Parker, a young commander who had been with him at Copenhagen, went off on a rural tour. They stayed a week at the Bush inn at Staines, on the Thames, where Lord William Gordon, the poetaster who had been at Emma's dancing of the tarantella, celebrated the occasion with four pages of doggerel addressed to her. Here are three lines depicting her and Nelson on the river:

> While Antony, by Cleopatra's side –
> While you, I mean, and Henry – in a wherry,
> Are, cheek by jole, – afloat there, making merry.

Henry was Nelson. It was a name they used occasionally in their letters. And since it was Emma who preserved these verses, she cannot have minded the allusion to Antony and Cleopatra.[1]

Nelson was much concerned with posterity. He had not been back a week when a Nelson namesake from Plymouth wrote to say he had named his new grandson Horatio. Nelson replied: 'I trust that the name of Nelson will remain with credit to our country for many ages, and ... I do not yet despair but that I may have fruit from *my* own loins.'[2] Such an heir for Nelson would require the deaths of William Hamilton and Fanny. But in the meantime, encouraged by Emma and by William, Nelson asked Addington to extend the remainder of his barony. As things stood, both his barony and viscountcy would become extinct on his death leaving no legitimate children. He asked for the remainder of the barony to be settled as he had settled the succession to the dukedom of Bronte – to his father, his brother and brother's son, and then to his sisters' children – and also that his foreign honours, the dukedom and the orders from Naples and Turkey, should be stated in the patent, since he was 'anxious to have them told to the world'. This cost the government nothing, and so a new barony was created, with the remainders and recitation of orders he requested, in 'consideration of the great and important services that renowned man, Horatio Viscount Nelson, hath rendered to Us and to Our Realm'.[3]

For Addington wanted something more of Nelson. Buonaparte had made a peace with Austria and Naples, which left him free to concentrate troops and gun-vessels along the English channel. London feared an invasion, or rather, as the opposition saw it, the government, in order that ministers should be unquestioningly obeyed as if they were generals, had created an invasion scare.[4] The result was the same. The renowned Nelson was needed to repel the French, and this new command was given to him. He did not want it, and several times tried to get rid of it. There was no agreement how to ward off invasion. Hood was for keeping defence squadrons along the English coast, and St Vincent for a blockade of French ports.[5] Nelson was for attack. He supposed that 40,000 Frenchmen were coming to attack London, half landing to the west of Dover and half to the east, sixty or seventy miles from the capital. They might come from Dunkirk or Ostend, but mostly from Boulogne, from where they might row over in twelve hours. Boulogne, he said, must be attended to. If the French got to sea in a calm they must be watched. 'If a breeze springs up, our ships are to deal *destruction*; no delicacy can be observed on this great occasion.' He was given orders to defend the mouth of the Thames, the coasts of Suffolk, Essex, Kent, and Sussex, and made commander-in-chief of a flotilla of thirty or so frigates, brigs, fire-ships, bomb-ketches, and flatboats. The Revd Edmund Nelson wrote to Catherine: 'Your brother recvd his commission this morning, and is gone to Sheerness this morning on a most important and honorable employment that any navall officer has been entrusted with for many many years, not since the Armada business.'[6]

Nelson attended to Boulogne on 4 August. From Dover the firing was heard all day. Thousands of spectators with telescopes lined the cliffs hoping to make out the French coast twenty miles away. Various reports said Nelson had destroyed the port and arsenal and then moved off to harass Calais and Dunkirk, Flanders and Holland. From the *Medusa* frigate Nelson wrote to Emma: 'Boulogne was evidently not a pleasant place this morning . . . but I hope and believe several hundreds of French are gone to hell this morning for if they are dead assuredly they are gone there.' His flotilla had gone nowhere but Boulogne and then withdrawn, having sunk a brig and three flatboats. It was an anti-climax. *The Chronicle* said public expectation had been wound up, and regretted that so great a commander as Nelson should have been employed in a business of no great importance. Nelson agreed. To Emma he wrote that he was vexed such a racket should be made of such trifling things as boats of fifty or sixty tons. To St Vincent he said he had no desire for anything else than to get clear of his present command.[7]

The *Chronicle* was becoming ever more sceptical about invasion, asking if anyone believed that there were 80,000 men at Boulogne, or 30,000 in Flanders. Buonaparte might want to march on London, but he was not such a driveller as not to weigh the dangers. Nelson himself was more than sceptical, and asked St Vincent where an invasion was to come from. The time for it had gone, and he did not think there were 2,000 men at Boulogne. He said he was laughed at for his puny boat warfare, but still intended a second attack on Boulogne, to take all the French gunboats lying outside the pier. He attempted the grandest of cutting-out expeditions, with fifty-five boats in four divisions, one commanded by Parker. The men in the boats were to be armed with pikes, cutlasses, and tomahawks, and each boat was to carry a 'carcase or other combustible' with which to set the French vessels on fire if they could not be brought off. The attack was to be at night, in silence, and with oars muffled. The watchword was to be NELSON, and the answer BRONTE.[8] The day before he launched this attack, Nelson repeated to Emma that this was no service for a vice-admiral.[9]

The essence of a cutting-out attack is surprise. The French, having been attacked once, were on their guard. Their vessels were chained together and to the shore, and not one was taken or burned. Forty-four of the attackers were killed and one hundred and twenty-eight wounded. Parker's thigh was smashed. 'The return of our squadron to Deal', said *The Morning Herald*, 'presented a very melancholy scene. Many of the gunboats were filled with the wounded, the dying, and the dead: each of the vessels was covered with an awning of sails and towed into harbour by row boats ... The men were all dressed in blue, and, that they might know one another, each wore a white belt round the middle.' A French report said: 'Nets spread and prepared aboard each of the vessels at night fall, and to a very great height, presented to them an obstacle which they did not expect. They entrapped themselves in them, they enmeshed themselves in them – they attempted to cut them, but all this time a horrible carnage was made among them, and the decks of our vessels were strewn with the fingers, hands, and wrists of the assailants, who fell into the sea.'[10]

Much was made of the chains, as if their use had been unfair. Nelson said that the moment the French had the audacity to unchain their vessels they would be captured or sent to the bottom.[11] St Vincent told Nelson, 'It is not given to us to command success' – exactly what he said after Tenerife, when a second attack on the same target also failed. The words are from Addison's heroic play of *Cato*. St Vincent was praising Roman virtues, but there was as little justification for a second attack on Boulogne as for a second on Santa Cruz.[12] At Deal, Nelson shed tears at the funeral of two midshipmen wounded in the action, was angered by the admiralty's refusal to let him come up to London to see Emma, and wrote to her that he longed to pay the French back, but *when, where, or how* he could not say. He had been stung by the general criticism, and not only the newspapers were damning. In *The Naval Chronicle* the passwords NELSON and BRONTE were seized on, and one old seaman was reported as asking another: 'I say Ben, do you know who this Bronte is that Nelson has got hold on?' And the reply came: 'No, I don't; all I can say is that he is a d–d fool, begging his pardon, for taking a partner ...'[13] And Nelson received a blackmailing letter from a Mr Hill saying that if did not want a seaman's account of the Boulogne attack to be published, he should send a bank note for £100 to be called for at the main London post office. He replied: 'Very likely I am unfit for my present command ... but you will, I trust, be punished for threatening my character. But I have not been brought up in the school of fear and therefore care not what you do. I defy you and your malice.' The admiralty tried to catch Mr Hill at the post office to which Nelson addressed this letter, but failed. Hill was offended by the reply he received, and in consequence compiled a statement of Nelson's conduct since the beginning of the war. It was published in part, seven weeks later, in the form of a letter to Nelson in *The County Herald and Weekly Advertiser*, which appeared in London on Friday evenings and on Saturday mornings, so it claimed on its masthead, in market towns within a hundred miles of London, as far afield as Norfolk, Hampshire, and Kent. It was more than a seaman's account of Boulogne. Giving only the heads of his argument, Hill wrote that Nelson's stopping to board the *San Josef* and *San Nicolas* at St Vincent, instead of pushing on to stop some of the other Spanish ships, was 'more calculated to acquire popularity in the newspapers than to add to the further success of the action'. He criticised the manner and timing of the attack at Tenerife. He said that, at the Nile, it was not because of any signal from Nelson that the ships went inside the enemy line; the captains themselves had done it. Going on to Copenhagen, he said 'the accidents which happened to so many of the ships' ought to have been prevented, and questioned '*the motives of humanity*' which induced Nelson to send in a flag of truce. The writer ended by saying that if Nelson did not wish the full manuscript to be published he should send small notes, to an amount he might think proper, in a sheet of brown paper, addressed to Mr J. Hill at a bookseller's shop on Ludgate Hill, near St Paul's. 'But if I do not hear from you *in two days*, I shall take it for granted that you have no objection to my printing the pamphlet, because you think your reputation too well established with the *public* to suffer from any thing I can say. But a plain statement of facts, supported by reasoning, the *opinion of seamen* – so different from that of the newspapers – and the failure at Boulogne, may, perhaps, have more weight than you imagine.'[14] No such pamphlet is known to have appeared. And the wonder is that the London daily papers did not pick up the letter from *The County Herald.*

Nelson continued unhappy. To Keith in the Mediterranean, with whom he had always been uneasy, he wrote a strangely confiding letter saying this 'curious command' of his was not giving him much strength, that he could hardly believe the French at Boulogne would be such fools as to make the attempt to cross and let themselves be caught 'half seas over', and that if he held his command three months longer he would be worn out. Then he wanted again to attack the

Dutch fleet at Helvoet, and St Vincent had to reply that, though he would be happy to place the whole of Britain's offensive and defensive war under his auspices, Nelson must be aware of the difficulties on that head. (There were commanders-in-chief of the Downs, the Nore, and the North Sea, on some of whose authority Nelson would be trespassing.) When Nelson replied tartly that he could then do nothing but lie at anchor and wait, St Vincent humoured him again: 'I differ with your lordship *in toto* as to the importance of the command you fill, and am of opinion it is not unworthy of the admiral of the fleet was he in a state of health and activity to fill it.'[15]

Nelson was also worried about money. There were no prizes in attacking invasion flotillas. On the same day that he complained to Keith about his curious command, he told Davison he had spent nearly £1,000 in six weeks. In that time he had drawn £600 in cash from his bankers. The Hamiltons came to stay at Deal for the first three weeks in September, and he paid for that.[16]

Poor Parker, whose thigh had been shattered in three places, was dying. He was only twenty-one. Nelson had taken more to him than to any other young officer. After the disaster at Boulogne, Nelson visited him whenever he was ashore, got the surgeon of the fleet to look after him, and wrote about his sufferings in letter after letter. The thigh was at last amputated, Parker seemed to recover, then the great artery burst, and on 27 September he died. St Vincent, when Nelson told him, said: 'What a war of devastation this has been.' The admiralty declined to pay for the funeral, so Nelson did.[17] Nelson by then was determined to be rid of a service he thought unworthy of him, and again wanted to get at the Dutch fleet. He wrote again to St Vincent, quoting from *Henry V*: 'I feel myself, my dear lord, as anxious to get a medal or a step in the peerage as if I never had got either, – for "if it be a sin to cover glory, I am the most offending soul alive," – I could lose only a few boats. If I succeeded and burnt the Dutch fleet, probably medals and an earldom.' But Nelson then gave the admiralty new reasons to take him away from the channel. It seemed that Mr Hill had been right to suggest that the opinion of seamen had weight, for Nelson wrote to St Vincent saying people in seaside towns had been very free in their talk, that the mayor of Deal had jailed a vagrant for saying he was careless with poor seamen's lives, and that the officers in the wardrooms were prating. And to Nepean he wrote that a diabolical spirit was at work, that posters had been put up warning seamen against being sent by Nelson to be butchered, and that at Margate men were asked, 'What, are you going to be slaughtered again?' He said – and this is remarkable from the abundantly self-confident Nelson – that he was not much liked by either officers or men, that if he ordered a boat expedition there was some doubt whether he would be obeyed, and that he really thought it would be better if he were removed from the command. 'If the thing succeeded the hatred agst me would be greater than it is at present, if it fail'd I should be execrated ...'[18]

He also told St Vincent he was 'low spirited from private considerations'. The trouble was with Emma and his family. Emma had charmed William and his wife, and was doing her malicious best to set them and the rest of the family against not only Fanny, which had already been achieved, but against their old father. It is not a pretty story. William had been easily seduced to Emma's camp, and was pressing his claims to preferment through her. Towards the end of August he was saying that if Jove got a higher title, it would be easy for him, William, now he was in the patent of the barony, to be advanced to greater honours. This he only mentioned between the two of them. Then he came back to his eternal desire for dead men's shoes in the church: 'I am told, there are two very old lives, prebends of Canterbury, in the minister's gift – near six hundred pounds a year, and good houses ... The deans of Hereford, Exeter, Lichfield and Coventry, York, and Winchester, are old men.' This in one letter. He habitually wrote out of greed, but with Emma he also had a ludicrously flirtatious vein. 'This morning comes your roguish, waggish letter, on a Sunday morning (amidst all my meditations for the good of my parishioners) about love, courtship, marriage, throwing the stocking, going to bed, &c – quite shocking to write to a country parson, who can have no idea of such things.'[19]

But the real difficulty was with Nelson's father. To please Nelson, most of the family were happy to shun Fanny and welcome Emma. The Revd Edmund Nelson was not. Fanny had looked after him for seventeen years, and he regarded her as a daughter. From Burnham Thorpe in August he wrote to her that whenever she had a house he would come to stay with her, in London or Bath. Then, when he had heard Nelson was buying a house at Merton, seven miles from London, he wrote to him as 'My dear Hor.', hoping that a new home might be a foundation of comfort. 'I long to see the time,' he said, 'when there shall be a door opened by which you may escape from present evill. *Carpe diem.*'[20] His father had never written so strongly before. Nelson could not see Emma as present evil. From the *Amazon*, he wrote to her. 'I had yesterday a letter from my father. He seems to think he may do something which I shall not like. I suppose he means going to Somerset Street [in London, where Fanny had taken a house]. Shall I to an old man enter upon the detestable subject? It may shorten his days but I think I shall tell him that I cannot go to Somerset Street to see him, but I shall not write until I hear your opinion ... but you shall decide.'[21]

Emma then wrote a vicious letter to Mrs William Nelson. First she said that Nelson loved his brother and most ardently wished to get him what he wanted. Ministers were deceitful animals and double dealers, but to keep them to their promises Nelson would, against his wishes, stay in the channel while peace talks went on. 'Nelson', she said, '*weighs* in the scales of politics very *heavy, counts* much.' Then she attacked Fanny and Nelson's father. 'His poor father is unknowing and taken in by a very wicked, bad, artful woman, acting *a bad part by so glorious a son*. The sin be on their heads ... And *your* father, Nelson's father, protects this woman and gives a mortal blow to his son. The old man could never hear her till now and now he conspires *against the saviour of his country* and his darling, who has risen him to such height of honour, and for whom? *A wicked, false, malicious wretch* who rendered his days wretched and his nights miserable; *and the father* of Nelson says, "I will *stab* my son to the heart."'[22] She went on and on. It was malicious, and there was not a shred of truth in it.

In late September, Fanny went to stay with the rector at Burnham Thorpe, a visit which she said called forth all her feelings. She had lived there with Nelson for the five years he was on the beach, and must, besides, have seen the rector's distress at the choice he was forced to make. So she then wrote to him, saying that though she would like them to live together, it would be too much for her to ask because – since he had in effect to make a choice between her and Nelson and the family he had gathered round him – it would deprive him of the pleasure of seeing his children, and this she thought would be cruel. She then said: 'I told Mrs M[atcham] at Bath that Lord Nelson would not like your living with me. "Oh my dear Lady Nelson. My brother will thank you in his heart for he knows no one can attend to his father as you do." I had seen the wonderful change past belief. She had not.'[23]

But the rector would not accept this sacrifice on her part. He wrote to Nelson: 'As a publick character, I could be acquainted only with what was made public respecting you. Now, in a private station possibly you may tell me where it is likely your general place of residence may be, so that sometimes we may have mutual happiness in each other, notwithstanding the severe reproaches I feel from an anonymous letter for my conduct to you, which is such, it seems, as will totally separate us. This is unexpected indeed.' He said he meant to spend the winter between London and Bath, and that if Fanny was by herself, gratitude required that he should sometimes be with her. 'But, my dearest son, here is still room enough to give you a warm, a joyful, and affectionate reception if you could find an inclination to look once more at me in Burnham parsonage.'[24] Who wrote the anonymous letter can only be guessed at. Nelson never did go to see his father. He immediately wrote to Emma, saying, 'I have [a letter] from my father which has hurt me, I shall not answer it till I hear from you.' And he enclosed to her the letter of reply he intended to send to his father.[25] Emma then wrote to Mrs William Nelson, enclosing an extract from Nelson's letter to the rector. Here is part of what she said he had written:

'My dear father, – I have received your letter and of which you must be sensible I cannot like for as you seem by your conduct to put me in the wrong it is no wonder that they who do not know me and my disposition should. But Nelson soars above them all and time will do that justice to my private character which she has to my public one. I that have given her [Fanny], with her falsity ... £2,000 a year and £4,000 in money and which she calls a poor pittance ... I could say much more but will not out of respect to you, my dear father, but you know her, therefore I finish.'[26] So Nelson, soaring above them all, told his father that Fanny had complained about a poor pittance, when she had thanked him for his generosity and said she could not in conscience have asked so much. Three days later, and this is the only thing remotely to Nelson's credit in the whole affair, he wrote again to Emma, saying he was sorry he had sent her his father's letter, and would not answer it.[27] But he was too late, since Emma had already put his letter to his father in the post.

On 17 October, Nelson's father wrote to Fanny again: 'My good madam, – Be assured I still hold fast my integrity, and am ready to join you, whenever you have your servants in the London house as at first thought of. In respect to this business, the opinion of others must rest with themselves, and not make any alteration with us. I have not offended any man and do rely upon my children's affection that notwithstanding all that have been said, they will not in my old age forsake me.'[28]

Peace came suddenly at the beginning of October, but Nelson was kept in the channel. From Downing Street, Addington wrote telling him he owed it to his own high character and to the interests of the nation to keep his flag flying until the definitive treaty had been signed. He would then be able to close with honour a career of unexampled success and glory. But if Nelson wanted to come on shore or even move to London for a few days, he could rely on the acquiescence of the board of admiralty. Their lordships did not acquiesce. 'The admiralty will not give me leave,' Nelson told Emma; 'What a set of beasts.'[29] Nor could he get George Tobin, one of the Nevis Tobins, made post. St Vincent refused in his silkiest manner: 'Encompassed as I am by applications and presumptuous claims, I have nothing for it, but to act upon the defensive, as your lordship will be compelled to do, whenever you are placed in the situation I at present fill.'[30] There was often a double edge to St Vincent's letters. It was less than a year since he had told Nepean that Nelson could never become an officer fit to command the channel fleet; now, to placate Nelson, he was implying that he might become first lord. Nelson did not strike his flag until the following April, but did get leave on 22 October, and went to Merton. Emma, who had so recently been damning Nelson's distressed father, began to write coaxingly to him, and after spending two weeks with Fanny in London, he did go on to Merton for a visit, but left before Christmas to winter in Bath.

In mid-December, Fanny made her last attempt at a reconciliation. She wrote to Nelson not at Merton but at Davison's house in St James's Square. 'My dear husband, – It is some time since I have written to you. The silence you have imposed is more than my affections will allow me and in this instance I hope you will forgive me in not obeying you. One thing I omitted in my letter of July which I now have to offer for your accommodation, a comfortable warm house. Do, my dear husband, let us live together. I can never be happy till such an event takes place. I assure you again I have but one wish in the world, to please you. Let every thing be buried in oblivion, it will pass away like a dream. I can only now intreat you to believe I am most sincerely and affectionately Your wife, Frances H. Nelson.'

This letter was returned to her, with a note scrawled on it: 'Opened by mistake by Lord Nelson, but not read. A. Davison.'[31] Davison had always acted decently to Fanny before, but he was Nelson's man, and perhaps this shows the dominance of Nelson over those closest to him.

Nelson meanwhile had been introduced to the House of Lords as a viscount. He made his maiden speech harmlessly praising Saumarez for an inconclusive action, off Algeciras, and then made his first substantial speech in support of the peace terms, of which, since they were so much to France's advantage, he cannot have approved. Britain gave back all her maritime conquests to France, Spain, and Holland, keeping only Trinidad and Ceylon. Malta, which Nelson had blockaded for so long, was handed back to the moribund knights, and the Cape of Good Hope to the Dutch. Emma, forgetting her years of flattery at the court of Naples, accused Nelson of being a time-server to Addington, at which he flared up, saying damn him if he was, that his intention was to show he could be as useful in the cabinet as in the field, that he wanted something for his brother, and that if you made yourself of consequence to politicians they would do what you wanted within reason. It would be a great bore to go to the Lords, and he would tell Addington when he saw him that he did it to please him, and not himself.[32]

But his second speech had been a sad affair. He said he had blockaded Malta to save it from the French, but by the treaty it was to be placed in the hands of a third power, and in any other hands but those of the French it was immaterial to Britain. As to the Cape of Good Hope, he had been there and considered it merely a tavern on the passage to the East. When the Dutch held it, a cabbage had cost twopence, but since it had been in our hands a cabbage cost a shilling. He therefore thought ministers had acted with prudence in giving up the Cape. He supported the peace. Could any man say that the republic of France was not as permanent as any state governed by one man?[33]

This would have sounded very well in the mouth of Fox, but from Nelson, who had hated the republicans of France and Naples, and had never stopped proclaiming his hatred, who that August had been sending Frenchmen to hell, and had been saying as recently as September that Buonaparte wanted to degrade Britain by making her give up all her conquests,[34] the speech lacked all credibility. As for the Cape, perhaps it was in Nelson's mind that the admiral who helped take it in 1795 had been Keith. For the rest of the speech there was no excuse. Having heard it, William Huskisson, who had been under secretary at war at the time of the Nile, told Henry Dundas, who later became first lord: 'I was obliged to Lord Nelson for giving me anything that could create a smile on such a grave and awful subject ... How can ministers allow such a fool to speak in their defence?'[35]

Later that month Addington used Nelson again, to second the address on the king's speech to both houses. He said he would not consent to sacrifice one jot of England's honour, spoke of the commerce, the grandeur, the resistless power, the unconquerable valour of the English nation, and then welcomed the sincere spirit of the peace.[36] It was dishonest, and Emma for once had been right. He was in the business of pleasing ministers. What Nelson wrote to his friend Captain Sutton of the *Amazon* about his maiden speech applied much more forcefully to his next two. 'Bad enough,' he wrote, 'but well meant – anything better than ingratitude. I may be a coward, and good for nothing, but never ungrateful for favours done to me.'[37]

Nelson and the Hamiltons were by then living at what Nelson called 'Paradise Merton', though it had only one and a half acres of land, no stabling, only one good bedroom, a library, and a scattering of other rooms. He was unlucky with houses. At Round Wood, which he had bought with Fanny in 1797, he had never spent a night. As for Merton he never saw it until he was at last given leave from Deal. Emma had chosen it, at a cost to Nelson of £9,000 he did not have. The prize case against St Vincent was still in the courts. He raised £1,511 from fragments of smaller prizes due, sold £3,371 worth of shares and some jewels which had been the present of grateful foreign sovereigns, and was able to raise £6,000 altogether. The rest he borrowed. He said it cost him every farthing.[38] Then they lived lavishly on more money he did not have. Lord Minto went there to dine. 'The whole establishment and way of life', he said, 'is such as to make me angry, as well as melancholy; but I cannot alter it and I do not think myself obliged or at liberty to quarrel with him for his weakness, though nothing shall ever induce me to give the slightest countenance to Lady Hamilton.

She looks ultimately to the chance of marriage, as Sir W will not be long in her way, and she probably indulges a hope that she will survive Lady Nelson: in the meantime she and Sir William and the whole set of them are living with him at his expense ... She goes on cramming Nelson with trowelfuls of flattery, which he goes on taking as quietly as a child does pap. The love she makes to him is not only ridiculous but disgusting: not only the rooms but the whole house, staircase and all, are covered with nothing but pictures of him and her, of all sizes and sorts, and representations of his naval actions, coats of arms, pieces of plate in his honour, the flagstaff of *L'Orient*, &c – an excess of vanity which counteracts its own purpose. If it was Lady H's house there might be a pretence for it; to make his own a mere looking glass to view himself all day is bad taste.'[39] And this is a description by a man who had been Nelson's greatest admirer.

Then Catherine wrote from Bristol to tell Nelson their father was extremely weak. He did not go to Bath to see him, and the old man, when he wrote, sent letters uncongenial to a hero. After Nelson accepted the obscure German knighthood of St Joachim and received another red ribbon from the sultan of Turkey, he wrote: 'My dear Hor, *This* is a title that, with me, will ever supersede all others which the empire of the world can ever give to you ...' In his next letter the rector wrote wishing his son internal peace such as he had never yet enjoyed. 'My strength', he said, 'returns very slow, yet still have hopes, I shall, with the assistance of the May sun shine, get able to travel, and smell a Merton rose, in June.'[40] His huge handwriting had become more straggling than ever, and he was making some punctuation mark every few words, or else just resting his pen on the paper, as if a few words were all he could write at a time. At Merton, on 2 April, 1802, the anniversary of Copenhagen, Emma composed a eulogy in which she addressed Nelson as 'the Victor of the Nile, the Conqueror of Copenhagen, the Terror and Stop of the Northern Confederacy, St Vincent's prop & the Hero of the 14 of Febry, the restorer of the King of Naples, the preserver of Rome, the avenger of Kings, the Guardian angell of England & the *man of men* who in this war as been in one hundred & 24 battles & come off loved with glory honner virtue & modesty the pride of his country & friend'.[41] By April his father was very ill, the doctors said in great danger. Mr Matcham wrote to tell Nelson, who replied: 'I have no hopes that he can recover. God's will be done. Had my father expressed a wish to see me unwell as I am I should have flown to Bath, but I believe it would be too late; however should it be otherwise and he wishes to see me, no consideration shall detain me a minute.'[42]

Nelson was not obliged to fly. His father died the same day. Fanny was with him. Nelson was not.

Two days later, having been informed of the death, Nelson wrote telling Mr Matcham that the body should be sent to Burnham, where his father should be buried with all that respect and attention becoming the beneficent pastor of his church for forty-five years. 'No proper expense shall be wanting and beyond that is not necessary. The minute parts of the ceremony my brother shall settle. I am not yet fixed whether I shall go to Burnham, my state of health and what my feelings would naturally be might be of serious consequence to myself . . .'[43] That same day Nelson had health enough to attend the christening at Merton of Emma's black Coptic maid, Fatima. The funeral was fixed for 11 May, more than two weeks after the rector's death. Nelson, who had not visited his father in his last four months, did not risk serious consequences to his feelings by attending the funeral either, and stayed at Merton. He paid the expenses.

Afterwards, Susannah Bolton wrote to Fanny: 'Your going to Bath my dear Lady Nelson was of a piece with all of your conduct to my beloved father . . . To me his loss is great indeed, even as a friend, but more as a parent. He had lived so long that when not with him we always flattered ourselves with a longer time still.' She said the church had been crowded, that six clergymen attended as bearers, and that the farmers of three parishes followed. Then she ended with the saddest of statements: 'I am going to Merton in a fortnight, but my dear Lady N we cannot meet as I wished for every body is known who visits you. Indeed I do not think I shall be permitted even to go to town.'[44] Susannah, who had advised Fanny to keep a house for Nelson, and who had said she as well as her brother had her pride, fell in with the rest of the family. She was the last to drop Fanny.

CHAPTER TWENTY-TWO

So Much for Gratitude

WHEN NELSON TOLD EMMA that the admiralty were a set of beasts, he did not have only St Vincent in mind. It is true that he doubted St Vincent's good faith in the matter of the prize money for the Spanish frigates. 'I will support him as a great sea officer,' he told Davison, 'but was he forty times as great, I will not suffer him to rob me with impunity.'[1] He was convinced his commanders-in-chief ran away with all the money he fought for. Let them, he said; he was content with honour.[2] Throughout 1801 St Vincent cajoled and flattered Nelson. During his time at Deal he wrote him thirty-one letters in four months, more than to the commanders-in-chief of the Channel, the North Sea, the Downs, and the Nore put together.[3] Nelson continued to suspect him, but he suspected Troubridge more deeply. This feeling was as bitter and irrational as any he ever conceived, for Troubridge had been his favourite captain in the Mediterranean, and they had known each other since they were boys.

They were the same age. Both joined the *Seahorse* frigate at the age of fifteen, within a few days of each other, and both went in her to the East Indies and the Persian Gulf. Troubridge became lieutenant at the age of twenty-three and was made post two years later. He was thus a fortunate young officer, but lacked the brilliant early interest of Nelson, and was five years his junior on the immovable list of post captains. After the American war he too was on half pay – for five years from 1785 – but in 1790, when Nelson was out of favour and had no earthly chance of a ship, Troubridge was given a frigate and again went to the far east. In

1793, when war came, he commanded a frigate off Toulon, but the following year was taken prisoner by the French fleet out of Brest.[4] He was exchanged, given a ship of the line, the *Culloden*, and in December 1794 at Spithead put down the first notable mutiny of the war. Troubridge seized ten of the ringleaders himself. Eight were condemned to death, of whom three were pardoned and five hanged on board. Fanny, at Bath, heard that a ship of the line had to be ordered to sink the *Culloden* before the people listened to reason.[5] Next year Troubridge and *Culloden* were in the Mediterranean. The commander-in-chief there was Jervis, who did not mince words about his officers. 'You should not', he told the admiralty, 'send out such creatures as this Sir John Colleton if they are so damnably afraid of gunboats, galleys &c . . .' He then gave a list of the captains whose services he prized. First on the list was Horatio Nelson. Troubridge was third. Among the rest were Foley, Fremantle, and Samuel Hood, all members of the band of brothers.[6]

In 1797–98, Nelson and Troubridge fought together in three actions. At St Vincent, Troubridge led the line from which Nelson famously broke away. He then went with Nelson's squadron on the disastrous raid on Tenerife, and, after Nelson was wounded, led the land attack and made terms with the Spanish governor. When Nelson returned to the Mediterranean the following year and was sent to reconnoitre off Toulon, it was Troubridge who was sent after him with reinforcements of ten ships of the line, to make up the squadron which fought the battle of the Nile. Since there were many captains senior to Troubridge, St Vincent's choice of him to take those ships to Nelson was almost as sharply criticised as his choice of Nelson to command the squadron. By then, Nelson was referring in his letters to 'dear Troubridge', and telling Sir William Hamilton that Troubridge was his 'honoured acquaintance of twenty-five years and the very best sea officer in his majesty's service'.[7]

At the Nile Troubridge led the line in the *Culloden*, but she went aground on the shoals of Aboukir and took no part in the battle. Nelson did not mention this in his dispatches home, and when St Vincent did learn, Nelson wrote to him fulsomely, saying Troubridge's conduct was as fully entitled to praise as any officer's in the squadron, that his services were eminent, and that he was a friend and a nonpareil. When it was proposed that the first lieutenants of only those ships *engaged* should be promoted, as was the custom, Nelson asked St Vincent for heaven's sake to get this altered to include the *Culloden*'s, and begged Spencer not to add misery to Troubridge's misfortune by not awarding him a Nile medal, since Troubridge on shore was superior to captains afloat. Nelson even wrote to St Vincent saying, 'I know he is my superior; and I so often want his advice and assistance.'[8] Troubridge then wrote Nelson a letter which ran: 'I am truly miserable. Do, pray, my lord, explain to Lord Spencer that my accident at Aboukir was not intentional, or through any fear of my *head*; for I assure you it preys in me so much that it would be a charitable act to *shoot me*.' Nelson passed these words on to Spencer, adding that such words from such a man made his heart bleed.[9] By the time this reached London, Spencer had already decided that Troubridge should get his medal with the rest. Nelson not only supported Troubridge but was pressing in his defence and extravagant in his praise.

By then, Nelson had encouraged the Neapolitans to march on Rome, provoked the French to march on Naples, and transported the court to Palermo. The savage year of 1799 began. Troubridge had always been draconic in his punishments, as he had shown with his mutineers, and in 1799 he and Nelson were at one in their severity. By March, Troubridge was in the bay of Naples recapturing the islands of Procida and Ischia, saying that if he had a few thousand soldiers they could have a glorious massacre, recommending the Italian judge with him to execute prisoners with no time for confession, so that they should go to hell, and offering to degrade priests by pissing on their damned Jacobin carcasses.[10] He also gave George Smith, seaman, three hundred lashes round the fleet for mutinous and blasphemous expressions. Nelson signed the order for the flogging.[11]

When Nelson went to Naples that June to restore the kingdom to Ferdinand, and found a treaty in force with the rebels which he repudiated, the captains he sent to parley with Ruffo were Troubridge and Ball. After Nelson's assurances brought the rebels from their castles, Troubridge was in charge of the marines who saw them on board the polaccas and then occupied the castles. He then led the assault on the fort of St Elmo, where the remains of the French garrison were holding out, and then on the forts of Gaeta and Capua, and took them all. At St Elmo he was summary. When he found Neapolitans selling his marines liquor he flogged them, cropped their hair, dressed them in seamen's cast off trousers, and in this get-up, in which they would be taken for Jacobins and lynched, thrust them back into the city.[12] This report came from a Scotsman doing the grand tour, who did not like what the English were doing, but it shows much the same Troubridge who, by his own account – in letters to Nelson – flogged a Neapolitan for selling adulterated bread, with a loaf round his neck the whole time, and then turned him on shore like that to show the people; or who lined up his own Swiss mercenaries blindfold in a square and went through the whole process of execution except the shooting.[13] Nelson praised his generalship in taking the French forts, gave him a commodore's broad pennant, and got him a baronetcy.[14]

Having been sent to take the surrender of Civita Vecchia from the retreating French, and accepted that of Rome as well when the French commander offered it, Troubridge was sent to oversee the blockade of Malta, where the French held only the port of Valletta and the rest of the population were nominally Neapolitan subjects. Troubridge found that Ferdinand did not much care if they starved, and would provide no grain. In January of 1800 he wrote letter after letter to Nelson, complaining that the people were dying off fast, and that Acton would send no food though there was plenty in Sicily. 'I am not very tender hearted,' he wrote, 'but really the distress here would even move a Neapolitan.' Then he seized two grain ships, and wrote again to Nelson: 'I have this day saved 30,000 people from dying; but with this day my ability ceases. As the king of Naples, or rather the queen and her party, are bent on starving us, I see no alternative, but to leave these poor unhappy people to starve, without being witnesses to their distress. I curse the day I ever served the king of Naples … We have characters, my lord, to lose; these people have none. Do not suffer their infamous conduct to fall on us.'[15]

At the same time, Troubridge wrote to Nelson warning him against being seen gambling into the night with Emma,[16] and in these letters from Malta he had touched Nelson on two of his most sensitive spots. He had damned the queen, whom Nelson still revered, and had spoken out about Emma. We do not have Nelson's reply, but it is plain he took offence, because Troubridge's next letter was distracted. He said he was tired and ill and trusted that this would acquit him of the smallest want of respect, of which Nelson's letter accused him. 'It really has so unhinged me, that I am quite unmanned and crying. I would sooner forfeit my life, my everything, than be deemed ungrateful to an officer

and friend I feel I owe so much to ... I [pray] your lordship not to
harbour the smallest idea that I am not the same Troubridge you have
known me.'[17]

He had jaundice. In this condition he continued at Malta, and continued to act savagely. After the *Guillaume Tell* was taken in March, he
found four wounded English deserters in her. 'Two died of their wounds
the other two are here one with both legs off & the other has lost his
arm, a court martial is ordered, if they will but live Monday, they will be
tryed and meet their deserts immediately, we *shot & hung* a Maltese for
carrying in two fowls & tomorrow I hope will be a gala day, for the old
lady who I have long been wishing to hang, that carried in intelligence.
She swore she was with child, and possibly she will try some stout
fellow: even then it will be good policy to destroy the breed.'[18] By
then, Nelson was writing to Troubridge about his own broken heart,
and, with Keith having taken over the command, was writing, '*We of
the Nile* are not equal to Lord Keith in his [Acton's] estimation, and
ought to think it an honour to serve under such a *clever* man.'[19] Both
Troubridge and Nelson were exhausted, physically and morally, and
should have been sent home long before. By May Troubridge was
spitting blood, and did go home, assuring Nelson no one loved and
respected him more, and hoping to see his flag in the channel fleet.[20]

He recovered, and by late 1800 was St Vincent's captain of the fleet
in the English channel, responsible for conveying the admiral's orders
to the fleet and for maintaining discipline, and taking a junior flag
officer's share of any prize money. That and his baronetcy were as much
preferment as could be given to an officer who was still not high on the
post captains' list. Then in February 1801, after Pitt's resignation and
the change of ministry, St Vincent wrote to Nelson, who was about to
go to the Baltic, saying he had just that instant come from the king, that
he would succeed Spencer as first lord, and that he would feel both pride
and pleasure in gratifying Nelson's laudable ambitions.[21] There were
seven lords of the admiralty, four of whom were civilians. One of those
was Sir Philip Stephens, who was seventy-five and had for thirty-two
years, until 1795, been secretary of the admiralty. Of the naval members,
St Vincent was first lord and a member of the cabinet. The other naval
members would usually have been admirals, but St Vincent, having all
the experience he needed in himself and Stephens, chose two relatively
young captains. One was Troubridge. St Vincent could not give him

a command, because not even a first lord could make a rear-admiral before his turn came on the captains' list, but he could take him to the admiralty. Now to be a lord of the admiralty did not make a man a lord, and one member of the board by himself had no great power. Three had to sign any admiralty order. But Troubridge turned out to be St Vincent's second. Nelson sensed this immediately, and wrote to Emma: 'Our friend Troubridge is to be a lord of the admiralty, and I have a sharp eye, and almost think I see it. No, poor fellow, I hope I do him an injustice; he cannot surely forget my kindness to him.'[22]

Nelson did have some small ground for suspicion. Miss Knight, the writer of flattering verses about Nelson to be added to the national anthem and generally to be sung by Emma, had lived with the Hamiltons in Palermo and returned across Europe with them and Nelson. She was a woman who needed to cherish her respectability – she later became lady companion to Queen Charlotte – and Troubridge advised her to break with the Hamiltons and go to live with the Nepeans, the family of the secretary of the admiralty. Nepean was the man St Vincent had written to about Nelson, saying he would create a *brouillerie* about getting Emma received at court, and Troubridge was St Vincent's man; someone as sensitive to slights as Nelson could sniff a plot in all this.[23]

But while Nelson was chafing to get off to the Baltic, it was St Vincent that he was most wary of. When he wrote to St Vincent that this might be his last service, he received a reply meant to soothe him but which probably did nothing of the sort. 'Be assured, my dear lord, that every *public* act of your life has been the subject of my admiration ...'[24] Every public act; what then of his private acts? In the three months after that he wrote more than twenty letters confiding his troubles to Troubridge, who had evidently advised him not to complain to St Vincent about Hyde Parker's delays.[25] Nelson appeared to agree, writing: 'As my own unhappiness concerns no one but myself, it shall remain forever fixed in my own breast.' But it did not remain in his own breast. He shared it not only with Emma but also with Troubridge. In the same letter in which he wrote saying he knew how angry the earl would be if he as second in command to Parker offered an opinion to the admiralty, he complained to Troubridge about his commander-in-chief's delays and the reasons for it: 'Consider how nice it must be laying abed with a young wife, compared to a damned

aw cold wind.' He repeated that he was unhappy; but let jealousy, cabal,
nd art conspire to do their worst, his ship would still be fit for battle.
Troubridge obviously conveyed some of this to St Vincent, since Parker
ent his wife away and cancelled a dance arranged for her, and Nelson
ronically thanked Troubridge for his and St Vincent's 'unpoliteness to
end gentlemen to sea instead of dancing with nice white gloves'. He
hen complained to Troubridge that Parker told him nothing, and that
xcept from the newspapers he did not even know they were going
o the Baltic.[26] When at last the fleet left Yarmouth and was in the
Baltic he criticised Parker's manoeuvres. 'It was never my desire to
erve under this man.' Himself, he would straightaway have placed the
leet off Copenhagen and the moment the Danish minister said war, he
vould have had enough of it. But the minister would have said peace.
Thus we should have peace with Denmark to a certainty either by fair
or foul means . . . Would it were all over. I am really sick of it.' He gave
Troubridge ten thousand thanks for his kind letters, assuring him they
had been burned so as not to fall into 'improper hands'. He complained
that Parker treated him with a haughtiness which his spirit could not
bear. He could hardly have been more open with Troubridge, whom he
called his old and faithful friend. After the battle it was Troubridge to
whom he confided that he was 'in a fright' what the government might
hink about the armistice he had concluded. It was Troubridge he first
asked to bring him home.[27]

Parker, however, was the one who was recalled, and Nelson then
wrote to St Vincent asking to be relieved of the Baltic command
he no longer wanted. The earl's reply appears to have put an end
to any cordiality between Nelson and Troubridge. What St Vincent
wrote was tactful, and harmless enough. 'To find a fit successor [for
the command], your lordship well knows, is no easy task, for I never
saw the man in our profession, excepting yourself and Troubridge, who
possessed the magic art of infusing the same spirit into others, which
inspired his actions . . .'[28] From then on all intimacy between Nelson
and Troubridge ceased. It was one thing for Nelson himself to call
Troubridge his superior, as he had two years before, but quite another
for St Vincent to name them as equals. From then on Nelson never had
a word to say about his friend that was not bitter. In the fall of that year
he was convinced that St Vincent and Troubridge conspired to keep
him in the channel or at Deal, and away from Emma, even though

the preliminaries of peace had been signed. One day in early October
he went ashore to call on Pitt, the late prime minister, at Walmer
where he was staying because he occupied the sinecure of warden o
the cinque ports. He found Pitt asleep, so left his card and went off along
a road which he and Emma had taken on her visit in September. 'And al
rushed into my mind,' he wrote, 'and brought tears into my eyes', and
he reflected that he had become a cipher, that Troubridge had gained a
victory over his spirit and kept him there, and away from her.[29] He told
Dr Baird, who had attended poor Parker until his death and would have
known what was going on, never to mention Troubridge's unfeeling
heart again. Nelson's state of mind was by then hardly rational. Pitt
had returned his visit that day, had even agreed with Nelson that it
was hard to keep him there any longer, and then asked him to dinner;
he refused the invitation because he was determined to dine with no
one until he was free to dine with Emma again.[30] To her he wrote
two letters in one day, complaining that Troubridge, who had written
recommending walks ashore, was laughing at him, and that 'Master
Troubridge' had grown fat while he had grown lean.[31]

When at last he was given leave he wrote Emma a letter that reached
the depths of bitterness. 'Tomorrow week all is over – no thanks to Sir
Thomas. I believe the fault is all his, and he ought to have recollected
that I got him the medal of the Nile. Who upheld him when he would
have sunk under grief and mortification? Who placed him in such a
situation in the kingdom of Naples that he got by my public letters
titles, the colonelcy of marines, diamond boxes from the king of Naples
1,000 ounces in money for no expenses that I know of? Who got him
£500 a year from the king of Naples? . . . Who brought his character
into notice? Look at my public letters. *Nelson*, that Nelson he now *lord.*
it over. So much for gratitude. I forgive him but by God I shall never
forget it. He enjoys shewing his powers over me. Never mind, although
it will shorten my days . . . I have been *rebuffed* so that my spirits are
gone, and the *great* Troubridge has what we call *cowed* the spirits of
Nelson, but I shall never forget it . . .'[32]

He never did. The rift lasted. Troubridge never visited Merton. He
and St Vincent held office for three years, until 1804. When they went,
Nelson wrote, again to Emma: 'But never mind; the late admiralty have
the execrations of the service for destroying as much as in them lay
the navy.'[33]

CHAPTER TWENTY-THREE

Planting Trees with One Hand

'IF YOUR UNCLE WOULD then die,' Nelson wrote to Emma in one of his coded letters in which her uncle was Sir William Hamilton, 'then he [Nelson] would instantly then come and marry you, for he doats on nothing but you and his child . . .'[1] But Hamilton lived, and together they occupied Merton. Since 1799 Nelson had lived with the Hamiltons when he was not at sea, and Hamilton had said the greatest pleasure he ever had was to have gained the friendship of this great man, though he had once let drop that he was a little tired of keeping open house.[2] Now he was living much of the time in Nelson's house, and sharing its running costs, while he still kept on his own house in Piccadilly so that he could easily visit the British Museum and the sale rooms.

Nelson was living beyond his income and Hamilton was living beyond his too, having been shabbily treated by the government in the matters of his pension and the property he had lost in Naples. He reckoned that in houses and pictures he had been despoiled of £8,000, and he never got a penny of it back. Months before he returned home he had written to Charles Greville, his nephew and heir and Emma's former lover, about his houses which had been torn to pieces by the French or the mob, and his horses and three carriages which had been stolen, and the expenses he had incurred in entertaining the British fleet. Thanks to his first wife, he said, he would never lack the comforts of life. And for the rest, he would lay his affairs before George III. 'The king, I have reason to think, has not forgot (as he never forgets) the many years passed with him in his early days.'[3] Hamilton's first wife had been Catherine Barlow, a gentle and congenial woman and also an heiress. She had died in 1782. As for the royal connection, Hamilton was the grandson of a duke, and his mother Jane had been at court where she had perhaps been the mistress of Prince Frederick, whose son became George III. However that may have been, she had certainly been mistress of the robes, and because of this the young Hamilton and the young man who was to be George III were for some years brought up together.

Whether or not the king forgot, his ministers did. While Hamilton was still in Palermo, Greville called several times at the foreign office on behalf of his uncle but was not received by Lord Grenville. He then wrote, enclosing copies of private letters he had received from Hamilton, which set out what had happened at Naples in 1799 rather more openly than Hamilton's official letters to the foreign secretary. He received no reply, became exasperated, and wrote that he did not suppose that Grenville was disposed to act on any but honourable principles, but that he would like to know the king's gracious determination. And he would like his uncle's letters back. There is no trace of a reply. Hamilton's letters were not returned, and still lie in the foreign office papers.[4] Poor Hamilton thought he had the promise of a pension of £2,000 a year, but in the end got £1,200, for his life only, with nothing to go to Emma. When he returned with Nelson, he did have the consolation of finding that many of his best vases, which he thought had sunk with the transport taking them from Naples to Palermo, had survived. He sold his pictures at Christie's for £5,025 and his vases privately for £4,000.[5]

Hamilton's quiet intention was that, having fagged all his life, he should spend his last days comfortably. 'Nothing', he told Greville, 'at present disturbs me but my debt, and the nonsense I am obliged to submit to here to avoid coming to an explosion, which would be attended with many disagreeable effects, and would totally destroy the comfort of the best man and the best friend I have in the world.'[6] He knew perfectly well what was going on, and he knew there was a child, but did he see her? Horatia was rarely brought to Merton, and then only on days when Hamilton was in London.[7] But there is one letter which suggests he did see her. Here is Nelson to Emma, going through the accepted fiction: 'Before we left Italy I told you of the extraordinary circumstance of a child being left to my care and protection. On your first coming to England I presented you the child, dear Horatia. You became, to my comfort, attached to it, so did Sir William, thinking her the finest child he had ever seen . . .'[8] So Hamilton knew there was a child of Emma's, but he would also have known the fiction, and that was probably part of the nonsense he accepted, letting it to be known that this adopted child was the finest he had seen. He did not see her often, but then neither did Nelson, since she was kept out at nurse.

While Hamilton was finding his interest was out of date, Nelson was pushing his to the utmost to get medals and prize money for Copenhagen, to get his own pension increased, and to get something for William. He pursued the lord mayor of London, the first lord, and the prime minister. When the City of London voted thanks to the British army that conquered the remains of Buonaparte's army at Alexandria he immediately wrote reminding the lord mayor of Copenhagen. He wrote to St Vincent, reminding the first lord of his promise of medals. St Vincent was terse, replying that far from promising medals he had advised Addington against them. Nelson told St Vincent he was thunderstruck, and then protested to Davison: 'Either Lord St Vincent or myself are liars.'[9] He tried again with Addington on three separate occasions.[10] He was quite unable to accept that this was a political decision, because Britain had not been formally at war with Denmark. It was probably a bad reason, but it was a reason of state. It reveals a lot about the deference to Nelson's status as a hero that no one told him enough was enough. And he, lacking all political sense, carried on. Shame on them, said Emma: ministers were vagabonds. Nelson still pressed for a deanery for William, which brought from Addington a note of the greatest good humour, in his own hand: 'My means are more limited than you imagine; the dean of Wells is living, nor have I heard that he is likely soon to create a vacancy: – but as I wish to tell you distinctly how I am circumstanced, & what are your brother's prospects, I should be glad if your lordship would take the trouble of calling in Downing Street at 1/2 past ten either on Friday or Saturday morning. The ecclesiastical atmosphere has been a very healthy one of late, & the succession has proved too slow, for even Christian patience.'[11]

In the summer and early fall of 1802 Nelson and the Hamiltons set out on a six week grand tour to Wales and the Midlands. It was a round trip of eight hundred miles, to Oxford, Gloucester, Monmouth,

Swansea, Worcester, Birmingham, Warwick, and Coventry, with *Rule Britannia*, fireworks, ironworks, cattle shows, presents of porcelain, feasts, mayors and alderman, freedoms of rotten boroughs, and horses unhitched and carriages drawn in triumph by locals all the way. At Oxford, Nelson and Hamilton were made doctors of civil law and William Nelson, who was hanging on, a doctor of divinity. At Blenheim, the seat of the Duke of Marlborough, the duke did not receive the party but coldly sent a servant with refreshments which were coldly declined, a welcome which brought from Emma the remark that the great duke of Marlborough who won at Blenheim had been rewarded because a woman reigned [Queen Anne] and women had great souls, and that if she [Emma] had been queen after Aboukir, Nelson should have had a principality compared to which Blenheim park would have been a kitchen garden.[12] Back at Merton, Emma continued to render the house a paradise by her tasteful arrangements, and Nelson planted shrubs with his one hand, assisted by Emma or Hamilton. One of the trees he planted was a mulberry which she thought would rival the celebrated mulberry planted by Shakespeare at Stratford upon Avon. Hamilton, however, felt that the nonsense he earlier complained of still continued, and he wrote her a long letter:

'I have passed the last 40 years of my life in the hustle and bustle that must necessarily be attendant on a publick character. I am arrived at the age when some repose is really necessary, & I promised myself a quiet home, altho' I was sensible, & said so when I married, that I shou'd be superannuated when my wife wou'd be in her full beauty and vigour of youth. That time is arrived, and we must make the best of it for the comfort of both parties. Unfortunately our tastes as to the manner of living are very different. I by no means wish to live in a solitary retreat, but to have seldom less than 12 or 14 at table, & those varying continually, is coming back to what was become so irksome to me in Italy during the latter years of our residence in that country . . . I have no complaint to make, but I feel that the whole attention of my wife is given to Ld N and his interest at Merton. I well know the purity of Ld N's friendship for Emma and me, and I know how very uncomfortable it would make his Lp, our best friend, if a separation shou'd take place, and am therefore determined to do all in my power to prevent such an extremity, which wou'd be *essentially detrimental* to all parties, but wou'd be more sensibly felt by our dear friend than by s ... but I am fully determined not to have more of the very silly ltercations that happen but too often between us and embitter the resent moments exceedingly. If really one cannot live comfortably ogether, a wise and well concerted separation is preferable; but I think, onsidering the probability of my not troubling any party long in this vorld, the best for us all wou'd be to bear those ills we have rather han flie to those we know not of ... therefore let us bear and forbear or God's sake.'[13]

In October, Nelson protested again to a newly elected lord mayor, eclining his invitation to a guildhall banquet on the old grounds, hat the city had not recognised Copenhagen, which he was now alling the most complete naval victory of any war.[14] He was also ursuing St Vincent for a gratuity in lieu of prize money for the Copenhagen captains, asking for £100,000 and getting £65,000. His wn share of this would have been about £1,500. And at last he got iis brother a prebendal stall, at Canterbury cathedral. William showed iis gratitude by complaining that Addington's conduct in not giving iim the *Winchester* stall was an additional proof of his insincerity. He iid thank Nelson for sending him a cask of sherry which had made iineteen dozen bottles and one. 'It is', he said, 'the more acceptable as rom the situation I am now in I am now in some measure *obliged* to ;ive dinners & good wine is required & expected of me in the double apacity of prebendary of Canterbury & Lord Nelson's *brother.*'[15]

William was always a grasping oaf. But at this period Nelson himself vas unbecomingly pressing about money, and he seems to have gained ome ascendancy over Addington. Admirals did not commonly bother irime ministers or frequent Downing Street. Nelson did. For the Vile he had been given a pension of £2,000 a year; this was paid mmediately and in 1802 formed the largest single item of his income. 'or their victories, St Vincent and Duncan (at Camperdown) had been oted £3,000 a year each. In March 1803 Nelson listed the details if his income and expenditure to the prime minister, down to £150 or assisting in educating his nephews, and demonstrated that he was eft with £768 a year to live on. This was not quite candid, since ie did not list his bits of prize money, which in 1802 amounted to €1,418, not much, since the dispute with St Vincent was still not esolved, but nearly twice his pay as a vice-admiral. He was asking or more, and he did so very directly. 'Was it, or not, the intention of

his majesty's government to place my rewards for services lower than
Lord St Vincent or Lord Duncan?'[16] Vice-admirals do not profitably ask
blunt, direct questions of prime ministers, but six weeks later Nelson
was back, repeating the same arguments, and adding that his needs
were greater, since St Vincent had made £100,000 in prize money
and Duncan not less than £50,000, while he, Nelson, had by the time
of the Nile not realised £5,000.[17]

In February, Nelson was subpoenaed to give evidence for an old colleague who was on trial for treason. This was Colonel Edward Despard
whom he had known as an artillery lieutenant in the Nicaraguan
expedition of 1780. Despard had been called back from central America
some years before to answer charges of cruelty against the settlers, had
been kept hanging about, and became so embittered that he plotted
with others to suborn the Guards regiment, seize the Bank of England
and assassinate the king by setting off a ceremonial cannon. Nelson,
described by Lord Chief Justice Ellenborough as a man on whom to
pronounce a eulogy would be to waste words, could only say at the
trial that he and Despard had been on the Spanish Main together,
slept many nights in their clothes on the ground, and that no man
could have shown more zealous attachment to his sovereign. Having
been convicted, Despard sent a petition to Nelson which he passed on
to Addington, and then he and six others were hanged and drawn, but
spared the quartering.[18]

This was also a time when the Naples affair of 1799 came back to
irritate Nelson. Alexander Stephens, who was writing a history of the
wars of the French revolution, wrote to him. Nelson warned Stephens to
be careful how he mentioned the characters of such excellent sovereigns
as the king and queen of Naples, said that Miss Williams's book on
Naples was either destitute of foundation or false, and invited Stephens
to call if he wished to have any conversation on the subject.[19] The book
he referred to, by Helen Maria Williams, had appeared in 1801, and
Nelson had a copy which he had annotated in ink in the margin. Miss
Williams had lived in France, had been a friend of the Girondists, and
was sympathetic to the French and Neapolitan republics, though she
did say in her preface that the political system most abhorrent to her
was that of terror, whether it were Jacobin terror in France or royalist
terror in Naples. She must have been anathema to Nelson, but he could
not ignore her since she was a well-known author, having published

poems on Peru, on peace, and on the slave trade, as well as books on he politics of France and Italy, and a bestselling translation of the novel *Paul et Virginie*. His annotations in the book are brief. Three times he marks 'not true' against her narrative of his search for the Toulon fleet before the Nile. Twice he writes 'lye', the first time when she states that his ship was dismasted as it carried the king to Palermo at Christmas 1798. He makes no comment on her account of Caracciolo's execution. When she describes the rebels as 'illustrious martyrs of liberty' and says that their attempt was 'sublime', he writes: 'Miss Williams has in my opinion completely proved that the persons she has named deserved death from the monarchy. They fail'd and got hanged or beheaded.'[20]

We do not know whether Stephens accepted Nelson's invitation to call, but his application is important because it induced Nelson to write a three-page memorandum on his conduct at Naples, which went into much greater detail than his markings in the Williams book, or his brief and incomplete reports to Keith, Spencer, and the admiralty at the time.[21] The memorandum is headed, 'PAGES WHICH ARE LIES'.[22] The pages he means are those of the Williams book, to which he evidently referred as he wrote. Here are some of Nelson's remarks, with the present author's comments on them in italics.

On the treaty with the rebels in Uovo and Nuovo: 'Capitulation not closed but negotiation broke off by Ld Nelson who would allow the rebels no terms but unconditional submission and this was regularly notified to the cardinal and he desired to acquaint the rebels of it, and this must have been done from the rebels coming out of the forts as prisoners and not as soldiers.' [*The capitulation was signed and closed, and Nelson knew it. Hamilton wrote to Ruffo on Nelson's behalf about the 'capitulation which your eminence has seen fit to conclude'.[23] Nelson at first purported to nullify it, and then to adopt it. He could have done neither if it did not exist. The rebels came out of the forts because Nelson told Ruffo he would do nothing to break the armistice'.*]

On Nelson's having promised protection to those who accepted his invitation to declare they had accepted employment under the republic: 'Protection not promised except from murder.' [*Would anyone knowingly have accepted so limited a 'protection'?*]

On Caracciolo's execution: 'He was tried by a board of Neapolitan officers, found guilty of rebellion, and hanged by order of Ld Nelson, whose dear friend he had been.' [*If Caracciolo was his dear friend, Nelson's summary hanging of him, that same day, looks even worse.*]

On Domenico Cirillo, the eminent naturalist and physician, whom Miss Williams describes as a friend of Buffon and Franklin, and also of Hamilton: 'Cirillo strange to say would *not* be saved he refused Sir William & Lady Hm's entreatys on the quarterdeck of the *Foudroyant.* When brought up for trial and asked who he was, he announced in the reign of the tyrant I was a physician, in the time of the republic I was a patriot and now I am a victim. He made his application for mercy too late or the queen would have begged his forfeited life from the king for the sake of his aged and good mother.' [*What entreaties made by the Hamiltons can Cirillo have refused? He was held not in the* Foudroyant *but in the Portuguese* San Sebastian, *from where he wrote a most undefiant letter to Emma Hamilton, saying he had attended the French only as a doctor, that he refused three times to join the legislative assembly but then was forced to do so, and that he never wrote or said a word against the king; he then asked her in the name of god to save his life, saying his gratitude would be eternal.*][24]

The more Nelson said, the more unconvincing it became. The business of Naples would not go away.

Then at the end of March 1803, Hamilton was taken ill at Merton and moved to his own house in Piccadilly. There, on the morning of 6 April he died. Nelson said it was in his arms and Emma's, without a sigh or a struggle, and that Lady Hamilton was desolate. In his will, Hamilton made this bequest: 'The copy of Madame Le Brun's picture of Emma, in enamel, by Bone, I give to my dearest friend, Lord Nelson, Duke of Bronte: a small token of the great regard I have for his lordship; the most virtuous, loyal, and truly brave character, I have ever met with. God bless him! And shame fall on those who do not say – *Amen.*' This is subtle, since Nelson already had Vigée Le Brun's original oil painting, made in Naples in 1798, having bought it from the auctioneer before Hamilton's sale of 1801, and then lent it back to Hamilton in 1802 for the enamel copy to be made.[25] It shows Emma as a bacchante reclining on a leopard skin. Was Hamilton saying that since Nelson had the original, in whatever sense, he could now have the copy as well?

As it happened, the artist herself was in London soon after. Emma called on her, wearing a dense black veil, and saying she would never be consoled. 'I confess that her grief made little impression on me, said Mme Le Brun, 'since it seemed to me that she was playing a part. I was evidently not mistaken, because a few minutes later, having noticed some music lying on my piano, she took up a lively tune and began to sing it.'[26] Hamilton was buried beside his gentle first wife, in a Welsh churchyard: it had been her wish, and he did not object, saying that the sea was undermining the church, and that they would roll together into Milford Haven.[27]

The peace of Amiens, concluded the year before on such uneasy terms, was never going to last, and by the spring of 1803 another war was inevitable. Nelson saw Addington and was offered the Mediterranean command. Horatia was hastily christened on 13 May, not at Merton but at St Marylebone, the parish in which Horatia's nurse lived. Horatia was more than two years old, and she was the only one of the seven children baptised that day whose parents were not named in the register. Neither Nelson nor Emma seems to have been present, and the child's date of birth was given falsely as 29 October 1800, to preserve the fiction that she had been born in Italy and later brought to England to be adopted by Nelson.[28] Then there was to be a family wedding, and Nelson's grand and long delayed installation as a knight of the Bath. The wedding was that of Nelson's niece Kitty Bolton, Susannah's daughter. She was marrying William Bolton, her cousin, a clergyman's son, whom Nelson had taken to sea as a midshipman on the *Agamemnon*, and whose promotion to lieutenant and to commander he had assisted. Bolton was fortunate in his connection. The wedding was set for 18 May, and Nelson's installation was to be at Westminster Abbey the following day. But Britain declared war on France on the very day of the wedding, and that morning Nelson left Merton for Portsmouth to take up his command. So he missed the wedding, and had to appoint a proxy for the ceremony of the order of the Bath, who would by convention be knighted himself. Nelson wanted Davison to stand in for him, but the king would not have it, on the grounds that he stood accused of bribery in the Ilchester election, which he had lost. So poor Davison lost his chance of a knighthood too, and Bolton stood as Nelson's proxy, thus gaining in two days a bride and a title.[29] He was also given a letter to deliver to St Vincent, in which Nelson candidly said: 'This will be presented to you by my nephew, Sir William Bolton, and now he stands in so near a situation to me, it must be my anxious wish to get him employed, and with me, and promoted.'[30]

Having left London at four o'clock in the morning of 18 May, leaving his niece's wedding and the reception of the Nelson and Bolton families to be conducted on his behalf by Emma, in her house in Clarges Street, Nelson travelled to Portsmouth where he hoisted his flag on the *Victory*. He had been at home for less than eighteen months. The commander-in-chief at Portsmouth was Admiral Lord Gardner, who as commodore at Jamaica in 1787 had tactfully avoided court-martialling Prince William's first lieutenant, whom Nelson had sent to him for that purpose. Gardner regretted the *Victory* was undermanned, but Nelson wished to lose no time and on the 20th weighed anchor and made sail out of Spithead in a heavy shower of rain, having told St Vincent that he would leave nothing undone, by an active exertion of the force under his command, to bring about a happy peace.[31]

THE CONSTANT WIFE

Frances Herbert Nisbet, daughter of a judge and the widow of a physician, married Nelson on Nevis in 1787, when they were both twenty-eight. She was an heiress and he an unknown captain. They lived contentedly until he became besotted with Naples and Emma Hamilton. After he left Fanny in 1801 she made three efforts at reconciliation. Her last letter was sent back marked 'Opened by mistake ... but not read.' She was a small, dark-haired woman who moved her hands rapidly as she talked. Hood and St Vincent admired her spirit, and St Vincent took her part against the Nelson family, whom he called 'vile serpents'. This miniature, attributed to Cosway, shows her in mourning, perhaps for her uncle, the former president of Nevis, who died in 1793, when she was thirty-five. She outlived Nelson by twenty-six years.

The lady of the admiralty

Lavinia, Countess Spencer was the wife of a grand whig who joined Pitt's government as first lord of the admiralty. As a girl she knew Johnson and Gibbon. As Lady Spencer she was a leader of London society. At a dinner she gave before Nelson returned to sea after losing his right arm, she noticed that he and Fanny were like lovers at table. After the Nile she wrote to him: 'Joy, joy, joy to you, brave, gallant, immortal Nelson ... My heart is absolutely bursting.' When Nelson and Fanny came to dinner again after Nelson's return from Naples in 1800, he treated his wife roughly, and Lady Spencer said she never saw so great a change. Nelson resented her sympathy with Fanny, and wrote sarcastically that 'the lady of the admiralty never had any cause for being cool to me ... I wish nothing undone ...' Mezzotint after Reynolds.

THREE ENGLISH
PORTRAITS

*Above: A grand, familiar, and lifeles[s]
portrait by Beechey, commissioned
by the city of Norwich in late 1800
and seen here as a mezzotint by
Edward Bell.*

*The other two are little known and
more revealing. Both were done in
late 1797 after Nelson lost his arm [at]
Tenerife.*
*Top left is a stipple by G. Keating
after a painting by Henry Singleton,
of whom Reynolds thought highly.
Left is a stipple by William Evans
after a drawing by Henry Edridge,
who catches the fragility of a man
still in pain. The ribbon-ties just
visible on the right arm enabled
the wound to be dressed without
removing the sleeve, which was slit.*

An English Caricature

This etching of October 1798, by James Gillray, shows Nelson extirpating revolutionary crocodiles at the mouth of the Nile. He has been given a hook to his right hand, which he never had. In the background one crocodile, representing the French ship L'Orient, blows up.

Two Italian Portraits from the Neapolitan Years

Above: Nelson in 1799, after Leonardo Guzzardi of Palermo. This fine engraving, by J. Skelton, was made for the frontispiece of Pettigrew's Life of Nelson, 1849. It clearly shows the triangular scar of the wound to his forehead which Nelson sustained at the Nile. Right: Drawing after an unknown Palermo artist, c1799.

The battle of Copenhagen, 2 April 1801

Pen and ink drawing, with watercolour over, by the Danish artist J. Bang, 1803. This is an emblematic and composite picture of the engagement between Nelson's division and the Danish defences in anchored ships, hulks, floating batteries, and land forts. The English ships are shown sailing both south (right to left) as on the day before the battle, and north, as during the battle itself. Bomb ships are lobbing shot into the city. In midstream, a launch is shown carrying the flag of truce. The Trekroner fort is on the shorefront below the first tall spire from the right.

NELSON'S
FAVOURITE
PORTRAIT

Nelson said of this line and stipple vignette (above), made after a sketch by Simon de Koster done in December 1800, that he 'rather thought' it was the most like him. It was reproduced many times in his lifetime and throughout the nineteenth century. On the left is the version now used by the Nelson Society in its publications.

Paradise Merton, *nine miles from London, which Nelson bought in the autumn of 1801 and where he lived with Emma, often surrounded by his family. Here he spent his last twenty-five days in England before he sailed for Trafalgar, days which he thought the happiest of his life. In the foreground is the canal he constructed and called the Nile.*

MERTON PLACE, SURREY.

The last portrait, *by Arthur William Devis,*
was done not from the life but from the death.
Devis went on board Victory *at Spithead, was*
present at the autopsy, and was commissioned by the
surgeon, Beatty, to paint a portrait. This engraving,
by Edward Scriven, was used as a frontispiece to
Beatty's Authentic Narrative of the Death of Nelson.
It is the only portrait to show the shade, attached to
the front hat-brim, which protected Nelson's good
eye from the glare of the sun.

The state funeral *This patriotic fabric shows*
Nelson shot on his quarterdeck, the shallop bringing
the body from Greenwich down the Thames, and the
car carrying the coffin to St Paul's. The scenes were
taken from aquatints published by Ackerman.

Inside St Paul's *the Bishop of Lincoln, who was also Dean of St Paul's, says the last prayers over the coffin. The Duke of Clarence is in the centre foreground, and the Prince of Wales, whom Nelson detested, is on his left. An engraving of 1808 by W. H. Worthington after W. Bromley.*

On the coffin, *besides his viscount's coronet, were laid a laurel wreath and the cocked hat worn by Nelson. It is a foul-weather hat, with the crown waterproofed.*

The ascension of Nelson *The Christ-like Nelson, wrapped in a shroud, is raised up by Neptune, supported by an angel, and offered to Britannia while cherubs hover. The artist was Benjamin West, president of the Royal Academy and historical painter to the king. His romantic work was engraved for the frontispiece to Clarke and M'Arthur's biography of 1809. The quasi-religious depiction of Nelson as saviour of his country is typical of the mood of the time, but compare Gillray's version of the death of Nelson (in the colour section) which shows Emma Hamilton as Britannia and George III and the Duke of Clarence as his supporters.*

CHAPTER TWENTY-FOUR

The Long Watch, and the Grand Race of Glory

'YOU SHALL NOT HAVE anything,' said the Duke of Clarence in the House of Lords, defying Britain's assorted enemies at the start of the new war, 'but what Great Britain pleases to give you.' France should not have Saint Domingue (Haiti) or Louisiana; Spain should not have the Floridas; the Dutch should not have the Cape of Good Hope. 'I wish', said the duke, 'to see Britain chastise France. It is not the first time that we have done so; and if the war be conducted with vigour and wisdom, I think it cannot last long.'[1] The war, as it happened, lasted another twelve years. Nelson, who had so praised the bad peace of 1801, rediscovered his old hatred and was soon calling Buonaparte that man of tyranny, that restless animal, whose tongue was that of a serpent oiled.[2]

The next two years in the Mediterranean – with the *Victory* as his flagship and Hardy his flag captain – were one long monotony, and Nelson longed for activity. When the lord mayor thanked him for blockading Toulon, he answered that the port had never been blockaded by him: 'Quite the reverse – every opportunity has been offered to the enemy to put to sea, for it is there that we hope to realise the hopes and expectations of our country ...'[3] The French wanted something different. The serpent Buonaparte might want the West Indies, or Ireland, or England, but a sea battle for its own sake was no use to him. Nelson wrote letters of grand strategy to the prime minister, saying Europe was degraded but that he was willing to die sword in hand; that he had only one arm but his heart was in the right trim; and please pardon this effusion but the words had flown from his pen as they had from his heart. At which Addington handed the correspondence over to his secretary at war, and Nelson continued unabated to him.[4]

His infatuation with the Neapolitan royal family deepened, if that were possible. He wrote to the queen addressing her for the first time as her *sacred* majesty, and assured the king that the last drop of his blood was at his disposal. 'A mouse assisted a lion,' he said, 'which is the only comparison I can make in arrogating to myself the power of assisting a king of the house of Bourbon.'[5] He was after a pension for Emma, and told the queen Hamilton had not left her enough to live on. Nothing came of it, and he then wrote to Emma that if the queen could forget her, he hoped god would forget the queen.[6] But he still wrote to the queen again, telling her this time – in a letter translated by his private secretary into formal French – that Hamilton had hardly left Emma enough to buy bread and cheese, and asking her to write personally to Addington on her sincere friend's behalf.[7] The queen did not write. This did not prevent Nelson holding out to her the spectacle of a battle in the bay of Naples, better than the Nile.[8] Maria Carolina still did nothing for Emma, and never did. Emma did have enough for bread and cheese. Hamilton had left her £800 a year, and Nelson allowed her another £1,200, but it was not enough for her high style.

For Nelson, day after day passed in the same way. Not once did he go ashore. When Emma offered to join him he discouraged her, saying she knew what a cruise off Toulon would be even in summer – a hard gale every week and two days' heavy swell.[9] He wrote to her constantly, mostly through a Quaker merchant at Rosas, north of Barcelona, who sent letters on through his agent in Bristol. Sometimes he listed to her the dates of his previous letters to assuage her jealous fears. In one letter he gave the dates of fourteen he had sent.[10] He called Horatia sometimes his adopted daughter and twice 'our dear child'.[11] 'I dreamt last night,' he wrote, 'that I heard her call papa.' In early 1804 Emma had another child. Nelson did not know this until he received a letter late in March, which told him the baby was dead but that the mother was recovering. Horatia too had been ill. He was thankful to god for sparing both her and Horatia; he was sure the loss of one, much more both, would have driven him mad.[12] He told Emma his soul was god's but his body hers.[13] His body was not well. He told Dr Baird his shattered carcase was the worst in the fleet. He had a sort of rheumatic fever, and felt the blood gushing up the left side of his head; he had a violent pain in his side, and night sweats.[14] The wound he sustained at St Vincent was a hernia, and violent coughing brought up a lump in his side the size of a fist.[15] To his old political friend of 1784, Admiral Sir Robert Kingsmill, he listed his wounds, and made three copies of this list, as if he were preserving it as a memorandum for himself:

> Wounds received by Lord Nelson
> His Eye in Corsica
> His Belly off Cape St Vincent
> His arm at Teneriffe
> His Head in Egypt
> Tolerable for one War.[16]

Facsimile of Nelson's list of his wounds received in the French war, c1802. From J.K. Laughton's Nelson and His Companions in Arms, *1896.*

He busied himself with minute orders. It is properly the business of a commander-in-chief to order that men with scurvy should receive six ounces of lemon juice and two ounces of sugar a day, but he ordered onions, leeks, pumpkins, sheep, and oranges, and concerned himself with a hogshead of tobacco that was shortweight and a bag of bread that had fallen overboard, every particle of which was to be 'particularly picked, and the dust wiped off', and anything edible to be put in charge of the purser.[17] He was indignant that his patronage was clipped by the admiralty who gave him too long a list of officers to be promoted – Lord Derby's and Lord Camden's nephews and Lord Hugh Seymour's son to be made lieutenants, and Lord Duncan's son to be a commander for his father's sake.[18] Only after admiralty promotions had been made could Nelson promote his own protégés, they would be confirmed only if they filled death vacancies, and no one was dying. He had procured a brig sloop for the fortunate Sir William Bolton, whom he had brought out expressly to promote, and sent him on cruises which should have brought him £30,000 in prizes, but he was lazy and took nothing. He even named him to command a captured Spanish frigate, which would have made him post, but Bolton, off on another cruise, returned so late that he missed her. Nelson was vexed and wrote to Susannah that he could move his fleet ten times as fast as Bolton could move his brig.[19] He was not a bad officer, as Nisbet had been, but he was another disappointment. Nelson could of course take young gentlemen to sea, and he made a midshipman of the son of Lord William Gordon, who had composed verses about Henry and Emma. But the few lieutenants he did make were unsure, even with his commendation, of further promotion. Silas Paddon, six times gallantly wounded, remained a lieutenant for twenty-two years, John Chrystie for twenty-nine, and Benjamin Baynton, 'one of the very best lads ever met with', for thirty-two.[20] He did save the career of another officer, Lieutenant Charles Tyler of the *Hydra* frigate, who had left his ship and run off with an opera dancer from Malta. He was the son of Captain Charles Tyler, who had been with Nelson on Elba and at Copenhagen, and in 1798 had been wrecked near Tunis as he carried dispatches to Nelson. Knowing that the lieutenant was adrift in Italy, probably at Rome or Naples and in prison for debt, Nelson wrote to the captain of the ship he had left in Naples bay saying the boy's father would pay his debts, that if a few pounds more were needed to liberate him he would pay that himself, and that all they wanted was to save him from perdition. After Nelson's intercession with the British ambassadors at Naples and Rome, Tyler was not struck off the list.[21] This was generous, but inconsistent with his previous threat in a fleet order that any deserter would be court-martialled, and any sentence of death most assuredly carried out.[22]

Nelson could not afford the £1,200 he was allowing Emma. His pay and pension did not cover both that and his allowance to Fanny. He had borrowed £4,000 from George Matcham, mortgaging Merton. His situation would have been desperate if he had not at last won his law suit with St Vincent. Lord Ellenborough, who at Despard's trial had remarked that Nelson was beyond eulogy, gave judgment in his favour, and he had £13,000. He said justice had triumphed.[23] But he was still a poor admiral. He would get his flag eighth of any prizes taken by the fleet, and when there were enemy merchant ships to be taken, he took them. The prize money was in their cargoes, not in the destruction of French men of war. But his whole instinct was that of the predator, he wanted the French fleet, and he was stating the truth when he told Davison that he attended more to that than to making captures. 'Not that I despise money – quite the contrary, I wish I had one hundred thousand pounds this moment, and I will do everything consistent with my good name to obtain it.'[24] He certainly did mind when someone else took what he thought rightly his, and this was what happened. Addington fell, Pitt was prime minister again, and St Vincent gave way as first lord to Lord Melville. When war with Spain once again became likely, Melville sent his favourite, Sir John Orde, out to Cadiz, cutting Nelson's Mediterranean command off at Gibraltar. Spanish prizes that would have been Nelson's were now Orde's.

Nelson protested to his friends. 'I have dreamt,' he told Ball at Malta, 'that I have done the state some service.'[25] To Hugh Elliot, Minto's brother and now ambassador at Palermo, he wrote that sending another admiral to take the whole harvest, after all his toils, was a little hard.[26] It was the harder because Orde was the admiral who in 1798 had so bitterly resented St Vincent's giving Nelson the squadron that won at the Nile, that he had challenged the earl to a duel. In spite of that, Orde was back in favour, and for some months reaped a golden harvest. He then got a pleasing comeuppance. Nelson appointed an agent for a prize at Gibraltar. Orde claimed the prize was his, and wrote a private letter to Melville, saying perhaps some other officer might find these circumstances less mortifying, and asking to resign his command into abler hands. He expected Melville to stroke his feathers, give him the disputed prize, and beg him to stay. But Melville, having been accused of peculation, was no longer first lord. His successor was Lord Barham, who was seventy-nine and went back so far that he had succeeded Nelson's uncle as comptroller in 1778, and only consented to become first lord because of the peerage offered with it. It was Barham who received Orde's letter to Melville, and he brought Orde home. Orde represented to Barham that he had not at all foreseen that his private letter would be considered public, shown to the board, and made the reason for an order to strike his flag. Barham was brief: 'If you was acquainted with the number of letters which come daily into the hands of a first lord of the admiralty you would not wonder at his wish to divest himself of every one of a public nature by transferring it to the board.' Orde persisted; he had indulged the flattering expectation of a command equally honourable. Barham did not reply. Orde was never employed again.[27]

In the Mediterranean in August 1804 Nelson felt he could not stand another winter at sea, and asked to come home. Maria Carolina invited him to spend the winter at Palermo, but without Emma that had no attractions. Then he reflected that there were so many admirals senior to him that if he went he would probably not be sent back; he was still only seventy-fourth on the flag list.[28] Then he reasoned with himself that the times were 'big with great events', which they were.[29] In May, the French senate and tribunate had enacted a change in the constitution which began with the curious words, 'The government of the republic is confided to an emperor ...', and Buonaparte in December crowned himself Napoleon I. Nelson was having second thoughts about going. He scented that the French fleet would break out, and determined to follow it, even to the East Indies. 'I have had a good race of glory ... but I cannot help, being at sea, longing for a little more.'[30] His views changed from day to day. By October 1804 he was hinting to Emma that he wanted to go to the admiralty.[31] In his cabin, with confidential friends, he talked of what he would do if he were in power. In November he abandoned the idea of going to England, and by Christmas, when he received permission to return, did not want it, kept it 'a profound *secret*', and stayed on.[32]

At home, Davison had been jailed for a year for bribing the electors of Ilchester. Nelson called it an honourable imprisonment and

looked forward to shaking his hand when he was released.[33] Catherine
Matcham saw Fanny at Bath, and wrote to tell Emma that the
viscountess looked at her 'in that *scornful way*'; she was sure there
was a strong party against Nelson.[34] The scorn was deserved. The
family was very thick with Emma, and Catherine often wished that
Fanny were in heaven.[35] *The Morning Herald* carried this paragraph:
'The Revd Dr Nelson expects a *dispensation* daily, to enable him to hold
his domestic chaplainship to Lady Hamilton, with his prebendal stall,
which gives *rise* to some extraordinary *Canterbury Tales*.'[36] Nelson wrote
to William saying that if he took another French fleet they might make
him a bishop.[37] Emma was importuning George Rose, Pitt's paymaster
general, for a pension. 'I did more than any *ambassador* ever did,' she
said, 'though their pockets were filled with secret service money, and
poor Sir William and myself never even got a pat on the back.' There
is even a suggestion that Emma's conscience was slightly worrying
her, but this has to be carefully looked at. It came from Richard
Bulkeley, the army captain who had been in Nicaragua with Nelson
and had since resigned his commission and settled in Shropshire. He
and Nelson had been young men in Jamaica together, and Bulkeley
wrote to him with frequent flattery and with a freedom which hinted
that on occasion they may have been on the town together. In 1800,
when there were rumours that Nelson was about to come home from
the Mediterranean, Bulkeley wrote to him saying: 'The fair sex ... *all*
impatiently await your return, each hoping that she may be one of
the select few who are to become slaves to your amorous passion – I
mention this that you may come back as determined to gratify your
own country women as much as you have by all accounts others in
your Italian states.' Nelson and Bulkeley remained friendly. Bulkeley
had a son, also Richard, whom Nelson took to sea as a midshipman, and
while Nelson was away, Bulkeley and Emma kept up a correspondence
which was also conducted with some freedom. It was in response to a
letter of hers in October 1804 that he wrote: 'You say, if it is a sin to
love him, you must sin on – I say sin on, it is a crime worth going
to hell for – you must either have him or be ungrateful – ingratitude
is a sin, and I would rather commit myself to the lash of the infernal
prince, for the one crime, than the other ...'[38]

In the Mediterranean, Nelson took up the cause of William Layman,
who had been with him as a lieutenant at Copenhagen and was one

of those young officers, like poor Parker, for whom he could not do too much. In 1804 he gave him a sloop, the *Weazle*, which he ran aground in a fog. The automatic court martial acquitted him of blame. On Nelson's recommendation he was given another sloop, the *Raven*, and confirmed in the rank of commander. He ran this second sloop ashore and this time the court martial placed him at the bottom of the commanders' list. Nelson then wrote the first lord a remarkable letter saying hardly any great things were done in a small ship by a man who feared the shore, and that he did not regret the loss of the *Raven* compared with the value of Layman's services, which were a national loss. 'You must, my dear lord, forgive the warmth which I express for Captain Layman ... [but] if I had been censured every time I have run my ship, or fleets under my command, into great danger, I should long ago have been *out* of the service, and never *in* the house of peers.' This was impetuously generous in a Nelsonian way, but Layman had lost two ships, was self-willed, and talked too much. As Nelson said of him, before he lost the first ship, it was Layman's venturing to know more about India than Troubridge that 'made them look shy upon him'. Nelson had found a dashing young man in his own image, but all his praise did not help. Layman was never promoted, and killed himself in 1824.[39]

Early in 1805, Napoleon's plans for the French fleets were grand. The English were to be decoyed towards both the East and West Indies, while Villeneuve's fleet from Toulon was first to join with the Spanish at Cadiz and then sail to Martinique, where it would rendezvous with the French fleets from Brest and Rochefort. The combined fleets of fifty to sixty sail would then recross the Atlantic and command the English channel while the British were still chasing chimeras in the far east, or India, or America. The end purpose was an invasion of England. The plan was so complex that it did have the virtue that no Englishman was likely to suspect it. In January the Toulon fleet did get out and Nelson, with 1798 and Egypt in his mind, searched as far east as Alexandria and found nothing. It did not matter, since storms had driven the French back to Toulon. At the end of March the French again escaped from Toulon, by 8 April were at Gibraltar, and then sailed westward. Once again Nelson stayed to protect the Mediterranean until he was sure the French were no longer there. But where then had they gone? On 20 April he was undecided between the East and West Indies. A week later he thought it might be Ireland. On 4 May, anchored off the Moroccan coast, he said: 'I cannot very properly run to the West Indies without something beyond mere surmise; and if I defer my departure, Jamaica may be lost.' By 10 May the lot was cast. He would go to the West Indies, but it *was* on little more than mere surmise. He had no idea, as how could he, of the French grand plan. He explained himself later in a letter to a friend in the West Indies: 'I was in a thousand fears for Jamaica, that is a blow which Buonaparte would be happy to give us. I flew to the West Indies without any orders, but I think the ministry cannot be displeased ... I was bred, as you know, in the good old school, and taught to appreciate the value of our West India possessions.'[40] He had twelve ships of the line, and Villeneuve twenty. He called first at Barbados, where he received a report from St Lucia that a fleet had been seen sailing south, perhaps to Trinidad. There he went, and found nothing. He sailed north to Grenada and then to Antigua, which he had last seen when he was engaged to Fanny. He did not set foot there or anywhere else in the West Indies. There had been a French and Spanish fleet in the Caribbean, and he had missed it, but his presence saved the islands.[41] He lamented that he had missed the battle he had sought – and in which he would have been greatly outnumbered – because of the mistaken message from St Lucia, and he never stopped saying so. The message had come from a General Brereton, who had not himself seen the supposed French fleet but simply passed the message on to Barbados. He had no reason even to know Nelson was there. But Nelson fulminated about Brereton's 'unfortunate', 'ill-timed', 'unlucky' message which had almost broken his heart. Damn Brereton, whose name would not soon be forgot.[42] 'But for General Brereton's damned information, Nelson would have been, living or dead, the greatest man in his profession that England ever saw.'[43] He pursued Villeneuve back across the Atlantic, but the French fleet was always to the north of him, never closer than a hundred miles. It had been a wild goose chase, but Napoleon's grand plan had not worked. The French fleet had never got out of Brest, so the fleets had not met at Martinique, and nor had they descended in mass on the English channel. When Nelson got back to Gibraltar he calculated that the run out had been 3,227 miles and the run back 3,459.[44] 'What a race I have run after these fellows', he wrote to Acton. To the sacred Maria Carolina he sent a few tamarinds and a little preserved ginger, which was all he had been able to get in the

West Indies. He went ashore at Gibraltar on 20 July, the first time he had set foot out of the *Victory* for only ten days short of two years.[45]

Two days later, to the north, off Finisterre, part of Villeneuve's combined fleet fell in with a squadron commanded by Sir Robert Calder. He took two of the Spaniards but night fell, and the next morning he did not harry the French, and was derided for it. Nelson, hearing the news, told Fremantle he was grieved John Bull was not content, and that it was insinuated that he (Nelson) would have done better. As he told his brother William: 'I might not have done so much with my small force. If I had fallen in with them, you would probably have been a lord before I wished; for I know they meant to make a dead set at the Victory.'[46]

Then he went home, struck his flag at Spithead, and went straight to Merton, arriving at six in the morning on 20 August. This is how Horatia's governess, Sarah Connor, a cousin of Emma's, described the homecoming. 'Thank God he is safe & well cold water has been trickling down my back ever since I heard he was arrived – Oh say how he looks & talks & eats & sleeps – never was there a man come back so enthusiastically revered . . . yet this is the man to have a Sr R. Calder & a Sr J. Orde sent to intercept his well earned advantages – I hope he may never quit his own house again.'[47]

Lord Minto met Nelson in Piccadilly in a mob. 'It is', he told his wife, 'beyond anything represented in a play or a poem of fame.' At Merton for dinner, he found Nelson again surrounded by William's and Catherine's sons and daughters.[48] One of Catherine's sons, George, who was almost sixteen, came later and kept a journal. '[3 September] On arriving at M. found them all in bed. Lady H. came out en chemise . . . Wednesday 4th Large company at dinner . . . Lost 11s 6d at cards. Lady H. presented me with £2 2s from Lord N. Friday 6th. Fished in the pond. Caught nothing. Sauntered about the grounds. HRH the duke of C[larence] dined here. Like the king . . . Introduced to the D. of C. Talked much. His deference to Lord N's opinion. Violent against Mr P[it]t; found out the reason. Seemed estranged from the K[ing].'[49]

Between Nelson and Emma, Minto found 'the passion as hot as ever'. She had in his absence bought from William Peddison, upholsterer, 'a large feather bed & bolsters fill'd with best goose feathers, and a new Kidderminster carpet for the bedroom'. Nelson paid the bill, for £32, promptly on his return. Peddison was both upholsterer and undertaker, and Nelson had left with him the coffin Hallowell had made for him after the Nile, from the timbers of *L'Orient.* When Nelson learned, after only two weeks at home, that the combined French and Spanish fleets were at Cadiz, he went to Peddison's shop in the Strand and asked for his name to be engraved on the coffin lid, saying he thought it highly probable he might need it on his return. He also bought from Barrett, Corney, and Corney, lacemen and embroiderers to their majesties, silver embroidered stars of the orders of St Ferdinand, the Crescent, St Joachim, and the Bath. They cost a guinea each, except for the Neapolitan star of St Ferdinand which, being grander, cost an extra four shillings. He bought five of each, to be sewn on his coats.[50]

CHAPTER TWENTY-FIVE

A Legacy to My King and Country

'I AM AGAIN BROKEN hearted,' Emma wrote, 'as our dear Nelson is immediately going. It seems as though I have had a fortnight's dream, and am awoke to all the misery of this cruel separation. But what can I do? His powerful arm is of so much consequence to his country.'[1] Nelson, who had so much feared the winter before that if he came home he would never be sent back to the Mediterranean, had found, when he returned from his long pursuit, that ministers looked to him and, as he put it, set him up for a *conjuror*; though he was still apprehensive that if he made one wrong guess the charm would be broken.[2] Where were the enemy? What should be done? But now the combined fleets were found it was obvious what was to be done and who was to do it. His return to England was treated as no more than a short leave, and he was to resume the Mediterranean command.

Emma's story is that she had seen how his health was better at Merton, surrounded by his family, that he told her he was happy, and that he would not have given sixpence to call the king his uncle. But she – and this is her account, which naturally casts her in a self-sacrificing light – replied that she did not believe him, that he was longing to get at those French and Spanish fleets which he considered as his own property, and that he must have them as the price and reward of his long watching, at which he exclaimed, 'Brave Emma! Good Emma! If there were more Emmas there would be more Nelsons.'[3] Emma was determined that much of the credit for his going back to sea should be hers.

Nelson spent only ten more days in England, and three of those were in London. He saw Barham, the first lord; Castlereagh, the new secretary for war; and Pitt, who was now prime minister again. Forgetting the speeches he had made for Addington, Nelson gave Pitt a lecture on political uprightness, saying that, not having been bred at court, he could not pretend to a nice discrimination between the use and abuse of parties, that he could not be expected to range himself under the political banners of any man, that England's welfare was his sole object, and that where the tendency of any measure to promote or defeat that object seemed clear he would vote accordingly; but that in matters where his judgment wavered he would be silent, as he could not reconcile to his mind the giving of a vote without full conviction of its propriety. He said Pitt listened with patience and good humour, and then wished that every other officer in the service would entertain similar sentiments.[4] Nelson was pleased when, after their interview, Pitt did him the compliment of seeing him to the door, and told Rose he came away with the conviction that Pitt knew that what the country wanted was annihilation of the enemy, 'not merely a splendid victory of twenty-three to thirty-six, – honourable to the parties concerned but absolutely useless in the extended scale to bring Buonaparte to his marrow bones'. It became a tradition in the Matcham family that Pitt considered Nelson as great a statesman as a warrior.[5] Emma, who had hopes of a pension from Pitt, returned the compliment: 'I call him', she said, 'the Nelson of ministers.'[6]

Nelson made two requests, but not of Pitt. He asked Rose to get Susannah's husband a commissionership in the customs or the navy office, and was put out when Rose enquired who he was, replying that Bolton was a gentleman in every meaning of the word, of more ability than many who had seats at those boards. And he again commended to the first lord the unfortunate Layman.[7] He got nothing for either. What he could do himself, and did do as soon as he got to the Mediterranean, was to take the young Sir William Bolton, his niece's husband, from the command of a hospital ship where his dilatoriness had left him, and give him a frigate.[8]

On what should have been his last day at Merton, Nelson went to Carlton House to pay his respects, as requested, to the Prince of Wales, and to take leave of Castlereagh. While he was waiting for the secretary of state he met in the waiting room a colonial major general, who many years later recalled the encounter: 'He could not know who I was, but he entered at once into a conversation with me, if I can call it conversation, for it was almost all on his side and all about himself, and in, really, a style so vain and silly as to surprise and almost disgust me. I suppose something that I happened to say may have made him guess that I was somebody, and he went out of the room for a moment, I have no doubt to ask the office keeper who I was, for when he came back he was altogether a different man, both in manner and matter. All that I had thought a charlatan style had vanished, and he talked ... like an officer and a statesman. The secretary of state kept us long waiting, and certainly, for the last half or three quarters of an hour, I don't know that I ever had a conversation which interested me more. Now, if the secretary of state had been punctual, and admitted Lord Nelson in the first quarter of an hour, I should have had the same impression of a light and trivial character that other people have had; but luckily I saw enough to be satisfied that he was really a very superior man; but certainly a more sudden and complete metamorphosis I never saw.' The soldier was Arthur Wellesley, who became the Duke of Wellington. He was thirty-five at the time, eleven years younger than Nelson. It was the only time the two men ever met.[9]

That afternoon Minto went to Merton. 'I stayed till ten at night,' he wrote to his wife, 'and took a final leave of him ... Lady Hamilton was in tears all yesterday; could not eat, and hardly drink, and near swooning, and all at table. It is a strange picture. She tells me nothing can be more pure and ardent than this flame.' And then he stated much the same conclusion as Wellesley had come to that afternoon: 'He is in many points a really great man, in others a baby.'[10] Nelson wrote in his journal that night: 'At half-past ten drove from dear dear Merton, where I left all which I hold dear in this world, to go to serve my king and country. May the great god whom I adore enable me to fulfil the expectations of my country ... If it is his good providence to cut short my days upon earth, I bow with the greatest submission, relying that he will protect those so dear to me, that I may leave behind. – His will be done: amen, amen, amen.' Next morning, at six, he arrived at Portsmouth. At two in the afternoon he embarked at the bathing machines on the beach, to be rowed out to the *Victory*, from which he had been absent 'only twenty-five days, from dinner to dinner'. The last letter he wrote in England, as he was about to get in the boat, was to a fellow admiral, George Murray, thanking him for a haunch of venison he had sent.[11]

That evening he dined on the *Victory* with Rose and with the young George Canning, then treasurer of the navy, many years later to be prime minister, the man who as an even younger minister at the foreign office, after the Nile, had thought it a bad decision to make Nelson only a baron. Next day he sailed. Off Portland, beating down the channel, he wrote to Davison reminding him to pay Maurice's 'poor blind Mrs Nelson' her annuity and house rent. Off Plymouth, at nine in the morning after a nasty blowing night, he wrote to Merton. 'I intreat, my dear Emma, that you will cheer up; and we will look forward to many, many happy years, and be surrounded by our children's children. God almighty can, when he pleases, remove the impediment. My heart and soul is with you and Horatia.'[12] The impediment was Fanny, whose removal he devoutly wished. A worldly priest he had known in Naples wrote a letter of hints about the queen's new lover, who to great scandal had been made a gentleman of the bedchamber, and Nelson in reply first asked him not to tell him about those little arrangements which raised a smile or gave a pang, and then said his brother William hoped he should meet the enemy's fleet so that somehow or other he might become a lord.[13]

When he joined the fleet off Cadiz he had to give Calder the admiralty's orders to return home. Calder wanted an inquiry, in which he believed he could prove it had been impossible for him to bring the combined fleet to battle, but said the order to turn him out of his flagship broke his heart. Nelson had no reason to feel tender to Calder, who had been captain of the fleet under Jervis at St Vincent, and was believed to have induced Jervis to remove his praise of Nelson from his dispatch.[14] But he let him return in his own ship, thus depriving himself of a ninety-gun second rate when a battle was in prospect, telling Emma that he had 'given way to his [Calder's] misery', and the admiralty he considered he had done right to a brother officer in affliction.[15] He also let Calder take two captains back to England as witnesses in his forthcoming court martial, so that at Trafalgar two ships of the line were commanded by their first lieutenants. They at least benefited from Calder's ticklish pride. After the battle they were not just promoted to commander, which would have been usual, but made post captains.[16]

Three days after he joined the fleet, Nelson suffered a spasm at four in the morning, which left him weak. Perhaps, he told Emma, it might not come again for six months, but he had no doubt what its effect would be one day. He then told her how he had been welcomed by the fleet:

> I believe my arrival was most welcome not only to the commander of the fleet [Collingwood] but also to every individual in it, and when I came to explain to them the Nelson touch it was like an electric shock, some shed tears all approved, it was new, it was singular, it was simple and from admirals downwards it was repeated it must succeed if ever they will allow us to get at them, You are my lord surrounded by friends who you inspire with confidence, some may be Judas's but the majority are certainly much pleased with my commanding them . . .[17]

If every individual in the fleet welcomed his arrival, who were the Judases? But Nelson moved rapidly from high exultation to deep suspicion, and from the ordinary to the exalted. The next day he ended a letter to Emma: 'I congratulate you on the fall of the wall and the opening prospect [at Merton]. I hope the kitchen is going on. God bless you, amen, amen, amen . . .'[18] Then he wrote to Rose that he verily believed the country would soon be put to some expense on his account, either for a monument or for a new pension and honours.[19]

The fleet prepared for action. Most captains were painting their ships *à la Nelson*, with yellow horizontal stripes on the line of the gunports and the ports themselves black, which gave a chequer effect. Nelson ordered the lower masts of all the fleet to be painted yellow, to distinguish them in the smoke and confusion of battle from the black hooped masts of the French.[20] Villeneuve, with the Spanish admiral Gravina and the combined fleets, waited at Cadiz. Napoleon, having abandoned the project of invading England, had ordered his admiral to take the fleet to sea, sail into the Mediterranean, land troops at Naples, and then return to Toulon. If he encountered a smaller British fleet he should fight a decisive action. Villeneuve was a gallant sea officer from an ancient military family, one of the few of the old regime to survive in the revolutionary navy. But he was demoralised. After his failure to carry out Napoleon's grand plan of decoying the British to the West

Indies and then doubling back to the channel, he had written to the minister of marine about his despair at the horror of the situation in which he found himself, saying that he had been obliged to give up the emperor's plans at a point when nothing could result but disasters and confusion. On 19 October he did put to sea from Cadiz, though it may have been out of no more than pride. He had learned that Napoleon was sending an admiral to replace him, and sailed before he could be removed.[21] A scouting English frigate saw the French and Spanish topsails, and the signal went along a line of frigates, *Sirius* to *Euryalus* to *Naiad*, and then to the line of battleships – *Defence* to *Colossus* to *Mars* – and in three hours Nelson, fifty miles from Cadiz, ordered a general chase to the southeast. The wind dropped, and it took a day before the combined fleets were well clear of Cadiz harbour. Nelson's frigates had told him where the enemy were, but they did not know where he was. The French and Spaniards were not looking for a fight, and a battle was not inevitable. They could slip back into Cadiz, or through the straits into the Mediterranean.

But by the night of 20 October, Blackwood in *Euryalus*, lying between the fleets and able to see the lights of both, knew there would be a battle the next day. At six in the morning, the fleets were nine miles apart. For six hours, in light winds, they slowly approached each other. Nelson took it as a good omen that it was the forty-eighth anniversary of his uncle Maurice Suckling's action against the French off St Domingue.[22] In his journal he wrote what has been called his last prayer, but it is part prayer, part log, and part simple statement of what was in his mind. He wrote that at daylight he had seen the enemy from east to east southeast, and that at seven the enemy wore in succession; then he asked the great god whom he worshipped to grant to his country and to Europe a great and glorious victory; then he resigned to god both himself and the just cause he was entrusted to defend; and he ended, as he had on two recent occasions, with the words Amen, amen, amen.[23]

Trafalgar[24] was named after the nearest point of land, a cape thirty miles southwest of Cadiz. The sea was smooth and the sun shone. Each fleet flew its ensigns – the French tricolour, the Spanish red and yellow, the British union flags. Each Spanish ship also hung to the end of her spanker boom a large wooden cross. Each fleet was under a full spread of sail. The British were outnumbered thirty-three to twenty-seven, but this was only a notional advantage and mattered the less because there would be no formal line of battle. Even at those odds it was an uneven combat, with the real advantage to the British, who had kept constantly at sea throughout the wars. The French and Spanish, apart from the break across the Atlantic, had kept to their ports. The British superiority in seagoing experience was great, and in gunnery even greater. The British rate of fire was twice that of the enemy. It was all calculated and bloody. Nelson's plan was that two spearheads of British ships would attack the rear and centre of the curving enemy line, concentrating the attack at those points and leaving the ten ships in the enemy's van untouched but unable to manoeuvre to help the rest of the fleet. This strategy gave the British a real advantage in numbers of twenty-seven to twenty-three. Nelson would lead the attack on the centre, breaking the enemy's line. It was not a commander-in-chief's place to do this. In the pell-mell that Nelson wanted, he would have no general view of the battle from there. In the smoke and confusion he would see nothing. Blackwood went on board *Victory* and suggested that Nelson should hoist his flag in *Euryalus*, where he could better see what was going on, but he refused. He then suggested that *Temeraire*, *Neptune*, and *Leviathan* should lead the attack, before *Victory*, giving that as his joint opinion with Hardy, but Nelson again refused, asked Blackwood to witness his will, and said goodbye.[25]

At 11.15am Nelson hoisted the signal, 'England expects that every man will do his duty'. He was in undress uniform, not wearing his full orders as he would have done in more formal dress, but Messrs Barrett, Corney, and Corney's silver embroidered stars – 'his unfortunate decorations of innumerable stars', as Blackwood put it – were every bit as conspicuous.[26] The Revd Dr Alexander Scott, his private secretary and chaplain, was anxious that he should cover them with a handkerchief but feared his displeasure if he made the suggestion. Beatty, the surgeon, said he would tell Nelson, but was ordered below before he could say anything. The French fired the first shots about twenty minutes before midday. The English held their fire. Before the *Victory* fired a single shot, Nelson's public secretary, John Scott, was killed by his side and thrown overboard, and a file of eight marines was killed by one cannon ball. Then, as *Victory* slowly broke through the French line, the carronade on the port side of her forecastle, containing one round shot and a keg filled with five hundred musket balls, fired right into the stern cabin window of the *Bucentaure*, Villeneuve's flagship. No two ships' logs agree on the precise time of this opening shot, which varies from 12.04 to 12.25. A disparity was usual. *Victory's* log says 12.04, and we shall follow her chronology of the action.[27] As *Victory* moved ahead, and this was all in slow motion, the fifty guns of her port broadside, all double- and some treble-shotted, were discharged in the same raking manner through *Bucentaure's* stern, killing men throughout the length of her. She then received, in succession, the broadsides of the English ships that followed, and was reduced to a wreck; in two minutes, four hundred of her people were killed and twenty guns dismounted. *Victory* then tangled with the *Redoutable*. So close were the two ships that their rigging touched as they rolled. All strategy ended when the line was broken. What followed was a massacre at point-blank range. Most of the *Victory's* men were on the gundecks below, and with them the lieutenants and midshipmen; on the quarterdeck of each ship, exposed by that position and made conspicuous by their uniforms, stood the captain, first lieutenant, and master. On the quarterdeck of the flagship there was also Nelson, most conspicuous of all, and unmissable. For him to stay there was a throwback to the choreographed formality of the eighteenth-century parade that had been the line of battle, every other step of which he had abandoned. It is extraordinary that a man whose entire aim was the cool annihilation of the enemy, should not coolly have seen that nothing was to be gained by exposing himself to this useless danger. The *Redoutable* had a captain, Lucas, who had trained his crew in small arms marksmanship, sent them aloft with grenades and muskets, and packed them into the tops. *Victory* and *Redoutable* were so much on top of each other that Lucas feared he might be boarded. It did not need marksmanship to hit an admiral covered in stars at fifty feet, and at a quarter-past one Nelson was shot from above.

It would have been astonishing if he had not been shot. The next most senior British officer to be killed was John Cooke of the *Bellerephon*. He wore his post captain's two epaulettes, declining his first lieutenant's advice to take them off, and he too was picked off.[28] Useless ornaments were commonly removed in battle, light shoes worn rather than boots, and silk stockings rather than socks, as likely to give less trouble to the surgeon. The ball struck Nelson's left epaulette, penetrated the shoulder, descended obliquely into the chest, ruptured a branch of the pulmonary artery, and entered the left side of the spine between the sixth and seventh vertebrae, where it was later found to have carried bits of epaulette with it.

He took until four o'clock to die. Dr William Beatty was with him for almost all that time and described everything.[29] The last hours and moments of Nelson's life were as minutely described as those of any man ever have been, and are as affecting as Dr Johnson's as described by Boswell. Nelson knew he was dying. 'They have done for me at last', he told Hardy. 'My backbone is shot through.' As he was carried down to the cockpit on the orlop deck, below the water line, where the surgeon was working on the wounded, he covered his face with a handkerchief so that the people should not see who it was. When Beatty was called over to him, Nelson said again that his back was shot through. While he was undressed down to his shirt, he said again that he was gone. As Beatty examined him he said once again that his back was shot through, that he felt a gush of blood every minute in his breast, and had no feeling in his lower body. Beatty saw the case was hopeless but told no one but his assistants, Captain Hardy, the purser, and Dr Scott. When the *Redoutable* struck fifteen minutes after Nelson was hit, *Victory*'s crew cheered, as they did whenever an enemy ship struck her colours. Once Nelson asked what the cheering was for. He became thirsty, frequently asked for a drink, and to be fanned with a paper. He was given lemonade, wine, and water. He repeatedly said, 'Fan, fan', and 'drink, drink'. The purser told him the enemy were defeated and hoped Nelson would himself be the bearer of the joyful news to his country, at which Nelson said it was nonsense to suppose he could live.

He then asked for Hardy, became impatient when he did not come, and insisted he must have been killed. A midshipman came down to say Hardy would be there as soon as possible. Nelson asked who the messenger was, was told it was Mr Bulkeley, and said, 'Remember me to your father'. The father was the Captain Bulkeley with whom Nelson had served in Nicaragua. George Westphal, a midshipman, was brought down and laid next to Nelson, whose discarded coat was rolled up and placed under his head as a pillow. Coagulated blood from his wound entangled his hair and the gold of the epaulettes, and when the coat was later cut away several bullions were left glued into his hair.[30]

Hardy came at last, more than an hour after Nelson was shot, and they shook hands. Both Dr Scott and the purser continued fanning, and Nelson often said that, god be praised, he had done his duty. When Beatty asked if the pain was still very great, he said it was so great he wished he were dead, but then, in a lower voice, 'One would like to live a little longer too'. A few minutes later he said, 'What would become of Lady Hamilton if she knew of my situation?' Hardy again came down into the cockpit and congratulated him on his victory, saying fourteen or fifteen enemy ships had surrendered. 'That is well,' said Nelson, 'but I had bargained for twenty.'

Then, knowing that a storm was blowing up, he told Hardy to anchor, at which he replied that he supposed Collingwood would now take upon himself the direction of affairs.

Nelson tried to raise himself, saying: 'Not while I live, I hope, Hardy.'

'Shall *we* make the signal, sir?'

'Yes, for if I live, I'll anchor.'

He asked Hardy not to throw him overboard, to take care of Lady Hamilton, and then to kiss him. It has been suggested often enough that Nelson said not 'Kiss me' but 'Kismet', meaning fate, but Beatty says Hardy did kiss him on the cheek, and then, after standing by him for a moment, knelt down and kissed him again on the forehead; and that the second time Nelson asked who it was. After Hardy left, Nelson told Dr Scott, 'I have *not* been a *great* sinner', and then, '*Remember*, that I leave Lady Hamilton and my daughter Horatia as a legacy to my country.' His thirst increased, and he said, rapidly and indistinctly, 'drink, drink', 'fan, fan', and 'rub, rub'. Dr Beatty insists that his last words were, 'Thank god I have done my duty', which he continued to repeat as long as he could speak. His hand and forehead became cold, the pulse went from his wrist, he opened his eyes, looked up, and then shut them again, and Dr Scott was still rubbing his chest when the surgeon told him Nelson was dead.

The battle lasted another hour. No British ship was lost. Of the eight French and Spanish ships that were the focus of the attack, six struck, one blew up, and one was devastated but escaped. In all, seventeen ships of the French and Spanish fleets were taken and sixteen escaped, many of them, in the van and the rear, having played little part in the action. Collingwood did not anchor. Blackwood, writing to his wife, said: 'Ever since last evening we have had a most dreadful gale of wind, and it is with difficulty that the ships who tow them [the prizes] keep off the shore. Three I think, must be lost, and with them, above 800 souls each. What a horrid scourge is war . . . I wish to god he [Nelson] had yielded to my entreaties to come on board my ship. We should all have preserved a friend, and the country the greatest admiral that ever was, but he would not listen to it . . . Villeneuve [who was captured] says he never saw anything like the irresistible line of our ships.'[31] The gales of the next four days were far worse than Blackwood had foreseen, and drowned more of the enemy than had been killed in the battle. Of the seventeen ships taken, twelve ran ashore or foundered, and only four survived to be taken as prizes to Gibraltar. It was a battle hard on admirals. Gravina died of his wounds, and Villeneuve, captured and then exchanged, committed suicide on his return to France.

News of the battle reached Paris before it reached London. Napoleon was absent in Austria, about to defeat the hopeless General Mack, he who had led the disastrous Neapolitan invasion of Rome in 1798. So Decrès, minister of marine, wrote to Louis Buonaparte, Napoleon's brother and governor of Paris, asking how to break the news to the French people. He was terse:

> *Aigle* and *Argonaute* have gone aground, and these ships, with *Héros*, *Pluton*, *Neptune*, and *Algeciras*, are the only ones that remain of those that composed his imperial majesty's fleet.
> Nelson is definitely killed.
> That is the state of affairs.
> It is hardly known in Paris.

Louis Buonaparte told Decrès to wait for Napoleon's orders before publishing anything. Conscripts were just leaving Paris for Austria, and should not be told about the scene at Cadiz while it was not generally known. It was, he wrote, possible that the emperor might not wish to give great publicity to what had happened.[32]

He did not. One French account of the battle which did appear is worth quoting because it shows just what the battle was not, in event or in spirit. It was from *Le Moniteur* of Paris, and had English seamen striking their colours and jumping overboard while French and Spanish admirals disputed the honour of first boarding Nelson's ship and taking him. 'They boarded the ship at the same moment – Villeneuve flew to

the quarter deck – with the usual generosity of the French, he carried
a brace of pistols in his hands, for he knew the admiral had lost his arm,
and could not use his sword – he offered one to Nelson: they fought,
and at the second fire Nelson fell; he was immediately carried below
– Oliva, Gravina, and Villeneuve attended him, with the accustomed
French humanity. Meanwhile fifteen ships of the line had struck – four
more were obliged to follow their example – another blew up – our
victory was now complete.'[33]

On the morning of the battle, Blackwood thought that the paper he and
Hardy had witnessed just before the battle was Nelson's will, and it is
generally called a codicil to his will, though the text nowhere states that
it is either a will or a codicil, and it is in effect Nelson's appeal to king
and country to look after Emma and Horatia. He says he asks this as a
favour. The document recites that it was made in sight of the combined
fleets, about ten miles distant, and lists the services of Emma Hamilton,
in particular that she had used her influence with the Queen of Naples
to procure supplies for his squadron in 1798 before the battle of the Nile.
'Could I have rewarded these services I would not now call upon my
country; but as that has not been in my power, I leave Emma Lady
Hamilton, therefore, a legacy to my king and country, that they will
give her an ample provision to maintain her rank in life. I also leave
to the beneficence of my country my adopted daughter, Horatia Nelson
Thompson; and I desire she will use in future the name of Nelson only.
These are the only favours I ask of my king and country at this moment
when I am going to fight their battle. May god bless my king and country,
and all those who I hold dear. My relations it is needless to mention; they
will of course be amply provided for. Nelson & Bronte.'[34]

Nelson's leaving Emma and Horatia as a legacy to the nation now
seems outlandish. But it would not have seemed so to him. The notion
of such a legacy was almost a custom of the navy, and had certainly
been familiar to Nelson since he was a very young officer. It was his
uncle Maurice Suckling, as comptroller of the navy, who got him his
commission as lieutenant and ensured, through Sir Peter Parker, that he
got the next two steps, so that he was a post captain at twenty. After
Suckling's death, Nelson wrote to his brother William Suckling, saying
he hoped to continue to prove himself worthy of the place in the service
of his country that Maurice Suckling had left him. 'I feel myself, to my

country, his heir; and it shall, I am bold to say, never lack the want of his counsel: – I feel he gave it to me as a legacy, and had I been near him when he was removed, he would have said, "My boy, I leave you to my country. Serve her well, and she'll never desert, but will ultimately reward you . . ." I beg your pardon for this digression, but what I have said is the inward monitor of my heart upon every difficult occasion.'[35]

Nelson was twenty-six when he wrote this. Many years later, in 1803, when he was commander-in-chief in the Mediterranean, he received an order from St Vincent, the first lord, that the son of Admiral Lord Duncan, the victor of Camperdown, should be promoted, and naming him as 'heir' to an admiralty vacancy as commander.[36] Nelson replied: 'I had not, my dear lord, forgot to notice the son of Lord Duncan. I consider the near relations of brother officers as legacies to the service.'[37] The same year, when Sir Peter Parker sent out his grandson, Nelson wrote: 'Nothing could be more grateful to my feelings than receiving him. I have kept him as lieutenant of the *Victory*, and shall not part with him till I can make him a post captain; which you may be assured I shall lose no time in doing. It is the only opportunity offered me, of showing that my feelings of gratitude are as warm and alive as when you first took me by the hand: I owe all my honours to you, and I am proud to acknowledge it to all the world.'[38] Nor was it necessary that a young man should be the son or grandson of an admiral to be so considered. St Vincent, naming the son of 'a worthy old lieutenant', stated it as his maxim that sons of brother officers should be promoted before any others. Recommending another lieutenant's son to Collingwood, he assumed that Collingwood would pay the same attention as he always had to 'the children of the service'.[39] And writing about the prospects of a young gentleman whose late father he had known, Nelson said again that he felt the children of departed officers were a natural legacy to the survivors.[40] There was always this sense of the continuity of the service, and of its traditions being handed down. The inward monitor of Nelson's heart led him to an almost feudal sense of reciprocal obligations, to the idea of service and reward. When his old friend Locker died in late 1800, Nelson wrote a letter of condolence to his son saying that the posterity of the righteous would prosper.[41] Locker had been the first captain with whom Nelson went to sea after passing his lieutenant's examination, and he would have considered himself part of Locker's posterity, just as he considered Emma and Horatia part of his, and naturally left them a legacy to his king and country.

CHAPTER TWENTY-SIX

State Funeral and
Empty Chariot

THE NEWS OF TRAFALGAR and of Nelson's death was sent ahead in the *Pickle* schooner, whose commander reached London at one o'clock in the morning of 6 November. William Marsden, secretary to the admiralty, received him and then had to take a candle and go and search for Lord Barham, the first lord, not knowing which room he was sleeping in. Secretary and first lord then stayed up all night writing to the king, the Prince of Wales, cabinet ministers, and the lord mayor, ringing the changes, as Marsden put it, a thousand times.[1] Pitt was told, and for the first time in his life could not get back to sleep after hearing momentous news, good or bad, and at length got up though it was only three in the morning. The king, when he was told, remained silent for five minutes.[2] Barham wrote to Fanny himself: 'It is the death he wished for & the less to be regretted on his own account – but the public loss is irretrievable.'[3] The comptroller of the navy sent a messenger to Emma, who screamed and fell back and, by her own account, could neither speak nor shed a tear for ten hours. *The Morning Chronicle* asked: 'What is likely to be the inward ejaculation of Buonaparte? – "Perish the twenty ships – the only rival of my greatness is no more!" ... He was, as a captain, equal in his own element of the sea, to what Napoleon, with a base degeneracy of motive, has proved himself to be on land.'[4]

Pitt was a dying man, and much affected. He had besides just received the news of Napoleon's victory at Ulm. He sent for Sir Isaac Heard, garter king of arms, the chief deviser of heraldry, and with him, three of his cabinet, and the first lord, conferred several times on the creation of a new order of knighthood for naval and military merit. There were to be knights chief, knights commander, and plain knights, according to the rank of the recipient. Masters, mates and midshipmen would be honoured with the gold medal of the order, and raised to knights when they were commissioned. The ribbon of the order would be four inches wide, of watered crimson, and the badge a sprig of laurel erect and a naval crown *or*. Barham asked Pitt, 'Have you ever thought of one for Lady Nelson during her life? She is as far as I have heard a valuable woman and irreproachable in her conduct. Such instances seldom occur and it does not add to the peerage.'[5] William Nelson was busy replying to letters of condolence. 'No titles,' he said, 'no distinctions which all the potentates of the earth can bestow, can make amends for the loss of such a man; – but it was the will of god and to his will we must submit.' He also submitted to an earldom. On Nelson's death his viscountcy had become extinct. His barony of 1801, with its special remainder, went to William, who became the second baron Nelson. But this was not thought enough, and his majesty was pleased to grant William, for the 'transcendent and heroic services' of his brother, the dignity of an earldom – a higher rank in the peerage than Horatio Nelson had ever held.[6]

The same ministers who made William an earl determined that the funeral should be at St Paul's cathedral, and for the same reason. Nelson's will directed that his body should be interred 'in as private a manner as may be' at Burnham Thorpe, next to his father and mother's, unless his majesty should signify his pleasure that it should be interred elsewhere.[7] On his ministers' advice, the king signified his pleasure that the burial should be at St Paul's, 'which the brilliancy of the victory seems to call for'. As Marsden said, 'All this . . . is a matter of the utmost importance, which people think more about than of the disasters on the continent; or the safety of our own troops.'[8] The Prince of Wales announced he would be chief mourner, at which William told him how deeply the family of his lamented brother was impressed with a sense of his royal highness's condescension. But government would have nothing to do with the earl's and prince's ambitious plans, and decreed that the chief mourner should be a sea officer, though his royal highness could still attend if he liked. The earl persisted, at which the matter was referred to the king, who of course did as his ministers advised and directed that the pall bearers should be admirals and the chief mourner either the first lord or Sir Peter Parker, who in the course of seniority had risen to be admiral of the fleet. There was no way the government could allow the Prince of Wales to play so conspicuous a part as chief mourner.[9]

Nelson's body was being brought home. On the day of the battle, after the action had ceased, Beatty traced the course of the bullet with a probe, but could not find the ball. He drew off some blood from the left side of the breast: none had escaped before. The hair was cut off, and the body undressed except for a shirt. It was then placed in a cask called a leaguer, the largest on board, which held one hundred and eighty gallons, and this was filled with brandy and stood on end on the middle deck. Three days later, in a storm, the body gave off so much air that the sentinel became alarmed when he saw the head of the cask rise. The officers spiled the cask to let the air escape. After a week, when *Victory* was towed into Gibraltar, the level of the brandy had dropped, some having been absorbed into the body, and the cask was topped up with spirits of wine. The *Victory* was fitted with jury masts and her rigging repaired, and she set off for a five week passage to Portsmouth against adverse winds, during which the spirit in the cask was twice renewed. All the time the Revd Dr Scott stayed near the body. On 4 December the ship arrived at Portsmouth. There were no instructions on what to do with the body, but Hardy had orders to sail to the Nore and there was a common report that Nelson would lie in state at Greenwich, 'literally exposed to the public'. Beatty therefore took the body from the cask, removed the bowels, and found the ball, which had passed through the spine and lodged in the muscles of the back. A piece of the coat and of the silk pad of the epaulette were found with it, and the gold lace or bullion of the epaulette was as firmly attached as it had been welded into the ball.[10]

It was then that John Tyson, who had been a friend of Nelson for more than twenty years, became agitated at the manner in which the body was to be treated. Tyson had been purser of the *Badger* brig, Nelson's first command. After the Nicaraguan disaster he had brought the desperately ill Nelson back from Jamaica to England. He had been his secretary in the Mediterranean and at Naples and had later lent him some £4,000. In 1805 he was clerk of survey at Woolwich dockyard.

'How', he asked Haslewood, one of Nelson's executors, 'is the body to be landed at Greenwich? In a cask of spirits and rolled into the Painted Chamber, or decently carried there in his coffin?' He then approached William, Nelson's other executor, who, as he discovered, was averse from doing anything. But surely, Tyson argued, in a second letter to Haslewood, Nelson should be buried in the coffin then at Peddison's, the one Hallowell had made from the timber of *L'Orient*. 'My only wish,' he wrote 'is that every attention may be paid to his remains – which I cannot agree with the earl, can be paid to it if it is not decently put into his coffin at the Nore on board the *Victory . . .* And if no attention whatever is paid to his remains by his relatives or friends they will be liable to much censure – the earl says that Dr Moseley [another Nicaragua veteran] is to go to Greenwich to see the painful ceremony performed and I presume he has come into this plan in order that Moseley may have the *éclat* of placing him in a coffin – you know my dear sir a physician is not wanted for the dead – all mere vanity this! for an undertaker is of more real use.' Tyson wrote a third time, insisting on the decency Nelson's heirs ought to observe towards the body, and saying that he had asked all his navy friends, who were unanimous that the body should be put in its coffin on *Victory*. He offered to fetch the coffin from Peddison's and take it to the Nore.[11]

William at the time was more interested in being presented to the king, and had made soundings at Windsor. He was told the etiquette was to wait until after the funeral.[12] On the passage round to the Nore, which took another two weeks, Beatty had already taken the corpse from its cask, removed the contents of the abdomen and chest, rolled the remains in cotton bandages, and put them in a leaden coffin filled with brandy, camphor, and myrrh. The body was in a perfect state of preservation. The face was swollen and Beatty tried to restore it by rubbing with a napkin but, as Scott told William, the features were lost and the face could not with propriety be exposed when the body lay in state.[13]

So there was to be no barrel rolled on shore, and no public exposure, and Tyson got his way about the coffin made from *L'Orient*'s timber. He collected it from Peddison's, then took the dockyard yacht from Woolwich and had to search for three days against a south westerly gale before he found the *Victory* in Nob channel at the Nore. In the presence of *Victory*'s officers, the body was dressed in shirt, stockings, and waistcoat, placed in Hallowell's coffin, and then soldered into an outer lead coffin. As the yacht came upriver with the body, all the forts and ships flew flags at half mast and fired minute guns. Tyson then had to get Nelson ashore. By the time he reached Greenwich it was the afternoon of Christmas Eve. Lord Hood, who was governor of Greenwich Hospital, wanted to leave the body on board the yacht over Christmas. Tyson objected that all London would come to see it. Hood asked if the coffin was so slung that six or eight men could carry it from the waterside. Tyson then went outside and told anyone who asked that the body would not be landed until the following Thursday. The crowd dispersed, and when the beach was clear the coffin was brought ashore at half-past six, in the dark. Not thirty people were there to see it.[14] Dr Scott stayed with the coffin, and was determined not to leave it until the interment. From Greenwich he wrote to Lady Lavington, a patron, to whom he had already sent a lock of Nelson's hair. It was the day after Christmas, and he told her: 'He did not intend to go to sea any more – he always said he would be in England by Xmas day *coûte que coûte* – & of truth his mind at the time took in the idea of what has happened.'[15]

By mid-December the news had come of a second Napoleonic victory, at Austerlitz, and the show of a great state funeral to celebrate a great sea victory was more than ever necessary. The heralds' office, which was responsible for the form of the funeral, consulted distant precedents – that of Sir Philip Sidney, soldier and poet, in 1586; that of James I in 1625; and the comparatively recent one of an Earl of Sandwich who in 1672 was killed in a naval battle with the Dutch. The resulting order of precedence offended many. The lord mayor of London claimed precedence within the city – and St Paul's is within the square mile – over all the king's subjects, even over the Prince of Wales. Garter king of arms conceded that at the funeral of James I, the lord mayor had taken precedence over the three lord chief justices, but that at Sir Philip Sidney's he had not seemed to be an integral part of the ceremonial, but had rather 'taken under his protection the nobility and others who attend'd the remains'. The king settled the dispute by sending a warrant to place the lord mayor between the prince and the great banner, in other words putting him before the prince without giving him precedence. It was a nice business. The speaker of the House of Commons, told that his place was among the privy councillors, protested 'in the name of all speakers past and present', quoted an act of parliament of 1689, and was promoted to be next to peers of the realm 'and of course before viscounts' eldest sons, earls' younger sons, etc.'. The new Earl Nelson made a greater fuss than anyone. He insisted that Garter should not give tickets to relations before he, William, had approved, and until they had fully satisfied Garter of their consanguinity by 'undoubted evidences of their pedigree'.[16] He also demanded no fewer than six mourning coaches, and a crape scarf for himself.[17]

All admirals who were in England were invited. One who declined was St Vincent. When the codicil leaving Emma as a legacy appeared in the newspapers, he had told his sister: 'The will of Lord Nelson has thrown a shade on the lustre of his services. That infernal bitch Lady H. could have made him poison his wife and stab me, his best friend.'[18] The admiralty asked him twice. To the second invitation he replied that in addition to the complaints set forth in his previous letter, he was attacked with a violent inflammation of the eyes which made it physically impossible for him to attend.[19] He had returned from the Mediterranean unwell in 1799, and as commander of the channel fleet had wintered ashore, but by 1805 was in better health than for the previous twenty-five years, and the day after the funeral he went riding for three hours.[20] But he would not come. Eighteen other admirals declined. Some were of course ill. But one said he could not come to town; three were suffering from fits of the gout; three, and this was two or three weeks before the day of the funeral, pleaded colds; and one said he could not conveniently come but that if any etiquette required his presence he would have no option but to obey. Thirty-six did attend, among them Sir Peter Parker, chief mourner, who was eighty-three, and Hood, who was eighty.[21]

At Greenwich the crowds gathered. Hood called them a tumultuous mob, 30,000 strong, and asked for cavalry.[22] The day before the funeral a procession of barges took the body upriver, in another gale, to Whitehall, where the crowd was happy to see Admiral Orde's hat blown into the river. He was believed to have made hundreds of thousands in prize money at Nelson's expense, and was no friend of his. But he had insisted on taking part for the glory of it, and in the ceremonies his rank made him chief pallbearer.[23] Marsden, secretary to the admiralty, was hardly reverent. 'The body', he wrote to his brother, 'has been deposited in the admiralty, and without any effort on my part, or intention of going the least out of my way, I have had a good view of the water procession from the top of the building, and of its entry into the court and house from my own window. The Mackenzies and the Wilkins are to be here at ten o'clock tonight (through the garden door) to be introduced to the tomb of the Capulets.'[24] Also at the tomb, very late, Dr Scott was still conferring with the undertakers, and after midnight on the morning of the funeral he wrote twice to Emma. In the previous day's procession, he said, he had seen many, tattered and on crutches, shake their heads in sorrow, and the very beggars had left their stands. He called Nelson the man of the century. Then he went on, at that hour and in that place, to ask her to intercede with the new earl to take him as his chaplain, saying it was 'not for any nasty material good of this world', and that he would never have urged it while dear Nelson remained unburied, except that he was afraid the earl might forget his prior claim.[25]

The next morning was extraordinarily fine for January. From eight o'clock 30,000 troops lined the route. The procession started at eleven. The body was drawn in a funeral car shaped fore and aft like the *Victory*, and took three and a half hours to reach St Paul's. A timber amphitheatre had been created inside the cathedral, seventeen tiers high, to seat 7,000. Seven royal dukes, sixteen earls, and forty-eight seamen were among the mourners. Neither Fanny nor Emma was there. Women were not invited, though some fashionable ladies found places in the organ loft. Boys perched on cornices of the dome, seventy feet high. Military bands played the 104th psalm – 'There go the ships, and there is that Leviathan.' The French and Spanish flags captured at Trafalgar stirred in the breeze from the west door. It was already dark by the time the service began, and the interior was lit by an octagonal cylinder ten feet deep, brought in for the occasion, suspended from the dome, and hung around with one hundred and sixty patent lamps. At half-past five the body was lowered by balancing machinery into the crypt twenty feet below, into an Italian marble sarcophagus which was originally made for Cardinal Wolsey but had been seized by Henry VIII after the cardinal fell into disfavour, and had ever since been at Windsor. Garter king of arms recited all Nelson's British, Sicilian, Turkish, and German titles and ranks over the grave. His staves of office as knight, baron, and viscount were then broken and thrown into the crypt, and so were the flags and ensigns of the *Victory*, except that the forty-eight seamen from her tore the largest flag into pieces in the cathedral, so that each had a fragment to keep.[26]

St Paul's was not cleared until after nine at night. In the coming week the four vergers made £300 a day by charging a shilling to view the catafalque.[27] The great car which had carried Nelson's body was sent to St James's palace, but the clerk of the king's stables objected to the prodigious crowds it attracted and said the sooner it was moved the better. The college of heralds tried to give it to the admiralty, the lord chamberlain objected that it was not theirs to give away, and it ended up at Greenwich hospital.[28] *The Morning Herald* called the descent of the coffin into the crypt a 'stage trick', and said the service ought to have been held at Westminster Abbey. *The Morning Chronicle* contrasted the 'meagre and monotonous' music of the ceremony with the grand public concert put on by the management at Drury Lane, where a cathedral set was built on stage.[29]

The moment of the service best remembered was the seamen's tearing up of the flag. The coach most remarked in the procession by *The Times* was 'the private chariot of the deceased lord – empty – the blinds drawn up – the coachman and footman in deep mourning, with bouquets of cypress'. *The Times* was mistaken. The carriage was Frances Lady Nelson's. She and Garter king of arms had silently arranged that it should take its place with the mourning coaches, and it carried his family arms and hers. It was the last gesture of a constant wife.[30]

CHAPTER TWENTY-SEVEN

The Founding of a Family

EVEN BEFORE THE FUNERAL, the clergyman father of a man Nelson had known in the Mediterranean asked the family if he could have back Boswell's *Life of Johnson* which he had lent him. He explained that the book itself was of no account, though he had known Boswell, but had become inestimable in his sight by Nelson's having had it in his cabin.[1] Earl Nelson demanded more. He took from Emma, giving her a formal receipt, the King of Naples's diamond-hilted sword, the collar of the order of the Bath, and the grand signior's diamond chelengk. Nelson had always intended the chelengk to go to his family 'as a memo that I once gained a victory', but William demanded them promptly from Emma, formerly his intimate friend, allowing her to keep on loan the bloodied coat in which Nelson died.[2] The insignia of the Bath he gave back into the hands of George III, with whom he had solicited an interview. The king fumbled with the ribbon, cut off William's pieties, and said what Barham had said, that Nelson had died the death he wished.[3]

The encomiums to Nelson were many. Minto said he had been a man to whom *impossible things* came easily.[4] The Duke of Clarence claimed to have lived with him with the intimacy of a brother. St Vincent was noticeably silent. In the Lords he mumbled a few words, but in so low a tone, said the reporters, that they could scarcely catch a word.[5] The new Earl Nelson was not admired. 'Nothing in him like a gentleman', said Collingwood, '. . . and here has fortune, in one of her frisks, raised him, without his mind or body having anything to do with it, to the highest dignity.'[6] The government which had raised William to that dignity then had to give him the means to support it, since Nelson had died a poor admiral. His will gave the house at Merton and everything in it to Emma (as well as an annuity of £500 on the Bronte estate), his telescopes to Captain Hardy, £200 to his friend Dr Scott, and an annuity of £1,000 to Fanny. To cover these legacies he had some farmland around Merton, £15,600 in government bonds, and £18,800 to come in prize money and back pay, which was all barely enough, and left nothing for the family.[7] So Parliament had to find the money to maintain the earl in the situation he expected to hold in society. As Castlereagh, the colonial secretary, put it, the individual was past gratitude, but the name remained.[8] The earl bargained with the prime minister, and what was settled was £5,000 a year tax free for the earl and his successors for ever, £90,000 to buy a house, £10,000 to furnish it, and £15,000 each for Susannah and Catherine.[9] When these grants came before the Commons, two members spoke against them. Colonel George Wood said that had Nelson himself been living, he should not have opposed a much greater grant, but the grant was not for Nelson, nor for any of his lineal descendants, but for his relations. As it was not Nelson who was to enjoy the rewards of his services, he thought £5,000 a year enough, and would not vote more until the national debt was reduced. George Rose, who had always been a good friend, compared Nelson to Marlborough, for whom a grateful country had built a palace at Blenheim, and he had possessed an immense fortune which Nelson had not: even at the Nile he had made only £3,090 in prize money. Mr Philip Francis took up the comparison: 'What makes the essential difference in the two cases is that the Duke of Marlborough was alive and had children living. He who received the reward, had earned it by acts of his own. Lord Nelson's collateral relations, personally, are unknown to the public, and can have no claim but what they derive from the accidental honour of bearing his name, and from services in which they had no share.' Lord Henry Petty, chancellor of the exchequer, answered this argument. There was, he said, perhaps no desire which operated more powerfully upon the minds of many men, than the desire of founding a family. It was the duty of Parliament to cherish and encourage this feeling, which formed such a prominent feature in the character of sea officers, who encountered dangers in order to leave to others the rewards they had no opportunity of enjoying themselves.[10]

Nobody mentioned Nelson's bequest of Emma to king and country. Petty described Nelson's sisters as having been thus bequeathed, which they had not been. Mr John Fuller, a member for Sussex, did appeal to the earl who was to receive profits and honours to show some degree of generosity and comply with Nelson's last wishes; this was taken to allude to Emma, but it did not.[11] He was reminding William that Nelson, and everybody else concerned, had expected him, on his ennoblement, to give up his prebend at Canterbury to the Revd Dr Scott, who had stayed with Nelson at the death. But William clung on to the stall and its stipend, claiming it was intended he should give it up only if he had been given preferment in the *church.* It seemed an earldom did not count.[12]

Fanny went into deep mourning for her husband – black silk and twill gowns, black crape turbans, black sarsnet cloak, black crape veil, and jet ornaments.[13] Pitt had died only two weeks after Nelson's funeral, the proposal for a new naval order of knighthood died with him, and so she did not receive the order of chivalry Barham had proposed for her. Parliament voted her a pension of £2,000 a year, which was as well since she had to sue William for the annuity Nelson had left her. When the earl delayed payment she asked St Vincent for help, which he promptly gave. He had resumed command of the channel fleet, but wrote from off Ushant to his sister recommending Fanny to take the advice of the solicitor general, one of the law officers of the crown, and saying: 'I love Lady Nelson dearly, & admire her dignified pride and spirit, which, I trust, will not be subdued by the infamous conduct of her late husband's brother, sisters, and their husbands, all of them *vile reptiles* ... Lady N. cannot be too quick in applying for the injunction.'[14] Faced with such opponents, William rapidly retreated, and funded the annuity. Then he refused to pay Fanny's legal costs, but had to give way on that too. Later that year, Fanny had to endure Harrison's biography of Nelson, which described the 'petrifying chill' with which she had greeted her husband on his return from Naples. This was Emma's false version, in a book she subsidised.[15] Fanny thought it the basest production ever offered to the public. St Vincent came to her aid again, saying Harrison deserved the pillory.[16]

Harrison's biography revived the whole business of Naples. In it, he characterised the treaty Nelson had annulled as 'infamous'. Captain Foote, who had signed that treaty, then published the papers he had collected in his defence in a pamphlet he called his *Vindication*: he said it was 'but too true that the garrisons of Uovo and Nuovo were taken out of those castles under the pretence of putting the capitulation . . . into execution', that when he had returned to England in 1801 all who regarded the character of Nelson or the reputation of the country 'saw the necessity of burying the whole transaction in oblivion', but that neither fame nor services, however shining, could justify laying one man's errors at the door of another. No one publicly challenged him, and his protest did him no professional harm. He had been in command of the royal yacht *Princess Augusta* since 1803, and he retained this command until he was given his flag in 1812.[17]

Before Harrison appeared, William was already busy ensuring that Nelson's official biography should be written to his satisfaction. John M'Arthur, formerly Hood's secretary and an editor of *The Naval Chronicle*, had been working on a biography for years. William, however, wanted it written by a 'person of rank'. M'Arthur replied that the reputation of Dr Johnson had not suffered from the lack of rank in his biographer. William retorted that he would surrender no papers. M'Arthur countered that Nelson's life was in the public domain. William then demanded to see the Prince of Wales, and ungraciously agreed, in accordance with the prince's wishes, 'not commands', that the life should be written jointly by M'Arthur and James Stainer Clarke, the prince's chaplain. He still protested that papers in his possession should not be 'indiscriminately examined', and insisted that Clarke's name, because of his connection to the prince, should come first on the title page. He achieved that much in the way of rank. Clarke was agreeable to this, and compliant, trusting that his conduct throughout the whole of the 'biographical task' would be such as William would approve, and assured him: 'You may rely, my lord, on my caution & my honor.'[18]

Petty had been right when he said Nelson had wanted to found a family. When in 1803 he had appointed Emma as Horatia's guardian, he had done so 'knowing that she will educate my adopted child in the paths of religion and virtue and give her those accomplishments which so adorn herself, and I hope will make her a fit wife for my dear nephew Horatio Nelson if he proves worthy in Lady Hamilton's estimation of such a treasure as I am sure she will be'.[19] Horatio was William's only son. When William and Lady Hamilton had been bosom friends, he had confided to her that he hoped to keep the line of the Nelsons with the true name and blood, without being obliged to go to others to assume a name which scarcely belonged to them. (He was here disparaging his own sisters' children, the Boltons and Matchams, who were in the line of succession.) He hoped Horatio would transmit a long line to posterity.[20] It did not happen. Early in 1808, when he was nineteen, Horatio died of typhoid. The earl was left with no male heirs.

Later that year, he pursued the deanery of Canterbury in a manner which it needs a Trollope to do justice to.[21] In August he wrote to his distant acquaintance John Fisher, by then bishop of Salisbury, saying the incumbent dean was so weak he might not get through the winter, that he did not want to let the chance of the deanery slip, and that if he did not get it himself he would keep his stall no longer than suited his convenience and would throw himself into opposing the government, in whose gift the deanery lay. Then he wrote to the prime minister, the Duke of Portland, saying that the worthy dean was in a precarious state. He recited that he was no common petitioner, and that it was not the additional emolument of seven or eight hundred pounds a year which induced him to make the application, but if another dean, certainly his inferior in rank, were put over his head, he would feel much hurt and degraded. His only wish was the deanery, and on his honour he assured his grace that if he were offered a bishopric the next day he would decline it.

The dean somehow survived the winter, but next April William was able to inform the duke that he was extremely sorry that his 'worthy friend the good dean' was dead, and trusted his grace had not forgotten his previous application. Next day, a Sunday, he somehow saw the duke at Downing Street, who briefly observed that he did not exactly see the line of promotion from prebend to deanery. So on Monday morning William wrote to him again, saying that the previous day he had been too agitated to make the point that this was as regular a promotion as from lieutenant to captain, citing the examples of five prebendaries who had become deans, and adding that he had already acted as vice-dean – 'So that I know the whole business & can do it. I have as it were already, I think with the Bow of Ulysses.' He trusted to his grace's candour to support his claim. This note he marked, 'Delivered at the gate myself . . . At ten o'clock'.

That same day the duke had the candour to reply that he had been so fortunate as to obtain information which had prevented him from communicating the dean's supposed death to his majesty. The dean still lived. At which the earl, dating his letter 'Monday 4 o'clock', desolately replied that he could not sufficiently express his concern; the good dean was indeed living – it was the dean's brother who had been found dead in the deanery garden.

Even that was not the end. By September, William was writing not to Portland, whose government was tottering, but to Lord Sidmouth, formerly Addington, confidently relying on the 'long friendship' of a man whom he had often abused but who, he hoped, might after a change of administration have influence with his majesty. The dean, he wrote, was *in extremis . . .*

William never got the deanery, and Emma never got a pension. She told her friend Lady Elizabeth Foster, the Duke of Devonshire's mistress: 'Let them refuse me all reward. I will go with this paper fixed to my breast, and beg through the streets of London, and every barrow woman shall say, "Nelson bequeathed her to us."'[22] She told Davison: 'All tho when I was in power many basqued in my sunshine [and] I have done the state no little service . . . all is now over and forgotten.' She ended one letter, *'Amen amen amen* as your dear friend Nelson used to say'. Across it Davison scribbled to his clerk, 'Let her have £100'.[23] Davison himself was sent to prison for a second time in 1808, having as a contractor defrauded the government of £8,800.

Spencer Perceval, who became prime minister in 1809, was importuned by two persons who invoked Nelson to support their claims, with unfortunate results for them. The first was Sir Sidney Smith, the navy captain and Swedish knight whom Nelson had resented and derided in the Mediterranean in 1799. Just before Nelson returned to Naples to put down the republicans, Smith, with a Turkish army, had repelled the stranded French troops who were storming the walls of Acre, on the shores of what is now Israel. After this defeat, Buonaparte abandoned the army he had taken to Egypt and returned alone to France. The Turkish sultan gave Smith a chelengk, like Nelson's. The British government gave him an annuity but no title. In 1810, having returned as a rear-admiral from the South American station, he was still asking Perceval for an Irish barony, saying Nelson had obtained a peerage for defeating a French fleet, and urging that his own services at Acre were the equal 'as to difficulties, risks, and results, [of] twelve hours hard fighting at the Nile . . .' He got nothing.[24] Nelson's was the wrong name to call in aid, as Isabella, Countess Glencairn later found. She petitioned Perceval for £15,000 spent gathering intelligence on the government's behalf by her first husband, in the Leeward Islands, as far back as the 1770s. She stated that she had met Nelson just before he sailed for Trafalgar, and that he had thought her claim just and had agreed she could use his name in pressing it. She had some interest, since she was the sister of Lord Chancellor Erskine, but she got nothing from Perceval either. Whereupon she published a pamphlet in which she cited him as replying to her: 'I am sorry to find, Lady Glencairn, that you rest so much on the force of Lord Nelson's opinion; with me you could offer no name of less weight. I never thought of the late Lord Nelson and his services as the world has . . .'[25]

The improvident Emma continued writing to anyone who would listen. She told the unfortunate Dr Scott, who never got his prebend, that she had been the representative of the Queen of England, and said of the world in general, 'My soul is above them. And I can make some of them tremble by showing them how he despised them, for in his letters he thought aloud.'[26] When sixty of Nelson's letters to her were published in 1814 she probably had no hand in it; most likely they were stolen from her.[27] But St Vincent said she had laid open a horrid scene, and what a diabolical bitch she was 'to expose the weakness of Lord Nelson, to say no more of it'. Five of St Vincent's own letters to her appeared in the same work – letters written before he knew her and in which he signed himself her devoted knight.[28]

Emma did bring up Horatia to speak Italian and German, and French like a Frenchwomen. She continued at first to live high, but without protectors – a Greville, or a Hamilton, or a Nelson – she wrecked herself with drink and debt. She sold William Hamilton's splendid library, which contained a copy of the Domesday Book, and she sold Merton. She mortgaged her annuities. She sold the Nelson coat the earl had lent her. To escape her debtors she fled to Calais where in 1815, at the age of fifty, she died of dropsy, drink, and want. Horatia was brought back to England and taken in by the Matchams. Legends grew round Emma and Horatia as they had around Nelson. The Earl of Guildford's son (and therefore a descendant of Lord North the prime minister) was reported to have bought Emma's body in a sack for sixty francs, and given it a decent burial.[29] In fact the British consul at Calais attended to this. Then Horatia was said not to have been Nelson's at all but to have been fathered by a man called Thompson and born to a woman on board ship during the battle of the Nile, and this story was attributed to captains Hardy and Berry.[30] The Thompson fiction adopted by Nelson himself was being elaborated. Another legend was assisted by the discovery of a statement in Emma's hand that the child was Nelson's true daughter, but that her mother was 'too great to be mentioned'.[31] The wild implication was that the mother had been Maria Carolina, though the queen would have been forty-eight at the time of conception. Horatia grew up knowing herself to be Nelson's daughter, but never accepting Emma as her mother, and married a clergyman.

Fanny, Viscountess Nelson, lived at Exmouth, which she and Nelson had first seen when they returned to England newly married. She appeared occasionally at court, and in 1814 was present at victory celebrations when the battle of the Nile was re-enacted in a grand *Naumachia* on the Serpentine in Hyde Park, which was irreverently reported in the press as 'park foolery'.[32] Josiah never had another command, even during the long wars when there were ships in plenty, and remained a half-pay post captain until 1825, when he resigned. Fanny later lived with him and his children in Paris, where he died before her.

St Vincent outlived Nelson by eighteen years. He was once asked for hush money to prevent the publication of more Nelson manuscripts, but scorned it. 'It is much wiser', he said, 'to stand the ridicule I may be exposed to for any nonsense I have written to his lordship, than to deal with the vendors of those papers.'[33] The only nonsense he had written to Nelson was the cajolery and flattery of 1801, to keep him in the channel – that the command was worthy of an admiral of the fleet, and that Nelson would one day be first lord of the admiralty. As soon as he really knew anything about Emma Hamilton, St Vincent had deplored her conduct, and Nelson's with her. His opinion of Nelson the man had not changed since he met him at Tor Abbey in late 1800, on his return from Naples, when he had seen him making a fool of himself, creating a great *brouillerie* to get Emma received at court. His estimate of Nelson as a sea officer had been formed in 1797, when he recognised him as a predatory genius. That opinion never changed either. St Vincent had long kept up a correspondence with Dr Andrew Baird, formerly physician to the fleet, who had also known Nelson well. We do not know what question or remark from Baird called this forth, but in

October 1814, a few months after the publication of Nelson's letters to Emma, he wrote him a letter about a dockyard, a breakwater, and the inhabitants of Baltimore, whom he characterised as bitter enemies of the mother country and closely connected with France. Then he added, in a postscript:

> Animal courage was the sole merit of Lord Nelson, his private character most disgraceful, in every sense of the word. – StV.[34]

After the death of his first wife in 1828, Earl Nelson disputed the bill of £92 for her burial in the vaults of St Paul's cathedral, and then within a year took as a bride the pretty young widow of a captain of hussars, winning her with a marriage settlement of £4,000 a year. He was seventy. She was twenty-eight.[35] He hoped for an heir but got no children by her, and so he knew that on his death the Nelson earldom would pass to the son of his sister Susannah, and only the Sicilian dukedom would remain in his own family, descending to his daughter Charlotte. Fanny died in 1831, at the age of seventy-three, and was buried at Exmouth. While William was there for the funeral his London house was burgled. A large diamond hoop, a ruby hoop, a topaz cross, several gold chains, collars, bracelets, emerald hoops and clasps were taken. But Nelson's chelengk, which he had wished his heir to have as a reminder that he once gained a victory, escaped the thieves though they might easily have laid their hands on it. The grand signior's chelengk, the most ostentatious and cherished of all Nelson's trophies, escaped, as the newspapers reported, because it was 'loosely wrapped in a piece of brown paper, and carelessly thrown into the bureau'.[36]

APPENDIX A: NELSON AT NAPLES, 1799

NELSON'S CONDUCT AT NAPLES in 1799 (see chapters 17 and 23) has been a matter of controversy ever since. Italian and French historians from that day to this have unanimously blamed Nelson, or Nelson and Hamilton. So have some English writers, though others have as vigorously defended Nelson. Here is a summary of the literature, and of manuscript sources.

ENGLISH: Opinion has always been divided. Charles James Fox said in the House of Commons on 3 February 1800 that what happened was a stain on the British name. *Captain Foote's Vindication*, London, 1807 and 1810, accurately quotes many letters by and to him; he signed the treaty which Nelson repudiated. The original papers he collected in his defence are in BL Add 36,873. He continued to deplore Nelson's actions. Helena Maria Williams's *Sketches of the State of Manners and Opinions in the French Republic*, 2 vols, London, 1801, is the work of a convinced republican: a copy of her book, annotated by Nelson, is at BL Add 34,991. Four sheets of Nelson's own comments on the events, previously unpublished, are at NMM PHB/P/19. Clarke and M'Arthur (1809) were somewhat troubled, writing that the matter was one of 'great delicacy and difficulty', that Nelson had some 'old fashioned ideas', and that he considered rebellion against a lawful sovereign 'as the sin of witchcraft'. They concluded that his error, even if admitted to be such, was not of professional integrity but of political judgment. Southey in his biography (1813) called the events at Naples a deplorable transaction, a stain on the memory of Nelson and the honour of England. James, in his standard seven volume *Naval History of Great Britain, 1822–24,* II 276, wrote: 'Here, then, was a gross infraction of the treaty, and by whom? By Lord Nelson.' If Nelson's fleet had been delayed, the unhappy victims of violated faith would have been on their way to Toulon and British honour would have been preserved untarnished. Henry, Lord Brougham (lord chancellor 1830–34) wrote in his *Historical Sketches,* 1839, II 171, that Nelson, whom he considered an illustrious hero, had nevertheless 'lent himself to a proceeding deformed by the blackest colours of treachery and murder'. Nicolas, 1845 (III 477–523) surveyed the English documents then known, and concluded that Nelson acted honestly and that nothing occurred inconsistent with his scrupulous sense of duty. Pettigrew (1849) also exonerated him. On the other hand, Clowes in his *Royal Navy,* 7 vols, 1899, was scathing, calling Nelson's conduct (IV 394) not quite that of a man of scrupulous honour. This view, as J.K. Laughton wrote in 1886 in the preface to his short edition of Nelson's *Letters and Despatches,* had by then become generally accepted: but it was a view that he attacked, calling it a 'story invented by Neapolitan traitors' and reproduced by a host of English writers of more or less repute. Laughton would hear no ill of Nelson, thinking the possibility of his guilt 'too absurd to be believed'. His views, and the concurring opinions of Mahan, were then attacked by F.T. Badham, a descendant of Foote's, and perhaps the fiercest critic of Nelson's good faith. In his *Nelson at Naples,* 1900, he examined the English and the then newly available Italian evidence. At the turn of the century H.C. Gutteridge was commissioned by the Navy Records Society to bring together the extant documents. He found in Naples not only Italian documents and transcriptions, but English documents previously unknown, or known only from their drafts in letter books or from the botched versions in Alexandre Dumas's ten volume *I Borboni di Napoli,* 1862–3. Gutteridge's *Nelson and the Neapolitan Jacobins: documents relating to the suppression of the Jacobin revolution at Naples,* NRS 25, 1903, collates 177 English and Italian documents, and is the single most important work on the subject. The editor gives less emphasis than he might to Foote's documents, but that is the only criticism of a splendid work. In an introduction of 112 pages, he exonerates Nelson. By then the controversy had become almost a personal matter between Badham on the one hand and Laughton and Mahan on the other. Laughton was professor of history at King's College, London, and founded the Navy Records Society in 1893, and Mahan was an historian of weight, but neither had mastered both the English and Italian evidence, and Badham, in his *Nelson and Ruffo*, 1905, got much the better of the argument which had, however, descended into bitterness.

Modern biographers have not followed the events of June 1799 day by day, and have not examined the authorities in detail. Oman (1947) gives some of the sources, but does not analyse the circumstances in which the rebels emerged from the castles on 26 June, which is the crux of the matter. Neither does Warner (1958), though he does call Nelson's conduct in support of the Neapolitan court 'shockingly unfortunate'. Pocock (1988) suggests that Nelson had tried to match Ruffo's own cunning, and quotes the saying: 'The Englishman who behaves like an Italian is the devil incarnate.' Hibbert (1994) gives only six lines to the events of 26 June.

ITALIAN: The British Library has a comprehensive collection, perhaps because Antonio Panizzi, librarian at the BM from 1831 and principal librarian from 1856, was an Italian patriot and exile. Transcriptions of original Italian documents are most easily found in the *Archivio Storico per le Province Napoletane*, published quarterly by the Societa di Storia Patria in Naples from 1876 onwards. Many of the early volumes are edited by B. Maresca and Benedetto Croce. There is a cumulative index. The contemporary accounts by Micheroux, De Nicola, Sacchinelli, and Vincenzo Coco are the most valuable. Micheroux was a Sicilian diplomat in Naples with the Russian troops, and his *Compendio*, published in *Archivo Storico*, anno xxiv, 1899, 456-63, is a report to Acton of events in Naples, 14 June–12 July 1799. There is also a biography, *II Cavaliere Antonio Micheroux nella Reazione Napoletana del 1799*, by Marchese Maresca, Naples, 1895. De Nicola kept a diary in Naples at the time. Abate Domenico Sacchinelli's was Ruffo's secretary, and his *Memorie Storiche sulla Vita del Cardinale Fabrizio Ruffo*, Naples, 1836, presents the cardinal's point of view. This work also contains comments on the earlier publications of Vincenzo Coco (*Sagio Storico* etc, 1799), Botta, and Pietro Colletta. Sacchinelli often appears to give the gist of documents rather than the text. There are also general histories by Croce and Luigi Conforti. The best Italian history in

English is *Naples in 1799: an account of the revolution of 1799 and of the rise and fall of the Parthenopean republic*, by Constance Giglioli (nee Stocker), London, 1903. The author is an Englishwoman who married into a celebrated Italian family. Her book is openly sympathetic to the republicans and hostile to Nelson, but draws on many Italian and English published sources to present a learned and entertaining picture of the time. Pietro Colletta's *Storia del Reame di Napoli* etc, 1838, was translated into English as *History of the Kingdom of Naples*, London, 1858, but his account of the events of 1799 is often inaccurate.

FRENCH: Alphonse de Lamartine (French foreign minister in 1848) in his *Vie des Grands Hommes*, Paris, 1856 – in which Nelson is counted as one of the great alongside Socrates, Joan of Arc, Gutenberg, Columbus, and Cromwell – says that Nelson shamed his country. So does Alexandre Dumas the elder in his ten volume history [in Italian], *I Borboni di Napoli*, Naples, 1862–3. [An apparently unpublished manuscript of c260 pages, *Documents sur l'histoire de Naples*, in Dumas's autograph and in French, covering Nelson's treatment of the rebels in 1799, is in the Pierpont Morgan Library, New York, at V 12 A. It appears to be part of the ten volume work which was published in Italian.] Paul Emile Durand Forgues, in his *Histoire de Nelson*, Paris, 1860, says Nelson was of a race apart, a heart of oak of indomitable courage, but narrow-minded, and that after Fox's condemnation no one dared defend him. The general French view is stated in Michaud's *Biographie Universelle*, c1856, in an article by H-Q-N. Hennequin, who says that this is an epoch in Nelson's life which it might be better to pass over in silence, but that a treaty so solemnly concluded could not be broken without dishonouring him who broke it. André Bonnefons, in his *Marie Caroline, Reine des Deux Siciles etc*, Paris, 1905, says that Nelson, had he been truly a genius, would have rebelled against playing the part of a torturer. He overestimates the influence of Emma Hamilton, as do most French writers.

GERMAN: Perhaps the most disinterested analysis is by a German, though translated into French. Professor Hermann Hueffer of the University of Bonn, in 'La Fin de la République Napolitaine' in *La Revue Historique*, Paris, vol 83, 243–276, Nov-Dec 1903, and 33–50, Jan–April 1904, concludes by asking from which point of view – legal, moral, or political – the conduct of the British in Naples and of the Sicilian court is most to be condemned. He blames Nelson but declines to blame him alone, saying that the king and queen and the Hamiltons all had a part.

Professors Marotta and Galasso (chapter 17) are quoted from *The Times*, 22 January 1999, and Professor Gargano from the London *Evening Standard*, 3 February 1999.

APPENDIX B: NELSON'S TEXT

NELSON WROTE FLUENTLY AND almost without punctuation, with hardly a full stop and with commas scattered here and there. He used capital letters at random. Semicolons or inverted commas in a transcript are a sure sign that his text has been tinkered with, as it has been by almost all editors. Here is a comparison of a passage from his 'Nelson touch' letter to Emma Hamilton, on the left as it was written (from the MS in BL Eg 1614), and on the right as it was reproduced in Nicolas (VII 60).

... and when I came to explain to them the Nelson touch it was like an Electric Shock, some shed tears all approved, it was new it was simple and from admirals downwards it was repeated it must succeed if ever they will allow us to get at them, You are My Lord surrounded by friends who you inspire with confidence, some may be Judas's but the majority are certainly much pleased with my commanding them ...;	and, when I came to explain to them the *'Nelson touch,'* it was like an electric shock. Some shed tears, all approved – 'It was new – it was singular – it was simple!'; and, from Admirals downwards, it was repeated – 'It must succeed, if ever they allow us to get at them! You are, my Lord, surrounded by friends whom you inspire with confidence.' Some may be Judas's; but the majority are certainly much pleased with my commanding them ...

The only thoroughly unreliable editors are Clarke and M'Arthur (see chapter 2, note 2) and their transcripts are avoided whenever there is an alternative. Pettigrew and Morrison often quote letters found nowhere else, but when their transcripts can be checked against the MSS they are almost always accurate as to the words, but never with the punctuation. The same is true of Nicolas. He and other editors also improve the grammar, for instance substituting *whom* for *who* in the passage above. The only editor to transcribe literally, punctuation and all, is Dawson in the catalogue of the Nelson collection at Lloyds. Where this book quotes from manuscripts, Nelson's own punctuation and spelling are followed, untidy though this may be, because that is how he wrote and the manner conveys his natural rapidity and spontaneity. Where passages are taken from Nicolas or other editors, their style is followed, and the source acknowledged in the notes. But whatever the source, capitals are used only for proper nouns. Like most others of his time Nelson scattered capital letters quite at random, with no consistency, and Victorian editors imposed a formal and schoolmasterly over-capitalisation which is both foreign to the original and strange to the modern reader.

From the *Lowestoffe's* journal, the first ship on which he served as a lieutenant

Typical right-handed signature of the 1780s

Left handed, after he lost his right arm at Tenerife in 1797

Signature as Baron Nelson, after the Nile, 1798

From letter of March 1800, after he was given the Sicilian title of Duke Bronté

From January 1801, after it was suggested his English title should come first

The many versions of Nelson's signatures, from 1777 to his last years.

H.M.S. Cambrian, *large frigate of 44 guns, 1797*

H.M.S. Royal George, *first rate of 100 guns, 1788*

APPENDIX C: SHIPS' RATINGS

THE LANGUAGE OF SHIPS and the sea in Nelson's time was often beautiful, and always vigorous. A *crank* ship was one that leaned, and was the less seaworthy because of it. A ship might also, from staying too long at sea without repair, become *crazy*. Sailors used these words of themselves. St Vincent, having temporarily retired ashore ill, described his own carcass as both crank and very crazy, and he did not mean he was mad. Many sea phrases have come into the language and are now so familiar that their origins are unrecognised. *Touch and Go*, as Admiral W.H. Smyth explains in his *Sailor's Word Book* of 1867, was said of anything within an ace of ruin, as when a ship under sail rubbed against the bottom with her keel without much diminution of her velocity. But I am no seaman and have avoided, wherever possible, the temptation to use sea terms any more obscure than *fore* and *aft*. When it became necessary, as in the description of the battle on St Valentine's Day, 1797, to say that Nelson *wore* his ship, I explained there and then that this meant he changed course by turning her head away from the wind, as opposed to *tacking*, in which he would have turned her head into the wind. But some terms of art necessarily appear in the letters of those I quote. Most are self-explanatory in the context, and rather than provide a glossary of these few terms I suggest that the reader should consult either Smyth, whose work has been lately reprinted, or *A Sea of Words*, by Dean King, with John B. Hattendorf (professor of maritime history at the United States naval war college) and J. Worth Estes. This is a lexicon and companion for

Patrick O Brian's splendid novels, and is easily found both in Britain and the United States.

But a word of explanation is needed about the rating of ships, because references abound throughout this book. Ships were rated according to the number of guns they carried.

A first rate, like *Victory*, carried 100 guns on three decks, and a crew of between eight and nine hundred. French and Spanish ships were commonly larger, rate for rate, than their English counterparts. No English first rate of the time was ever as big as the French *L'Orient*, 120, at the Nile, or the Spanish *Santissima Trinidad*, 130, at Trafalgar.

A second rate carried 90 to 98 guns on three decks. Few were built. They had neither the power of the first rate nor the agility of many third rates.

A third rate could carry anything from 64 to 80 guns on two decks. Nelson's *Agamemnon*, which he commanded for the first three years of the revolutionary wars, from 1793, was a 64. The *San Josef*, captured from the Spanish at St Vincent, was a fine 80 which was briefly Nelson's in early 1801. The classic British third rate was the 74. All Nelson's ships of the line at the Nile were 74s. They carried crews of 6–700.

A fourth rate carried 50 guns on two decks. This type was obsolete in Nelson's day, though Bligh (of the *Bounty*) commanded a 50, the *Glatton*, at Copenhagen.

Ships of the first to the fourth rate were called ships of the line because they could stand in the line of battle.

Fifth and sixth rates were frigates, carrying anything from 20 to 44 guns on a single deck. They were commerce raiders and fast, scouting ships, 'the eyes of the fleet'. The only remaining frigates, the USS *Constitution*, now at Boston, and the *Constellation*, at Baltimore, are likely to mislead the visitor. *Constitution*, though laid down in 1797, is an immense frigate, almost the length of *Victory*, and twice as powerful as any frigate in which Nelson went to sea. His first frigate, the *Hinchinbrook*, carried 28 guns and a crew of 200.

Ships of the line and frigates were commanded by post captains. Sloops of war, smaller vessels of 12 to 20 guns, were commanded by officers with the rank of master and commander. A sloop could be three masted, or brig-rigged like the *Mutine*, which had a distinguished history. She was a French corvette captured in 1797 at Spanish Tenerife by Lieutenant Hardy, to whom St Vincent then gave command of her.

When Nelson in the Mediterranean promoted Hardy to be his flag captain he first gave the *Mutine* to Paget, a favourite of the first lord of the admiralty's wife, and then to Hoste, his own protégé.

Vessels smaller than sloops, like cutters, were lieutenants' commands.

NOTES AND SOURCES

THE PRINCIPAL SOURCES OF manuscripts, and of printed transcripts of manuscripts, used in this book are as follows. The abbreviations are those used in the notes:

BL: British Library manuscripts room. The principal BL collection, bought in 1895 from the Bridport family, into which Nelson's niece Charlotte married, is contained in ninety-one bound volumes at Additional manuscripts (Add) 34,902–34,992, each containing about 200 documents. There are letters received by Nelson, his drafts, letter books, journals, and logs. Other Nelson papers are in the Egerton (Eg) collection, and many in the sixty volumes of the papers of St Vincent.

NMM: National Maritime Museum, Greenwich. More than 2,500 Nelson papers are contained in the Stewart (STW), Bridport (BRP), Phillipps (PHB), Nelson-Ward (NWD), Trafalgar (TRA), Girdlestone (GIR), Parker (PAR), Elliot (ELL), Matcham (MAM), Croker (CRK), and Hood (HOO) papers, and there are scattered letters in the Autograph (AGC) collection. Others are in the plentiful Nepean (NEP), Hamilton (HML), and Keith (KEI) papers; 26 unpublished letters of Nelson's are in KEI 18/4 alone.

PRO: Public Record Office, Kew. Letters to and from Nelson, documents, and logs in Admiralty (ADM) papers, and others scattered in Colonial Office (CO) and Foreign Office (FO) files.

Monmouth: The Nelson Museum, Monmouth. Eight hundred letters and documents, largely the collection of Nelson's wife, brought to light in 1898 and bought for the museum in 1914. Far and away the most important source of manuscripts outside the state collections. Many letters remain unpublished.

Nicolas: The Dispatches and Letters of Vice Admiral Lord Viscount Nelson, with notes by Sir Nicholas Harris Nicolas, seven vols, 1844–46. The standard printed record; 3,500 letters, and many valuable notes and appendices. The transcription is accurate, but heavily punctuated and capitalised in a Victorian style foreign to Nelson's manner.

Pettigrew: Memoirs of the Life of . . . Nelson, by Thomas Joseph Pettigrew, two vols, 1849. A biography, with partial but accurate transcripts of 600 letters from Lady Hamilton's collection, many found nowhere else since Pettigrew sold the letters at auction in 1853 and they were scattered. Some have appeared at auction, two notable items in New York in the 1980s. A much underrated source.

Morrison: The Collection of Autograph Letters and Historical Documents formed by Alfred Morrison: the Hamilton and Nelson Papers, two vols, 1893–4: transcripts of 1,067 letters, with other documents, some from Pettigrew. Again, a primary source for many letters.

Lloyds: The Nelson Collection at Lloyds [of London] ed. Warren A. Dawson, London, 1932. A faithful and literal transcript of 496 letters.

Naish: Nelson's Letters to his Wife and other documents 1785–1831, ed. [Commander] George P. B. Naish, London, 1958. Accurate transcript, though with modernised punctuation, mostly of the Nelson–Fanny letters at Monmouth, with some from other sources.

NRS: Navy Records Society. Since 1894 the society has published transcripts of the papers of St Vincent, Hood, Keith, Spencer, Barham, and of many others.

Notes to Chapter One: NATURAL BORN PREDATOR

[1] *Instrument of God:* Nelson's letters to Lord Spencer and to William Nelson, 25 September 1798, Nicolas III 129, 131. Nelson to Hamilton, 8 August 1798, *Letters of Lord Nelson to Lady Hamilton . . .,* 2 vols, 1814.

[2] *Invincible:* Nelson to his wife Fanny, 4 August 1798, Naish 487. *All that is left:* Nelson to Kingsmill, 4 August 1804, Nicolas VI 133. *Heaven above earth:* Nelson to victualling board, 14 November 1799, Nicolas IV 100.

[3] *Fixed as fate:* Nelson to Davison, about his separation from Fanny, 23 April 1801, Naish 587. *Annihilation:* Nicolas III 110 and IV 222 (both to Minto), IV 452 (to admiralty), VII 80 (to Rose), and many other instances.

[4] Nelson to Suckling and to Locker, Nicolas II 253, 255; *Sun,* 20 March and *Times,* 13 March 1897. Colonel Drinkwater's narrative, Nicolas II 347, Harrison I 154–65.

[5] Clarke, James Stanier, and M'Arthur, John, *Life of Admiral Lord Nelson etc,* 2 vols, London, 1809. West's 'Immortality of Nelson' was exhibited at the Royal Academy, 1807.

[6] *The Life of Nelson,* by Robert Southey, London, 1813 and many later editions. 'Cat in pantry': *Letters of Robert Southey,* London, 1856, 315; also BL Add 30,927.

[7] Wellington (1769–1852) was prime minister 1828–30. He and Nelson met once, in 1805; see chapter 25 note 9. But it is Nelson who remains the archetypal hero. When Paul Johnson, a historian of great verve and scope, wished to put forward his conviction that our greatest lack today is of heroes, and that a genuine, old-fashioned

hero is a spiritual weapon and a source of strength to a country, it was Nelson he chose as his exemplar. (*Spectator*, London, 9 June 2001.)

[8] Nelson never wore an eye patch, only a green eyeshade, attached to his hat, which could fold down to shield his good eye from the sun. See *Nelson Dispatch*, 6 July 1999, 486, article by Dr K.S. Cliff, with sketch from Lock the hatters.

[9] *Times* and *Daily Telegraph*, 22 January 1999. *Evening Standard*, 3 February 1999.

[10] *Boatswain*: Nelson to Davison, Nicolas VII cci. Commander Layman: Nelson to Melville, Nicolas VI 353.

[11] Pay certificate, 31 December 1785, NMM BRP 6 (Bridport papers).

[12] Fanny to Nelson, 18 June 1799, Naish 529.

[13] *Convulsed*: *Life of Sir James Macintosh* II 137. *Jewels*: Pettigrew I 258. *Flogging*: captain's log of *Boreas*, 1786–7, PRO ADM 51/120.

[14] *Christmas day*: Nelson to Calder, 9 July 1797, Nicolas II 409. Copenhagen truce, see chapter 20.

[15] Colomb on Nelson in *From Howard to Nelson etc*, ed. J. K. Laughton, London, 1899.

[16] Nelson to Hamond, 8 September 1797, Nicolas II 443.

[17] Nelson to Emma, 22 February 1801, Pettigrew I 430.

[18] See 'There is But One Nelson', by Colin White (deputy director RNM), *Nelson Dispatch*, July 1999, 492.

[19] *L'Orient*: *The Friend* III, essay IV [on Captain Ball], 1809–10. *Facts*: S. T. Coleridge, *Notebooks*, ed. Kathleen Coburn, London, 1962, 2122.

[20] *Predatory raider*: St Vincent to Nepean, 30 November 1800, *The Spencer Papers* IV NRS 59, London, 1924, 21. Spirit: St Vincent to Nelson, 31 May 1801, Nicolas IV 373 note.

[21] St Vincent to Baird, 18 October 1814, NMM PAR 167c.

Notes to Chapter 2: WELL THEN, I WILL BE A HERO

[1] The Revd Edmund Nelson kept a 'Family Historical Register' up to 1784, which is in NMM NWD/34. See also Nicolas I 15–18.

[2] Nicolas, in his preface, said no reliance could be placed on the literal fidelity of any one extract in Clarke and M'Arthur. Thomas Case, president of Corpus Christi, Oxford, who later examined many MSS they had used, deplored their 'travesties' and said they omitted, interpolated, transposed, improved, and 'committed almost every kind of literary immorality possible': see *Literature* (a predecessor to the *Times Literary Supplement*), 26 February 1898.

[3] Clarke and M'Arthur I, 8.

[4] Letters of William Nelson, M'Arthur, and Clarke, 11 and 16 February, 31 March, 4 April, and 28 May 1806, and two undated. BL Add 34,992.

[5] Bloodline, William Nelson to Emma, 6 September 1801, BL Eg 1614.

[6] Clarke and M'Arthur I, 6.

[7] Clarke and M'Arthur I, 9. Details of Nelson's ratings, Nicolas I 5 note.

[8] *Bear*: The bear story appears to come from Captain Lutwidge of the *Carcass*, who said he fired a gun to scare off the animal. But he could not have heard Nelson say to his companion on the ice floe (as is reported in Clarke and M'Arthur I, 11), 'Never mind, do but let me get a blow at this devil with the butt-end of my musket and we

shall have him.' *Cutter*: Nicolas I, 3ff; Nelson's 'Sketch of My Life'. The MS is in the Rosenbach Museum and Library, Philadelphia.
9 Nicolas I 5.
10 Clarke and M'Arthur I 9.

Notes to Chapter 3: THE WHOLE GLORY OF THE SERVICE

1 *Princes of the blood: Letters of Admiral of the Fleet the Earl of St Vincent*, vol 1, NRS, 1922. Letter of 6 April 1801 to Mrs Montagu. *Friend's grandson*: St Vincent to Nelson, 17 June 1803, NMM CRK/11.
2 For the powers of the comptroller, *The Barham Papers*, NRS 39, 1911. Lord Barham, as Charles Middleton, was comptroller 1778–90, after Suckling.
3 *The British Admiralty*, by Leslie Gardiner, 1968, 171.
4 Lord Sandwich's personal papers are at the NMM, catalogued as SAN 1/1–6 and SAN/V/3–4.
5 NMM SAN V/3.
6 NMM SAN/3, p33.
7 Acknowledged by Vice-Admiral Sir James Douglas, c-in-c Portsmouth, in letter to Admiralty of 29 September 1776. PRO ADM 1/952.
8 PRO ADM 1/2390, Captains' Letters. Capt. Mark Robinson to Philip Stephens, 16 April 1777. Also Nicolas I 6 for details, from Robinson's diary, of Nelson's time with him.
9 Nelson's 'Sketch of My Life' 1799. Nicolas I 6.
10 PRO ADM 107/006 [Lieutenants' passing certificates]. Also Nicolas I 21.
11 Biographical details of Captains Campbell and North from Charnock's *Biographia Navalis*.
12 PRO ADM 107/006, p386.
13 The story first appeared in Clarke and M'Arthur's *Life of Admiral Lord Nelson etc*, London, 1809.
14 Nelson to William Nelson, 14 April 1777. Nicolas I 21.
15 PRO ADM 107/006. Names taken from Philip [Gidley] King, who passed on 3 April 1777 to George Irwin (7 May 1777). Their later careers from Pitcairn-Jones list, PRO.
16 Nelson to William Nelson, 14 April 1777. Nicolas I 22.
17 Pitcairn-Jones list, PRO.
18 The 78 letters to Locker are now in the Huntington Library, San Marino, Calif.
19 Nelson's 'Sketch of My Life' given in October 1799 to John M'Arthur, Nicolas I 3.
20 BL, Add MS 34,988. Nelson to Capt. Suckling, 19 April 1778.
21 *Dictionary of National Biography* (DNB).
22 *Parliamentary History of England*, vol xxvii, 1788–89, 286, 18 April 1788.
23 *Social History of the Navy*, by Michael Lewis, London, 1960, 212.
24 PRO ADM 1/241, Admirals' Letters, 'List of commissioned and warrant officers made and removed by Sir Peter Parker', 21 June to 23 September 1778.
25 Nelson to his father, 24 October 1778. BL Add MS 34,988.
26 PRO ADM 1/241. Admirals' Letters. Parker's 'List of vessels seized', May 1778 to May 1779.

[27] Nelson to Locker, 12 September 1778; Nicolas I 25. Also Nicolas I 24.

[28] PRO ADM 1/241. Admirals' Letters. 'List of commissioned and warrant officers made, removed, or appointed by Sir Peter Parker', 29 September 1778 to 21 February 1779.

[29] 'Sketch of My Life', Nicolas I 8.

[30] Nelson to Locker, 7 June 1795. Nicolas I 29.

[31] St Vincent to Sir William Parker, 19 December 1798. St Vincent Papers, BL Add 31,166.

[32] PRO ADM 1/241. Parker to Admiralty, November 1778. He calls the French prize *Laestric*. *Repertoire des Navires de Guerre Français*, by Jacques Vichot, Paris, 1967, shows that she was *L'Astrée*, and was built the year she was captured.

[33] Nelson to William Nelson, 8 February 1782, Nicolas I 57–8.

[34] Nelson to the Earl of Carysfort, 24 August 1804, Nicolas VI 169.

Notes to Chapter 4: THE REDUCTION OF THE NEW WORLD

[1] Nelson to Locker, Nicolas I 31.

[2] Dalling's message of 13 August 1779 was reprinted in *The London Chronicle* of 11–13 January 1780. This and Germain's rebuke of 2 February 1780 are in PRO CO 137/76.

[3] Dalling to Dalrymple, 20 October 1779, PRO CO 137/76.

[4] Nelson to Locker, Nicolas I 32.

[5] Both doctors published accounts of the expedition: *A Treatise on Tropical Diseases; on military operations; and the climate of the West Indies*, by Benjamin Moseley, 1792, and later editions up to 1803; and *A Brief History of the Late Expedition against Fort San Juan etc*, by Thomas Dancer, Kingston, 1781.

[6] Dalling to Germain, 4 February 1780. PRO CO 137/76.

[7] Germain to Dalling (Secret), 1 March 1780. CO 5/263.

[8] Nelson's 'Sketch of My Life', Nicolas I 10.

[9] Polson to Dalling, 30 April 1780. CO 137/76.

[10] St Vincent to Nelson, 31 May 1801. BL Add 31,169. St Vincent's Letter Books.

[11] Details of the campaign are from Polson's journal, in his letter to Dalling, see note 9 above; and also from Moseley's and Dancer's accounts.

[12] Polson to Dalling, see note 9.

[13] Dalling to Germain, 3 June 1780, CO 137/78.

[14] Dalling to Germain, 23 June 1780. CO 137/78.

[15] Dalling to Nelson, BL Add 34,903, f8.

[16] Nelson to Ross, Nicolas I 34.

[17] Nelson to General Villettes, 12 November 1804. Monmouth E158.

[18] A copy of Dalling's note of 29 June 1780 commending Nelson is in the Nelson Papers, BL Add 34,903. Nelson later sent another copy to Sydney on 20 March 1785, in CO 152/64.

[19] Parker to Admiralty, 5 September 1780, and doctors' report to Parker 1 September 1780; PRO ADM 1/242.

[20] The Revd Edmund Nelson to Nelson, 12 June 1801, NMM CRK 9 (N9–20).

[21] 7 September 1780. Christie's sale, New York, December 1986; now in Karpeles Manuscript Library, Santa Barbara, Calif, which has 23 Nelson items.

[22] Germain to Dalling, 13 January 1781, CO 137/79; and 7 December 1780, CO 137/78.

[23] These are Nelson's figures, in a passage he wrote for the 1803 edition of Moseley's book (see note 5). Nicolas I 9.

[24] Lady Dalling to Nelson, 13 June 1799, BL Add 34,913.

Notes to Chapter 5: FAIR CANADA, AND THE MEREST BOY

[1] Nelson to Locker, Nicolas I 35, 37.

[2] *London Gazette*, 18 July 1780.

[3] Nelson to Locker, Nicolas I 38.

[4] DNB.

[5] Jenkinson to Sandwich, 12 February 1781. BL Add 38,308.

[6] Nelson to Locker, Nicolas I 39–42.

[7] Nelson to William Nelson, Nicolas I 42.

[8] 'A Family Historical Register', by the Revd Edmund Nelson, 1781. NMM NWD 1/34.

[9] Nelson to William Nelson, and to Locker, Nicolas I 43–7.

[10] Nelson to Locker, Nicolas I 48.

[11] Captain's log of *Albemarle*, PRO ADM/51/24. Nautical date in log is 6 November.

[12] Nelson to William Nelson, and to Locker, Nicolas I 53–6.

[13] Sandwich's patronage books. NMM SAN/6.

[14] Nelson to Locker, Nicolas I 61–2.

[15] Nelson to Locker, and to his father, and the text of Nelson's certificate to the American, Nicolas I 65–7.

[16] Clarke and M'Arthur, I 76.

[17] PRO ADM 51/24.

[18] Nelson to his father, Nicolas I 67.

[19] Nelson to Locker, Nicolas I 68.

[20] Clarke and M'Arthur I 53, 'from minutes of a conversation [about 1809] with Duke of Clarence [formerly Prince William, later William IV]'. Nicolas I 70.

[21] As note 20.

[22] Nicolas I 90.

[23] Nelson to Hood, Nicolas I 73.

[24] For Bastia, see Nelson to Duke of Clarence, Nicolas II 300. For Tenerife, Nelson to commandant of Canary Islands, Nicolas II 419. For Naples, 'Nelson. Statements by Lord Northwick', 7 February 1846; BL Add 30,999, 75–80.

[25] Nelson to Locker, Nicolas I 75.

Notes to Chapter 6: SUBJECTS OF THE GRAND MONARQUE

[1] *Journal of a Lady of Quality* [Janet Schaw of Edinburgh] 1774–76, ed. E.W. Andrews, Yale, 1921.

[2] *A Farewel Address etc*, by James Tobin Esq, Salisbury, 1788; and *Cursory Remarks upon the Reverend Mr Ramsay's Essay* ... [by James Tobin]. Copies in the BL are inscribed, 'For Sir Joseph Banks'.

[3] 'Lady Nelson's Memorandum', written c1806 for the Revd J. Clarke. Monmouth E687. Naish 61.

[4] *A West India Fortune*, by Richard Pares, 1950. History of the Pinney sugar plantation on Nevis, based on Pinney papers in Bristol University library.

[5] *The Golden Rock*, by Ronald Hurst, 1996, compiled from original papers.

[6] *The First Salute*, by Barbara Tuchman, London and New York, 1989.

[7] Pinney to Pretor, 30 June 1781. Pinney papers.

[8] Pinney to Pretor, 17 November 1781. Pinney papers.

[9] Herbert to Shirley, 16 February 1782. PRO CO 152/62. See also *Nevis and St Christopher 1782–1784; Unpublished documents*, Paris, 1928 (?), by Arthur P. Watts. The papers, cut out of the islands' minute books, were found at the Bancroft Library, University of California.

[10] Hood to Jackson [a friend at the admiralty], 24 June 1781, in *Letters of Samuel Hood*, NRS 3, 1895, ed. David Hannay.

[11] Hood to Jackson, 16 April 1782. In Hannay.

Notes to Chapter 7: RUNNING AT THE RING OF PLEASURE

[1] Nelson to Locker, Nicolas I 76–7.

[2] *A Social History of the Navy*, by Michael Lewis, London, 1960. Tables of pay, 294–5, 301, and 308–9; and of half pay, 313.

[3] Nicolas I 77.

[4] Nelson to William Nelson, Nicolas I 78, 82.

[5] Nelson to Earl of Cork, Nicolas I 249. (The earl had asked what accomplishments his midshipman son needed. In his reply Nelson put French second only to navigation.)

[6] Nelson to Ross, and to William Nelson, Nicolas I 80, 86.

[7] Nelson to William Nelson, Nicolas I 86.

[8] Nelson's first accounts of his journey in France are in his letters to William and to Locker, Nicolas I 85, 86, 89.

[9] Nelson to Locker, Nicolas I 89.

[10] Nelson to William Nelson, Nicolas I 91. More on Deux Ponts, Nicolas I 90.

[11] Nelson calls her only Miss Andrews. Tom Pocock discovered her Christian name for his *Nelson's Women*, London, 1999.

[12] Nelson to William Nelson, and to Locker, Nicolas I 93–4. The couplet is from Gay's *The Hare and Many Friends*.

[13] Nelson to William Suckling, Nicolas II 479.

[14] The Revd Edmund Wilson to Nelson, 24 February 1800. BL Add 34,906.

[15] Nelson is quoting from Sterne's *Sentimental Journey*. Yorick, newly arrived in Paris, looks out from his hotel room: 'I walked gravely to the window in my dusty black coat, and looking through the glass saw all the world in yellow, blue and green, running at the ring of pleasure – The old with broken lances, and in helmets which had lost their vizards, – the young in armour bright which shone like gold, beplumed with each gay feather of the east – all – all tilting at it like fascinated knights in tournaments of yore for fame and love.'

[16] Nelson in 1798 told Cornelia Knight, daughter of an admiral, writer, and later royal governess, that he had not gambled since he was a midshipman. Nicolas III 475.

[17] Nelson to William Nelson, Nicolas I 96.

[18] Nelson to Locker, and to William Nelson, Nicolas I 96–7.

[19] Nelson to Locker, Nicolas I 96.

[20] Nelson to William Nelson, Nicolas I 98.

[21] Nicolas I 96.

[22] Deux Ponts to Nelson, dated Paris, 23 March [1784]. BL Add 34,903. This must be a second letter, since Nelson mentions an invitation as early as November 1783. Deux Ponts did become Elector of Bavaria in 1799 and then, the Holy Roman Empire being dissolved, became in 1806 King of Bavaria, as Maximilian I.

[23] Nelson to William Nelson, Nicolas I 101.

[24] Nelson to William Nelson, Nicolas I 105.

[25] Nelson to Locker, Nicolas I 100.

[26] Nelson to Stephens, admiralty secretary, and to Locker, Nicolas I 103–5.

[27] Nelson to Locker, Nicolas I 105.

[28] This has to be conjecture. Nicolas (I 105) says it does not appear what Nelson meant by land-frigate. Carola Oman, in her *Nelson*, 1947, takes it to mean Kingsmill's constituency, but his seat was at Tregony in Cornwall, not Plymouth. However, *A Dictionary of Buckish Slang, University Wit, and Pickpocket Eloquence*, London, 1811, derived from Francis Grose's *Classical Dictionary of the Vulgar Tongue, 1785*, defined *frigate* as 'a well-dressed wench'.

[29] Nelson to Locker, Nicolas I 105, 107.

Notes to Chapter 8: LET MY HEART SPEAK FOR ME

[1] 'Walking the *Boreas*' quarter deck on the 30th May 1784, at 7 in the evening.' Nelson's autograph. Nicolas I 107, 108 notes.

[2] According to James Wallis, first lieutenant of the *Boreas*. About 1806 he gave an account of the passage to the West Indies and of Nelson's stay there to Clarke and M'Arthur, who used much but not all of it in their biography. There are 25 large sheets in his hand in BL Add 24,990. Wallis's promotion by Nelson to be commander of the *Rattler* sloop in 1787 was not confirmed. He was eventually made commander in 1794, post captain in 1797, and died before 1809.

[3] Harrison I 80. For a note on the reliability of this biography, see Bibliography.

[4] Wallis, see note 2.

[5] Nelson to Locker, Nicolas I 112–13; and to William Nelson, I 151.

[6] Nelson to Locker, Nicolas I 156.

[7] Nelson to Locker, Nicolas I 113.

[8] Nelson to Locker, Nicolas I 156.

[9] Wallis, see note 2.

[10] Nelson to Hughes, 9 January 1785, BL Add 34,961.

[11] Nelson to Locker, Nicolas I 156. And 'Nelson's Narrative', perhaps sent to Prince William, Nicolas I 179.

[12] Nicolas I 118 note. DNB.

[13] Wallis, see note 2. Also Nelson to Hughes, 9 January 1785, BL Add 34,961.

[14] Nelson to Locker, Nicolas I 110; Nelson to William Nelson, Nicolas I 123, 126.

[15] The letter book of the *Boreas*, containing copies of Nelson's in and out letters, is in BL Add 34,961. It was not used by Nicolas, though he did print some of the original letters from other sources. Some unpublished letters put a different complexion on Nelson's conduct towards Moutray.

[16] Wallis, see note 2. This part not used by Clarke and M'Arthur.

[17] Nelson to Hughes, 9 January 1785. BL Add 34,961, f9.

[18] Nelson to Hughes, second letter of 9 January 1785. BL Add 34,961.

[19] Nelson to Locker, Nicolas I 156.

[20] Nelson to Philip Stephens, Nicolas I 121.

[21] Nicolas I 118.

[22] Nelson to William Nelson, Nicolas I 124.

[23] Nelson to Locker, Nicolas I 114.

[24] Nelson to Sydney, 20 March 1785. PRO CO 152/64. 'Leeward Islands 1785–1786', in 'miscellaneous' section at end. Nicolas I 129.

[25] PRO CO 152/64. Nicolas I 134.

[26] Sydney to Nelson, 4 August 1785. As note 24.

[27] Nelson to Sydney, 29 September 1785. BL Add 34,961, f26.

[28] Nelson to Collingwood, Nicolas I 143.

[29] Nelson to William Suckling, Nicolas I 144.

[30] Clarke and M'Arthur I 70.

[31] Sydney to Shirley, 9 April 1785. PRO CO 152/63.

[32] Nelson to Locker, Nicolas I 159.

[33] Compare Vice-Admiral Philip Colomb on Nelson in *From Howard to Nelson* ed. J. K. Laughton, London, 1899. He also thought Nelson a fanatic for duty.

[34] Nelson to Radstock, Nicolas VI 391.

[35] *Smile*: Nelson to St Vincent, 25 January 1799. *Heaven*: Nelson to St Vincent, 7 May 1801. *Child of day*: Nelson to Minto, 11 January 1804. All Nicolas III 238, IV 359, V 367.

Notes to Chapter 9: I PERCEIVE THE CONTRARY EFFECT

[1] Clarke and M'Arthur I 113, who give no source. Lady Nelson reluctantly supplied a few letters for this biography, which are quoted inaccurately.

[2] *The Nisbets of Carfin* by John A. Inglis, 1916. A copy of Nisbet's MD thesis, *De Rheumatismo Acute . . .* subjicit Josias Nisbet ex India Occidentalis [Edinburgh 1768] is in the BL.

[3] *Salisbury and Winchester Journal*, 8 October 1781, Wiltshire Record Office, Trowbridge. Nelson told Suckling that Nisbet was insane; Nicolas I 160. Midshipman William Hotham, later an admiral, wrote that Nisbet died 'deranged'. (*Pages and Portraits from the Past*, London, 1919.)

[4] *Salisbury and Winchester Journal*, 15 July 1782.

[5] John Pinney to James Tobin, 31 August 1783. Pinney Papers, Bristol University library.

[6] Captain James Wallis's account, BL Add 34,990.

[7] Nelson to Fanny, 19 August 1785, Naish 16. See note 13 below.

[8] Nelson to Fanny, Naish 19. MS at Monmouth.

[9] Nelson to William Nelson, Nicolas I 134.

[10] Log of *Boreas* 24 March 1784–30 November 1787. Monmouth. Nelson continued to fail to learn French for many years. Four sheets written with his left hand, and therefore dating from 1797 or later, show him noting that *orgeuil* is pride, *paysages* are landskips, *riant* is smiling or pretty, and that *que je m'aimasse* means 'that I loved myself'. BL Add 34,902, f216.

[11] Nelson to William Nelson, Nicolas I 204.

[12] Harrison II 461.

[13] Almost all of Nelson's letters to his wife, and of hers to him which survived, were not found until 1897. They were quoted from and analysed in seven long articles, 'New Nelson Manuscripts', probably by Thomas Case, president of Corpus Christi College, Oxford, in successive editions of *Literature*, a weekly review published by *The Times*, from 19 February to 23 April 1898. They were bought for the Monmouth collection in 1914.

[14] Harrison II 270.

[15] Nelson to Suckling, Naish 53.

[16] *Debrett's Peerage.*

[17] Nelson to Fanny, Naish 18.

[18] Pay certificate in NMM BRP/6 (Bridport Papers).

[19] Nelson to William Nelson, Nicolas I 197.

[20] Nelson to Fanny, Nicolas I 167.

[21] Nelson to Directors of the East India Company, 5 May 1786. Nicolas I 167.

[22] Nelson to Locker, Nicolas I 198.

[23] Nelson to Fanny, 19 August 1786, Naish 33–4. This section of the letter is dated 21 August in the Monmouth MS. The *Boreas*'s log for that day records, 'Hot calm weather'.

[24] Wallis's account, see note 6 above.

[25] Nelson to Stephens, Nicolas I 202.

[26] Prince William to Prince of Wales, 23 July 1784. Royal Archives 44,664.

[27] Same, 1 April 1785. Royal Archives 44,674.

[28] Nelson to Locker, Nicolas I 205.

[29] Nelson's draft account of his meeting with Prince William in December 1786. BL Add 34,902. Naish 57.

[30] Nelson to Stephens, Nicolas I 207.

[31] DNB.

[32] Nelson to William Nelson, Nicolas I 204.

[33] Nelson to Fanny, Naish 39–40.

[34] Nelson to Locker, Nicolas I 205.

[35] Nelson to Fanny, Naish 41.

[36] Nelson to Commodore Alan Gardner, 'Private', 13 May 1787. Nicolas I 237. This is the second letter, accompanying his briefer official letter, which Nelson sent Gardner on the same day. This was common navy practice.

[37] Prince William to Hood, 9 February 1787. See 'Prince William and Lieutenant Schomberg etc.' and article on the Hood Papers in the NMM by B. McL. Ranft; NRS 92, 1952, 272.

[38] Nelson's general order, Nicolas I 210. Nelson to Locker, Nicolas I 214.

[39] *Letters of Sir T. Byam Shaw*, vol I 25–84. NRS, 1902.

40 Hotham, see note 3.

41 Nelson to Fanny, 25 February 1787, Naish 45.

42 Nelson to Fanny, 6 March 1787, Naish 50.

43 Prince William to Hood, NMM, Hood Papers, Naish 56.

44 Nelson to Prince William, Nicolas I 275.

45 John Pinney, Nevis, to Simon Pretor, Bristol, 29 April 1787. Pinney Papers, letter book 8, Bristol University Library.

46 Wedding certificate, BL Add 28,333, and Naish 55.

47 Nelson to Gardner, Nicolas I 237.

48 Nelson to William Nelson, Nicolas I 213.

49 Nelson to Locker, Nicolas I 219.

50 Hotham, see note 3.

51 Nelson to Prince William, Nicolas I 235. Also Hotham.

Notes to Chapter 10: NELSON FOUND WANTING

1 Captain's log of *Boreas*, PRO ADM 51/120.

2 Admiralty to Nelson, Nicolas I 240.

3 Prince William to admiralty, 27 December 1786. PRO ADM 1/491.

4 Nelson to Stephens, Nicolas I 242.

5 Commodore Gardner to admiralty, 5 June 1787. PRO ADM 1/243.

6 Prince William to Gardner, 26 May and 5 June 1786; Gardner to Prince William, 6 June 1787. Hood Papers, NMM, and *Naval Miscellany* IV, NRS 92, 1952,

7 Lords of the admiralty to Gardner, Sawyer, and Hughes, 27 May 1786. PRO ADM 2/1342. Secret Out Letters.

8 Nelson to Stephens, Nicolas I 243, 245, 246 note.

9 Nelson to Stephens, Nicolas I 246, 253.

10 Nelson to Stephens, Nicolas I 255.

11 Nelson to Wilkinson and Higgins, Nicolas I 269.

12 Letters of Nelson to Middleton and to Rose, Nicolas I 264–65.

13 Nelson to Prince William, Nicolas I 250.

14 Nelson to Prince William, Nicolas I 250 note.

15 Prince William to admiralty, PRO ADM 1/2677. Howe to Hood, 24 July 1787, NRS 92, 1952, 287.

16 *Eleven hundred men*: The Revd Edmund Nelson to his daughter, Catherine. *The Nelsons of Burnham Thorpe*, by M. Eyre Matcham, 1911, 45. All family details in this chapter are from this source. *Johnson*: Boswell's *Life*, 16 March 1759.

17 Nelson to William Nelson, Nicolas I 258.

18 Nelson to Locker, Nicolas I 259.

19 Captain's log of *Boreas* for 10 October 1787. PRO ADM 51/120.

20 Prince William to Nelson, Naish 59. NMM 37 MS 1625, AGC.

21 Shorthand report of *R. v Carse*, Old Bailey Sessions papers 1788, and *Trafalgar Chronicle, Year Book of the 1805 Club*, 1993.

22 Captain's log of *Boreas* from 1 April 1786 to 30 November 1787. PRO ADM 51/120.

23 Clarke and M'Arthur I 102. Nicolas I 262.

[24] Lady Nelson's Memorandum, given c1806 to Revd J. Clarke. Monmouth E 687. Naish 61.

[25] Entry under John Elphinston in DNB. See also *John Paul Jones*, by Samuel Eliot Morison, New York, 1959, 363.

[26] Eyre Matcham 47.

[27] Nelson to Locker, Nicolas I 266.

[28] See the journal of his passage from Halifax to Cork, 12 November to 3 December 1787, enclosed with letter to admiralty of 3 December 1787. PRO ADM 1/2677.

[29] Prince William to admiralty, 23 April 1787. PRO ADM 1/2677.

[30] Hood Papers, NMM, in *Naval Miscellany* IV, NRS 92, 1952. Prince William to Hood, 26 December 1787.

[31] Same. Hood to Prince William, 1 January 1788.

[32] Same, p 291. Prince William to Hood, 5 January 1788.

[33] Same, p 292. Hood to Prince William, 8 January 1788.

[34] Nelson to Prince William, Nicolas I 276.

[35] Lady Nelson's Memorandum, Naish 61.

[36] *Steel's Navy List*, January 1790.

[37] Nelson to Prince William, Nicolas I 234.

[38] Nelson to Howe, [May 1788.] BL Add 34,903. Nicolas I 274.

[39] Nelson to Stephens, and to Fanny, Nicolas I 276.

[40] Cornwallis to Nelson, October 1788. BL Add 34,903. Nicolas I 177 note.

[41] Chatham to Nelson, 24 March 1789. BL Add 34,903. Nicolas I 282.

[42] Revd Edmund Nelson to Catherine, January 1790. Eyre Matcham 71.

[43] George Forbes to Nelson, 12 July 1789. BL Add 34,903.

[44] Nelson to Locker, Nicolas I 281.

[45] Hood to Nelson, 8 November 1789, Monmouth E 540.

[46] Hood to Alexander Hood, 5 June 1792. BL Add 35,194, Bridport Papers IV.

[47] Lady Nelson's Memorandum, Naish 61. Nicolas I 287 note.

[48] George III to Clarence, 25 May 1789. *The Letters of George III* ed. Bonamy Dobree, London, 1935.

[49] Hood to Nelson, 9 July 1790. NMM Hood papers. NRS 92, 1950, 364.

[50] Nelson to Stephens, to Prince William, and to Chatham, Nicolas I 287–9.

[51] Eyre Matcham 72.

[52] Revd Edmund Nelson to Nelson, 11 October 1790, Naish 62.

[53] Hood to Alexander Hood, letters of 11 and 15 December 1790. BL Add 35,194.

[54] *Steel's Navy List* December 1790, January 1791, and June 1791.

[55] Eyre Matcham 88.

[56] Nelson to Duke of Clarence, and Clarence's reply, Nicolas I 292–3.

[57] Nicolas I 294 note.

[58] Clarence to Nelson, 6 December 1792. BL Add 34,903. Part in Nicolas I 294 note 1.

[59] Nelson to Clarence, Nicolas I 294.

[60] Eyre Matcham 96.

[61] Nicolas I 12.

[62] Howe (first lord) to Hood (c-in-c Portsmouth), 2 July 1787. Hood Papers, NMM. NRS 92, 1952, 287.

[63] Hood to Alexander Hood, 7 December 1792. BL Add 35,194.

[64] Nelson to Fanny, Naish 72.

[65] Nelson to Fanny, 4 March 1793, Monmouth, Naish 73, who also prints a facsimile.

Notes to Chapter 11: THE HORROR, AND THE BENEFIT TO THE NATION

[1] Nelson to Fanny, Nicolas I 309.

[2] Nicolas I 309.

[3] Nelson to Fanny, to Locker, and to his father, Nicolas I 318–20.

[4] List of French ships in Nelson's hand, Nicolas I 321.

[5] 'Nelson's Sea Journal', 23–26 August 1793, NMM, Croker Collection. Naish 128ff.

[6] *London Gazette Extraordinary*, 14 September 1793, BL Add 35,194.

[7] Nelson to Fanny, 7–11 September 1793. Monmouth, Naish 89.

[8] 'Nelson's Sea Journal', 11–16 September 1793. See note 5.

[9] Emma to Hamilton, Morrison 157.

[10] *Travels in Italy*, Johann Goethe, London, 1892, 314.

[11] Hamilton to Banks, 6 April 1790. BL Add 34,048.

[12] Hamilton to Orford, Morrison 208.

[13] Emma to Greville, Morrison 215.

[14] Maria Carolina to Emma, 9 February 1793. BL Eg1615.

[15] Nelson to Fanny, Nicolas I 326.

[16] 'Corsica 1794', NRS 92, 1952, 363.

[17] Nelson to Maurice Nelson, 23 December 1793. Monmouth papers IV.

[18] Nelson to Clarence, Nicolas I 343.

[19] Nelson to Fanny, Naish 97.

[20] Nelson to Hood, Nicolas I 352.

[21] For Corsica campaign see Fortescue's *History of the British Army*, IV; and also 'Corsica 1794', ed. Admiral J. H. Godfrey, NRS 92, 1952, 359–422, hereafter called Godfrey.

[22] *Diary of Sir John Moore*, London, 1904. Moore himself became a hero in Wellington's peninsular campaign. C. Wolfe's lines on his burial, beginning, 'Not a drum was heard, not a funeral note/ As his corpse to the ramparts we hurried . . .' remained until well into the twentieth century one of the best-known patriotic poems in the language.

[23] Nelson to Fanny, Naish 103–6.

[24] Nelson's Journal B, Nicolas I 367.

[25] Hood to Nelson, 24 April 1794, Godfrey 389.

[26] Hood to Dundas, letters of 6 and 7 March 1794; Dundas to Hood, 8 March 1794; Hood to Nelson, 9 March 1794; Moore's diary, 13 March 1794. All in Godfrey. See also Nicolas I 358 note.

[27] Moore's diary, 21 March 1794; Godfrey 379.

[28] Nelson's Journal B, Nelson to William Nelson, to Hamilton, and to Suckling, Nicolas I 375–81.

[29] Nelson to Fanny, Naish 108; Moore to Elliot, Moore's diary, 27 April and 3 May 1794, Godfrey 391–2; Hood to Nelson, 15 May 1794, Godfrey 396; Nelson to Fanny, Naish 109, 112.

[30] Moore's diary, 31 May 1794; Godfrey 402. Nelson to Fanny, Naish 112.

[31] Stuart to Elliot, 24 June 1794; Naish 170; Hood to Nelson, 18 July 1794; Godfrey 407 and Nicolas I 445 note; Nelson to Fanny, Naish 114.

[32] Fremantle's diary entry, for 19 April 1794, from *The Wynne Diaries*, ed. Anne Fremantle, London, 1952, chapter 19.

[33] Nelson to Hood, Nicolas I 432; Nelson to Thomas Pollard, Nicolas I 436; Nelson to Suckling, Nicolas I 438. Hood's dispatch, Nicolas I 399 note.

[34] Nelson to Clarence, Nicolas I 474; Nelson to Hood, Nicolas I 477; Nelson to Fanny, Naish 118; Elliot to Portland, 28 August 1794, Godfrey 417.

[35] Nelson to Fanny, Naish 119; Moore's diary, 20 August and 26 October 1794, Godfrey 416 and 418.

[36] Nicolas I 482.

[37] Nelson to Fanny, Naish 119.

[38] Nelson to Suckling, Nicolas II 4. Nelson to Windham and his reply, Nicolas II 43–4 and note.

[39] Nelson to Hood, and to Suckling, Nicolas I 483–6. Nelson to Fanny, Naish 123.

[40] Nelson to Fanny, Naish 97.

[41] *Wynne Diaries*; Fremantle's diary entries of 3 December 1794, 28 August and 27 September 1795.

[42] *Female friend*: Nelson to Thomas Pollard, 6 February 1795, Sotheby's catalogue, 16, 17 November 1925. *Opera Singer*: n.d., Huntington Library, San Marino, California, HM 34180.

[43] Nelson to Locker, Nicolas II 20.

[44] From 'Transactions on board his majesty's ship *Agamemnon* and of the fleet, as seen and known by Captain Nelson', Nicolas II 10–17.

[45] As 44 above.

[46] Nelson to William Nelson, Nicolas II 24.

[47] As 44 above.

[48] Hotham's dispatch, Nicolas II 13 note.

[49] *Histoire de la Marine Française sous la Premiere Republique*, par F. Chevalier, capitaine de vaisseau, Paris 1886, V 177.

[50] Nicolas (II 10 note) calls James's omission of Nelson's account imperfect and unjust, and quotes from the log of the *Agamemnon*, which bears out Nelson's account of what his own ship did, and when, but cannot explain why he should have minimised the part played by Fremantle. Nicolas also prints a letter of 20 March 1795 from William Hoste, a midshipman on the *Agamemnon*, to his father. Log and letter are in Nicolas II 463, appendix, note A. Clowes does not give Nelson's account.

[51] The *Illustrious* was badly damaged and ran ashore in a gale. Nicolas II 22 note.

[52] Nelson to Fanny, Naish 202.

[53] Nelson to Fanny, Naish 204.

[54] *The Life and Letters of Sir Gilbert Elliot*, by Countess of Minto, 3 vols, 1874 II 299.

[55] Chevalier V 172–3, 182.

[56] Nelson to William Hamilton, 1794, Morrison.

[57] *Pages and Portraits from the Past* [the papers of Admiral Sir William Hotham],

London, 1919. This younger Hotham, a nephew of the Hotham who was commander-in-chief, Mediterranean, in 1795, also says in these papers that he had as a midshipman thought that Nelson, as senior captain at Antigua, had 'not much the appearance or the manners of a gentleman'.

[58] Nelson to Hamilton, Nicolas I 377.

[59] Nelson to Fanny, Naish 123.

[60] Fanny to Nelson, Naish 264.

[61] Nicolas II 28 note.

[62] Nelson to William Nelson, Nicolas II 42.

[63] Nelson to Spencer, first lord, Nicolas II 27, and note.

[64] Nelson to Clarence, Nicolas II 52.

[65] Nelson to Elliot, Nicolas II 67.

[66] Nelson to Clarence, Naish 236.

[67] A year later, on 3 October 1796, Clarence wrote to Nelson that he had suggested to the king that he, Clarence, should become first lord. BL Add 34,904.

[68] Nelson to Fanny, Naish 224.

[69] Nelson to person unnamed, Nicolas II 94.

[70] Nelson to William Nelson, Nicolas I 98.

[71] Nelson to Fanny, Naish 291.

Notes to Chapter 12: I SHALL COME LAUGHING BACK

[1] Jervis to Tucker (his secretary), November 1801. *Memoirs of Earl St Vincent etc*, by Jedediah Stephens Tucker, London, 1844, II 38.

[2] Minto II 257, 284–5, 347.

[3] Nelson to Locker, Nicolas II 131.

[4] Nelson to Fanny, Naish 293.

[5] Minto II 354.

[6] Nelson to William Nelson, and to Locker, Nicolas II 187, 299.

[7] Nelson to the governor of Finale, Nicolas VII lxvii.

[8] Jervis to Nelson, 25 July and 22 August 1796. NMM Minto Papers. Naish 339–40.

[9] Nelson to Fanny, Naish 291, 295, 299.

[10] Nelson to Fanny, Naish 319. Prize money listed in Nelson's own hand, Nicolas II 178–9.

[11] Nelson to Clarence, Nicolas II 300. Nelson to Fanny, Naish 307.

[12] Nelson to Locker, Nicolas II 298.

[13] Nelson to Fanny, Naish 305.

[14] Minto II 363–6.

[15] Nelson to Fanny, Nicolas I 309.

[16] Jervis, as he then was, to Coffin, 25 July 1798. BL Add 31,166, St Vincent's letter book (Secret).

[17] Jervis to Spencer, Nicolas II 335.

[18] Nicolas II 340. *The Sun*, 20 March 1797.

[19] Nicolas II 344. Naish 317. *The Times*, 13 March 1797.

[20] Nelson to Suckling, and to Locker, Nicolas II 253, 255. *Naval Chronicle* II 500. Nicolas III 172–80.

[21] *The Times*, 13 March 1797. See also Fanny to Nelson, Naish 354.

[22] Nicolas II 347. Drinkwater's *Narrative of the Proceedings of the British Fleet, commanded by Admiral Sir John Jervis etc*, published anonymously, 1797, reprinted 1840. A long extract is in Harrison I 154–65.

[23] Minto II 377. Elliot to Nelson, and Nelson to Elliot, Nicolas II 349–50.

[24] St Vincent to Nepean, 22 March 1797. BL Add 36,708. (St Vincent papers.)

[25] Parker to Nelson, Nicolas II 471, and *Naval Chronicle* xxi 300.

[26] Nicolas II 438.

[27] Minto II 379.

[28] Nicolas II 467, appendix C.

[29] The Revd Edmund Nelson to Nelson, 11 June 1797. BL Add 34,988.

[30] Nelson to Elliot, and to William Nelson, Nicolas II 349, 351.

[31] Fanny to Nelson, 11 March 1797. Naish 351. But Fanny's wedding day was 11 March, the same day she wrote the letter (see her wedding certificate in BL Add 28,333, Naish 55).

[32] Letters of Nelson to Fanny, Naish 318, 321, and 323.

[33] Clarence to Nelson, Nicolas II 386–8 and note.

[34] Nelson to Jervis, Nicolas II 403–7 and notes.

[35] Nelson to Jervis, Nicolas II 407.

[36] Nelson to Hoste, Nicolas 401.

[37] Peard to St Vincent, 5 July 1897; PRO ADM 1/396. The court martial is in ADM 1/5340, 7–8 July 1797. It was no time to be court-martialled. At another trial in the squadron on 10–11 July, two men were acquitted of mutiny because the charges were only 'proved in part', but were still flogged.

[38] Nelson to Calder, Nicolas II 409.

[39] St Vincent to Nelson, Nicolas II 377 note.

[40] Nelson to Clarence, Nicolas II 364.

[41] Nelson to St Vincent, Nicolas II 378.

[42] Nelson to M'Arthur, Nicolas II 371.

[43] Nelson to St Vincent, Nicolas II 392, 395, VII cxlii.

[44] Nelson to Troubridge, Nicolas II 416. Nelson to governor, II 419.

[45] *Wynne Diaries*, II 185.

[46] Nicolas II 411.

[47] The Spanish accounts are set out by J. D. Spinney in *Mariner's Mirror* 45, 207–223. He quotes from *Relacion circunstanciada de la defensa que hizo la plaza de Santa Cruz etc*, by Don Jose de Monteverde, Madrid, 1798, and from *Ataque y derrota de Nelson en Santa Cruz de Tenerife*, by D. Francisco Lanuza Cano, Madrid, 1955. Mr Spinney wrote as a great great great grandson of Captain Waller of the *Emerald*, which took part in the attack.

[48] Nelson to Don Antonio Gutierrez, Nicolas II 421.

[49] In his first report to St Vincent, of 27 July 1797, Nelson did not mention his own wound. A detailed account of how Nelson received this wound and of the amputation is in Nicolas II 422 note. Fanny's account, Naish 374.

[50] Nelson to Hamond, Nicolas II 433. Colin White, in his book *1797: Nelson's Year of Destiny*, Royal Naval Museum, 1998, gives a detailed account of the actions at Tenerife, and argues that suggestions that Nelson's decisions were based on overconfidence and personal pride are unfair, and that he decided on a second attack

after a council of war with his captains. 'Council of war' was Betsy Fremantle's expression. Nelson did call his captains together but most probably to tell them what he was going to do, and his letter to Hamond speaks for itself.

[51] Nelson to St Vincent, Nicolas II 424.

[52] Nelson to Catherine Matcham, 3 March 1797. NMM MAM/1.

Notes to Chapter 13: THE MAKING OF THE LEGEND

[1] St Vincent to admiralty, 16 August 1797, *London Gazette*, 2 September; Nicolas II 434.

[2] Nelson to Captain Ralph Miller on 'the last action being the best', Nicolas II 456.

[3] Nelson to St Vincent, Nicolas II 434.

[4] Nelson to St Vincent, and St Vincent's reply to Nelson, 16 August 1797. BL Add 34,902, Nicolas II 435.

[5] Nelson to Fanny, 5 and 16 August 1797. BL Add 34,988. Naish 332.

[6] *Gown and sashes*: Naish 290, 325. *Silk shawls*: Nicolas II 327–8. *Revolutions in dress and sunshine*: Naish 359, 348. '*Sits easy*' and '*laughing come back*': Naish 367, 360.

[7] Fanny to Suckling, Nicolas II 440 note. Fanny to Locker, Nicolas II 449–51, and facsimile. *Five surgeons*: Nicolas II 445.

[8] Nelson to St Vincent, Nicolas II 444.

[9] Most reports of the king's words are apocryphal. Lord Eldon, later lord chancellor, related the king's claim for a bit more of Nelson. Nicolas II 448.

[10] Nicolas II 445–6.

[11] Note dated 8 December 1797, marked 'For next Sunday', Nicolas II 455.

[12] In his letter to St Vincent, Nicolas II 448, Nelson says '£712 with the deductions': the full pension was £923. *St Paul's: Annual Register*, 1797.

[13] Nelson to Captain Ralph Miller, Nicolas II 456, 458 note.

[14] Parker to Bingham, 1 September 1797. *Naval Chronicle* xxi 301, Nicolas II 470.

[15] Nicolas II 422–3, and 'Lady Nelson's Memorandum of The Events of July 1797', Monmouth V, Naish 374.

[16] See *The Nelson Portraits*, by Richard Walker [former curator of the government art collection], Royal Naval Museum, 1998; *A Portrait of Lord Nelson*, by Oliver Warner, London, 1958, appendix; and 'The Engraved Portraits of Nelson', by Commander C. N. Robinson, *Print Collector's Quarterly*, vol 17, No 4.

[17] Minto III 2.

[18] Fanny to Nelson, Naish 357.

[19] Clarence to Nelson, Nicolas II 441.

[20] Fanny to Nelson, Naish 353.

[21] Nelson to Loughborough, 12 October, and Loughborough to Nelson, Oct 1797; BL Add 34,906.

[22] William Nelson to Nelson, Naish 375.

[23] William Nelson to Nelson, 11 November 1797. Monmouth IV.

[24] William Nelson to Nelson, 30 November 1797. As above.

[25] Nelson to his father, and to William Suckling, Nicolas II 32–3.

[26] DNB for Spencer. Diana Spencer, Princess of Wales, later came from this family.

[27] *The Diary of Frances Lady Shelley 1787–1817,* ed. Richard Edgcumbe, London, 1912, 77–8.

[28] Eyre Matcham 146, 151.

[29] Sale catalogue, 26 September 1797, BL Add 30,170.

[30] Nelson to Thomas Lloyd, Nicolas III, 3.

[31] Nelson to Berry, Nicolas II 453, 456.

[32] Fanny to Nelson, Naish 430.

[33] Fanny to Nelson, Naish 422.

[34] Lavinia Spencer to St Vincent, 31 March 1798. NMM PAR/251. Lady Spencer's recommendation was attended to. Mr Capel was highly favoured, and lived to become a full admiral.

Notes to Chapter 14: THE NILE, AND THE HAPPY INSTRUMENT OF GOD

[1] Minto to Nelson, *Memoirs of Earl St Vincent,* by Jedediah Stephens Tucker, 2 vols, 1844, II 348.

[2] Fanny to Nelson, 4 and 15 April 1798, BL Add 34,988. Naish 421, 426. Nelson to Fanny, Naish 395–6.

[3] St Vincent to Spencer, Tucker II 435. Nelson to St Vincent, Nicolas III 14–16.

[4] Nelson to Fanny, Naish 396.

[5] Admiralty letter of 2 May 1798 and private letter from Spencer of 29 April, both received by St Vincent on 19 May. Nicolas III 24–27.

[6] St Vincent to Emma Hamilton, 22 May 1798, BL Add 31,166. St Vincent to William Hamilton, Tucker II 443–5, where the letter to Emma also appears in part.

[7] *Emma Hamilton and Sir William,* by Oliver Warner, London, 1960, 146.

[8] St Vincent to Parker, 19 December 1798. BL Add 31,166, St Vincent Papers.

[9] Orde published a pamphlet in 1798, setting out the whole business. The MS, of 117 folio pages, is at Lloyds of London; Lloyds 64–114. Orde's remarks on the service 'of the greatest eventual importance to the world' are on p90.

[10] Tucker II 37.

[11] Listed with others in Nelson's orders to his captains, Nicolas III 23.

[12] St Vincent to Nelson, Nicolas III 24–7 note.

[13] *Steel's Navy List,* January 1798.

[14] He received his next orders, from St Vincent, on 15 August 1798. Nelson to Nepean, Nicolas III 105.

[15] Nelson to St Vincent, Nicolas II 27, 45.

[16] Nelson to Spencer, Nicolas III 98.

[17] Nelson to St Vincent, Nicolas III 30.

[18] Nelson to Spencer, Nicolas III 31.

[19] Nelson to Hamilton, Nicolas III 43. PRO FO 70/11.

[20] Fanny to Nelson, Naish 439–41.

[21] William Nelson to Nelson, 7 June 1798. BL Add 34,988.

[22] *Times,* 9 September 1798.

[23] *Morning Herald,* 13 September, 1798.

[24] *Morning Chronicle,* 11 September 1798.

[25] The first mention of Egypt in any orders was in those sent after Nelson on 2 June

1798 by Captain Foote in the *Seahorse* in which St Vincent says the destination of the French fleet is 'differently spoken of: Naples, Sicily, the Gulph of Alexandria, with a view to taking possession of Egypt; lastly and most probably to pass the straits, and take the circuitous route to Ireland'. But Foote did not reach Nelson until after the battle of the Nile. St Vincent Papers, BL Add 31,166.

[26] Nicolas III 48.

[27] *Repertoire des Navires de Guerre Français,* by Jacques Vissot, Paris, 1967.

[28] Nicolas III 55.

[29] The French side of the battle is taken from 'Account of the Battle of the Nile by the Adjutant of Rear Admiral Blanquet', Pettigrew I 456–60.

[30] The British view of the battle is taken largely from *An Authentic Narrative etc* [of the battle of the Nile] published anonymously in London late in 1798, but by Captain Sir Edward Berry. Parts are reprinted in Nicolas III 48–54.

[31] The assertion that the idea was Foley's was first made in the *Annual Register,* 1798 [published 1800] p 143, which says: 'The passing round the bow of the enemy's van and inside of their line appears to have originated with the leader, Captain Foley, as no signal was made to direct such a manoeuvre … The idea was followed by four other of those who composed the van, and the advantage which derived from that manoeuvre may best be calculated by a reference to the result.' This statement in the *Annual Register* is as public as could be, and it was not denied. See also *Royal Naval Biography* by John Marshall [Lieutenant RN], 1823, I, part 1, 365: 'It had long been a favourite idea with Captain Foley, which he had mentioned on the previous evening to Captains Troubridge and Hood [both dead by 1823], that a considerable advantage would arise, if the enemy's fleet were found moored in line-of-battle with the land, to lead between them and the shore, as the French guns on that side were not likely to be manned, or to be ready for action. The original plan which Sir Horatio Nelson had intended to have adopted, if Captain Foley had not judged it expedient to lead within the French line, was to have kept entirely on its outer side; and to have stationed his ships, as far as he was able, one on the outer bow and another on the outer quarter of each of the enemy.' Major General Sir Charles Napier in *The United Services Journal,* August 1837, said of Foley's tactic: 'The action was great in itself, and would have been great, even in the great Nelson, but it was greater in the subordinate than in the chief.' Napier was the conqueror of Sind, and his statue stands in Trafalgar Square. Foley had married his cousin. And in 1845, Rear-Admiral Sir Thomas Browne, who had been first lieutenant of the *Elephant* under Foley, wrote to Nicolas (III 474) saying he had been in the constant habit of conversing with him about the Nile, and that Foley had stated that he acted without previous orders or arrangement. Much of this is discussed in Nicolas III 62–5. And in 1863, writing sixty-four years after the event in *Memoirs of Admiral the Honble. Sir George Elliot, written for his children* (of which the NMM has a copy), Elliot said that he was on the quarterdeck of the *Goliath* as a midshipman when he heard Captain Foley say to his master that he wished he could get inside the leading ships of the enemy's line, and this was done. He heard Foley say he would not be surprised to find the French unprepared for action on that side. Elliot was Lord Minto's son.

[32] Nicolas, III 54, says this information came from Berry's widow.

[33] Blanquet, see note 29 above. Also Nicolas III 68.

[34] Two who died were her captain, Casabianca, and his ten-year-old son, who was celebrated in Felicia Hemans's lines: 'The boy stood on the burning deck/ Whence all but he had fled . . .'

[35] Account of the battle of the Nile given by M. Vivant Denon in his 'Travels in Upper and Lower Egypt'. Pettigrew I 460.

[36] *The Friend*, by S. T. Coleridge, London, 1818, III 310. See note 43 below.

[37] Nelson to St Vincent, Nicolas III 56.

[38] Nelson to Fanny, Naish 399.

[39] Howe to Nelson, and his reply, Nicolas III 84 and 230.

[40] Nelson to Minto, Nicolas III 110. See also Nicolas III 65.

[41] Nelson to Minto, Nicolas III 111. See also *Times* and *Daily Telegraph* of 28 June 1999, for reports of the finds of French archaeologists and divers who found the wreck of *L'Orient* in Aboukir Bay. See also *Napoleon's Lost Fleet*, by Laura Foreman and Ellen Blue Phillips, New York and London, 1999.

[42] Nelson to Locker, Nicolas II 90.

[43] *The Friend*, a weekly literary magazine, vol III, essay IV, 1809–10. Reprinted in two volumes in 1818.

[44] *The Friend*, 1818 ed, III 281–2.

[45] *The Notebooks of Samuel Taylor Coleridge*, ed. Kathleen Coburn, New York and London, 1962, vol 2, text, 1804–1808, item 2138.

[46] Pettigrew I 130.

[47] Nelson's plan, 15 August 1801, Nicolas IV 461. Nelson to St Vincent, 3 October 1801, Nicolas IV 504. Definition of a carcase from *Sailor's Word Book*, by Admiral W. H. Smyth, London, 1867.

[48] At the Nile the first lieutenant of the *Minotaur* was not promoted until 1802, and Lieutenant Yule of the *Alexander* not until 1805. Clowes IV 370.

[49] Nelson to Capel, Nicolas III, 103. And see Capel in DNB.

[50] St Vincent to Rear-Admiral Markham, Tucker II 280.

[51] St Vincent to Nelson, Nicolas III 84.

[52] Lady Spencer to Nelson, Nicolas III 74.

[53] Nelson's letters to Spencer and to William Nelson, Nicolas III 129,131. Nelson to Hamilton, 8 August 1798, Letters 1814.

[54] Hallowell to Nelson, Nicolas III 88 and note.

Notes to Chapter 15: THE FAMILY, AND THE GREAT STAGE OF LIFE

[1] *Times* and *Morning Herald*, 21 September 1798, both quoting *Le Redacteur* of 15 September.

[2] *Morning Chronicle*, 22 September 1798, quoting *Le Clef du Cabinet* of 16 September.

[3] *Times*, 1 October 1798.

[4] *Times* and *Morning Herald*, 2 October 1798.

[5] Hood to Nelson, 15 October 1798, Nicolas III 85.

[6] *Times*, 3 October 1798

[7] Lady Spencer to St Vincent, 7 October 1798, NMM PAR/251.

[8] *Times*, 3 October 1798.

[9] Eyre Matcham 160.

[10] Fanny to Nelson, Naish 447.

[11] Nelson to Fanny, Naish 399.

[12] Catherine Matcham to Nelson, 6 October 1798. BL Add 34,988.

[13] *Morning Chronicle,* 4 October 1798.

[14] For correspondence about Jervis's peerage, see *Spencer: Private Papers* II NRS 46, 1913, Pitt to Spencer, 6 March 1797, and pp96, 98, 383, 388, 393. Pitt first thought to make Jervis a viscount, but then agreed with Spencer that it 'would not be at all too much' to make him an earl. See also Tucker I 225.

[15] Hood to Nelson, Nicolas III 85.

[16] Fanny to Hood, Naish 458. NMM HOO/28(2).

[17] Windham to Spencer, 4 October 1798. *Spencer Papers* III NRS, 1923.

[18] Maurice Nelson to Fanny, Naish 452–3.

[19] Spencer to Nelson, Nicolas III 75.

[20] Hood to Nelson, Nicolas III 85.

[21] Goodall to Nelson, Nicolas III 86.

[22] Eyre Matcham 161.

[23] Fanny to Hood, Naish 458–9.

[24] Maurice Nelson to Fanny, Naish 454.

[25] 'Maurice Nelson, purser, recommended by Mr Suckling, appointed to the Swift.' She was a sloop built in 1777 and surrendered in 1780. NMM, Sandwich's personal papers, SAN/ 3 53.

[26] Maurice Nelson was clerk (Bills and Accounts) at the navy office 1 November 1775–25 December 1793; then assistant commissary to the forces under Lord Moira; then returned to the navy office in his previous post 27 April 1797; then chief clerk (Bills and Accounts) 27 March – 24 April 1801. *Navy Board Officials 1660–1832,* by J. M. Collinge, London, 1978. See also NRS 55, 1922, 93.

[27] Maurice Nelson's letters to his wife, 24 December 1793 to 3 June 1794. NMM CRK/22 (HAM 81).

[28] Maurice Nelson to Nelson, 25 November 1798. BL Add 34,988. Nelson's letter saying the fleet had appointed Davison full agent for the Nile was dated 12 August 1798. Nelson wrote: '. . . whatever assistance you may give Davison or whatever he may wish to serve you in, I beg that you may never be considered, directly or indirectly as having anything to do with the agency.' BL Eg 2240.

[29] William Nelson to Fanny, 1 April 1799, Naish 467.

[30] *Catalogue of Political and Personal Satires,* by M. Dorothy George, VII 1793–1800.

[31] Charlotte Nelson to Nelson, Naish 466.

[32] House of Lords, vote of thanks to Nelson, 21 November 1798. Nicolas III 78.

[33] On Walpole and Pitt's duel (with George Tierney) see DNB.

[34] Commons debate, 22 November 1798. Nicolas III 79.

[35] *Morning Chronicle,* 11 October 1798.

[36] Fanny to Nelson, Naish 443–7.

[37] Draft inscription in Pinney papers, Bristol University library.

[38] Revd Edmund Nelson to Nelson, 2 July 1798. BL Add 34,988. The allusion is to Gray's *Elegy,* stanza 15: 'Some village Hampden, that with dauntless breast/ The little tyrant of his fields withstood,/ Some mute inglorious Milton here may rest,/ Some Cromwell guiltless of his country's blood.'

[39] Canning to Windham, Downing Street, 23 October 1798. BL Add 34,902.

Notes to Chapter 16: FIDDLERS, POETS, WHORES, AND SCOUNDRELS

¹ Account of the battle of the Nile by Vivant Denon in his *Travels in Upper and Lower Egypt.* Parts are in Pettigrew I, appendix, and Harrison I 291.

² Nelson's Journal on the *Vanguard,* 2–21 August 1798. Nicolas III 105–7.

³ Nelson to Hamilton, Nicolas III 116.

⁴ Nelson to Wyndham, minister at Florence, Nicolas III 108.

⁵ Nelson to Wyndham, and to Eden, minister at Vienna, Nicolas III 190, 194.

⁶ Admiralty to St Vincent [and similar orders to Nelson] 3 October 1798; Lloyds 307 gives a transcript of the MS admiralty minute. Also Nicolas III 143.

⁷ Nelson to St Vincent, Nicolas III 107.

⁸ Nelson to St Vincent, 19 August 1798. NMM PAR/251 f74. Part of this letter, without the first page, is in Nicolas III 107, who took it from Clarke and M'Arthur.

⁹ Nelson to St Vincent, Nicolas III 100. *Splitting:* Nelson to St Vincent, Nicolas VII clxii.

¹⁰ Nelson to Hamilton, Nicolas III 101. Hamilton to Grenville, 7 September 1798, PRO FO 70/11.

¹¹ Nelson to St Vincent, Nicolas III 128.

¹² St Vincent to George III, 17 July 1798. BL Add 31,166. St Vincent's Letter Book (Secret).

¹³ Maria Carolina to Emma [in French], 3 September 1798, BL Eg 1615. Printed in *Carteggio di Maria Carolina etc, documenti inediti,* by Raffaele Palumbo, Naples, 1877.

¹⁴ Nelson to Fanny, Naish 399.

¹⁵ Nelson to Spencer, Nicolas III 129.

¹⁶ Nelson to Fanny, Naish 401.

¹⁷ *Autobiography of Miss Cornelia Knight . . . with extracts from her journals and anecdote books,* 2 vols, London, 1861, I 116. Miss Knight was born in 1757 and as a girl knew Johnson, Goldsmith, Burke, and Reynolds. She wrote a sequel to Johnson's *Rasselas.* Later lady companion to Princess Charlotte. Her autobiography was assembled from her journals and published after her death. Nicolas occasionally gives direct quotations from the journals themselves (as in III 475), which are more valuable.

¹⁸ Hamilton to Grenville, foreign secretary, 25 September 1798. PRO FO 70/11.

¹⁹ Knight's journal; Nicolas III 475 note.

²⁰ Nelson to Fanny, Naish 401–4.

²¹ Nelson to Spencer, Nicolas III 137.

²² Nelson to St Vincent, Nicolas III 138.

²³ Memorandum from Smith, minister at Constantinople, to foreign secretary, passed on to Fanny. Naish 405.

²⁴ Hamilton to Nelson, Nicolas III 72.

²⁵ Nelson to St Vincent, Nicolas III 144.

²⁶ St Vincent to Emma, 28 October 1798. Monmouth E 415.

²⁷ Emma to Nelson, 30 June 1798, Letters 1814.

²⁸ Nelson to Fanny, Naish 478. The MS at Monmouth bears a note in Fanny's handwriting, in parts illegible: 'Notwithstanding the previous conduct of Earl St Vincent, Lord Nelson had [?] at Naples embedded the seeds of distrust and

suspicion; and there were some moments when forgetting all that he once thought of his respected commander in chief, he [???] believed the great man [?] which [?] and distorted every object he beheld.'

29 Nelson to St Vincent, Nicolas III 148.

30 Nelson to Spencer, Nicolas III 171.

31 Nelson to Clarence, Nicolas III 168.

32 Nelson to Hamilton, Nicolas III 182.

33 Troubridge to Nelson, Nicolas III 182.

34 Nelson to Wyndham, Nicolas III 190.

35 Nelson to Spencer, Nicolas III 195.

36 Nelson's letters to Ball and to Troubridge, Nicolas 201–2.

37 Nelson to William Nelson, Nicolas III 176.

38 Emma Hamilton to Nelson, 26 October 1798. BL Add 34,989. Naish 420.

39 Nelson to Spencer, Nicolas III 188.

40 Harrison, 1806, I 373. This early biography was subsidised, and perhaps in part dictated, by Emma.

41 Nelson to Fanny, Naish 478. This letter, abbreviated and tinkered with, is in Clarke and M'Arthur II 132, omitting these words about St Vincent: 'I am got he fancies too near him in reputation.'

42 Nelson to the Turkish grand vizier, Nicolas III 203.

43 Nelson to J. Spencer Smith, Nicolas III 205.

44 Nelson to St Vincent, Nicolas III 210.

45 Knight I 125.

46 Emma to Greville, Morrison 370. Emma's draft petition for pension [March 1813], Morrison 1046.

47 Maria Carolina to Emma, 18 December 1798. BL Eg 1615.

48 Journal of *Vanguard*, 19–26 December 1798. Nicolas III 209.

49 Acton to Nelson, 20 December 1798. BL Eg 1623.

50 Nelson to St Vincent, 28 December 1798. Nicolas III 210.

51 Maria Carolina to Emma, 21 December 1798; BL Eg 1615. There are c150 letters from the queen to Emma, in two bound volumes, at the BL, and another 136 at the NMM, in CRK/21. A few are in Italian and the rest in French. The queen never punctuated or used accents, wrote in a stream of consciousness, addressed Emma as 'chere miledy', and more often than not did not sign or date the letters. She did date almost all her letters during the two critical periods of the escape in December 1798 and the retaking of Naples in the summer of 1799. Emma's letters to the queen seem not to have survived.

52 William Hamilton to Grenville, foreign secretary, 28 December 1798; PRO FO 70/11. Emma to Greville (her former lover), Morrison 370; her more detailed account of 1813, in support of her claim for a pension, Morrison 1046; and Harrison I 383. Nelson to St Vincent, 28 December 1798, Nicolas III 210.

53 Nelson's memorandum (to his captains?) 20 December 1798; Nicolas III 206. Lists in Pettigrew I 183, and in BL Eg 1613, ff 8–10. *Cardinals*: Harrison I 383.

54 Hamilton to Grenville, see note 52.

55 Giglioli 99.

56 *The Queen of Naples and Lord Nelson*, by John Cordy Jeaffreson, London 1889, vol 2, 48. Jeaffreson is not wholly reliable and gives no source for this, but he is so

emphatically royalist that any anecdote he gives *against* the king may have some substance.

[57] Nelson to St Vincent, 28 December 1798, Nicolas III 213.

[58] Captain W. H. Smyth, who was present during the escape, in an article in 'The United Services Magazine', May and July 1845. Part in Pettigrew I 177.

[59] Nelson to St Vincent, Nicolas III 213.

Notes to Chapter 17 THE SICILIFYING OF MY OWN CONSCIENCE

For details of the works referred to in these notes (Giglioli, Gutteridge, Rushout, Micheroux, Sacchinelli and others) see appendix A.

[1] Nelson to Fanny, 2 January 1799. Naish 479.

[2] Nelson to J. Spencer Smith, Nicolas III 373.

[3] Nelson to St Vincent, 31 December 1798, Nicolas III 215. St Vincent to Nelson, 17 January 1799, BL Add 34,940. Nelson to Sidney Smith, Nicolas II 284.

[4] Nelson to Fanny, 17 January 1799, Naish 481. St Vincent to Nelson, 10 January 1799, BL Add 24,940. St Vincent to Nelson, 27 February 1799. BL Add 34,940.

[5] Nelson to Lady Parker, 1 February 1799, Nicolas III 248.

[6] Nelson to St Vincent and to Davison, Nicolas III 239, 272. Nelson to Lady Parker, III 248, to Goodall, III 246, to Locker, III 260. See also *The Nelson Portraits* by Richard Walker, Royal Naval Museum, 1998, 78–91, 223–6.

[7] Nelson to Minto, Nicolas III 236. *The Locks of Norbury* by the Duchess of Sermoneta, London, 1940, 152, for Charles Lock's letters home.

[8] For the Italian literature on the Naples revolution, see appendix A.

[9] Giglioli 131.

[10] Gutteridge 28, 33.

[11] Troubridge to Nelson, 4,12, and 13 April 1799. BL Add 34,910. Nicolas III 333 prints parts, but omits Troubridge's threat to 'piss on the d–d jacobins carcass' and his advice to hang rebels without a mass so that they shall go to hell.

[12] Nicolas III 329, 334, 341, 358, 360.

[13] Nelson to Foote, Nicolas III 376. Nelson to Acton, Gutteridge 16: Gutteridge prints forty letters of Nelson to Acton, January–May 1799, from Grande Archivo di Stato di Napoli, 3 riservato, fasc. 624, which appear nowhere else. Nelson to Minto, Nicolas III 452.

[14] Nelson to Troubridge, Nicolas III 334.

[15] Giglioli 149.

[16] Foote to Nelson, 4 June 1799. BL Add 36,873.

[17] Maria Carolina to Gallo, 17 May 1799, *Correspondance Inedite de Marie-Caroline Reine de Naples et de Sicile avec le Marquis de Gallo*, by M.H. Weil and Marquis C. di Somma Circelo, Paris, 1911, II 92. Acton to Hamilton, 20 June 1799, BL Add 34,912, Gutteridge 143.

[18] Nelson to Keith, 16 June 1799, Nicolas III 380. '*Must go*' – Nelson to Hamilton, 20 June 1799; Nicolas VII clxxxv.

[19] Maria Carolina to Emma, BL Eg 1616; Gutteridge 105.

[20] Commandant at Castellamare to Foote, and his reply, 15 June 1799. BL Add 36,873. This volume of MSS contains papers which were later published in *Captain*

Foote's Vindication etc, London, 1807 and 1810. Gutteridge 29, 30.

[21] Ruffo to Foote, 17 June 1799, Gutteridge 35.

[22] Gutteridge 110.

[23] Micheroux to Ruffo, 19 June 1799, from Sacchinelli, Gutteridge 124. Also Foote to Micheroux, 23 June 1799, Gutteridge 177.

[24] Foote to Clarke, Nicolas III 486 note.

[25] Capitulation of the Forts of Uovo and Nuovo [the terms]. BL Add 34,944. Nicolas III 488. The queen's scrawled comments in the margin of the treaty are in BL Add 30,999. Gutteridge 159.

[26] Foote to Nelson, 23 June 1799. BL Add 36,873.

[27] Nelson's 'Opinion', 24 June 1799. Nicolas III 384.

[28] Foote's report to Nelson, 16 June 1799, BL Add 36,973. Hamilton to Acton, 24 June 1799, Gutteridge 207.

[29] Master's log of *Foudroyant*, Gutteridge 202. Rushout: 'Nelson statements [made to Panizzi on 9 February 1846] by Lord Northwick'. BL Add 30,999. Hamilton to Charles Greville, 4 August 1799, PRO FO 70/12, not in Morrison, as Hamilton's earlier letter of 14 July is.

[30] At the foot of the 'Opinion' (Nicolas III 386) a note is added in Nelson's hand: 'Read, and explained, and rejected by the cardinal.' Nelson to Duckworth and to Keith, Nicolas III 387, 392. Micheroux's *Compendio*, 24 June 1799, Gutteridge 114.

[31] Emma to Charles Greville, 19 July 1799, Morrison 411.

[32] *Carteggio di Maria Carolina con Lady Hamilton*, by Raffaele Palumbo, Naples, 1877. Letter not dated.

[33] Hamilton to Grenville, 14 July 1799, 'Separate and Secret'. PRO 70/12. Hamilton enclosed twelve letters of the queen to Emma, asking for them back. They were numbered up to 22. He said the queen had particularly requested Emma to go with him and Nelson to Naples, and that the letters did much honour to the queen's understanding and heart.

[34] Nelson to Duckworth, 25 June 1799, Nicolas III 387.

[35] Micheroux, 25 June 1799. Gutteridge, 182, cites De Nicola, whose *Diario Napoletano dal 1798 al 1825* is published in Archiv. Stor. Anno XXIV and XXV. See appendix A.

[36] Harrison II 101.

[37] Sacchinelli 251. Gutteridge 218. Not dated.

[38] Marshal Micheroux (a cousin) to the Chevalier Micheroux, 26 June 1799. BL Add 34,950. Gutteridge 236.

[39] Ruffo to Massa, Sacchinelli 252; De Nicola 25 June 1799. Gutteridge 222, 184.

[40] De Nicola and Micheroux, Gutteridge 186, 116.

[41] Hamilton to Ruffo; Sacchinelli 255, Gutteridge 231.

[42] Nelson to Ruffo, 26 June 1799, not 28 June as in Nicolas III 394. BL Add 34,963. Gutteridge 233.

[43] Sacchinelli 256; Gutteridge 234. Sacchinelli says Troubridge and Ball stated in writing to Ruffo that Nelson 'does not oppose' [non impedisce] the execution of the capitulation. He then gives what he calls a facsimile of the statement, which says that Nelson 'will not oppose [non si opporà] the embarkation of the rebels'. The facsimile is not in an English hand and is probably what an interpreter wrote. Sacchinelli is

not scrupulously accurate, and this may be an example of his carelessness. But since it is here that Sacchinelli says Ruffo suspected bad faith, the difference between promising not to oppose the execution of the treaty (which would have allowed the rebels to sail to Toulon) and simply not opposing the embarkation (which could be taken to mean no more than that) is of some importance, though since both Hamilton and Nelson had given Ruffo their own written statements that day, it does not affect the case for or against Nelson.

[44] Micheroux, 26 June 1799, Gutteridge 116.

[45] As note 29 above.

[46] Micheroux, Gutteridge 117; and Minchini's statement, Gutteridge 239.

[47] Hamilton to Acton, 27 June 1799. There are slight differences between the draft (NMM HMI/21 and Naish 504) and the letter as sent (in the Naples foreign office, Gutteridge 249.) The draft says that if one cannot do what one wants, 'one must make the best of a bad bargain'. The letter Acton received says that 'one must do the next best thing'.

[48] As above.

[49] Hamilton to Acton, 29 June 1799, Gutteridge 277.

[50] Hamilton to Acton, 29 June 1799 (second letter that day), Gutteridge 279.

[51] Nicolas III 499–504 gives an account of the trial and execution, largely relying on Clarke and M'Arthur.

[52] *Nelsonian Reminiscences etc* by G.S. Parsons, Lieut RN, Boston, Mass., 1843; London 1905.

[53] Northwick, BL Add 39,999. Compare T. A. Evans's printed pamphlet on the Nelson coat, 1846, which gives much the same account but does not name Northwick as the witness cited; New York Public Library, A. p.v. 889–6.

[54] Northwick to Pettigrew, 26 October 1848. Pettigrew papers, Monmouth.

[55] Nelson to Nepean, 27 June 1799, Nicolas III 389.

[56] Naish 504. NMM HML/21.

[57] De Nicola, Gutteridge 189; and Hamilton to Acton, Gutteridge 277.

[58] Acton to Hamilton, 25 June 1799 (one of Acton's three letters to him that day), BL Eg 2640. Gutteridge 227.

[59] Maria Carolina to Emma, 25 June 1799. BL Eg 1616. Pettigrew I 233. Gutteridge 210.

[60] De Nicola, Gutteridge 191. Acton to Hamilton, 29 June 1799, Gutteridge 279.

[61] Acton to Hamilton, 27 June 1799 (two letters, both received 30 June); BL Eg 2640. Gutteridge 257, 258.

[62] Hamilton to Acton, 30 June 1799. NMM HMI/21. Naish 506. Gutteridge 286.

[63] Nelson to Acton, 29 June 1799, Gutteridge 278. Nelson to the king, 30 June 1799, Gutteridge 287.

[64] Giglioli 273.

[65] Acton to Hamilton, 20 June 1799, Nicolas III 391; and Nicolas III 504.

[66] 'List of Jacobins . . . some very private papers', 1799. NMM GIR/3a.

[67] Maria Carolina to Emma, 2 July 1799, with Emma's endorsement, BL Eg 1616.

[68] Cirillo to Emma, 3 July 1799, Morrison 403. Letters: BL Eg 1621. Nelson to Mrs Cadogan, 17 July 1799, Monmouth E 448. Nelson to Troubridge, 6 and 9 July 1799, Nicolas 401–2. John Jolly to Emma, 6 July 1799; NMM CRK/22 (HAM 80.)

[69] Emma to Charles Greville, 5 August 1799, Morrison 417.

70 *Lady Hamilton*, by A. Fauchier-Magnan, Paris, 1910, 221.
71 Keith to Nelson, 12 July 1799, Nicolas III 419.
72 Maria Carolina to Emma, 18 July 1799, Pettigrew I 266.
73 Nelson to Fanny, 4 August 1799, Naish 487.
74 Nelson to Foote, 19 May 1799. *Captain Foote's Vindication*.
75 Acton to Hamilton, 25 June 1799. BL Eg 2640, f 271. Gutteridge 224.
76 Hamilton to Grenville, 14 July 1799. PRO FO 70/12. Giglioli 401.
77 See Appendix A for the continuing history of this controversy.
78 Nelson to Keith, 27 June and to Spencer, 13 July 1799. Nicolas III 393, 406.
79 Albanese's memorial, 29 June 1799. Sacchinelli 262. Gutteridge 282.
80 *Racconti Storici* etc by Gaetano Rodino, Arch. Stor. anno VI. Giglioli 348.
81 Moreno to Nelson, BL Add 34,945, f 20. Apart from the petitions in the BL, another 166 petitions were listed in the catalogue of Pettigrew's sale of 1853 at Sotheby's (NMM CRK/21).
82 L'Aurore to Nelson, undated, BL Add 34,950, f 69.
83 From vessel *La Stabia* to Nelson, undated, BL Add 34,950, f 71.
84 Sacchinelli 256 [26 June 1799]. Gutteridge 234.
85 Ferdinand to Nelson, 10 June 1799. Gutteridge 62. Nicolas III 491, 522.
86 Nelson to Sidney Smith, 8 March 1799, Nicolas III 284.
87 Hamilton to Grenville, 14 July 1799. PRO FO 70/12. Giglioli 399.
88 Hamilton to Charles Greville, 14 July 1799. PRO FO 72/12. Morrison 405.
89 Hamilton to Charles Greville, 4 August 1799. PRO FO 70/12, f 223. Not in Morrison.
90 Nelson to Clarence [13 August 1799]. Nicolas III 410.
91 Nelson to Gibbs, 11 August 1803. Nicolas V 160.
92 Parsons, see note 52 above.
93 Nelson to Addington [8 May 1801], Nicolas IV 360.
94 Nelson to Troubridge, 17 July 1799, Nicolas III 413.
95 *The Locks of Norbury* 170. See note 7.
96 Officers of the *Leviathan* to Emma, 17 July 1799. Pettigrew 278. Morrison 409. Morrison does not transcribe the name of the nine signatories. Pettigrew does.
97 Giglioli 350.
98 *Storia dei Popoli della Luciana e Basilicata*, by Giacomo Racioppi, II 277, 1868.

Notes to Chapter 18: INACTIVE AT A FOREIGN COURT

1 Hamilton to Grenville, 19 December 1799. PRO FO 70/12. 'Secret. No 32'.
2 Harrison II 146.
3 Harrison II 142–9.
4 Nelson to Fanny, Naish 486.
5 Keith to his sister Mary Elphinstone, 31 May 1799. *Keith Papers*, NRS 1950, 38.
6 Letters from Keith to Nelson, Nelson to Keith, and Nelson to Spencer in Nicolas III 408–18.
7 Nelson to Spencer, 1 August 1799, Nicolas III 427.
8 Hamilton to Charles Greville, Morrison 405; Nelson to Smith, Nicolas III 417.
9 Nelson to Davison, 23 August 1799. Nicolas III 460.
10 Spencer to Nelson, 18 August 1799, NMM Croker papers, Naish 511.

11 Three letters, all 20 August 1799; Nepean to Nelson, Nicolas III 409; orders to take acting command, Pettigrew I 293; Nelson to Nepean, Nicolas IV 23. *Piece of glass* – Nelson to Spencer, 21 September 1799, Pettigrew I 281.

12 Keith to Admiralty, 10 August 1799. PRO ADM 1/400. *San Josef:* Nelson to Fanny, Naish 490.

13 Nelson to Spencer, Nicolas IV 56. Lock to his father, 27 July 1799, *Sermoneta* 174. Nelson to victualling board, Nicolas IV 100.

14 Lock to his father, 9 August 1799, *Sermoneta* 179.

15 Foote to Keith, 20 July 1799, PRO ADM 1/1798. Foote did not print this letter in his *Vindication*.

16 *Memoirs . . . of Sir W. Hoste*, 1833, I 115. Nelson to pope, 24 June 1800, BL Add 34,902, Nicolas IV 259.

17 Maria Carolina to Gallo, 8 September 1799, in *Correspondance Inedite de Marie Caroline Reine de Naples avec le Marquis de Gallo*, by M-H Weil and Marquis C. di Somma Cicelo, Paris, 1911, 2 vols.

18 *Letters of Mary Nisbet of Dirleton, Countess of Elgin*, ed N. Hamilton Grant, London, 1926, 18.

19 Lady Minto to Lady Malmesbury, 6 July 1800, repeating what Rushout told her. Minto III 138.

20 Troubridge to Emma Hamilton, Pettigrew I 339, 343.

21 *Times*, 14 November 1799.

22 Goodall to Nelson, Nicolas IV 204.

23 Nelson to Spencer, Nicolas IV 90.

24 Nelson to Duckworth, to Spencer, and to Jackson at Turin, Nicolas IV 113, 117, 124.

25 Clarke and M'Arthur and Nicolas I p3.

26 These references are from seven of Fanny's letters to Nelson, from 8 September 1799 to 23 February 1800, Naish 532–550.

27 Revd Edmund Nelson to Nelson, 24 February 1800. BL Add 34,906.

28 Nelson to Fanny, Pettigrew I 220, Naish 482; sold at Sotheby's, London, 1853; now in the collection of Mr and Mrs Harry Spiro, New York.

29 William Nelson to Nelson, 8 November 1799 and 18 January 1800. BL Add 34,906.

30 Maurice Nelson to Nelson, 10 November 1799. BL Add 34,906.

31 Nelson to Maurice Nelson, Nicolas VII exciii. Spencer to Nelson, Nicolas IV 225.

32 Nelson to Fanny, 20 January 1800. Naish 494.

33 Nelson to Emma Hamilton, 29 January [1800]. This was probably in Pettigrew's collection. It is on the same size laid paper as that used by Nelson for his journal at the time (Pettigrew I 305, BL Eg 1614.) Pettigrew did not print any part of it. He says in his preface that the only liberty he took with the letters he transcribed was 'to omit numerous expressions of endearment which might be offensive to the general reader'. He did omit whole chunks, and may have considered this letter one long endearment. It was probably sold in Pettigrew's sale at Sotheby's, London, 1853. It resurfaced at Christie's, New York, as lot 200 in a sale of 19 December 1986, where it sold for $16,000. No provenance was given. It is now in the collection of Mr and Mrs Harry Spiro, New York.

[34] Keith to his sister Mary Elphinstone, 9 February 1800. NMM Keith Papers, KEI/46.

[35] Hamilton to Grenville, 26 February 1800, in which he reports the *Généreux* has been taken, and encloses an extract from a letter of Nelson's to Emma 'which was a sort of journal'. PRO FO 70/13.

[36] Nelson to Minto, Nicolas IV 193.

[37] Minto to his wife, 23 March 1800. Minto III 114.

[38] Nelson to Keith, Nicolas IV 207.

[39] Nelson to Nepean, 4 April 1800, enclosing Berry's letter. PRO ADM/401. Nicolas IV 218.

[40] Nelson to Spencer, Nicolas III 99.

[41] *Parliamentary History of England* 34, 1391–6: Debate on peace overture from France, 3 February 1800. *Morning Chronicle*, 4 February 1800. *Whitehall Evening Post*, 5 February 1800.

[42] *Captain Foote's Vindication of his Conduct . . . in the Bay of Naples in the Summer of 1799*, London, second edition, 1810. This edition is more useful because it has copies of letters between Foote and Clarke, on statements made in Clarke and M'Arthur. Clarke mentions Keith's disapproval of Nelson at Naples.

[43] BL Add 36,873. 'Correspondence between Ld Nelson and Captain Foote'. A collection of letters and papers which Foote printed in his *Vindication*. These words are written on the back of a letter to a Mr Stone, who had got Foote a report of Fox's speech.

[44] Nelson to Davison, Nicolas IV 232.

[45] Nelson to Davison, Nicolas IV 233.

[46] Nelson to Elgin, 31 March 1800; Pettigrew I. Nelson to Hamilton, Nicolas IV 213.

[47] Keith to Nepean, 18 April 1800. PRO ADM 1/401. Nelson to Keith acknowledging this order, 9 May 1800, NMM KEI/18/4.

[48] Nelson to Elgin, Nicolas IV 214.

[49] Nelson to Goodall, Nicolas 206.

[50] Grenville to Hamilton, 22 December 1799, PRO FO 70/12. Hamilton to Grenville, 22 March 1800, FO 70/13.

[51] Young to Keith, 30 March 1800. Keith Papers, NRS 1950, 214.

[52] Spencer to Nelson, Nicolas IV 242.

[53] *Autobiography of Miss Cornelia Knight etc*, two vols, London, 1861, I 146.

[54] Nelson was at Torbay on 1 February 1801 when he received news of the birth in London of Horatia.

[55] Nelson to Davison, Nicolas VII cxcvii. Nicolas IV 241 note.

[56] Nelson to Spencer, Nicolas VII cxcviii.

[57] Keith to Nelson, 17 June 1800. Keith Papers, NRS 1950, 116.

[58] Hamilton to Keith, 16 June, and Keith to Nelson, 19 June 1800; Keith Papers 116–7. Nelson had earlier written to Keith saying he was sure he would not be sent home in a store ship or anything less than a large frigate. (Nelson to Keith, 3 April 1800, NMM KEI/18/4.)

[59] Keith to Admiralty, 22 June 1800. Keith Papers, NRS 1950, 117.

[60] Pettigrew I 380.

[61] Pettigrew I 374

[62] Nelson to Keith, 1 July and two letters of 11 July 1800. Keith Papers 122–3. NMM KEI/18/4.

[63] Spencer to Keith, Naish 525.

[64] Keith to Addington, 15 May 1802. NMM KEI L/36.

[65] Keith to Paget, 20 June 1800, Keith Papers 62. Spencer to Keith, 18 August 1800, Naish 526.

[66] *Diary of Sir John Moore*, ed J. F. Maurice, London, 1904, I 367.

[67] Minto III 140.

[68] Moore I 366.

[69] Knight I 319–23. These details of the journey come from a letter written by Miss Knight to Sir Edward Berry from Leghorn, Ancona, and Trieste from 2 July to 9 August 1800. This letter (Nicolas IV 263) is likely to be more reliable than the rest of Miss Knight's account, which was put together after her death from her many journals and from an unfinished autobiography.

[70] Barge's crew to Nelson, Nicolas IV 262. Nelson on the king's ounces of silver, Nicolas III 270.

[71] Minto III 147

[72] *Remains of the Late Mrs Richard Trench*, London, 1862, 106–13.

[73] *Meine Freuden in Sachsen* by Thomas Kosegarten, Leipzig, 1801.

[74] Knight I 152.

[75] *Sanfelice*: Giglioli 379. *Morning Post*, 15 September 1800. *Füger*: Walker 104.

[76] Walker 236.

[77] Harrison II 262.

[78] *Naval Chronicle* 1800, III 180.

Notes to Chapter 19: THE HOMECOMING

[1] Codicil to Nelson's will and other accounts, 6 March 1801, Morrison p 405.

[2] Knight I 162.

[3] Nelson to Fanny, Naish 495.

[4] Nelson to Fanny, Naish 496.

[5] *Morning Post*, 8 November, and *Whitehall Evening Post*, 6–8 November 1800.

[6] *Morning Chronicle*, 13 November and *Whitehall Evening Post*, 6–8 November 1800; Harrison II 272 and 274; *Bell's Weekly Messenger*, 16 November 1800, and *Morning Post*, 20 November 1800.

[7] Pettigrew I 400.

[8] Nicolas IV 278 note. W.H. Bourne to J. Spencer Smith [received 3 January 1801]. Monmouth.

[9] Nelson to Heard, Nicolas IV 81, and Nelson to Heard, 20 September 1800, Monmouth E 79.

[10] *Diary of Frances, Lady Shelley*, ed. Richard Edgcumbe, two vols, 1912, 78.

[11] *Morning Chronicle*, 19 and 20 November 1800.

[12] 'Smoking Attitudes', 18 November 1800. Reproduced in catalogue to the exhibition *Vases and Volcanoes*, British Museum, 1996, 299.

[13] *Morning Post* and *Morning Herald*, 25 November 1800.

[14] *Bell's*, 7 December; *Whitehall Evening Post*, 4–6 December; *Morning Post*, 4 December 1800.

[15] *Naval Miscellany* 2, NRS, 1912, 329. Compare Captain W.H. Smyth in *Colburn's United Services Magazine*, May 1845, 25, where he says Nelson 'was never very nice about a ship or its kilter'.

[16] *Lieutenants:* St Vincent to Nepean, 22 September 1800, NMM NEP/5. *Bowen:* St Vincent to Nepean, 28 November 1800, BL Add 36, 708, and St Vincent to Emma Hamilton, Pettigrew I 166.

[17] St Vincent to Nepean, 25 October 1799, NMM NEP/5.

[18] Henry Trollope, who passed for lieutenant in the examination next after Nelson's, was in command of the cutter *Kite* in 1779 when he took two prizes laden with timber. Since he was under direct admiralty orders no flag officer took a share, and Trollope took his full three-eighths of the value. He thus gained £30,000. He died in 1839 a full admiral and a knight of the Bath.

[19] DNB.

[20] St Vincent to Nelson, 20 November 1800, BL 31,167, St Vincent's Letter Book (Secret). Prize money £13,000, Morrison 542.

[21] St Vincent to Nelson, Tucker II 115, Pettigrew 408.

[22] *Morning Post*, 1 and 11 December 1800.

[23] *Morning Herald*, 5 January 1801. Castelcica to Grenville, 30 December 1800, PRO FO 70/14. The letter said, in the diplomatic French of the time: 'Le roi ... a donné a milord Nelson la faculté de designer pour son successeur telle personne qu'il voudra, en le choississant même hors de ses parents, et cela dans le cas que des descendants de son corps existent ou qu'ils n'existent point.'

[24] Eyre Matcham 181.

[25] Morrison 673, 678.

[26] St Vincent to Nepean, 30 November 1800, *Spencer Papers* IV, NRS 59, London 1924, 21.

[27] Harrison II 278.

[28] Pettigrew I 392. Original in the Mr and Mrs Harry Spiro collection, New York.

[29] Nelson to Spencer and to Nepean, Nicolas 273–4.

[30] Nicolas VII 392, giving Haslewood's account of 1846.

[31] Nelson's account with Marsh, Page & Creed shows a payment to Fanny of £400 on 13 January 1801. Six other sums were paid to her that year, making £1,500 in all. From the beginning of 1802 she was paid quarterly sums of £400; Morrison II 392–8. Apart from this, he gave her the income on the £4,000 left to her by her uncle Herbert, making £1,800 a year in all. He stated in a holograph memorandum (BL Add 28,333, Naish 580, 4 March 1801) that he was allowing her half his annual income, which was £3,600 after tax. A draft of Fanny's letter of thanks, undated, is at Monmouth (E 981), Naish 588.

[32] Nicolas (II 353) does not name Mrs (later Lady) Berry, quoting 'the widow of one of [Nelson's] bravest followers', but he often quotes her on other topics, and the context and manner strongly suggest her.

[33] St Vincent to Nelson, 15 December 1800, NRS 55, 1922, 319.

[34] St Vincent to Nepean, 17 January 1801, *Naval Miscellany* II, NRS, 1912.

[35] St Vincent to J. Kaye, 17 January 1801. BL Add 31,167, f177.

[36] Nelson to St Vincent, Nicolas VII ccxxxvii.

[37] St Vincent to Nelson, 21 January 1801, BL Add 31,167, f179. Nelson to Davison, Nicolas VII cci.

[38] Nelson to Emma, 1,3,4, and 5 February 1801. Morrison 504–5 and 507–8.

[39] Nelson to Emma, Morrison 528.

[40] *Horatia Nelson*, by Winifred Gerin, Oxford, 1970, 289, for Horatia's view of the foundling as expressed to Nicolas, 7 November 1844, when she was Mrs Philip Ward, the wife of a clergyman. See also Nicolas VII 369–96 appendix. Commander J.G.B. Swinley wrote to *The Times* on 19 August 1999 saying that when he was director of the foundling hospital in the 1970s he examined the records and found that no girl admitted was born within three months of Horatia, but that Sir William and Lady Hamilton did attend the foundling chapel soon after Copenhagen, and that to mark the event a baby born Mary James was sponsored by Lady Hamilton and christened Emma Hamilton, it being usual for children to be given their sponsor's name. See also 'Horatio Nelson and Lady Hamilton's Twins', by Lesley Edwards, *Mariner's Mirror*, September 2000. She also believes the twin to be mythical.

[41] Nelson to Emma, Pettigrew I 449.

[42] Emma Hamilton to Davison, 24 July 1804. BL Add 40,739.

[43] Nelson to Emma, [8 February 1801] Morrison 511.

[44] *Scolding words and black stockings*: Morrison 514–15.

[45] Nelson's letters 8–20 February 1801, passim. Morrison 511–26.

[46] Hamilton to Nelson, 19 February 1801, Naish 576.

[47] Nelson to Emma, Morrison 530.

[48] *Love-begotten*: Nelson to Emma, 10 [?] March 1801, Nicolas VII 374. *Dear wife*: Nelson to Emma, 1 March 1801, Morrison 532.

[49] Betsy Wynne, 3 March 1801, *Wynne Diaries*.

[50] Nelson to Fanny, 4 March 1801. The draft is in NMM AGC, Morrison 536, and Naish 580. The original, with Fanny's endorsement, is in BL Add 28,333 (a collection of documents which includes Fanny's wedding certificate) where the top half of the letter, referring to Josiah's wishing to break Nelson's neck, is cut off, and the fragment begins, '. . . or am left in the Baltic . . .'

[51] On Nisbet in the Mediterranean, see master of *Thalia* to Nisbet and to Navy Board, Naish 516–19. Also Nelson to Troubridge, 7 and 11 March and 27 April 1801, NRS 20, 1902, 415, 419, 430.

[52] William Nelson to Emma, I Pettigrew 429.

[53] Naish 578–9.

[54] Susannah Bolton to Fanny, Monmouth E669, Naish 582.

[55] Susannah Bolton to Fanny, Monmouth E670, Naish 587.

[56] Revd Edmund Nelson to Fanny, Naish 583.

Notes to Chapter 20: CHAMPION OF ENGLAND IN THE NORTH

[1] Nelson to Emma, Morrison 504.

[2] Nelson to Emma, Pettigrew I 439.

[3] Nelson to Nepean, Nicolas VII cciv.

[4] *Morning Post*, 31 January 1801. See also *Morning Chronicle*, 20 December 1800.

[5] Nelson to Emma, Morrison 532, 533.

6 Nelson to Emma, parts in Pettigrew I 443, 445. Full text of dream letter, 17 March, NMM MON/1, collection of Nicholas Monsarrat, author of *The Cruel Sea*.

7 Nelson to Davison, Nicolas IV 294.

8 Nelson to Parker, Nicolas IV 295.

9 Orders for attack, Nicolas IV 304.

10 Nicolas IV 315.

11 From Thomas Wallis, purser of *Elephant*, Nicolas IV 310 note.

12 Nicolas IV 316.

13 Clowes V 438.

14 Nelson to Emma, 2 April 1801. BL Eg 1614.

15 Nicolas IV 326

16 Nelson to Davison, 4 April, Nicolas VII ccv. Nelson to Emma, 2 April 1801, BL Eg 1614 f 34.

17 Nelson to Addington, 4 April, Nicolas IV 332. A minute of Nelson's conversation with the prince, and eighteen letters between Lindholm and Nelson, are in the William L. Clements Library, University of Michigan.

18 Nelson to Emma, 4 April, BL Eg 1614.

19 Nelson to Emma, 4 April, Pettigrew II 654.

20 Nicolas IV 326.

21 Nelson to Lindholm, Morrison 558, 562.

22 Nelson to Emma, 9 April, BL Eg 1614.

23 Tyson to Nelson, 8 April, BL Add 34,918 f28.

24 The nature of Parker's signal is explored in *The Great Gamble etc*, by Dudley Pope, London, 1972, appendix I, 514.

25 Young to Keith, 21 May 1801, *Keith Papers II*, NRS, 1950, 373.

26 Stewart to Clinton, 6 April 1801. NMM AGC/14/27.

27 *Cumloden Papers*, see note 30.

28 Harrison II 295, account of Fergusson, surgeon of *Elephant*.

29 Clarke and M'Arthur II 266–7, 'by an officer who was with Lord Nelson'.

30 Southey, *Life of Nelson*, 1813 and many later editions, chapter VII. Southey collated the accounts of Harrison and Clarke and M'Arthur, and attributed the resulting version to Fergusson. Stewart's letter to Clinton is in NMM AGC/14/27. His contemporary journal was reprinted in *The Cumloden Papers*, Edinburgh, 1871. The Hon. William Stewart (1774–1827) was the second son of the Earl of Galloway. At the time of the Baltic expedition he was twenty-seven. He was MP for Saltash, Wigtonshire, later fought with Wellington in the Peninsula, was knighted in 1813, and rose to be a lieutenant general.

31 *Cumloden Papers* 25.

32 Nicolas IV 311.

33 Nelson to Emma, 2 April 1801, BL Eg 1614.

34 *Wynne Diaries* III 41, 43.

35 Fischer to crown prince, 3 April, Nicolas IV 320. Nelson to Addington, 8 May, Nicolas IV 360.

36 *Morning Chronicle*, 21 April. Fischer's letter was printed in London newspapers of 17 April.

37 Nelson to Addington, 4 April, Nicolas IV 332. 'It was by your own desire that I trouble you with a letter ...'

[38] Nelson to Emma, 4 April 1801, BL Eg 1614.

[39] Nelson to Addington, 8 May 1801 (a copy), Nicolas IV 360; and Nelson to Emma, the original, with his additions, BL Eg 1614.

[40] Young to Keith, 21 May 1801, *Keith Papers* II, NRS, 1950, 373.

[41] *The Life of Nelson etc*, by Captain A.T. Mahan, USN, London, second edition, revised, 1899, 486.

[42] *Historical Memoirs of My Own Time*, by Nathaniel Wraxall, London, 1815, I 230.

[43] *Morning Chronicle*, 17 April 1801.

[44] Same.

[45] *Morning Post*, 22 April, and *Morning Chronicle*, 22 and 25 April 1801.

[46] *Sole merit*: St Vincent to Rose, NRS 55, 1922, 63. See also Nelson to Addington, 5 May 1801, Nicolas IV 355.

[47] Minto II 219.

[48] Nelson to Davison, Nicolas IV 416.

[49] Nelson to St Vincent, and to Davison, Nicolas IV 336, VII ccvii.

[50] Spencer to Fanny, Naish 584. Fanny to Nelson, Monmouth E980, Naish 585. Nelson to Davison, 23 April 1801, Nicolas VII ccix. Nelson to Emma, 23 April 1801, BL Eg 1614. Fanny's letter exists only in draft, with two other letters in which she made overtures for a reconciliation, but the Monmouth MSS also includes her note that Nelson returned her last letter (see note 31, chapter 21) but kept the previous two; so the letter of 23 April was sent.

[51] Nelson to Emma, 5 May 1801, BL Eg 1614.

[52] Nelson to St Vincent, Nicolas IV 371. Nelson to Emma, 5 April 1801, BL Eg 1614.

[53] Maurice Nelson to Catherine Matcham, NRS 55, 1922, 93. *Navy Board Officials 1680–1832*, ed. J. M. Collinge, London, 1978, shows that Maurice became chief clerk (Bills and Accounts) on 27 March.

[54] St Vincent to Nelson, 25 April 1801, Letter Book, BL Add 31,169. Rose 347.

[55] Revd Edmund Nelson to Davison, three letters, 7 April 1801 and after, NMM CRK/22 (HAM 82). Nelson to Davison, Nicolas IV 378 and 391. Nelson, codicil to will, Nicolas VII ccxxxviii, and Nelson to Mrs Maurice Nelson, Morrison 605.

[56] Russian admiral and Pahlen (Russian minister) to Nelson, Nicolas IV 377, 393.

[57] Nelson to St Vincent, 7 May, Nicolas IV 359; Nelson to Ball, 4 June, Nicolas IV 401. *Spasm*: Nelson to Emma, 8 June 1801, BL Eg 1614 f8. *Nails*: Nelson to Emma, 13 June 1801, Pettigrew II 101.

[58] Nelson to St Vincent, 12 June 1801, Nicolas IV 412.

[59] Revd Edmund Nelson to Nelson, 12 June 1801, NMM CRK 9 (N 9–20.) The verse is from *Hebrews* III 13, AV, 1611.

Notes to Chapter 21: NOT SINCE THE ARMADA BUSINESS

[1] BL Eg 1623 f27. Nelson called himself Henry in his letter to Emma, 2 April 1801, Laughton II 16.

[2] Nelson to R. Nelson, Nicolas IV 421.

[3] Patent of Barony of Nile and Hilborough, Nicolas IV 539.

[4] *Morning Chronicle*, 8 August 1801.

[5] Nelson to Addington, Nicolas IV 475.

[6] *Destruction*: Nelson memorandum, Nicolas IV 425 and note. *Armada business*: Revd Edmund Nelson to Catherine, 27 July 1801, Eyre Matcham 190.

[7] *Morning Herald*, 7 August 1801; *Morning Chronicle*, 6 August 1801; Nelson to Emma, 4 August 1801, BL Eg 1614; Nelson to Addington, Nicolas IV 439; *Morning Chronicle*, 8 August 1801; Nelson to Emma, Morrison 612; Nelson to St Vincent, Nicolas IV 450.

[8] *Morning Chronicle*, 13 August 1801; Nelson to St Vincent, Nicolas IV 456; Nelson's plan, 15 August 1801, BL Add 31,182 and Nicolas IV 460.

[9] Nelson to Emma, Morrison 614.

[10] *Morning Herald*, 19 August 1801; unnamed French source from *Morning Herald*, 28 August 1801.

[11] *Morning Chronicle*, 25 August 1801.

[12] St Vincent's message: newspapers of 17 August 1801, Nicolas IV 471.

[13] *Naval Chronicle*, VII 32, January–July 1802.

[14] Letters of Nelson to Hill (6 September 1801), and to St Vincent, Nepean, and Davison, Nicolas IV 484–9. Hill's second letter appeared in *The County Herald and Weekly Advertiser* [London], No. 515, 31 October 1801. No copy is in the BL newspaper library. Mr Anthony Cross, of the Warwick Leadlay Gallery, Greenwich, has a copy, which he kindly allowed me to see. Other documents are in NMM CRK/14, 50–53. In one note, Hill tells Nelson that a relation of his was killed at Boulogne, where his life and 'many others' were 'thrown away'.

[15] Nelson to Keith, 14 September 1801, NMM KEI 18/4; Helvoet – Nepean to Nelson, Morrison 619; St Vincent to Nelson, 14 and 22 September, BL Add 31,169.

[16] Nelson to Davison, Nicolas IV 489. Nelson's accounts for 1801, Morrison II p 394.

[17] Nelson to Baird, St Vincent, and Davison, Nicolas IV 497; St Vincent to Nelson, 29 September 1801, BL Add 31,169.

[18] Nelson to St Vincent, 23 September 1801, Nicolas VII ccxxx. And to Nepean, NMM CRK/15, September 1801.

[19] William Nelson to Emma, 23 August and 6 September 1801, *Letters* 1814.

[20] Revd Edmund Nelson to Fanny, 21 August 1801, Naish 500, and to Nelson, 23 September 1801, NMM BRP/5.

[21] Nelson to Emma, 26 September 1801, Naish 590.

[22] Naish 592.

[23] Fanny to Edmund Nelson, [October 1801], Naish 594. This is from a draft in Fanny's hand at Monmouth, E 689. At the end she wrote, and then crossed out, the following passage: 'Be assured if at any time my attentions or my house can afford the least accommodation I shall be happy in rendering it – and I think I may promise you shall always find me the same. And thank god I have not been led into temptation.' There is nothing in her other letters of the time to elucidate the last sentence.

[24] Revd Edmund Nelson to Nelson, 8 October 1801, Morrison 632.

[25] Nelson to Emma, 10 October 1801. NMM MAM 1.

[26] Emma to Mrs William Nelson, [11 or 12 October] Naish 595.

[27] Nelson to Emma, 13 October 1801, Monmouth E112.

[28] Revd Edmund Nelson to Fanny, 17 October 1801, Naish 595.

[29] Addington to Nelson, 8 October 1801, Nicolas IV 507. Nelson to Emma ('set of

beasts'), 15 October 1801, extract from letter in Sotheby's catalogue of 6–7 May 1858, NMM CRK/21.

[30] St Vincent to Nelson, 29 September 1801, BL Add 31,169 f46. Tobin was made post in 1802.

[31] Fanny to Nelson, 18 December 1801. Monmouth E 979. Naish 596, who also prints a facsimile.

[32] Nelson to Emma, 20 October 1801, Nicolas IV 515.

[33] *Parliamentary History of England*, London, 1820, vol 36. Nicolas IV 487.

[34] Nelson to Ross, Nicolas IV 487.

[35] Russell, 248.

[36] As note 33, 23 November 1801.

[37] Nelson to Sutton, 31 October 1801, Nicolas IV 520.

[38] Morrison II, p395. Nelson to Davison, 14 September 1801, Nicolas IV 489.

[39] Minto III 242.

[40] Catherine Matcham to Nelson, 14 February 1802, Morrison 655. Revd Edmund Nelson to Nelson, 26 February and 23 March 1802, NMM CRK/9: the second is printed in Naish 598.

[41] BL Eg 1623 f32.

[42] Eyre Matcham 194.

[43] Nelson to Matcham, 28 April 1802, NMM MAM/1.

[44] Susannah Bolton to Fanny, (15 May 1802), Monmouth, Naish 599.

Notes to Chapter 22: SO MUCH FOR GRATITUDE

[1] Nelson to Davison, Nicolas VII ccii.

[2] Nelson to Davison, Nicolas VII ccvi.

[3] BL Add 31,168 St Vincent letter book (commanders-in-chief).

[4] Pettigrew I 86.

[5] Clowes IV 167. Fanny to Nelson, Naish 265.

[6] Jervis to Nepean, 4 October 1796. NMM NEP/7.

[7] Nelson to St Vincent and to Hamilton, Nicolas III 27, 30.

[8] Nelson to St Vincent, Nicolas III 150, 183. Nelson to Spencer, and to St Vincent, Nicolas III 188, 133.

[9] Nelson to Spencer, Nicolas VII clxxi.

[10] Troubridge to Nelson, letters of March and April 1799, BL Add 34,910.

[11] Nelson to Troubridge, 20 March 1798, BL Add 34,910.

[12] *Personal Memoirs etc*, by Pryse Lockhart Gordon, 2 vols, London, 1830, I 226.

[13] Troubridge to Nelson, Nicolas III 358–9.

[14] Nelson to Troubridge, Nicolas IV 34. Spencer to Nelson, Naish 511.

[15] Troubridge to Nelson, letters of 1, 5, 7, and 8 January 1800, Nicolas IV 166–7 notes.

[16] Troubridge to Emma, Morrison 441.

[17] Troubridge to Nelson, Nicolas IV 195 note.

[18] Troubridge to Nelson, 7 April [1800], BL Add 34,917 f 112.

[19] Nelson to Troubridge, Nicolas IV 206.

[20] Troubridge to Nelson, Naish 523.

21 St Vincent to Nelson, 14 February 1801, BL Add 31,167 St Vincent letter book (secret).
22 Nelson to Emma, Morrison 516.
23 Naish 558. Knight I 158.
24 St Vincent to Nelson, Nicolas IV 291 note.
25 Nelson wrote 22 letters to Troubridge from 7 March to 23 June 1801. The series is now in the Huntington Library, San Marino. It was printed in *Naval Miscellany*, NRS 20, 1902, 414–35.
26 Same. Nelson to Troubridge, 7, 8, 10, 11 March 1801.
27 Same. Nelson to Troubridge, 13, 20 and 29 March, 9 and 23 April 1801.
28 St Vincent to Nelson, 31 May 1801, Nicolas IV 373.
29 Nelson to Emma, Nicolas IV 509.
30 Nelson to Emma, Morrison 634.
31 20 October 1801, Nicolas IV 515–16.
32 Nelson to Emma, Pettigrew II 222.
33 Nelson to Emma, 13 August 1804, Morrison 777.

Notes to Chapter 23: PLANTING TREES WITH ONE HAND

1 Nelson to Emma, Morrison 513.
2 Hamilton to Minto, Naish 513, 522. Hamilton to Greville, Morrison 444.
3 Hamilton to Greville, 4 August 1799. PRO FO 70/12.
4 Greville to Grenville, 4 January 1800 and to Frere (under secretary at the foreign office), 30 January 1800. PRO FO 70/13.
5 Morrison 550, 552, 554. An account of Hamilton's paintings and sales, by Kim Sloan, forms chapter 5 of *Vases and Volcanoes*, London, 1996, the catalogue of an exhibition at the British Museum of Hamilton and his collections.
6 Hamilton to Greville, Morrison 651.
7 *Horatia Nelson*, by Winfred Gerin, Oxford, 1970, 41.
8 Nelson to Emma, Morrison 779.
9 Seven letters to and from Nelson, St Vincent, Addington, Davison, and lord mayor, 20 November–18 December 1801. Nicolas IV 524–534 and notes.
10 Nelson to Addington, Nicolas IV 534 and V 3.
11 Addington to Nelson, 30 May 1802. NMM BRP/6. Emma to Bedford, 13 February [1802], BL Add 31,182.
12 Harrison II 382.
13 Hamilton to Emma, Morrison 684.
14 Nelson to lord mayor, Nicolas V 34.
15 William Nelson to Nelson, 25 March 1803. NMM CRK/9 (N 5–8).
16 Nelson to Addington, Nicolas V 47. Nelson's prize money and accounts, Morrison II 395–9.
17 Nelson to Addington and to Rose, Nicolas V 59 and 65.
18 Nelson to Davison, Nicolas V 42.
19 Nelson to Stephens, 10 February 1803. He took some care with this letter. Three versions exist. A draft in Emma's hand is at Monmouth, and a transcript in NMM TRN 30/3. A draft in Nelson's hand, and a clerk's copy with one interpolated sentence and an added postscript (as in Nicolas V 43), are at NMM PHB/P/19.

20 *Sketches of the State of Manners and Opinions in the French republic etc*, by Helen Maris Williams, London, 1801, 2 vols, is in BL Add MS 34,991, with ink notes in Nelson's hand in the margins.

21 Nelson to Keith, Spencer, and Nepean, Nicolas III 392, 406, 410.

22 'Pages which are lies'; memorandum in NMM PHB/P/19.

23 Hamilton to Ruffo, 24 June 1799. Sacchinelli, facsimile, and Gutteridge 205.

24 Cirillo to Emma Hamilton, 3 July 1799. Morrison 403.

25 Bone's enamel is now in the Wallace Collection, London. The collection's *Catalogue of Miniatures*, London, 1980, 306, gives the provenance and history of the enamel and the oil. But it has also been suggested that the painting Nelson bought was that of Emma as St Cecilia, by Romney. See Nelson to Emma, Morrison 543; and Nelson to Davison, Nicolas VII cciii.

26 Gérin 61.

27 Hamilton to Sir Joseph Banks, 13 September 1799. BL Add 34,038.

28 Gérin 62. Also Nicolas VII 377, where the history of Horatia, as far as it was known in 1846, is given.

29 Nicolas V 51. *A Brief Memoir of the Life and Writings of William Marsden* [admiralty secretary], London, privately published, 1838.

30 Nelson to St Vincent, 19 May 1803, Nicolas V 67.

31 Nelson to Gardner, 19 May, and to St Vincent, 18 May 1803, and log of *Victory* 20–21 May 1803. Nicolas V 66–7 and V 68 note.

Notes to Chapter 24: THE LONG WATCH, AND THE GRAND RACE OF GLORY

1 *Parliamentary History of England*, vol 36, 23 May 1803.

2 Nicolas V 67, 187, 453; VI 71.

3 Nelson to lord mayor, 1 August 1804, Nicolas VI 125.

4 Nicolas V 406

5 *Sacred majesty*: Nicolas V 84. *Mouse assisted lion*: Nelson to Acton, Nicolas V 99. *Last drop of blood*: Nelson to Ferdinand, Nicolas V 331.

6 Nicolas V 84, 118.

7 Nicolas VI 31.

8 Nicolas VI 317.

9 Nicolas V 254.

10 Eyre Matcham 209. Morrison 232.

11 Morrison 713 and 778. In a letter of 9 September 1804, Nelson tells Emma he hopes to live happily 'many many years with you and my dear Ha'; the last three words are crossed out by some hand in the MS but just legible: BL Eg 1614 f106.

12 NMM Phillipps papers 29,914, where there are 55 letters from Nelson to Emma.

13 Nelson to Emma, 6 October 1803. Morrison 733.

14 Nicolas VI 41.

15 Nicolas VI 279.

16 Nelson to Kingsmill, 4 October 1804, Nicolas VI 133. Two other versions, listing only the wounds, as quoted here, are in NMM TRN 30/3 (transcript of MS at Monmouth), and in BL Eg 1614 f91, on black edged mourning paper, dated, in pencil, 1802. The last is the one reproduced in facsimile.

[17] Nicolas VI 19,126.

[18] St Vincent to Nelson, 22 and 29 November 1803, 21 December 1803, 25 January 1804, and 4 March 1804. BL Add 31,169.

[19] Morrison 813.

[20] Nicolas V 512 and 180, and VI 483.

[21] PRO ADM 1/410, f490. See Nicolas VI 416 and VII 58 (Nelson to Sotheron at Naples), who suppresses the names of the lieutenant and his father. Captain Tyler commanded the *Tonnant* at Trafalgar and was badly wounded, but lived to become a knight of the Bath and a full admiral. His absconding son served in the East Indies from 1809, was given his only real promotion, to commander, in 1812, was made post captain on his retirement in 1844, and died 1846. See O'Byrne.

[22] Nicolas V 285.

[23] Nelson to Davison, 13 January 1804, Nicolas V 370. Judgment in King's Bench, 14 November 1803, reported in *Naval Chronicle*, x 432. A copy of the pleadings is at Monmouth. Transcripts of Nelson's brief, memorials and letters of Keith, St Vincent, and Nelson, counsels' opinons etc are in the National Archives, Washington DC, Record group 45, 448B.

[24] Nicolas V 219; VI 244, 307.

[25] Nelson to Ball, 5 December 1804, Nicolas VI 286. 'Done the state some service' – *Othello* V, 2.

[26] Nicolas VI 289.

[27] Orde to Melville, 27 March 1805, and admiralty endorsement; Orde to Barham, 20 and 22 May 1805; Barham to Orde, 21 May 1805. *Letters and Papers of Lord Barham*, III, ed. J. K. Laughton, NRS, 1911, 303–9.

[28] Nicolas VI 148, 149, 156, 168, 176, 192, 221.

[29] Nicolas VI 214.

[30] Nelson to Gen. Villettes, Nicolas VI, 189.

[31] Morrison 783.

[32] Nelson to admiralty, 30 December 1804, acknowledging permission, Nicolas VI 307; and to Hugh Elliot, 'profound *secret*', 13 January 1805, Nicolas VI 320.

[33] Nicolas VI 307.

[34] Morrison 806.

[35] Morrison 819.

[36] *Morning Herald*, 18 August 1804.

[37] Nicolas V 363, 252.

[38] *Pat on back*: Rose I 241. Bulkeley to Nelson, 12 March 1800, and to Emma, 26 October 1804: both in Houghton Library, Harvard, MS Eng 196.5 PF.

[39] Nelson to Melville, 10 March 1805, Nicolas VI 353. Also V 7, 171, 481, 487 note, VI 348.

[40] Nelson to Simon Taylor of Jamaica (whom he had known for 30 years), 10 June 1805, Nicolas VI 450.

[41] Nicolas VI 414, 419, 431, 455.

[42] Nicolas VI 460, 472, 478 and VII 12. Brigadier general Robert Brereton had served as a major with Nelson at Calvi in 1794. His message was after all forgotten, and he rose to be a lieutenant general.

[43] Nelson to Davison, 24 July 1805, Nicolas VI 494.

[44] Nelson's diary, Nicolas VI 471.

[45] Nelson's diary, Nicolas VI 475.

[46] Nicolas VII 5, 13.

[47] Sarah Connor to Emma, 'tuesday' [20 August 1805], Morrison 828. The MS is in the Nelson collection at Lloyds of London, in whose catalogue it is more correctly transcribed at p 211, and that is the text used here.

[48] Minto III 362.

[49] Eyre Matcham 230.

[50] Bills for feather bed and carpet, paid 10 September 1805, and for embroidered stars, paid 7 September 1805, Monmouth E178 and E400. Coffin, Harrison II 468.

Notes to Chapter 25: A LEGACY TO MY KING AND COUNTRY

[1] Emma to Lady Bolton, Nelson's niece, Nicolas VII 28 note.

[2] Nelson to Captain Keats, Nicolas VII 15.

[3] Harrison II 458.

[4] Nicolas V 371 note. This is on the authority of Haslewood, Nelson's solicitor, who gave this account to Nicolas forty years later. He said Nelson told him of this conversation with Pitt the day after it took place. Haslewood is perhaps not the most reliable of witnesses. He also told Nicolas that Lady Hamilton was not Horatia's mother, and that he knew the mother's name but was prevented by a sense of honour from disclosing it. (Nicolas VII 369.) He may of course have believed this.

[5] *Seeing to door*: Eyre Matcham 233. Nelson to Rose, Nicolas VII 80. *Statesman and warrior*: Eyre Matcham 235 note.

[6] Emma to Rose, 4 November 1804, Rose I 242.

[7] Nicolas VII 18, 28, 29.

[8] Nelson to admiralty, Nicolas VII 98.

[9] *Correspondence and Diaries of John Wilson Croker* [friend of Canning; later secretary to admiralty], London, 1885, II 233.

[10] Minto III 370.

[11] Nicolas VII 25, 54, 36.

[12] Nicolas VII 39, 40.

[13] Abbé Campbell to Nelson, Morrison 834; Nelson to Campbell, Nicolas VII 92.

[14] Nicolas II 337.

[15] *Misery*: Nelson to Emma, 11 October 1805, Pierpont Morgan Library, New York, MA 321. *Affliction*: Nicolas VII 57.

[16] Nicolas VII 142.

[17] Nelson to Emma, 1 October 1805, BL Eg 1614 f121. Nicolas VII 60. See appendix B.

[18] Morrison 843.

[19] Nelson to Rose, 6 October 1805, Nicolas VII 80, now in Karpeles MSS Library, Santa Barbara, Calif.

[20] Nicolas 71 note, 131.

[21] Troude, *Batailles Navales de la France*, III, cites Villeneuve's correspondence.

[22] Clowes III 165.

[23] Nicolas VII 139.

[24] There are a hundred accounts of the battle of Trafalgar. Those drawn on here are from Nicolas VII, who relies mainly on James but also cites other English accounts,

and quotes at length from the logs of many ships. He also gives a full French report from *Monumens des Victoires et Conquêtes*, and a translation of seven Spanish accounts and documents. In the centenary year of the battle, *The Times* published two series of articles from 14–21 July and from 19–30 September 1905. An excellent modern account of the battle, its strategy and tactics, is in *The Price of Admiralty*, by John Keegan, London and New York, 1988. Another is *Trafalgar: the Nelson Touch*, by David Howarth, London, 1969.

[25] Nicolas VII 147, 225.

[26] Blackwood to his wife, 22 October 1805, Nicolas VII 224. See also H. Wells who wrote from the *Thunderer* at Gibraltar to his wife (?) on 29 October 1805: 'I very much fear his honours were the cause of his death as he evidently was picked off from the rest wearing his stars in action, which in my opinion was rather indiscreet': Monmouth E 464.

[27] On different times, Nicolas VII 157–8 note. The *Spartiate's* log gives the time as 12.59, an extraordinary difference, but adds a note that the watch by which the times of the action were taken appeared to be 34 minutes fast. The times recorded by different ships at the Nile were just as various.

[28] Lieut Pryce Cumby, *Lloyds*, 455 note.

[29] Beatty's account of the death, Nicolas VII 244–54.

[30] Capt Sir George Westphal to Nicolas, in 1844. Nicolas VII 249 note.

[31] Nicolas VII 226.

[32] Decrès to Louis Buonaparte, 23 brumaire, an 14. NMM AGC/18/24

[33] *Morning Herald*, 9 November 1805, quoting *Le Moniteur*, Paris.

[34] Codicil, Nicolas VII 140. Lady Hamilton often claimed she had seen to the provisioning of the Nile squadron. It is more likely that Acton quietly allowed Hamilton to provision at Sicilian ports; and in any case Nelson had orders to take anything he needed. Emma probably influenced the decision, but no more, but Nelson believed her claim. On 17 May 1798, Nelson did write to Emma (BL Eg 1614) saying he had kissed a letter from the queen, which Emma had sent him, but we do not know what the letter said. Emma endorsed Nelson's reply: 'This letter I received after I had sent the queen's letter for receiving our ships in their ports – for the queen had decided to act in opposition to the king who would not then break with France & our fleet must have gone down the Mediterranean to have watered & the battle of the Nile would not have been fought for the French fleet wou'd have got back to Toulon.' Emma's claims became greater with each successive petition for a pension. By 1813 she was memorialising the prince regent that she had also enabled Ball to hold Malta, 'which he cou'd not do but for the prompt supply of grain provided by the memorialist at her own expence!' (Lloyds 232.) There is no evidence she did anything of the sort. See Walter Sichel, *Emma, Lady Hamilton*, 1905, 201–22 and 486, and Oman, 694–5 note, who both consider this matter in detail.

[35] Nelson to William Suckling, Nicolas I 186.

[36] St Vincent to Nelson, 22 November 1803. BL Add 31,169.

[37] Nelson to St Vincent, Nicolas V 364.

[38] Nelson to Parker, Nicolas V 245.

[39] Undated note, BL Add 29,914 f303; and St Vincent to Collingwood, 19 July 1806, BL Add 31,167 (St Vincent's letter book, secret), f232.

[40] Nelson to Thompson, 23 February 1804. NMM TRN 30/3.

41 Nelson to John Locker, Nicolas IV 271.

Notes to Chapter 26: STATE FUNERAL AND EMPTY CHARIOT

1 *Brief Memoir of . . . William Marsden*, ed. Elizabeth Marsden, London, 1838.
2 Nicolas VII 302.
3 Barham to Fanny, 6 November 1805. BL Add 28,333.
4 Hamond to Emma, 6 November 1805, Karpeles Manuscript Library, Santa Barbara, Calif. *Morning Chronicle*, 7 November 1805.
5 Heard to Spencer, 9 June 1806, BL Add 38,378, in which are enclosed coloured designs for the arms and insignia of the order. Barham to Pitt, 9 November 1805; *Barham Papers* III, NRS, 1911.
6 *Will of God*: William Nelson to 'My Lord Duke' [probably Hamilton], BL Add 34,992 f28. Nicolas VII 304.
7 Nicolas VII ccxxi.
8 King to Pitt, 11 November 1805, *Letters of George III*, Bonamy Dobree, 1935. Marsden to his brother Alexander, 8 January 1806, as 1 above.
9 William Nelson to Prince of Wales, 18 and 21 November 1805, and Hawkesbury (home secretary) to William Nelson, 12 December 1805, all NMM STW/8.
10 Beatty's report, Nicolas VII 254–62.
11 Tyson to Haslewood, 6, 11, and 12 December 1805, Monmouth E 214, 215, 217.
12 Bishop of Exeter to William Nelson, 12 December 1805, BL Add 34,992.
13 Beatty to Scott, 15 December 1805, and Scott to William Nelson, 20 December 1805, BL Add 34,992.
14 Nicolas VII 259. Tyson to Haslewood, Christmas Day 1805, Monmouth E 222.
15 Scott to Lavington, 26 December 1805. Monmouth E 474.
16 College of Arms RRG LXIII A, ff 22, 27, 29, 32, 33, 61.
17 William Nelson's note, 7 January 1806, NMM STW/8.
18 St Vincent to his sister, 3 January 1806, BL Add 29,915.
19 St Vincent to admiralty [December 1805], PRO ADM 1/581 f 434.
20 *Riding*: St Vincent to Baird, 10 January 1806, NMM PAR 167c.
21 PRO ADM 1/581, December 1805, 'Admirals Unemployed'.
22 Hood to Hawkesbury, 6 January 1806. Monmouth E 387.
23 PRO ADM 1/158. *Morning Chronicle* 7 November 1805 and 11 January 1806. *Morning Herald* 9 January 1806.
24 Marsden to his brother, 8 January 1806, as note 1.
25 Scott to Emma, two letters, 12.30am and later, 9 January 1806. He said of Nelson: 'Lui même fait le siècle.' Morrison 860, 861.
26 *The Times, Morning Post, Morning Chronicle, Morning Herald*, 10 January 1806, and Nicolas VII 406–18.
27 *Morning Chronicle*, 11 January 1806. Scott to Lavington, 14 January 1806, Monmouth E 475.
28 College of Arms RRG XVIIIA, ff 91, 94, 95.
29 *Times* 11 January, and *Chronicle* 10 January 1806.
30 *Times*, 10 January. College of Arms RRG LXIII A; Fanny to Heard, 1 January, endorsed by Heard; and Heard to Fanny, 5 January 1806; Heard advised the

coach should bear Nelson's arms and Fanny's (those of the Woolwards) in a lozenge.

Notes to Chapter 27: THE FOUNDING OF A FAMILY

[1] Revd C. Este to Lady Charlotte Nelson, Morrison 867.

[2] Nelson to Emma, 17 February 1801, BL Eg 1614 f12. Morrison 868.

[3] *Dearest Bess: the Life and Times of Lady Elizabeth Foster*, by Dorothy M. Stuart, London, 1955, 133.

[4] Minto III 374.

[5] *Parliamentary Debates*, 1806, 36, 82.

[6] Warner, *Trafalgar* 168.

[7] Will; Nicolas VII ccxxi. Nelson's estate; Marsh & Creed to Haslewood, 16 December 1805, Monmouth E219.

[8] *Debates* 1806, 101.

[9] Lloyds 225. Nicolas VII 330–42.

[10] *Debates*; Wood, Rose, Francis, Petty, 1806,1149–52.

[11] *Debates* 263.

[12] *Recollections of the life of the Revd A. J. Scott, D.D., Lord Nelson's chaplain*, ed. Margaret and Alfred Gatty, London, 1842, 203ff, 220.

[13] Fanny's dressmaker's bill, Naish 614.

[14] Fanny's legal correspondence, Naish 610–613. St Vincent to his sister, 9 June 1806, BL Add 29,915 f82.

[15] Morrison 890.

[16] Naish 615. St Vincent to sister, 21 January 1807, BL Add 29,915.

[17] *Captain Foote's Vindication of His Conduct . . . in the Bay of Naples etc*, 1807 and 1810; 'but too true', see 1810 edition, p82, and Nicolas III 515.

[18] Letters of William Nelson, M'Arthur, and Clarke, 11 and 16 February 1806, 31 March, 4 April, 28 May, and two undated, BL Add 34,992.

[19] Nelson to Emma, 6 September 1803, NMM STW/1. Nicolas V 260.

[20] William Nelson to Emma, 6 September 1801, BL Eg 1614.

[21] Correspondence between William Nelson, Fisher, and Portland in NMM BRP/2 and BL Add 34,992 ff188, 190, 194. Fisher, a canon of Windsor, married c1787 Dorothea Scrivener, a cousin of the Nelsons; he was a favourite of the king and became bishop of Exeter (1803) and then of Salisbury (1807). Nelson also knew him (Nicolas V 252).

[22] *Dearest Bess etc*, by Dorothy M. Stuart, 1955, 133.

[23] Emma's letters to Davison, NMM LBK/7. *Sunshine*: Emma to William Smith, 22 March 1809, Collection of Morris Wolf, Philadelphia, 1934, NYPL, AN nc 15.

[24] Smith to Perceval, 2 and 3 January 1810, BL Add 38,244.

[25] *A Letter to the Right Hon. Spencer Percival* [sic] *. . . containing an appeal to the British nation on the most wanton and invidious aspersions made by him . . . on the character of the late, ever to be lamented, Lord Nelson*, by Isabella, Countess of Glencairn, Bristol, 1812. BL 814. I. 26. Her memory was inexact: she quoted Nelson as telling her that intelligence reports had been important to him in finding the French fleets at Aboukir in 1798 and in the Caribbean in 1805, which was manifestly not so. Perceval was murdered in the Commons lobby in May 1812 by a bankrupt with a personal grudge.

26 Emma to A. J. Scott, 7 September 1806, *Chambers's Journal*, 2 April 1904, 279.

27 *Letters of Lord Nelson to Lady Hamilton* ... two vols, 1814. Morrison 1054.

28 St Vincent to Baird, 23 May 1814. NMM PAR/167b.

29 Undated cutting from *St James's Chronicle* [?], and Mrs Butt to Pettigrew (biographer), 26 September 1849. Monmouth.

30 Elwin to Pettigrew, 9 September 1849. Monmouth E 351.

31 Nicolas VII 388. The paper, dated 30 August 1805 and given by Emma to a silversmith when she ordered a silver cup for Horatia, said Horatia was Nelson's daughter and that her mother was too great to be mentioned. It was seen by Nicolas c1845.

32 *Times* and *Morning Chronicle*, 1, 2, and 4 August 1814.

33 St Vincent to Keith, 1 March 1817, Monmouth E550.

34 St Vincent to Baird, 18 October 1814, NMM PAR/167c. St Vincent had also said something very like this in an earlier letter to his sister (30 January 1807; NMM AGC/J/3), in which he wrote, soon after the publication of Harrison's biography, that he was much disgusted by the letters quoted in which Nelson unjustly censured every person who had not worshipped Lady Hamilton, and that he had thrown away the first volume in disgust. 'The publication will reflect eternal disgrace on the character of Lord Nelson, which will ultimately be stripped of every thing but animal courage, of which he certainly had an abundant share.'

35 DNB. Also *Nelson's Friendships*, by Hilda Gamlin, London, 1899, II 260–64.

36 *Times* and *Morning Chronicle*, 16 May 1831.

SELECT BIBLIOGRAPHY

THIS BOOK IS BASED almost entirely on manuscripts or on the published transcriptions of manuscripts, which have been listed in the introductory paragraphs to Notes and Sources. Apart from these, the Nelson literature is enormous, and this bibliography does not attempt a complete list of printed books. Those referred to in the text are acknowledged in the chapter notes and their titles are generally not repeated here. What follows is a list of early works which contain original material; of books frequently referred to in the notes; of books remarkable for their value or (twice, as examples) for their uselessness; of general works on the naval history of the period; and of the standard biographies.

The Nelson legend has been self-propagating, and has been handed down, often with advantages, from book to book. It is, however, true that no single biography has traduced Nelson as thoroughly as John Paul Jones, a contemporary American hero, was traduced by Augustus C. Buell, whose widely accredited biography of 1910 is less accurate than the wildest film script. (See *John Paul Jones*, by Samuel Eliot Morison, New York, 1959.) Buell makes Jones into a slave-owning Virginia plantation owner, none of which he was. He invents not only a whole correspondence between Jones and Louis XVI but also a statement by Napoleon that Jones should have been employed to oppose Nelson, when Napoleon, at the time of Jones's death, was an artillery lieutenant. Buell's most famous invention is Jones's letter stating that he would water the struggling roots of the US navy with his blood, which was for some years required reading for midshipmen at Annapolis, the US naval academy: there can be few better illustrations than this of the power of legend.

In this list, the titles of works referred to in the notes by one word, for example NICOLAS or CLOWES, are preceded by that same single word. For the English, Italian, and French literature of Nelson at Naples in 1799 see Appendix A.

Early works

HARRISON: *The Life of . . . Horatio Lord Viscount Nelson*, by Mr [James] Harrison, 2 vols, London, 1806. The first biography of any consequence. Has often been scornfully dismissed because it was subsidised and perhaps in part dictated by Emma Hamilton. Harrison used many of her papers and there is much information, particularly about Nelson in England in 1800 and after, which appears nowhere else. Valuable, once Emma's influence is discounted: almost all statements in it about Nelson's wife are false.

CLARKE AND M'ARTHUR: *The Life of Admiral Lord Nelson ... 2* vols, 1809 (and 1840 edn in three vols) by the Revd James Stainer Clarke, librarian and chaplain to the Prince of Wales, and John M'Arthur, former secretary to Lord Hood. The 'official' biography, whose authors were uncritically credulous, but who knew many of Nelson's contemporaries. (See chapters 1 and 27 of this book for the story of the book's commissioning.)

SOUTHEY, Robert: *Life of Nelson,* 1813, and a hundred editions to this day. Mostly an epitome of Clarke and M'Arthur. This is the single most influential biography, because of its author's literary reputation, Southey having become poet laureate. It is also the biography written with the least knowledge of its subject (see chapter 1 of this book), but the innocent Southey was invested with such authority that he was often quoted by those such as Nicolas whose own authority was infinitely greater.

LETTERS 1814: *The Letters of Lord Nelson to Lady Hamilton, with a supplement of interesting letters by other distinguished characters* [St Vincent, Earl of Bristol, William Hamilton] 2 vols, 1814. The first publication of their letters, in which Emma probably had no hand.

TUCKER: *Memoirs of Earl St Vincent,* by Jedediah Stephens Tucker, 2 vols, 1844. A quick and sanitised skip through his letter books, but revealing about St Vincent's discipline and his summary way with those officers who did not devote themselves 'soul and body' to the service.

NICOLAS: *The Dispatches and Letters of Lord Nelson,* by Sir Nicholas Harris Nicolas, 7 vols, 1844–46; reprinted by Chatham Publishing, London, 1997. Abundant, accurate, the essential framework for any study of Nelson. Nicolas described his work as 'the most genuine and truthful portrait of a public character that the world has ever seen'. See Notes and Sources.

PETTIGREW: *Memoirs of the Life of ... Nelson,* by Thomas Joseph Pettigrew, 2 vols, 1849. Prints about 600 Nelson letters, some still unknown elsewhere, and gives many biographical notes of Nelson's officers. Also many letters from Maria Carolina to Emma Hamilton. Pettigrew had all of Emma's papers, which he thoroughly censored, but he was the first biographer to show that she was Horatia's mother. See Notes and Sources.

ROSE: *The Diaries and Correspondence of the Rt Hon George Rose,* ed. I. V. Harcourt, 2 vols, 1860. Rose held government office for thirty years, knew Nelson, his brother Maurice, and Emma Hamilton, and was their faithful friend.

MINTO: *Life and Letters of Sir Gilbert Elliot,* ed. Countess of Minto, 3 vols, 1874.

Gilbert Elliot, first Earl Minto, was active in politics from 1786, and later became governor general of India. From his time as viceroy of Corsica in 1793 he was Nelson's friend, admirer, and patron. Many Nelson references.

G. LATHOM BROWNE: *Nelson, the Public and Private Life* ... 1891 (Dedicated to Queen Victoria). Though written with access to the mass of the Nelson papers which soon afterwards went to the British Museum, this book is most remarkable for its blindness. Long after Pettigrew and Morrison settled the matter, Browne insisted, on the grounds that Nelson had said that Horatia was adopted, and on the *a priori* assumption that he could not act or speak a lie, that relations between Nelson and Lady Hamilton were innocent, that Emma was not Horatia's mother, and that Nelson was not her father by Emma or any other woman. He asserted that Nelson's conduct at Naples was 'cruelly misrepresented'.

LAUGHTON: *The Nelson Memorial: Nelson and His Companions in Arms,* 1896. Sir John Knox Laughton served with the navy in the Crimea and China, was a pioneer of naval history, became professor of history at King's College, London, and wrote most of the naval entries for the *Dictionary of National Biography*. But he was an uncritical purveyor of the legend and intolerant for instance of the work of Pettigrew ('Written without any knowledge ... crammed with errors'), when Pettigrew's biography is worth ten of his. See also appendix A.

MAHAN: *The Life of Nelson, the Embodiment of the Sea Power of Great Britain,* by Capt A[rthur] T[hayer] Mahan [USN], 1898, 2 vols, 1897, and second edition, revised, 1899. A classic biography, whose title states its scope. His second edition notices but discounts Italian sources on Naples and the then newly-found letters of Nelson's wife. A disciple of Laughton, but an historian of much greater substance. See also Appendix A.

EYRE MATCHAM: *The Nelsons of Burnham Thorpe,* by M. Eyre Matcham, 1911. Family history, valuable mostly for the letters of Nelson's father and his sister Catherine. Good on 1787–93.

General works on the Georgian navy

CHARNOCK, John, *Biographia Navalis,* 6 vols, 1794–98.

CHEVALIER, E., capitaine de vaisseau, *Histoire de la Marine Française sous la Première République,* 5 vols, Paris, 1886. Standard French history.

CLOWES, William Laird, *The Royal Navy,* 6 vols, 1899, reprinted by Chatham Publishing, London, 1997. Standard history. Relies heavily on James for Nelson's period. Good maps.

GARDINER, Robert, editor, *Fleet, Battle, and Blockade, the French Revolutionary War 1793–1797,* and *Nelson Against Napoleon, from the Nile to Copenhagen 1798–1801,* published 1996 and 1997 by Chatham, in association with the NMM, with contributions by Roger Morriss, Nicolas Tracy, and David Lyon. Heavily illustrated and authoritative.

GUÉRIN, Leon, *Histoire Maritime de France*, 6 vols, Paris, 1851.

JAMES, William, *The Naval History of Great Britain* [1793–1830], 6 vols, 1837. Standard history.

LAVERY, Brian, *Nelson's Navy: the Ships, Men, and Organisation, 1793–1815*, London, 1989, with a foreword by Patrick O'Brian. A scholarly, lavishly illustrated, beautiful book by the curator of ship technology at the NMM.

LEWIS, Michael, *A Social History of the Navy*, London, 1960. A pioneer work, still unique in its scope, should be read alongside Lavery. Where sea officers came from, what and how they were paid, how they rose or fell.

LYON, David, *The Sailing Navy List*, London, 1990. Comprehensive details and plans of naval vessels.

MARSHALL, John, *Marshall's Naval Biography or Memoirs of Services etc* [of officers down to the rank of commander, still on the list in 1823], 4 vols, 1833.

MORRISS, Roger, *Guide to British Naval Papers in North America*, 1994. A guide to the increasing number of MSS in American public collections.

PARKINSON, C. Northcote, *Britannia Rules: The Classic Age of Naval History, 1793–1815*, London 1977, reprinted 1994. Brief, sceptical of the legend, sure of Nelson's genius.

O'BYRNE, William, *A Naval Biographical Dictionary* [of all sea officers living], 1849.

RODGER, N. A. M., *The Wooden World: an Anatomy of the Georgian Navy*, London, 1986. The best work of its kind, learned and original. The navy it analyses is that of the Seven Years' War, before Nelson's time, but the structure remained much the same. The author is now professor of naval history at the University of Exeter.

WALKER, Richard, *The Nelson Portraits: an inconography* ..., RNM, 1998. Standard work on Nelson paintings and engravings by a former curator of the government art collection.

WHITE, Colin, ed., *The Nelson Companion*, London, 1995, in association with the RNM, of which Mr White is deputy director. An authoritative survey of Nelson literature, portraits, relics, monuments, and letters.

The line of modern biographies

The works of Carola Oman, Oliver Warner, and Tom Pocock all exhibit a deep knowledge of the original materials, and each in its turn has added to the sum of knowledge.

OMAN: *Nelson* by Carola Oman (Lady Lenanton), the author of biographies and many historical novels, appeared in 1947 and was instantly successful. Here is a traditional Nelson, but portrayed more in the round than in any previous biography, since she was the first to make use of Lady Nelson's papers, though they had been discovered fifty years before. A biography of splendid narrative sweep.

WARNER: *A Portrait of Lord Nelson*, by Oliver Warner, 1958. Warner served at the admiralty 1941–47, published studies of Collingwood, Marryat, and Conrad, and was an authority on marine painting. His is a biography written with great modesty. He believed Nelson had suffered from both idolatry and attack, and that the duty of the biographer was 'to rediscover not perfection, but the extent of the man's genius'.

POCOCK: *Horatio Nelson*, by Tom Pocock, 1988. Pocock is a former naval correspondent of *The Times* and foreign correspondent with *The Evening Standard*, and the author of other biographical works on the young Nelson, William Hoste, and Sidney Smith. He suggests that one reason for Nelson's abiding appeal may be that, as the saviour of his people, sacrificed for their sake, he is an echo of the Christian tradition. Pocock is very strong on a sense of place, having travelled almost everywhere Nelson served, even to the Rio del Norte in Nicaragua.

Other modern works

Beloved Emma, by Flora Fraser, 1986.

Horatia Nelson, by Winifred Gérin, 1970. Impeccable sources. Revealing about Emma 1800–15.

Nelson: the Immortal Memory, by David and Stephen Howarth, 1988.

Nelson: a Personal History, by Christopher Hibbert, 1994. By the accomplished biographer of George III, Wellington, Queen Victoria, and Edward VII, but not in the line of Oman–Warner–Pocock, though Hibbert owes much to Pocock, whom he thanks for the loan of his papers; 63 of his notes cite Pocock as his authority, and another 77 cite the works of other modern authors.

Nelson's Band of Brothers (in US as *Nelson's Captains*), by Ludovic Kennedy, 1951. The author, who served as a lieutenant RNVR in the war, picks out the stories of Hardy, Foley, Fremantle, Troubridge, Ball, and others. It is a work which is complementary, as Kennedy intended, to the Nelson biographies.

The Great Gamble: Nelson at Copenhagen, by Dudley Pope, 1972. Particularly valuable for the Danish material.

Nelson and the Hamiltons, by Jack Russell, 1969. The most detailed study of the *tria juncta in uno*, from 1800 onwards almost day by day. Deeply researched, with wide use of newspapers, but without notes.

INDEX

A NOTE ON THE AUTHOR

TERRY COLEMAN is an historian and journalist. As special correspondent for the *Guardian* and *Daily Mail* he has reported from seventy countries, interviewed eight British prime ministers, from Macmillan to Blair, and in 1988 was named Journalist of the Year. His previous books include a biographical study of Thomas Hardy; *Passage to America*, a history of nineteenth-century emigration; and historical novels set in early Australia, in seventeenth-century New England, and in the Texas Republic.

A NOTE ON THE TYPE

The text of this book is set in a digitised version of Bell, a very English face originally cut in 1788, when Nelson was a young frigate captain. It was designed by Richard Austin for John Bell, bookseller, publisher, and the founder of half a dozen newspapers, among them *The Morning Post*. When Dominick Serres, marine painter to George III, published his *Liber Nauticus* in 1805, it was set in Bell, which remained until the 1950s the typeface in which Oxford University Press set many of its books.